LIBRARY IN A BOOK

HATE CRIMES

Tom Streissguth

Facts On File, Inc.

HATE CRIMES

Facts On File, Inc.
132 West 31st Street
New York NY 10001

Library of Congress Cataloging-in-Publication Data
Streissguth, Thomas, 1958-
    Hate crimes / by Tom Streissguth.
      p. cm.—(Library in a book)
    Includes bibliographical references and index.
    ISBN 0-8160-4879-7
    1. Hate crimes—United States. I. Title. II. Series.
HV6773.52.S768 2003
364.15—dc21   2002155862

Facts On File books are available at special discounts when purchased in bulk quantities for businesses, associations, institutions, or sales promotions. Please call our Special Sales Department in New York at (212) 967-8800 or (800) 322-8755.

You can find Facts On File on the World Wide Web at http://www.factsonfile.com

Printed in the United States of America

MP Hermitage 10 9 8 7 6 5 4 3 2 1

This book is printed on acid-free paper.

CONTENTS

———————

PART I

OVERVIEW OF THE TOPIC

CHAPTER 1

INTRODUCTION TO
HATE CRIMES

"Hate crime" as a legal category is a recent invention, but bias-motivated violence has a long history. Since antiquity, humans have been selecting other humans for assault, injury, and murder on the basis of certain personal characteristics: different appearance, different color, different nationality, different language, different religion. Individuals as well as nations and governments have carried out what would be defined in the 21st-century United States as hate crimes. The Romans murdered Christians; the Nazis persecuted Jews; Muslims were singled out for imprisonment, torture, rape, and mass execution by Christians in the former Yugoslavia.

For a period of more than three centuries, beginning in the 16th century, Native American tribes were methodically destroyed by Dutch, French, Spanish, and British colonists, and then by American citizens, who had the conquest and cultivation of a new land in mind. The American settlers also carried out extrajudicial executions of those whites holding different political views, an act that came to be known as lynching. The verb *lynch* originates with an 18th-century Virginia planter named Charles Lynch who, with a group of like-minded colonists, would sometimes take the law into his own hands and punish Tories (those who sympathized with the British colonial government), most often by tarring and feathering them but also by carrying out summary hangings.

Generally, lynching has come to be defined as an execution that is done outside of the ordinary system of justice. A lynching represents a breakdown of order and a defiance of the law. The victim is chosen either because of a suspected crime, or simply (and most commonly) because of his or her race. No trial is held, and no jury passes sentence. After the American Revolution, lynching became an expedient way to deal with suspected criminals in places where the police authority was weak or nonexistent. On the western frontiers,

3

lynch mobs punished the crimes of horse and cattle stealing, kidnapping, robbery, and murder, commonly by hanging.

CUSTOMARY PREJUDICE

The English Protestants who made up the majority of North American colonists brought their customary prejudices and habits of mind to the New World. One of the strongest such prejudices was directed against Catholics, who in most areas of the British colonies (with the exception of Pennsylvania and Maryland) were banned outright. Catholics were suspected of conspiring to undermine or overthrow established governments in the name of their church, they were accused of a wide variety of other crimes and conspiracies, and they were the frequent target of violence and bigotry. The colonies were also a hostile place for Jews, whose numbers in North America remained small through the 18th century. The Jewish communities of New York, Newport, Savannah, and Charleston largely isolated themselves from the surrounding society, whose members often treated them with contempt as craven usurers and—a prejudice remaining from the medieval age—as the killers of Christ and of good Christians.

Bigotry was not only directed at Catholics and Jews. The British colonies were separated from each other by long distances as well as by important cultural and religious differences. The Dutch of New York and New Jersey strongly distrusted the English Puritans of Massachusetts. Anglicans, who belonged to the national Protestant church of England, disliked the breakaway sect of Puritans as well as the Presbyterians, whose country of origin was Scotland. The American Revolution brought forth a wide variety of new loyalties and hatreds among the colonists. Support for the revolution was by and large divided along the old religious differences, with Anglicans opposing the revolt and Baptists and Presbyterians supporting it. The Quakers of Pennsylvania professed pacifism and refused to give their allegiance or their military service to either side. For this they were despised and maltreated by members of both factions outside of Pennsylvania. After the Revolution, many Loyalists, who refused to join the movement for separation from England, were driven from the colonies; those who remained saw their property confiscated and their legal rights to sue in court, to vote, to collect debts, and to sit on juries promptly ended. Many colonies required their citizens to swear an oath of allegiance to the new United States; those who refused were relegated to a second-class legal status.

The Revolution did not end the rivalries among the 13 British colonies. Fears of a new monarchy or dictatorship and mistrust of a strongly centralized government had great influence on the writers of the U.S. Constitution. The states were allowed to pass and enforce their own laws, but the Constitution also required the states to maintain republican (nonmonarchal) forms of local government, and to grant newcomers from other states the same legal rights as longtime residents. The Constitution also prevented religious tests for public officeholders. By the Bill of Rights—the first 10 amendments to the Constitution—the citizens of the United States were guaranteed freedom of speech, freedom of religious worship, the right to petition, and other rights seen as essential to prevent the return of tyranny and arbitrary rule. The First Amendment was written in part as a check on the government's power to interfere in organized religion.

But many state constitutions read quite differently. Only Protestants were granted full citizenship in some states, and in most places Catholics and Jews were prevented from holding public offices. New Jersey allowed only Protestants to hold public office, while Massachusetts simply required all officeholders to repudiate the authority of the pope. In addition, the rights and privileges of the federal Constitution did not extend to slaves of African origin or to Native Americans. On the contrary, Indian tribes were forced from their ancestral homes and driven further west, beyond the Appalachian Mountains. Black slaves were kept in bondage, while a provision in the Constitution allowed a period of 20 years (until 1808) before the importation of slaves would be legally ended.

Most Americans considered slavery to be the natural condition for Africans, whom they saw as inferior, half-human beings who were not, and never would be, worthy of constitutional rights and full citizenship. Article IV of the Constitution allowed for the extradition of runaway slaves, who were to be returned to their legal owners. In addition, as the vast majority of slaves lived in the South, the framers of the Constitution took care not to see the southern states gain greater power through congressional representation, which was based on population. For the purpose of representation in the Congress, a slave was counted as only three-fifths of a white inhabitant.

Political rivalries between Federalists and Republicans led to the writing of new federal laws such as the Alien and Sedition Acts of 1798. By these laws, all those found to be speaking or writing scandal or treason against the new government were subject to fines and imprisonment. Those considered dangerous to the government could be deported from the country. Written and passed by a Federalist-dominated Congress, the Alien and Sedition Acts originated in suspicion towards the new Republican faction, which was seen by Federalists as a dangerously revolutionary and atheistic mob that threatened to repeat the violent, disastrous revolution that had just taken place in France. But in the opinion of many, the acts represented a direct infringement of the Bill of Rights; the laws were repealed during the administration of Republican president Thomas Jefferson.

IMMIGRANTS AND KNOW-NOTHINGS

In his book *Legacy of Hate*, author Philip Perlmutter describes the development of racial, religious, and ethnic bigotry in 19th-century America as follows:

> *When economic depression, labor strife, war or the threat of war developed . . . Americans struck out against the supposed enemy within—alien or radical. Generally, the worse the conditions, the more the vituperation against religious, racial, and ethnic groups, each of whom was charged with inability to assimilate, lowering wage standards, strikebreaking, and taking jobs away from the native-born. . . . The result was an ever-repeating pattern of majority-group members disliking minority ones and the latter disliking each other.*[1]

In the first half of the 19th century, the settlement of the frontier and the development of the country's vast natural resources and new industry called for a permissive immigration policy. Most newcomers arrived from northern Europe, particularly the British Isles, Germany, Holland, and Scandinavia. Later, new groups arrived from Italy, Greece, Austria-Hungary, Russia, Spain, and Poland. Two major immigrant groups developed: northern and southern European. As the population increased, and as these newcomers began competing for jobs and living space, bitter rivalries broke out among them. The cities and settled regions of the country were the scene of violence against immigrants and Catholics from Ireland and southern Europe. New immigrants were feared for their willingness to work for low wages and despised for their unfamiliar social and religious customs, for their strange accents and foreign languages. They often suffered what would today be described as "hate crimes," such as mob assaults, burning of property, random acts of violence, and murder. These attacks took place most often in times of economic distress, when jobs and money were scarce and the public sought out scapegoats for punishment. The response on the part of the authorities was to establish city police departments, which were charged with investigating crime, arresting criminals, and keeping public order.

The formation of the Know-Nothing Party in 1845 came as a direct result of the widespread fear and mistrust of new immigrants, many of whom were arriving as a result of a famine then sweeping through the largely Catholic nation of Ireland. The Know-Nothings, whose official name was the American Party, formed lodges, invented secret rituals and handshakes, wrote inflammatory books and pamphlets, and ran for (and in many northeastern states, won) public office. The goal of the Know-Nothings—who considered Protestantism as the true faith of genuine American citizens—

was to rid the government and business institutions of all Catholic and foreign influence. The Know-Nothings suspected Catholics of voting at the direction of their priests and pope, and of plotting to overthrow the American government and replace it with a religious dictatorship, a government controlled from the papal headquarters in Rome.

The Know-Nothings were heartily supported in this program by workers who feared the loss of their jobs and a depression in their wages through the influx of cheap laborers. Samuel Eliot Morison, in his *Oxford History of the American People*, describes this period as follows:

> *This wave of immigration enhanced the wealth and progress of the country, yet encountered bitter opposition, as did Asiatics half a century later. Sudden influxes of foreigners with strange ways and attitudes always do that, everywhere. In part, the antagonism was religious, since most of the Irish and many of the Germans were Roman Catholics. . . . The greater number of immigrants, however, only wanted an opportunity to work; but their need for work was so desperate that they cut wages at a time when native-born mechanics were trying to raise their standard of living through the labor unions.[2]*

The result was a series of violent riots and crimes committed against Catholic immigrants in the eastern cities where they congregated. Irish immigrants were attacked in the streets; their homes and churches were vandalized and burned; they were prevented from obtaining work by bigoted employers; they were suspected of carrying disease and bringing crime and the general degradation of public morals. (The bigotry worked two ways, however, as the Democrats enlisted Irish Catholics to intimidate voters inclined to vote against the Democratic Party in presidential and municipal elections.)

The rising resentments and a long-burning conflict over the use of the (Protestant) King James Bible in the public schools brought about an explosion in Philadelphia, Pennsylvania, in May 1844, in which several dozen Catholic homes as well as two Catholic churches were burned to the ground. State militia were called out to restore order, but the Protestant/Catholic riots, the worst religious outbreak in American history, brought the deaths of 30 people.

The Know-Nothings were a largely northern phenomenon, as the southern tier of states had largely been sheltered from the great influx of European immigrants. But in the middle of the 19th century, as conflict over slavery intensified between the North and South, African Americans were singled out for violence because of their race. The activities of abolitionists in the northern states brought a reaction from those in the South who saw such opinion as an attack on a valued, traditional way of life, in which each segment of society knew and remained in its proper place.

In an attempt to resolve the thorny issue of slavery in new states and territories, Congress passed a series of compromises. In 1820, Missouri was admitted as a slave state and Maine as a free state; in addition, all territory north of a latitude of 36 degrees, 30 minutes was closed to slavery. In 1850, another compromise admitted California as a free state, while in New Mexico and Utah the residents were allowed to decide for themselves whether or not to permit slavery. The 1854 Kansas-Nebraska Act allowed the residents of these new territories to decide on slavery; while Nebraska peaceably banned it, Kansas became the scene of widespread bloodshed, as abolitionists combatted proslavery factions.

Many Southerners, even those who did not own slaves, heartily supported the institution as the best possible for those of African origin, who otherwise would find themselves at the mercy of ordinary employers who would hold them in perpetual economic bondage through low wages and poor working conditions. Prejudice against blacks persisted in northern states where slavery had been banned since the late 18th century. Black residents were kept strictly apart from whites in public places such as theaters and inns. Black workers could not ordinarily join labor unions. They could not vote and they could not worship in white churches. In the cities, they were restricted to black neighborhoods, which were sometimes attacked by white mobs. By the 1857 Supreme Court decision in *Dred Scott v. Sanford,* black slaves were held to be an inferior class without the normal rights of U.S. citizens. By the Emancipation Proclamation of 1863, President Lincoln freed African Americans from slavery—but only in those states that had seceded from the Union. In July of the same year, the drafting of unemployed laborers for service in the Union army in New York City brought an explosive riot among workers who opposed the Union cause and feared the loss of their jobs and status to free blacks. Hundreds of black residents of the city were attacked, beaten, lynched, or burned alive.

After the Civil War ended in 1865, a veteran Southern officer, Nathan Bedford Forrest, met with a group of tradition-minded brothers in Pulaski, Tennessee, to form a secret society that would return the South to the virtues of the past and fight, with any means available, against Reconstruction, northern interference, and the pretensions of newly freed slaves. Members of the group, who rode at night under cover of terrifying masks and robes to commit their mayhem, gave themselves the appropriately obscure name of Ku Klux Klan. Their darkest deed, carried out only after appropriate warning was given, was the kidnapping and hanging of their victims—a lynching done in the name of the Old South.

THE CIVIL RIGHTS ACT OF 1866

The era of Reconstruction followed the ravages of the Civil War. In the view of the defeated Confederate states, Reconstruction was an attempt by the North to subjugate them completely and subvert the old order of things by elevating former slaves to a place of equality. In the view of the federal government, the South would have to accept the terms of its defeat, which had been accomplished at such a terrible cost in Union army lives. To this end, the Freedmen's Bureau was organized in March 1865 to relieve the situation of the ex-slaves. A government bureau created by the War Department but largely staffed by civilians, the Freedmen's Bureau issued food rations; built hospitals; founded schools; set up courts to resolve disputes over labor, wages, and working conditions; and attempted to integrate freed slaves into southern society. The problem of blending Negro and white populations occupied President Lincoln in the last days of his administration, when military victory was imminent. The possibility of colonization, or allowing the freed slaves to occupy a new western territory, was debated, but most southern blacks did not want to leave the states where they already lived, where whites sought to keep them as a permanent underclass and an inexpensive source of labor.

During Reconstruction, civil governors were appointed in the former Confederate states. These governors assembled constitutional conventions in their states; the representatives were elected by all voters willing to take an oath of allegiance to the United States. Blacks were not allowed to vote, nor were certain classes of white citizens, including former Confederate officials and military officers, unless they agreed to swear allegiance and petition for a pardon.

The state conventions struck down the original ordinances of secession, formally abolished slavery within their borders, amended their state constitutions, and arranged for new elections. Although the Civil War was ceremoniously and formally ended, a new era had begun in the South. Freedmen were allowed to own property, to testify in court, to move about freely, to legally marry, and to inherit property. But the new laws passed by the southern states also included "black codes," which barred Negroes from voting, from serving on juries, or even owning a gun. Some states restricted the jobs a freedman could hold and also carefully controlled where he could live and what kind of property he could buy or own. The black codes were an attempt to make a permanent underclass of freed slaves in the South, and although the Freedmen's Bureau had the power to overturn some of these laws, its efforts were largely futile.

The new laws, codes, and social pyramid were enforced by a constant threat of violence with the purpose of keeping the newly freed slaves in their place.

THE ANTI-KLAN LAWS

The Congress that began its session in December 1865 took a direct hand in the drive to establish universal suffrage. By the Fourteenth and Fifteenth Amendments to the Constitution, passed in 1868 and 1870, respectively, all those born or naturalized in the United States were given the right to equal protection and due process of the law. As citizens, blacks were given the right to vote, although they were unable to exercise this right wherever election officials raised barriers, such as a literacy requirement. By the Civil Rights Act of 1870, it was made a federal crime for two or more persons to conspire against the right of any citizen to vote.

Southern representatives were forbidden to hold seats in Congress until their states ratified the Fourteenth Amendment. Throughout the South, the reaction to these new laws and to the constitutional enfranchisement of blacks was intensified bigotry and racial violence. A race riot erupted in Memphis, Tennessee, in May 1866, with white citizens rampaging through the city, attacking blacks and those whites seen as sympathetic to the freed slaves. The riot resulted in at least 46 deaths. Another such riot erupted in New Orleans, Louisiana, in July, while the state governor, James Wells, made a determined effort to ensure black suffrage in the state by reconvening the constitutional convention and rewriting the state constitution.

The New Orleans and Memphis race riots accompanied increasing racial violence in the South in reaction to the new constitutional amendments, the doctrine of equal protection, the drive for black suffrage, and the imposition of state governments by what was seen as a hostile Republican administration. Fearing social equality as a threat to their livelihoods and standing, white southerners banded together and singled out their black neighbors for vandalism, floggings, and lynchings. In response to the murder and general terrorism perpetrated by the Ku Klux Klan and other vigilante organizations, the federal government passed the Ku Klux Klan Act of 1871. As it was originally written, the Ku Klux Klan Act would have made federal crimes of such acts as murder and arson. This radical shift in legal jurisdiction from the states to the federal government ignited fierce opposition among Democrats—the party of southern interests at the time—and even by moderate Republicans who favored a strong federal role in the Reconstruction effort. The law was eventually amended to provide criminal penalties only for those acts that interfered with the normal rights of citizens.

The next and final piece of postwar civil rights legislation was the Civil Rights Act of 1875, a bill that was debated and amended for several years after its introduction by Senator Charles Sumner in March 1871. By the time the bill was passed, support for sweeping equal rights protection was fading; the Republican administration of President U.S. Grant, which supported the bill, was immersed in a series of scandals and the problems of an economic panic that struck in 1873. The Senate finally passed the bill on May 22, 1874, and the Civil Rights Act became law in February 1875. The final language of the bill simply prohibited discrimination in public places, but also provided for federal prosecution in matters that had traditionally been handled by state statutes. The debate over states' rights and federalism would continue to be a central issue in future civil rights laws and hate-crime statutes.

JIM CROW LAWS

The last federal troops were withdrawn from the South on the order of President Rutherford B. Hayes in 1877, and the era of Reconstruction came to an end. In an attempt to restore some semblance of the old order, the southern state governments passed a sweeping series of new laws, known as "Jim Crow," that effectively separated the white and black populations. In his book *The Strange Career of Jim Crow*, historian C. Vann Woodward explains the impetus behind the new segregation laws:

> *The public symbols and constant reminders of [the Negro's] inferior positions were the segregation statutes, or "Jim Crow" laws. They constituted the most elaborate and formal expression of sovereign white opinion upon the subject. In bulk and detail as well as in effectiveness of enforcement the segregation codes were comparable with the black codes of the old regime, though the laxity that mitigated the harshness of the black codes was replaced by a rigidity that was more typical of the segregation code. That code lent the sanction of law to a racial ostracism that extended to churches and schools, to housing and jobs, to eating and drinking. Whether by law or by custom, that ostracism extended to virtually all forms of public transportation, to sports and recreations, to hospitals, orphanages, prisons, and asylums, and ultimately to funeral homes, morgues, and cemeteries.[3]*

The Jim Crow laws adopted in the South prevailed and were supported by a series of Supreme Court decisions that gradually shifted lawmaking power from the federal government back to the states. Segregation was given the highest legal sanction in 1896 by the Supreme Court's decision in *Plessy v. Ferguson*, which held that segregated public facilities did not violate the equal protection clause of the Fourteenth Amendment, provided that the separate facilities were "equal." The doctrine of "separate but equal" reigned in the South until the civil rights era of the 1960s.

While Jim Crow laws began the segregation era, the Klan's campaign to restore the pride and customs of the white South was carried out first against freed slaves and their families, and then against African Americans in general. Beginning in the 1890s, the practice of lynching blacks for suspected crimes or insults against white citizens began in earnest. But the Klan had many other ways of enforcing its views. Targets were kidnapped and horsewhipped; their homes were vandalized; they were branded and beaten; and their property was destroyed. Cross burning, the Klan's ceremonious way of warning and threatening its enemies, occurred in front of homes, businesses, and churches, in this way extending the Klan message to an entire neighborhood or community.

The Klan specialty of lynching took place most commonly in the South, where racial tensions continued long after the war between the states. Blacks were often targeted for lynching when economic times were hard; they were chosen whenever progress was threatened in the area of civil rights and equality before the law; they were lynched for "unacceptable" behavior such as whistling at white women. Lynching was carried out by small groups in the middle of the night; it was also attended by large mobs in full daylight.

In the meantime, the late 19th century saw another wave of anti-immigrant bias, directed against Italian Catholics, eastern Europeans (particularly Jews) and, on the West Coast, Asians (Chinese, Japanese, Koreans, and Filipinos) who had been recruited to work in the mines and on the railroads of the western United States. Eastern Europeans were suspected of fomenting revolution and socialism; Finns were accused of drunkenness; Jews were viewed as greedy and dishonest, although intelligent; Italians were believed to be naturally violent. In 1881, 11 Italian residents of New Orleans were arrested at random and accused of the assassination of a police official, found not guilty, then promptly lynched, after which several hundred Italian residents fled the city.

Asians suffered on the basis of their foreign customs, language, appearance, and religions. Throughout the country, the prevailing view was that Asians could never assimilate in American society, that they were clannish, and that they would always remain an insular and dangerous foreign element, one that would pose a dire threat to public morals, to established Christian religions, and to the jobs of ordinary laborers. Chinese immigrants were subjected to discrimination, violence, and murder. A mob lynched 22 Chinese residents of Los Angeles in 1871. After the western railroad network was completed, the fear of widespread unemployment and cheap Asian labor was so strong that the Chinese Exclusion Act was adopted in 1882, banning immigration completely from China for 10 years. By the Scott Act of 1888, more than 20,000 Chinese workers who had left the country temporarily were forbidden to return, even though they held proper reentry documents. In 1902, the Chinese Exclusion Act was made permanent.

At this time, white Protestant Americans formed the dominant social and political group, particularly in the eastern United States. Feeling what they considered to be "their" country threatened by immigrants, some authors advanced new theories of race, which held Anglo-Saxons and northern Europeans to be the most advanced "races" on Earth, intellectually and morally superior to lesser breeds such as Asians, Africans, Native Americans, and southern Europeans. Many authors grew alarmed at the fact that these lesser races seemed to be reproducing at a faster rate, and predicted the day would come when the traditional white and Protestant caste that had dominated the United States since the American Revolution would have to submit to new customs, laws, and religions upheld by the new majority—thus threatening personal liberties and the country's constitutional basis.

THE NEW KLAN

World War I, which the United States entered in the spring of 1917, had been seen throughout the United States as an exclusively European affair. The country entered the war on the side of Allies and against Germany only after much debate among federal lawmakers and within the executive branch. Violence and discrimination against Germans took place; the fear of infiltration and espionage on the part of Germany and its allies prompted the passage of new federal laws in direct conflict with the provisions of the First Amendment, reminiscent of the Alien and Sedition Acts of the late 18th century. The Espionage Act of 1917 banned all speech tending to obstruct the war effort or give aid and comfort to the enemy. In 1918, the Sedition Act made speech considered disloyal or critical of the government punishable by a long prison term. Certain magazines or newspapers held to be critical or unsupportive of the war effort were banned from the mails by the postmaster, while hundreds of suspected spies (nearly all of them immigrants) were arrested, convicted under the new laws, and imprisoned on New York's Ellis Island, an important entry point for European immigrants. The general fear and disdain of African Americans manifested itself in stricter segregation laws, which spread under a deliberate policy of President Wilson into the federal government, in which black employees were restricted to separate facilities.

Meanwhile, a revived Ku Klux Klan spread beyond the South. The organization was marketed to the general public by professional publicity agents, who built the Klan into a widely popular national secret society. The strange costumes, the mysterious rituals, the special vocabulary and titles, and above all the message of "100 percent Americanism" appealed to many people who feared the disruptions of a modernizing world. The Klan stood opposed to what its members saw as the mongrelization of American society by Catholics, Jews, and foreigners generally. In New England, the Klan targeted French Canadian immigrants for random attack. In the Southwest, Klan members harassed Mexicans and Asians.

As new waves of immigrants arrived after World War I, the general fear of immigrants increased along with America's political isolationism. As the conflict between whites and blacks continued, race riots erupted throughout the Midwest. In 1919, when a young black swimmer entered a whites-only area along the shores of Lake Michigan in Chicago, a riot broke out, ending only after two weeks and the deaths of several dozen black and white Chicagoans and the razing of entire black neighborhoods. Lynching carried out or inspired by the Klan spread from the South to the Midwest.

In response to Klan violence, or white-on-black violence that was not prosecuted in many regions of the South, the federal government passed new laws. The first of these laws, passed in 1870 as 18 U.S. 241, criminalized conspiracies of two or more people to "injure, oppress, threaten, or intimidate any person. . . . In the free exercise of any right or privilege secured to him by the Constitution. . ." The statute did not mention race or prejudice and did not address the issue of bias violence per se. It was simply formulated as a guarantee of the free exercise of constitutional rights, no matter the race, color, religion, or ethnic origin of the criminal or the victim.

A second federal statute, 18 U.S. 242, was more explicit in its language: "Whoever, under color of any law . . . subjects any person . . . to the deprivation of any rights . . . secured or protected by the Constitution or laws of the United States, or to different punishments, pains, or penalties, on account of such person being an alien, or by reason of his color, or race . . . shall be fined . . . or imprisoned." This statute was intended to protect the people from abuses of constitutional rights by public officials, and in particular by police officers, under the guise of enforcing the law.

The rivalry among social and ethnic groups that had long simmered within the United States was given free rein during the Great Depression of the early 1930s and during World War II. Immigrants were again blamed for the economic malaise, and in communities where different ethnic groups came in contact there were frequent scenes of violence. In Los Angeles, Mexicans were randomly attacked on the streets; thousands of Mexican laborers were forcibly repatriated to Mexico.

The declaration of war by the United States after the Japanese attack on Pearl Harbor in December 1941 inspired patriotic fervor across the country. Japanese-Americans were confronted and attacked, particularly on the West Coast, where after Pearl Harbor many people feared an invasion. An entire community of U.S. citizens of Japanese descent was rounded up and interned in California during the war.

Wartime prejudices were not limited to the Japanese. On the East Coast, German Americans were seen as a third column of Nazi sympathizers. Jews, now the target of Germany's murderous Nazi government, heard very strong echoes of the anti-Semitism that was sweeping across Germany and the rest of Europe. In the United States, Jews were accused of starting the war as an insidious internationalist plot against the United States and its ancestral nations in Europe. Jews serving in the military experienced these prejudices outright. Leonard Dinnerstein, in *Anti-Semitism in America*, reports that:

> *Jewish chaplains in the services found that a number of their Christian peers also harbored strong prejudices. Some of the ministers denounced Jews as "Godless Communists," believed that there were too many of them in government in Washington, and thought that "all of you Jews are good business executives."[4]*

These sentiments did not end with the successful conclusion of the war against Germany and Japan. The campaign against Communist influence in the federal government, which reached a high tide during the 1950s, brought a strong wave of anti-Semitism among a general public fearing an international conspiracy to bring down the United States and its democratic institutions. The fear found its darkest expression in incidents of violence and vandalism directed against Jews and their homes and families.

THE CIVIL RIGHTS ERA

Nevertheless, the postwar period also saw the issue of discrimination come to the forefront. In 1948, President Harry S. Truman signed an executive order banishing segregation in the armed forces. Although Jim Crow laws remained in force in the South long after World War II. During the Eisenhower administration, the country's political leaders were focused on the outside Communist menace rather than the domestic undercurrent of troubled race relations. Yet segregation of the races did meet with challenges, starting with the decision of the U.S. Supreme Court on May 17, 1954, in the case of *Brown v. Board of Education*, in which the justices unanimously declared that "separate but equal" public education violated the equal protection clause of the Fourteenth Amendment. On May 31, 1955, the court handed down a decree ordering the implementation of its decision in a "reasonable" time under the authority of federal district courts, which would hear and resolve cases brought on the issue of school desegregation.

This decision sounded the knell for years of protest and violence against the doctrine of racial segregation, while the reaction intensified and took many forms. In Mississippi, "citizens' councils" were formed to defend segregated public facilities. While the federal courts handed down decisions in favor of school desegregation, the citizens' councils spread outside of Mississippi. On the other side, black Americans were organizing as well, and a new sense of urgency and militancy, as described by author Philip Perlmutter, arrived:

> *Civil rights organizations began changing their tactics and goals, with calls made for stressing group rights rather than individual rights; self-interest politics rather than coalitional politics; color-conscious justice rather than blindfolded justice; and preferential treatment rather than equal opportunity.*[5]

One of the first important events in the campaign for civil rights was the yearlong boycott of the public buses of Montgomery, Alabama, which began in 1955. The Montgomery bus boycott brought Martin Luther King, Jr., founder of the Southern Christian Leadership Conference (SCLC), to the forefront of a long struggle against segregation, a struggle that brought the worst period of racial violence in the country's history.

A violent reaction against university desegregation began on February 6, 1956, over the admission of Autherine Lucy to the University of Alabama. In the meantime, several southern states passed new laws in an attempt to enforce segregation in the public schools, and thus nullify the Supreme Court's *Brown v. Board of Education* decision. In September 1957, Governor Orval E. Faubus of Arkansas called out the National Guard in an attempt to prevent nine black students from enrolling in Little Rock's Central High School. The confrontation led to the calling out of federal troops, and for an entire school year the school remained under heavy guard. Still defiant of the federal government and the Supreme Court, Faubus simply closed all of Little Rock's high schools for the school year 1958–59. In the meantime, the federal Civil Rights Act of 1957 further bolstered the right of black citizens to vote by removing several of the legal obstacles to voting adopted by the southern states. Local officials who refused to register qualified voters were subject to fines and imprisonment. Another civil rights law passed in 1960 authorized federal referees to oversee registration and voting. Both of these laws were considerably weakened by compromises in the course of congressional debate, and their enforcement by the Justice Department did not, by and large, overcome the determined effort of southern officials to deprive African Americans of the right to vote.

On February 1, 1960, four black students of the Agricultural and Technical College of Greensboro, North Carolina, staged a sit-in at a local Woolworth's lunch counter when they were refused service. This was the first of many sit-ins, in which black youths would nonviolently protest the written and unwritten Jim Crow laws that separated the races and relegated African Americans to second-class status. Boycotts and sit-ins occurred at movie theaters, bus stations, public libraries, and swimming pools. They were countered by mass arrests, which were in turn struck down by the U.S. Supreme Court in the decision of *Garner v. Louisiana* (1961), in which it was found that the act of peaceably occupying a facility such as a lunch counter did not constitute a breach of the peace.

A violent reaction began in May 1961, when a group of Freedom Riders, protesting the segregation of interstate buses, were attacked by white mobs in Anniston and Birmingham, Alabama. The state of Mississippi, however, took first place in its determined opposition to desegregation. Historian C. Vann Woodward observed:

> *Mississippi, however, easily maintained its historic priority in racism. . . . Its Negroes lived in constant fear and its whites under rigid conformity to dogmas of white supremacy as interpreted by a state-subsidized Citizens Council. In 1955 three Negroes were lynched, the first in the country since 1951, and one was a fourteen-year-old boy, Emmett Till. No one was punished, nor were any of the lynchers who took another victim in 1959. Less than 2 per cent of the Negroes over twenty were registered voters. Law enforcement was in the hands of bigots, and bigotry was respectable.*[6]

The battle over civil rights in Mississippi reached its climax on the campus of the University of Mississippi at Oxford, where in September 1962 a federal court order paved the way for the enrollment of James Meredith. Governor Ross Barnett defied the order by instructing state police to arrest any federal officials interfering on Meredith's behalf. On October 1, federal marshals who accompanied Meredith into a university dormitory came under attack by mobs of students, with Mississippi state troopers standing by. The general campus riot that followed left two dead and hundreds injured.

Racial violence continued throughout the Deep South. In the spring of 1963, Birmingham, Alabama, police chief Theophilus Eugene "Bull" Connor closed parks, swimming pools, and other public facilities in defiance of court-ordered desegregation. The leaders of the SCLC convened a series of sit-ins and demonstrations, opposed by the police and furious mobs of white citizens, as well as by Governor George Wallace, a determined opponent of desegregation. On May 11, after a bomb planted by the Ku Klux Klan exploded at the home of Dr. Martin Luther King's brother, rioting raged out of control for several days. That fall, Governor Wallace followed the example of Governor Barnett by stationing himself in front of the University of Alabama to block the enrollment of black students. Tension continued as public high schools prepared for their first year of court-ordered desegregation.

Although the first week passed in relative calm, the uneasy truce was shattered on September 15, when a bomb exploded at the Sixteenth Street Baptist Church, killing four young black girls.

Such incidents, broadcast nationwide, caused a sense of frustration and outrage among the public at large, and spurred a commonly held view that only action at the federal level would solve the issue of discrimination and the growing problem of racial violence. At the same time, the domination of the country's elite institutions by white Protestants began to end. Edward Brooke became the first black senator since the Reconstruction era; John F. Kennedy, a Catholic, was elected president; Thurgood Marshall became the first African American appointed to the U.S. Supreme Court. Discrimination in legislative representation was effectively ended by the Court in the 1962 decision of *Baker v. Carr*, which held that such representation must be determined without reference to race, sex, economic status, or place of residence within a state. The Twenty-fourth Amendment to the U. S. Constitution banned poll taxes in federal elections.

In the meantime, President Kennedy was throwing his determined support to passage of a new federal civil rights bill. In June 1963, the White House proposed a sweeping new civil rights bill, and President Kennedy signed Executive Order 10925, which established "affirmative action" as a principle in which all applicants for government jobs be treated without regard to race, creed, or color. The debate over civil rights law continued until November 22, 1963, the day of Kennedy's death, an event that gave new impetus to the legislation as it was taken up by Kennedy's successor in office, Lyndon Baines Johnson of Texas. In his speeches on civil rights, Johnson would insist on "equality as a result," not just "equality as a right." The next summer, during a presidential election year, the voter registration drive resumed with the arrival of white volunteers from the North, organized by the SNCC for what became known as Freedom Summer. On June 21, three of these northern volunteers—Michael Schwerner, Andrew Goodman, and James Chaney—were arrested, thrown in jail, released, then abducted and murdered. Their bodies were discovered on August 4. The murders gained nationwide press attention; the killing of northerners in Mississippi sounded a faint echo of the terrible war fought a century earlier. The deaths spurred passage of the Civil Rights Act of 1964; in the meantime an extensive investigation was ordered by J. Edgar Hoover, the director of the Federal Bureau of Investigation (FBI), who until that time had been most reluctant to get his agency involved in civil rights cases. The arrest of white suspects in the case marked a change from past practice in the South, where white police and juries had been slow to investigate and prosecute whites for crimes of violence against blacks. (The murder trial that followed this crime ended on October 20, 1967, with the convictions of seven members of the Ku Klux

Klan. This was one of the first trials in the nation's history to result in convictions for a violation of civil rights.)

While the 1964 Civil Rights Act banned preferential treatment for minorities, in 1965 affirmative action and other antidiscrimination measures were given a new emphasis. Federal regulations not only banned discrimination by those doing government business but also encouraged affirmative action programs among employers, educational facilities, government agencies, and other institutions. These organizations were urged to actively recruit and prefer members of racial minorities in order to show a proportional number of minorities hired or trained—objective proof of an end to the often-subjective phenomenon of discrimination.

The ongoing battles and the eventual victories of the Civil Rights movement spawned a new era in American social history. This era was described by authors Valerie Jenness and Kendal Broad in their book *Hate Crimes: New Social Movements and the Politics of Violence:*

> *Early advances by the modern civil rights movement spurred more than awareness, however. They also defined for other constituencies the potential of mobilization. As a model and ground-breaker, the Black struggle . . . facilitated the mobilization of future movements in the United States . . . by sensitizing opinion makers, polity members, authorities, and the wider public to the challenges, promises, and consequences of protest.*[7]

The direct result of this awareness was the founding of new organizations that fought for civil rights for other ethnic and national minority groups, for homosexuals, for women, and for religious faiths. These organizations include the Anti-Defamation League of B'nai B'rith (ADL); the Southern Poverty Law Center (SPLC); and the National Organization for Women (NOW). In addition, the founding of the National Organization of Victim Assistance (NOVA) in 1975 and the National Victim Center (NVC) in 1985 marked the rise of an entirely new criminal justice field, that of victims' rights. NOVA and NVC arranged for the national coordination of local and state victim assistance programs, lobbied for new legislation expanding the rights of crime victims in the justice system, and sponsored a wide range of educational programs designed to make crime victims aware of these rights.

Many of these groups took on the battle against bias violence as one of their most important functions. They used the Civil Rights movement as a model, and applied their protests, their mobilization of public opinion, and their lobbying efforts to the newly perceived, but in fact ancient, social problem of hate crimes.

HATE CRIME LEGISLATION

The U.S. Congress opened the modern era of hate-crime legislation with a federal statute, 18 U.S. 245, a law passed in 1968 as part of the landmark Civil Rights Act. The law made it illegal to, by force or by threat of force, injure, intimidate, or interfere with anyone who is engaged in six specified protected activities, by reason of their race, color, religion, or national origin. The prosecution of such crimes must be certified by the U.S. attorney general.

This law was an attempt to address the wave of violence that was occurring in response to the Civil Rights movement. The murders of civil rights workers by their opponents in the South had brought a call for action from legislators determined to see the Civil Rights Act put into full effect. Like the earlier statutes, the law enumerates "protected" activities. These include "enrolling in or attending a public school or university; participating in any benefit, program, service or facility provided by a state or local government; applying or working for any state or local government or private employer; serving as a juror; traveling in or using any facility of interstate commerce, or using any vehicle, terminal, or facility of any common carrier; or using any public facility, such as a bar, restaurant, store, hotel, movie theater, or stadium. . ."

While attention focused on the struggle of African Americans for their civil rights, bias violence was not limited to confrontation between blacks and whites. Philip Perlmutter outlines the varied ethnic and nationalistic prejudices that have often manifested themselves in recent decades by assaults and killings:

> *Immigrants, particularly illegal ones, were viewed as economic threats. More Blacks than Whites in 1979 believed illegal immigrants deprived them of jobs. . . . Tensions also erupted in Florida between Cubans and Haitians, who believed that "the government gives the Cubans financial assistance to get started, while we get deported." In Hawaii, Filipinos, Puerto Ricans, Koreans, Samoans, and native Hawaiians complained about Japanese being overly represented in government and education. . . . In West Philadelphia, in the early 1980s, Black students assaulted Asian ones for allegedly receiving preferential treatment in schools. In Denver, Mexican-Americans reacted violently to Vietnamese obtaining apartments in a housing project for which they were on the waiting list. In Long Beach, California, resentments and gang wars took place between Mexicans and Cambodians.[8]*

The year 1978 brought the passage of the first state hate-crimes statute, California's Section 190.2, providing for penalty enhancement in cases of murder motivated by prejudice. This law defined four varieties of "protected status": race, religion, color, and national origin. The range of protected statuses increased with the passage of new hate crimes laws in Washington in 1981 (ancestry); in Alaska in 1982 (creed and gender); and then disability, sexual orientation, and ethnicity. By the 1990s, in a few states protected status extended to age, marital status, membership in the armed forces, and membership in civil rights organizations.

In addition, with the passage of time new state laws expanded the range of criminal acts that could be considered as hate crimes, depending on circumstances and evidence: aggravated assault, assault and battery, vandalism, rape, threats and intimidation, arson, trespassing, stalking, and many other acts, until finally, in 1987, new California hate-crimes legislation included "all crimes" as possible hate crimes.

The states have adopted a wide variety of hate-crimes statutes, including penalty enhancement laws that increase the sentence of a convicted criminal when it can be shown that he or she was motivated by prejudice; ethnic intimidation, institutional vandalism, cross-burning, and hood-wearing statutes; reporting statutes that require statewide data collection on hate crimes; compensation statutes that provide money awards to victims of bias crimes; statutes providing for civil lawsuits against those convicted of hate crimes; and statutes that provide for parental responsibility when the offender is a juvenile. Each state also must decide on what constitutes a hate crime, which protected attributes (race, religion, sexual orientation, and so on) a hate crime may be directed against, the range of sentence enhancements, and whether or not prosecutors may ask for hate-crime penalty enhancements when charging defendants under ordinary criminal statutes (such as laws against assault or vandalism, for example). When a conviction is won under such statutes, penalty enhancement may be achieved either by lengthening the sentence or upgrading the "offense category," a method commonly used to determine criminal penalties.

Concurrent with the writing of new hate-crimes laws came the founding of grassroots and nongovernmental organizations (NGOs) seeking to deal with the issue of hate crimes on a local level through education, mobilization, and lobbying. This form of activism grew directly out of and was frequently modeled on that of the civil rights groups that had successfully pushed for equal rights for African Americans in the 1950s and 1960s. The new groups organized crisis intervention, victim assistance, legal services, watch services and street patrols, counseling, and hot lines for those in fear of or experiencing hate crimes.

Among the largest of such organizations were the Anti-Defamation League of B'nai B'rith, the National Gay and Lesbian Task Force, the National Institute Against Prejudice and Violence, and the Southern Poverty Law Center. These groups released statistics, collected with a wide variety of methods, that purported to show hate crimes on the rise. Yet rather than support a consensus for new laws, the statistics often gave rise to further debate over whether the country was actually experiencing some kind of hate-crime epidemic, or whether these and other advocacy groups were merely spinning an epidemic out of inflated numbers in order to strengthen their presence in the media and among the public.

TROUBLE IN NEW YORK

The multiethnic "melting pot" city of New York paved the way in the handling of what would become known during the 1980s as hate crimes. In 1980, the New York City Police Department (NYPD), under its commissioner Robert McGuire, established the Bias Investigation Unit, later renamed the Bias Incident Investigation Unit, or BIIU. The unit's task was to investigate criminal acts motivated by prejudice against race, religion, or ethnicity (in 1985, this list was expanded to include sexual orientation, and in 1993 to disability). The BIIU also collects and disseminates statistics on hate crimes, provides victim assistance programs, provides a liaison agency between the NYPD and community and interest groups, and conducts training programs for police officers in handling suspected bias crimes. The BIIU became a model for many other big-city police departments over the ensuing 20 years.

While New York's police department developed this response to hate crimes, a troubling death that gave strong impetus to the modern hate-crimes debate took place in the Howard Beach neighborhood of the New York City borough of Queens on December 19, 1986. A white, largely Italian working-class enclave, Howard Beach was typical of many areas of New York City, a place where neighborhood ties were close and those of different social or economic background were seen as unwanted, uninvited outsiders. On that December night, three black men had been driving along Cross Bay Boulevard, a main thoroughfare through Howard Beach, when their car broke down. While wandering through the neighborhood, they stopped at the New Park Pizzeria, where they exchanged taunts with a group of white men. Later, after midnight, the locals returned with weapons—baseball bats and a tire iron—and gave chase. One of the black men, 23-year-old Michael Griffith, ran onto the Belt Parkway and was struck and killed by a speeding car. A year later, assailants Jon Lester, Scott Kern, and Jason Ladone were found guilty of having "recklessly caused the death of another," and a fourth was charged and convicted of assault in a plea-bargain deal. As yet, New York had no statute punishing crimes motivated by racial bias.

While the Howard Beach incident simmered in New York, the debate over the true facts of the hate-crime debate, and the desire for a systematic method of recording hate crimes in order to reach a conclusion about their prevalence brought about passage of the Hate Crimes Statistics Act (HCSA). In 1983, the U.S. Civil Rights Commission had recommended the establishment of a nationwide reporting system in order to gauge the extent of crimes based on racial or religious prejudice. In 1985, the Anti-Defamation League and other organizations had asked Congress for a new statute to mandate hate-crime reporting. Vigorously lobbying for the bill were private and public civil rights groups, including the ADL, the American Civil Liberties Union, the Coalition on Hate Crimes Prevention, and the International Association of Chiefs of Police.

One issue arising during the debate over the HCSA was inclusion of gender as a protected status for the purpose of defining hate crime. Few states included gender in their hate-crimes provisions; nor did the ADL include gender as a protected status within the model legislation it created in 1981. Women's groups argued that gender bias is often the basis for crimes of violence such as spousal battery and rape, and that female crime victims are most often victimized by men. They also argued that inclusion of gender bias in the bill would serve its most useful purpose in raising public awareness of the prevalence of gender-motivated crimes.

However, other organizations lobbying for passage of the bill opposed the inclusion of gender bias. Opponents maintained that because violence against women was often motivated by a personal relationship between two individuals, the victim of such violence could not be considered as being selected because of her membership in a group. Also, the broader definition of hate crime to include gender bias would turn the spotlight away from hate crimes motivated by racial or religious prejudice, the concern of organizations such as the ADL and the NAACP.

In their book *Hate Crimes: New Social Movements and the Politics of Violence*, Valerie Jenness and Kendal Broad describe the problems that arose with gender and the HCSA:

> *Prior to the passage of the HCSA, the Coalition on Hate Crimes Prevention contemplated promoting the inclusion of gender as a protected status in the HCSA, but eventually decided against it for a variety of reasons. First, some members of the coalition believed that the inclusion of gender would delay, if not completely impede, the (timely) passage of the HCSA. Second, some members of the coalition argued that the inclusion of gender in the HCSA would open the door for [the protected status of] age, disability, position in a labor dispute, party affiliation, and/or membership in the armed forces provisions. Third, some believed that including gender would make the enactment of the HCSA too cumbersome—if not entirely impossible—since violent crimes against women are so pervasive . . . opponents feared that adding*

gender as a victim category would simply overwhelm the data collection ef-
forts of law enforcement agencies and human rights organizations that track
hate crimes . . . [and that] the large number of crimes against women would
overshadow statistics on hate crimes against members of other groups.[9]

Although the House of Representatives had first passed the bill in 1985, Congress had adjourned before a Senate vote, and debate continued for five more years before the bill's final passage in 1990. An important point of debate was the inclusion of antihomosexual violence in the bill—the HCSA was the first federal civil rights law to mention sexual orientation. Led by Senator Jesse Helms of North Carolina, a group of lawmakers opposed the inclusion of antigay violence in the HCSA and the designation of homosexuals as a "protected group."

A compromise was reached with a passage in the bill that expressed the finding of Congress that "1. American family life is the foundation of American society. 2. Federal policy should encourage the well-being, financial security, and health of the American family. 3. Schools should not deemphasize the critical value of American family life." The addition of this language paved the way for passage of the HCSA in 1990 and its final signing by President George H. W. Bush in April 1990.

This seemingly innocuous "reporting statute," which carried no criminal penalties or sanctions for bias-motivated violence, turned out to be a watershed in the field of hate-crimes law. The law gave responsibility to the attorney general for establishing guidelines and collecting data on certain crimes from state and local law enforcement officials—crimes that manifested "evidence of prejudice based upon race, religion, sexual orientation, or ethnicity." The crimes included murder, manslaughter, rape, aggravated assault, simple assault, intimidation, arson, and vandalism. The statistics, which at first were given voluntarily, would be published as part of the Uniform Crime Report (UCR) program of the FBI. In 1991, the FBI issued its *Training Guide for Hate Crime Data Collection* to aid public officials in the collection and reporting of hate-crimes statistics.

For legislators, policy makers, and journalists, the annual UCR represents the nation's crime score—the statistical guidebook to trends in the occurrence and type of crime and, since hate crimes appeared as a new category in the UCR in January 1991, to the issue of hate-crimes legislation. The 1991 report consisted of a single page of statistics on hate crime as recorded in 1991. Data from 32 states and 2,771 law enforcement agencies was presented; a grand total of 4,558 hate crimes were recorded, out of a total of 14 million crimes reported (by 12,805 agencies) in the comprehensive UCR.

At that time, the number of law enforcement agencies actually reporting hate crimes was low—about one in five, and those from mostly urban departments where bias crimes had already been acknowledged as a problem. Gradually, the reporting improved. In 1992, the number of reporting agencies jumped to 6,865, representing 42 states; in that year the number of reported hate crimes increased to 7,466. By the late 1990s, nearly every jurisdiction in the country was involved. In 1999, 12,122 agencies from 49 states reported 7,876 hate crimes. Most of the states had passed laws mandating such reporting, and as the recording of hate crimes became more common, the statistical picture came to be seen as more accurate. The effect of requiring hate-crime reporting was to make police officers aware of hate crime, and the effect of publishing statistics on hate crime was to provide reinforcement to those demanding action on the issue.

For many, however, the issue of hate crimes was not so cut-and-dried as simply checking a box on a police incident report. Many police departments did not have the time, personnel, or inclination to investigate hate crimes. Some saw the reporting of hate crime as a blemish on their community, and thus underreported it. On the other hand, a high (and inaccurate) reporting of hate crimes sometimes backed up a demand for the hiring of more police officers, or the granting of additional public funds for equipment and salaries. Above it all lay the possibility that the raw numbers could be manipulated—hate crimes could be shown to be "increasing" or "insignificant"—to support or denigrate a certain point of view. The raw statistics of hate crime gradually turned into a debating point for both sides of the overriding issue: whether hate-crimes laws are necessary, effective, or constitutional.

THE CROWN HEIGHTS RIOT

In the meantime, racial tensions continued to simmer in New York. To the north of Howard Beach, in the Brooklyn neighborhood of Crown Heights, there had been longstanding tension between a newer community of conservative Hasidic Jews and a long-established group of African Americans. The two groups separated themselves as much as possible and carried out their disputes in relative peace, most often over the issues of housing and schools. But the rising tension needed only a spark to bring open violence, and that spark was struck on August 19, 1991, when a seven-year-old African-American boy, Gavin Cato, was killed by a car that was part of a Hasidic Jewish motorcade. In the riots that broke out subsequently, a Jewish student, Yankel Rosenbaum, was chased down by a mob and stabbed to death. Rosenbaum identified his killer before dying in a hospital a few hours later.

The Crown Heights riots enveloped the administration of Mayor David Dinkins in controversy. The mayor, an African American, was accused of not doing enough to calm the situation and with instituting a "no arrest" policy that brought about a state of near anarchy. Norman Rosenbaum, the brother of Yankel Rosenbaum, and members of the Crown Heights Jewish community brought suit against the city. The suit was settled under the subsequent administration of Mayor Rudolph Giuliani, who made a public apology and extended a financial settlement to the family.

In the meantime, the criminal trials proceeded. Lemrick Nelson and Charles Price were brought up on criminal charges by the state of New York. Lemrick Nelson, who was 16 years old at the time, was charged in Rosenbaum's murder, while Price was charged with incitement to riot, after being videotaped calling on a crowd to "kill the Jews." Lemrick's attorney argued that he committed the killing in the heat of the moment and without premeditation. The prosecution dismissed this defense, pointing out that others in the mob had not been inspired to murder. But on October 29, 1992, Lemrick Nelson was found not guilty of the murder of Yankel Rosenbaum.

Nelson and Price were then charged in federal court with violating Rosenbaum's civil rights. In 1997, these charges brought convictions; Nelson was sentenced to the maximum 19 years, six months; Price was sentenced to 21 years, 10 months. But the Crown Heights verdict was overturned in January 2002 by the U.S. Second Circuit Court of Appeals. The decision was based on the attempts by District Court judge David G. Trager to select a jury representative of the community—from both a racial and religious standpoint. The appeals court found that such race-based selection of jurors was impermissible. A new trial was ordered, and in April 2003, a trial of Nelson began in Brooklyn's federal court. This time Nelson admitted to the killing but claimed he committed the murder while drunk and not because of his anti-Semitic views.

Through the 1990s, the hate-crime debate continued in New York City, a kaleidoscopic, often balkanized metropolis that has centuries of experience with violence between rival nationalities, religions, and interest groups. Many murders, assaults, arsons, and other crimes were quickly transformed into political debates, in which politicians seeking support from one group or the other either characterized or dismissed the act in question as a hate crime. These debates involved high civic officials: city and borough council members, the mayor, the commissioner of police, and public and private organizations. In turn, the hate-crimes debates in New York, the nation's media capital and a place where local events can be magnified to national proportions, rippled across the United States, bringing the subject of hate-crimes laws sharply into focus for the public and for legislators.

THE SUPREME COURT AND HATE CRIMES LAW

A series of decisions made by the U.S. Supreme Court supported the expansion of criminal and civil penalties for discrimination and bias-motivated violence. In the 1987 decision of *Shaare Tifila Congregation v. Cobb*, the Court allowed the members of any ethnic group to sue for compensation and punitive damages under the provisions of the 1866 Civil Rights Act.

In the same year as the passage of the HCSA, an incident occurred that resulted in one of the Supreme Court's most far-reaching judicial decisions over hate crimes. It was an act of petty vandalism that happened in the evening of June 21, 1990, in the front yard of Mr. Russ Jones, a new black resident of a mostly white East Side neighborhood of St. Paul, Minnesota. Hearing a noise from his front yard, Jones looked out to see a small cross, made from two broken sticks of furniture, burning in front of his house.

Seventeen-year-old Robert Viktora was arrested and charged with violating St. Paul's Bias-Motivated Crime Ordinance. The ordinance banned the display of any "symbol, object, appellation, characterization, or graffiti" that "arouses anger, alarm, or resentment in others on the basis of race, color, creed, religion, or gender." Adopted in 1982, the ordinance went beyond the ADL model statute, which punished bias-motivated crimes against persons or property, to punish bias-motivated expression, which would be treated as a misdemeanor synonymous with "disorderly conduct." The law was amended in 1989 to include burning crosses and Nazi symbols such as the swastika. The charge against Viktora was the first prosecution brought by the city under the ordinance.

Arguing that the law violated the First Amendment, Viktora's attorney, Edward J. Cleary, appealed the conviction in Ramsey County Juvenile Court, where Viktora was originally convicted. The judge agreed with Cleary and the conviction was overturned. The court cited an opinion rendered in a 1989 U.S. Supreme Court case, *Texas v. Johnson*, in which the Court ruled that Dallas could not outlaw flag burning solely for the unpalatable sentiments it expressed. In the same way, St. Paul could not outlaw cross burning on the grounds that the expression was racist, unpleasant, or socially unacceptable.

St. Paul then appealed to the Minnesota Supreme Court, which upheld the conviction. The opinion stated that cross burning was not an expression that deserved free-speech protections. This decision was based on the "fighting words" verdict reached by the U.S. Supreme Court in 1942 in the landmark case of *Chaplinsky v. New Hampshire*, which held that expression that tends to incite disorder is not protected by the First Amendment. Finding that cross burning was a comparable act, the Minnesota Supreme Court decided it was also not protected by the Constitution, upholding the St. Paul ordinance and the conviction of Robert Viktora.

The U.S. Supreme Court reversed this decision on June 22, 1992, in a unanimous decision. The Supreme Court found the law too broad, but the justices split on whether cross burning was a form of speech that should be protected by the First Amendment. Four justices took the position that the law could be struck down as it was overbroad; five took the position that the law unconstitutionally singled out specific expressions on the basis of their content. This majority argued that laws passed against expression cannot select certain viewpoints and not others for prohibition. The five-to-four vote was split along "conservative" and "liberal" lines in the Court.

Writing about *R.A.V. v. City of St. Paul*, columnist Nat Hentoff, a frequent commentator on First Amendment issues, described the case as follows:

> *It was the First Amendment, not cross-burning, that powered this case. At issue was a municipal ordinance so overbroad that its effect, if adopted by other cities and states, would have chilled the speech, both verbal and symbolic, of large numbers of protesting citizens.*[10]

WISCONSIN V. MITCHELL

A second landmark Supreme Court decision was reached in 1993 with *Wisconsin v. Mitchell*. The case arose out of an assault that took place in Kenosha, Wisconsin, on October 7, 1989, when a group of African-American youths, enraged by a scene in the movie *Mississippi Burning*, attacked and beat a white youth, nearly killing him. One of the defendants, Todd Mitchell, had been convicted of aggravated battery and charged under Wisconsin's statute 939.645, which provides for "penalty enhancement" when the accused selects a victim for a crime based on the victim's "race, religion, color, disability, sexual orientation, national origin or ancestry of that person." The evidence for conviction under the statute was not a criminal action, but instead Mitchell's choice of words just before the attack took place: "Do you all feel hyped up to move on some white people? . . . You all want to f—k somebody up? There goes a white boy; go get him."

The enhanced sentence was challenged all the way to the U.S. Supreme Court on the grounds that it represented a constitutional ban on free speech. The defendants, and the many briefs that were filed in this case on their behalf, claimed that the Wisconsin statute was broadly unconstitutional in the same manner as the St. Paul city ordinance that was struck down in *R.A.V. v. St. Paul*. But on June 11, 1993, the nine justices unanimously upheld the sentence and therefore passed a favorable verdict on all similar penalty-enhancement statutes in the United States. In the Court's opinion, ". . .Whereas the ordinance struck down in *R.A.V.* was explicitly directed at expression, the statute in this case is aimed at conduct unprotected by the First Amendment." Since the decision of *Wisconsin v. Mitchell*, the Supreme Court has not found it necessary to certify any further cases for argument on the subject of penalty-enhancement statutes.

HATE CRIMES IN THE COURTROOM

Through the early 1990s, as state legislatures wrote new hate-crime statutes, and as law enforcement began recording, investigating, and prosecuting hate crimes, criminal and appeals courts throughout the country faced the task of interpreting the new statutes. There were a wide variety of legal challenges to hate-crimes law: vagueness and arbitrary arrest and prosecution in violation of the Fourteenth Amendment; unconstitutional restriction of free speech and opinion in violation of the First Amendment; and denial of equal protection before the law, also in violation of the Fourteenth Amendment, as the statutes singled out certain ethnic, religious, and other groups for preferential protection.

Hate-crimes laws survived their earliest challenges in 1991, with several state appeals court decisions finding in support of the laws. The Wisconsin Court of Appeals decision in *Wisconsin v. Mitchell*, for example, upheld Wisconsin's penalty-enhancement law on the grounds that the statute condemned criminal conduct and not protected speech. In 1992, however, a series of decisions—including the U.S. Supreme Court opinion in *R.A.V. v. St. Paul*, the Ohio Supreme Court decision on that state's ethnic intimidation law in *Ohio v. Wyant*, and the Wisconsin Supreme Court's overturning of the earlier appeals court decision in *Wisconsin v. Mitchell*—found hate-crimes laws to be overbroad and an unconstitutional restriction of speech. These decisions, most of which cited *R.A.V. v. St. Paul* in their support, found that those accused of hate crimes were being punished not for conduct, but for opinion and motive. These decisions cast the future of hate-crimes legislation into serious doubt on constitutional grounds.

Over the following two years, however, hate-crimes laws survived a series of important challenges. In the 1992 decision in *Dobbins v. Florida* in the Florida Court of Appeals, the judges upheld the laws as legal restriction not only on criminal conduct but on discrimination, which the state had a compelling interest in combatting through new statutes. Over the next few years, statutes similar to Wisconsin's penalty-enhancement law have withstood nearly all the legal challenges presented to them in state courts. By the late 1990s, hate-crimes legislation grew increasingly standardized across the country, as the courts moved away from the basic constitutional issues and delivered more focused instruction on what constituted punishable behavior on the part of hate-crime offenders. Nevertheless, hate-crimes law still had its vociferous critics, who maintained that such statutes remained vague, redundant, and unconstitutional. The debate continued as new federal legislation was proposed increasing the range of offenses punishable as hate crimes.

THE VIOLENCE AGAINST WOMEN ACT

After the passage of the HCSA, women's groups frustrated in their efforts to include gender bias in the definition of hate crime began lobbying Congress for a new bill specifically targeting such crimes. The lobbying effort won a sympathetic hearing on Capitol Hill, and the effort to draft a new bill specifically targeting gender-based hate crimes emerged in 1990, the year of the HCSA's final passage. Senator Joseph Biden, who introduced the Violence Against Women Act, stated in Judiciary Committee hearings in 1992 that:

> *Title III [of the VAWA] seeks to put gender-motivated bias crimes against women on the same footing as other bias crimes. Whether the attack is motivated by racial bias or ethnic bias or gender bias, the results are often the same. The violence not only wounds physically, it degrades and terrorizes, instilling fear and inhibiting the lives of those similarly situated.[11]*

The new law was included in an omnibus bill known as the Violent Crime Control and Law Enforcement Act, which passed the House and Senate in 1993 and then was signed by President Bill Clinton. Title I of the Violence Against Women Act provided for a budget of $300 million for special units of police and prosecutors and public-safety measures, such as lights and security cameras. Title III of the act allowed plaintiffs to bring civil suit against defendants for violence motivated by gender, even if no prior criminal complaint or conviction existed. Title IV dealt with campus security measures for women; Title V provided for training programs on the issues of gender-motivated violence for state and federal judges.

HATE CRIMES GAIN NATIONAL PROMINENCE

Hate crimes took an ever-increasing share of news headlines through the mid-1990s. In Fayetteville, North Carolina, three Fort Bragg soldiers were charged with the bias-motivated slaying of an African-American couple in December 1995. At the same time, newspapers were reporting a rash of church arsons, as well as vandalism of synagogues, across the South.

The rising prominence of the issue inspired widespread discussion and analysis of hate crimes and the psychology of hate-crimes perpetrators among academics. Surveys showed that the incidence of hate crimes tends to rise with difficult economic conditions or with dramatic changes of the socioeconomic makeup of affected neighborhoods. In addition, racist speech and discourse on the Internet, talk radio, and in the media can prompt what the academics called a "climate of hate," in which racial tensions are rising and a single confrontation or incident between members of different racial or religious groups can spark a wave of bias-motivated violence. The sharp rise of hate crimes in the early 1990s was put down to an economic recession and competition from foreign producers; the issue of immigration, especially immigration from Latin America and the Caribbean; and certain nationally prominent incidents such as the beating of black motorist Rodney King by several Los Angeles police officers in March 1991.

JAMES BYRD AND HATE-CRIMES LAW IN TEXAS

On June 7, 1998, while driving their pickup truck along a dirt road in Jasper, Texas, three white men—Shawn Allen Berry, Lawrence Brewer, and John King—picked up a black hitchhiker, James Byrd, Jr. The three men beat Byrd, chained him by the ankles to the back of the pickup truck, and dragged him along two miles of the road, killing him and mutilating and dismembering the body. On July 7, the three men were indicted on a charge of first-degree murder. John King was convicted of murder and kidnapping on February 23, 1999, and sentenced to death. Lawrence Brewer was found guilty of murder, although on the witness stand he had claimed to be only a bystander to the crime. He was also sentenced to death. Shawn Berry was found guilty as well, but was spared the death penalty.

The death of James Byrd touched off a long dispute over hate-crimes legislation in Texas. The debate revolved around a proposed law known as the James Byrd, Jr., Hate Crimes Act, a penalty-enhancement law that would have affected anyone convicted of a crime against race, religion, or sexual preference. The statute would have enhanced certain categories of crimes, although not first-degree felonies or capital murder. For vandalism, the law would have enhanced a Class C misdemeanor, which in Texas carries a maximum fine of $500 and no prison sentence, to a Class B misdemeanor punishable by a maximum fine of $2,000 and up to six months in prison.

The bill had vehement supporters and opponents. Opponents argued that the proposed bill would violate the legal principle of equal protection and confer special rights on certain classes of citizens. They also argued that Texas already had a hate-crimes statute. This law, passed in 1993 in response to vandalism against Texas synagogues, set down enhanced penalties for those convicted of crimes against members of "a group."

Supporters of the new bill believed this statute was too vague and largely ineffective in fighting bias crimes. In their opinion, the new law improved on the old one by specifying broad categories such as race, religion, and sexual orientation, giving prosecutors a better focal point for investigation and prosecution of bias crimes. They also pointed out that by avoiding the naming of any group such as Jews, African Americans, or homosexuals, the James Byrd, Jr., Hate Crimes Act avoided the constitutional bans against unequal protection of the laws. In 1999, the bill passed the Texas House but was killed in a Senate committee. In early 2000, the bill again came up for a hearing before the Texas House Judicial Affairs Committee. During this hearing, Stella Byrd, the mother of James Byrd, testified about the crime and pleaded with lawmakers to pass the bill as a testament to her son. Opponents brought their witnesses forward as well. A retired air force major challenged the bill and demanded that hate crimes against members of the military be included.

A change in membership on the Senate committee, giving Democratic members a four-to-three majority, helped its chances in 2001. The Senate committee, chaired by Senfronia Thompson, a Democrat and a sponsor of the bill, finally approved the bill.

In "The Hate Debate," an article in *Texas Monthly* discussing the Texas hate-crimes bill, author John Spong succinctly described the hate-crimes debate as follows:

> *Most lawmaking involves familiar questions of politics and policy, matters that are worth fighting over but are nevertheless well removed from basic ideas of what kind of society we want and what role our laws should play in shaping it. There is a certain amount of government intrusion when the state sets a speed limit or requires cars to be inspected, but it does not have the same impact as a law that says society disapproves of a certain thought or belief, or one that says that some victims need more protection than others from similar crimes. Hate crimes laws seem to draw just these sorts of lines, which is one reason they stir up so much emotion. At issue are two of the most elemental principles of American law, free speech and equal protection of the laws—the kind of things that first-year law students argue about among themselves in the first week of law school.[12]*

MATTHEW SHEPARD

A second high-profile hate-crime case began on October 6, 1998, when Matthew Shepard, a gay University of Wyoming student, was beaten, tied to a fence post, and left for dead outside Laramie, Wyoming. Following the murder, the state of Wyoming indicted Russell Henderson and Aaron McKinney for aggravated robbery, kidnapping, and attempted murder. When Shepard died, five days after the incident, Henderson and McKinney were both charged with first-degree murder, a charge that can bring the death penalty in Wyoming. At the time of the indictments, Wyoming did not have a hate-crimes statute.

In the months between Shepard's murder and the trial of Henderson and McKinney, the crime sparked a nationwide debate on the issue of hate crimes. Competing demonstrations were held in state capitals and in Washington D.C., with one side calling for tougher and more comprehensive hate-crimes legislation and the other protesting the same.

The trial of Russell Henderson began on March 24, 1999. The defendant pled guilty to the charges of kidnapping and murder and was given a sentence of two consecutive terms of life in prison. McKinney, whose trial began on October 11, 1999, attempted to defend his actions by reason of panic induced by Shepard's homosexual advances. The judge barred this defense, however, and McKinney was found guilty of felony murder (and acquitted of premeditated murder). Through the intercession of the parents of Matthew Shepard, McKinney was spared the death penalty and sentenced to life in prison without parole.

The Matthew Shepard murder brought the spotlight onto another aspect of hate crimes: violence directed against individuals on the basis of their sexual orientation. Both inside and outside of legal institutions, homosexuals have always been singled out for violence in many different societies. Although the inclusion of such acts in the legal definition of "hate crime" was contested through the 1990s, many state and federal statutes have been adopted or expanded to include them. In the same way, crimes that involve prejudice against the disabled have been added, state by state, to the legal definition.

In the late 1990s, the introduction of new hate-crimes legislation became an annual event in the U.S. Congress. The Hate Crimes Prevention Act of 1998 would have expanded federal jurisdiction over hate crimes by allowing federal authorities to investigate all hate crimes, and not just those in which the victim was exercising a federally protected right such as the right to vote, attend a public school, and so on. The legislation also expanded the definition of hate crimes to include those committed over gender, sexual orientation, and disability. The new law died in committee, however, while the debate over the necessity for new hate-crimes legislation continued.

In March 1999, Representative John Conyers of Michigan introduced the Hate Crimes Prevention Act of 1999. The new law would have expanded the definition of hate crimes to include those committed against homosexuals. With more than 200 cosponsors and support from both political parties, the bill passed the Senate in July 1999, but failed in the House of Representatives.

THE YEAR 1999

Hate crimes again took the national spotlight in 1999. On February 19, 1999, a gay man named Billy Jack Gaither was murdered by Charles Monroe Butler and Steven Mullins in Sylacauga, Alabama. Both of the killers were given life sentences. Over the Fourth of July weekend of 1999, white supremacist Benjamin Smith went on a shooting rampage in Illinois and Indiana. The spree began in West Rogers Park, a mostly Jewish Chicago neighborhood, on the evening of Friday, July 2, 1999, when Smith opened fire on Dr. Michael Messing and his 16-year-old son Ephraim. Both men escaped unhurt. But Smith was not finished. Later he drove to Skokie, a Chicago suburb, where he opened fire on Ricky Byrdsong, an African-American former Northwestern University basketball coach, killing Byrdsong immediately. He then drove to the suburb of Northbrook, where he shot an Asian-American couple he found in a car.

The rampage continued on the next day, Saturday, July 3. Smith shot and wounded an African-American man in the state capital, Springfield, then shot a black minister in Decatur. He then drove to the campus of the University of Illinois in Urbana, where he fired on a group of Asian-American students, injuring one of them. On Sunday, July 4, Smith arrived in Bloomington, Indiana, where he opened fire on a group of Korean Americans while they were leaving Sunday church services. One of the targets, an Indiana University student, was killed. Smith fled the scene in a stolen car as the local police gave chase. When finally stopped and cornered, Smith killed himself.

Another rampage occurred a month later in Los Angeles. On August 10, 1999, Buford Furrow began shooting at a Jewish community center, then killed Joseph Ileto, a Filipino postal worker. Furrow surrendered the following day and was charged by a federal grand jury with five separate hate crimes. On March 1, 2000, Ronald Taylor, an African American, killed three white men and wounded two others in Wilkinsburg, Pennsylvania. Taylor was arrested and charged with murder, arson, aggravated assault, and "ethnic intimidation."

HATE CRIMES AND THE ELECTION OF 2000

During the 2000 presidential election, the issue of hate crimes again came to the fore. The hate-crimes issue followed Texas governor George W. Bush as he entered the race. The NAACP called on its members to work against Bush for his opposition to the hate-crimes statute in Texas, opposition that the NAACP largely blamed for the defeat of the bill. A television commercial, showing a chain being dragged behind a pickup truck, alluded to the

Byrd crime and suggested that Bush was insensitive to black voters and to the issue of bias violence against African Americans.

Governor Bush was finally declared president by the U.S. Supreme Court after a bitterly contested vote recount in the state of Florida. Early the next year, the momentum within the Texas legislature began to swing back in favor of the James Byrd, Jr., Hate Crimes Act. With the unanimous support of Democratic representatives in the Texas House of Representatives, the bill passed the House on April 24, 2001, by a margin of 87 to 60. An editorial in the *Dallas Morning News* on May 2 urged the Texas senators to pass the bill:

> *Opponents mischaracterize the issue when they claim that hate crimes legislation distinguishes one victim from another. It is more truthful to say that what is being differentiated are not the victims but rather the crimes. Not all crimes are equal. What separates them are not just the varying degrees of damage and human suffering they cause but also whether those damaged or made to suffer are individuals or a whole group of people.*
>
> *When a person is attacked because of the essence of who he is, the attacker intends to do harm that goes beyond the individual victim. The perpetrator intends to send a message—a violent one—to others who share the same characteristic: You could be next.*
>
> *Now, the Texas Senate has a chance to send a message of its own—that this sort of intimidation will not be tolerated.[13]*

On the next day, the Senate committee passed the bill 5 to 1, and on May 7, the bill passed the Senate by a vote of 20 to 10, despite the addition of amendments by Senator Florence Shapiro intended to derail the legislation. When the bill was returned to the House, it was passed by a vote of 90 to 55, and on May 11, Governor Rick Perry signed the bill.

COUNTERING HATE CRIMES: COMMUNITY RESPONSE

While federal lawmakers wrangled over new hate-crimes legislation, state and local authorities formulated a variety of responses to the issue. The federal Bureau of Justice Assistance included the following three programs in its report "Promising Practices Against Hate Crimes: Five State and Local Demonstration Projects," published in May 2000.

In San Diego, the Victim Assistance Project set down a strictly defined procedure in which police officers first call in an Anti-Defamation League "crisis interventionist" to work with victims at the scene of the crime. On the following day, a police detective contacts the victim to follow up on the investigation, while the interventionist begins working with the Victim Assistance Project office to determine what services the victim may need: repairing or repainting vandalized property, one-on-one counseling, moving to a new home, and so on. Two to four weeks after the incident, a coordinator again determines the needs of the victims, making the appropriate referrals, while the detective provides an update on the investigation and prosecution of the crime.

Another Southern California project, the Juvenile Offenders Learning Tolerance (JOLT) program, focuses on hate crime among youth in Antelope Valley, a community lying 80 miles northeast of Los Angeles. Throughout the 1990s, the area suffered one of the highest youth hate-crime rates in the region. The JOLT program includes two-day workshops for school faculty and administrators at the Simon Wiesenthal Center's Museum of Tolerance in Los Angeles; full-day workshops in the schools in which teachers are trained in the use of hate-crime prevention curricula; and an early intervention program for juveniles 12 to 18 years of age who have participated in some kind of bias crime or incident. After the incident takes place, the juveniles are given the choice of expulsion/suspension or participating in the program, in which they go through an intensive antihate curriculum, attend an anger-management and conflict-resolution program, write letters of apology to the victims, and carry out a restitution agreement, if appropriate. If they successfully complete the program, the offenders stay in school and avoid the filing of a criminal petition against them in juvenile court.

The state of Massachusetts has come up with one of the most comprehensive responses to hate crimes, under the aegis of the Massachusetts Governor's Task Force on Hate Crimes. In the fall of 1999, the state established civil rights teams in seven Massachusetts high schools. The teams include 12 to 18 students who work to promote tolerance and lessen prejudice and bias-motivated harassment. The task force also established a web site, www.stopthehate.org, that gives public information and is also accessible to the school civil rights teams, who are allowed through the use of a password to communicate with similar teams working in other states.

In a statewide campaign, Massachusetts also designated May 1–7, 2000, Stop the Hate Week. The task force provided schools throughout the state with antibias curricula and arranged workshops and community forums.

THE HATE CRIMES DEBATE

Sociologists, criminologists, psychologists, and journalists have all added their considered opinions to the discussion on hate crimes. All acknowledge the existence of such acts, and many have suggested what inspires such crimes. A few generally agreed-upon points have emerged.

First, hate crimes by and large are committed by individuals, not groups. The existence of "hate groups" may play an important role in the thought and motivation of hate-crime perpetrators, but if the leaders of such groups direct a conspiracy to commit a hate crime they risk a civil lawsuit and very heavy financial punishment. For example, the White Aryan Resistance, a neo-Nazi organization headed by Tom Metzger, was subject to a multimillion-dollar judgment in the wake of a race-motivated murder in Portland, Oregon. Second, hate crimes are the acts of the young, and more particularly the young male. Such perpetrators often act out of boredom, peer group pressure, and a desire to prove themselves through an act of violence committed against a despised group.

What are the motivations? One is resentment over the perceived threat of a different class of people to another group's success and standing in the community. Such resentment arrives when blacks move into a white neighborhood, when immigrants appear in the workplace, or when women or homosexuals march or protest against discrimination. Prejudice is sometimes given a legal stamp of approval, such as when the U.S. Congress passed the Chinese Exclusion Act of 1882. At this time, Chinese laborers made up a majority of foreigners brought into the United States for work on the western railroads; when railroad construction began to slow, American-born citizens saw a threat to their jobs and clamored for the government to close the immigration gates.

The success of immigrants can be deeply resented by those who have long-established roots in the community, and whose prejudice and antagonisms are aroused when an economic threat is perceived. Such was the case for Hispanic victims of hate crimes, who in the late 1990s made up the largest single ethnic group victimized when an ethnic prejudice was involved. Violence against Hispanic immigrants in the southern tier of the United States, and particularly in California, Florida, and Texas, has given rise to what many local law enforcement officials are reporting to the FBI as hate crimes. The legal status of the victim—as a resident alien, naturalized citizen, or illegal alien—often makes no difference to the perpetrator.

Another spark for the commission of a hate crime may be a perceived slight or injury by a member of the targeted group. A tense or violent encounter between two individuals may lead to a thirst for retribution or revenge on some randomly selected stranger, who represents the enemy only through his or her appearance. The same may occur when a national or international event, and in particular a war, commences and a certain ethnic group becomes an official national enemy. During the two Gulf wars between Iraq and U.S.-led coalitions of European and Arab allies, Arab Americans were subject to increased violence and harassment throughout the United States.

The perpetrator of hate crimes is most often not a habitual offender or career criminal. In the American Psychological Association report entitled *Hate Crimes Today: An Age-Old Foe in Modern Dress*, the authors found that: "Most hate crimes are carried out by otherwise law-abiding young people who see little wrong with their actions. Alcohol and drugs sometimes help fuel these crimes, but the main determinant appears to be personal prejudice, a situation that colors people's judgment, blinding the aggressors to the immorality of what they are doing."[14]

Alcohol or drugs may influence an individual or group to simply leave aside the normal social inhibitions and allow fears and anger to come to the surface, inspiring an act of violence. Hate crimes range from such random acts, to premeditated injury inflicted on a chosen individual, to those perpetrated by what criminologists term the "mission offender," an individual who carries out a crusade, sometimes carefully planned, against the hated group.

THE ROLE OF LAW

The essential debate over hate crimes revolves around the necessity, effectiveness, and constitutionality of hate-crimes statutes. Those supporting hate-crimes laws explain that such laws are a necessary defense of public order, which is threatened more seriously when the issue of race prejudice is involved. According to the Anti-Defamation League, an organization that saw its model legislation widely adopted by the states: "Hate crimes demand a priority response because of their special emotional and psychological impact on the victim and the victim's community. . . . By making members of minority communities fearful, angry, and suspicious of other groups—and of the power structure that is supposed to protect them—these incidents can damage the fabric of our society and fragment communities."[15]

Another argument for hate-crimes laws claims it as a logical extension of widely accepted laws that prohibit discrimination based on race, gender, religions, nationality, and so on. Nadine Strossen, in "Yes: Discriminatory Crimes," a 1993 article published in the *American Bar Association Journal*, explains this viewpoint as follows:

> *[The] fundamental distinction between protected thought and punishable conduct is central to both free speech jurisprudence and anti-discrimination laws. . . . Anti-discrimination laws long have prohibited discriminatory acts that would not otherwise be illegal—for example, refusing to hire someone—because of society's consensus that such discriminatory acts cause special harms, not only to the immediate victim but also to the racial or other societal group*

to which the victim belongs, and to our heterogenous society more generally. Why, then, shouldn't the law treat discriminatory criminal acts more severely than other criminal acts?[16]

Opponents see the demands of certain groups for legal protections and civil rights as inspiring a backlash among those who oppose such protections. They also view hate-crimes laws as a cynical tool of politicians seeking to curry favor with the voters. James Jacobs, a prominent opponent of hate-crimes laws, states in *Hate Crimes: Criminal Law and Identity Politics*:

> *Politicians have fully endorsed the existence of a hate crime epidemic. Passing laws denouncing hate crime provides politicians with an opportunity to decry bigotry. They can propose hate crime legislation as a quick-fix solution that's cheap and satisfying to important groups of constituents.[17]*

As for legal principles, opponents believe that punishing prejudicial beliefs, no matter how obnoxious they may be, violates a fundamental constitutional right to freedom of expression and belief. In his article "Should Hate Be a Crime?" Jacobs responded as follows:

> *To fragment criminal law into specialized laws recognizing a moral hierarchy of motives and offender/victim configurations will have little, if any, crime-control benefit, while carrying serious risks for race relations and social harmony. . . . The new hate crime laws both reflect and contribute to the politicization of the crime problem and the criminal justice process, especially around issues of race, and thereby exacerbate social divisions and social conflict.[18]*

HATE CRIMES AND SEPTEMBER 11, 2001

The long-term effects of the devastating terrorist attack of September 11, 2001, may well extend to the nation's laws and criminal justice system. On that morning, 19 hijackers, all of them Muslims, commandeered four passenger jetliners in the eastern United States, disabled the pilots and crew, and used the planes as guided missiles against targets that to them symbolized American power, imperialism, and arrogance. One plane crashed into the Pentagon in Washington, D.C., and two others hit and destroyed the twin towers of the World Trade Center in New York City. A fourth plane, in which the passengers apparently overcame the hijackers, crashed in rural Pennsylvania before reaching its target. Approximately 3,000 people were killed in the attacks.

Almost immediately after the attacks took place, they were attributed to the al-Qaeda terror network masterminded by Osama bin Laden, a Saudi exile who ran the organization from a headquarters in Afghanistan. In the wake of the attacks, Arab Americans became the target of violent assaults, and in some cases outright murder—crimes unquestionably motivated by the bias of the perpetrator against the nationality or appearance of the victim. Virulently anti-Arab statements and proclamations appeared on the Internet, while government officials, including President George W. Bush, called for calm and tolerance. While the panic and shock over the September 11 attacks slowly subsided, occasional violence continued. An assailant shot and killed an Indian gas station owner in Mesa, Arizona. A gunman in a ski mask fired more than 20 shots at Hassan Awdah, a Yemeni native and U.S. citizen, in Gary, Indiana. Awdah was saved by a thick screen of bulletproof glass. The Islamic Institute of New York received daily threats against its 450 students. The incidence of "profiling," or selective questioning or investigation of individuals according to their race or nationality, also became commonplace. In Providence, Rhode Island, while searching for terrorists on an Amtrak train, police removed and questioned a group of 10 people who appeared to be of Arab descent.

The anti-Arab backlash after September 11 illustrated an important aspect of hate crimes: They are often motivated not by personal animosity or prejudice but by events well outside the daily life and experience of both perpetrator and victim. Fall 2001 echoed the last weeks of 1941, when after the attack on Pearl Harbor many Japanese Americans were attacked, beaten, harassed, and vilified by complete strangers who, in ordinary times, would concern themselves little with the presence of Asians in their midst.

EXTENDING HATE-CRIMES LAW IN THE 21ST CENTURY

As of May 2003, the hate-crimes debate had been largely overshadowed by other national concerns. Yet legislators continue to debate proposed extensions and innovations in hate-crimes law. Whether or not homosexuals should be covered by a comprehensive law that considers them as a protected group is an important point of contention. In addition, lawmakers are considering new laws that would extend hate-crimes protection on a federal level to the disabled. A ban on employment discrimination has already been written into federal law as the Americans with Disabilities Act (ADA), and a vigorous "disabilities rights" campaign has inspired a variety of new laws and ordinances on the local level. Should such protection be extended in the form of a new federal statute criminalizing bias-motivated assaults against the disabled?

Introduction to Hate Crimes

In their article "Examining the Boundaries of Hate Crimes Law," authors Valerie Jenness and Ryken Grattet summarize the moral principles underlying such an extension of hate-crimes laws:

> ... [criminals] often expect—with good reason—that the criminal justice system will share the view that such victims are unworthy of vigorous enforcement of the law. The stereotypes and biases upon which these views are based are, in turn, residues of historical relations of subordination, inequality, and discrimination, which criminals capitalize upon and reinforce. Moreover, like the school-yard bully who preys upon the small, the weak, and the outcast, crimes against the disadvantaged are increasingly understood to possess a distinct moral status and evoke particular policy implications.[19]

Those arguing against such an extension of hate-crimes laws maintain that extending protected status to the disabled will set them off from the rest of society, further isolating them and reinforcing society's rejection and indifference. In turn, say opponents, such isolation will breed further bias crimes, committed by those who see the disabled as vulnerable prey, and bring about the opposite effect intended by any new law.

Hate-crimes laws, and the creation of new protected-status groups, lies at the heart of much current public policy debate. On one side, a redress of past grievances and discrimination is called for, and the country's history of bigotry and racism is cited. Lawmakers are called upon to live up to the original promises of the Declaration of Independence and the Constitution, to allow citizens "life, liberty and the pursuit of happiness" and to bring about "equal justice for all." The creation of new laws is seen as one possible remedy for the problem of crimes motivated not by greed or malice, but by prejudice—a pernicious moral component that affects society as a whole, and thus should be more severely punished.

On the other side are those who protest at the fragmentation of society into distinct groups, each with its own claim to certain rights and legal redress. Opponents view this process as a threat to the historic ideals of the United States, in which people of all backgrounds should be considered American citizens first, and members of ethnic and socioeconomic groups second, with all living under a common law.

---

[1] Philip Perlmutter, *Legacy of Hate: A Short History of Ethnic, Religious, and Racial Prejudice in America.* Armonk, N.Y.: M. E. Sharpe, 1999, p. 58.

[2] Samuel Eliot Morison, *The Oxford History of the American People.* New York: Oxford University Press, p. 481.

[3] C. Vann Woodward, *The Strange Career of Jim Crow.* New York: Oxford University Press, 1955, p. 7.

41

[4] Leonard Dinnerstein, *Anti-Semitism in America.* New York: Oxford University Press, 1994. p. 138.

[5] Perlmutter, p. 192.

[6] Woodward, pp. 173–174.

[7] Valerie Jenness and Kendal Broad, *Hate Crimes: New Social Movements and the Politics of Violence.* New York: Aldine de Gruyter, 1997, p. 24.

[8] Perlmutter, pp. 203–204.

[9] Jenness and Broad, pp. 142–143.

[10] Quoted in Cleary, Edward J. *Beyond the Burning Cross: The First Amendment and the Landmark R.A.V. Case.* New York: Random House, 1994, p. xiv.

[11] Jenness and Broad, p. 147.

[12] John Spong, "The Hate Debate." *Texas Monthly*, April 2001, p. 64.

[13] Editorial, *Dallas Morning News.* May 2, 2001, p. 14A.

[14] American Psychological Association, *Hate Crimes Today: An Age-Old Foe in Modern Dress*, p. 2.

[15] Anti-Defamation League, "Hate Crimes Laws: Introduction." Available online. URL: http://www.adl.org/99hatecrime/intro.html. Downloaded on May 30, 2001.

[16] Nadine Strossen, "Yes: Discriminatory Crimes." *American Bar Association Journal*, May 1993, p. 44.

[17] James Jacobs and Kimberly Potter, *Hate Crimes: Criminal Law and Identity Politics.* New York: Oxford University Press, 1998, p. 52

[18] Jacobs, James. "Should Hate Be a Crime?" *The Public Interest*, vol. 113, Fall 1993, p. 14.

[19] Valerie Jenness and Ryken Grattet, "Examining the Boundaries of Hate Crime Law: Disabilities and the 'Dilemma of Difference.'" *The Journal of Criminal Law and Criminology*, vol. 91, no. 3, Spring 2001, p. 598.

CHAPTER 2

THE LAW OF HATE CRIME

FEDERAL LEGISLATION

Many legal scholars trace the origins of modern hate-crime legislation to federal statutes passed just after the Civil War. The new laws were intended to put in place an evenhanded and colorblind system of justice, as supposedly guaranteed by the Fourteenth Amendment, end the vigilante "justice" dispensed by the Ku Klux Klan, and end the arbitrary and discriminatory arrests, trials, and convictions of former slaves in the South. The first of these statutes, 18 U.S.C. (United States Code) Section 241, banned conspiracies to deprive citizens of their rights secured by the Constitution:

If two or more persons conspire to injure, oppress, threaten, or intimidate any inhabitant of any State, Territory, or District in the free exercise or enjoyment of any right or privilege secured to him by the Constitution or laws of the United States, or because of his having so exercised the same; or

If two or more persons go in disguise on the highway, or on the premises of another, with intent to prevent or hinder his free exercise or enjoyment of any right or privilege so secured;

They shall be fined under this title or imprisoned not more than ten years, or both; and if death results from the acts committed in violation of this section or if such acts include kidnapping or an attempt to kidnap, aggravated sexual abuse or an attempt to commit aggravated sexual abuse, or an attempt to kill, they shall be fined under this title or imprisoned for any term of years or for life, or both, or may be sentenced to death.

The second of these statutes, Section 242, is directed at public officials, such as police and judges, who deprive citizens of their constitutional rights "under color of any law." It states:

Whoever, under color of any law, statute, ordinance, regulation, or custom, willfully subjects any inhabitant of any State, Territory, or District to the *deprivation of any rights, privileges, or immunities secured or protected by the Constitution or laws of the United States, or to different punishments, pains, or penalties, on account of such inhabitant being an alien, or by reason of his color, or race, than are prescribed for the punishment of citizens, shall be fined not more than $1,000 or imprisoned not more than one year, or both; and if bodily injury results shall be fined under this title or imprisoned not more than ten years, or both; and if death results shall be subject to imprisonment for any term of years or for life.*

The statutes did not mention protected groups or statuses, or punish crimes committed on the basis of prejudice. In modern times, these statutes have most often been enforced against public officials such as the police, for example in prosecuting the Los Angeles police officers accused of beating black motorist Rodney King in 1991.

THE CIVIL RIGHTS ACT OF 1968

A new law passed within the Civil Rights Act of 1968, 18 U.S.C. Section 245, was enacted during a turbulent era in which federally protected civil rights became an important focus of new laws. This law deals specifically with the criminal offense of interfering with a person's enjoyment of a federally protected right on the basis of their race, color, religion, or national origin. These protected rights are listed as follows:

A. Voting or qualifying to vote, qualifying or campaigning as a candidate for elective office, or qualifying or acting as a poll watcher, or any legally authorized election official, in any primary, special, or general election;

B. Participating in or enjoying any benefit, service, privilege, program, facility, or activity provided or administered by the United States;

C. Applying for or enjoying employment, or any perquisite thereof, by any agency of the United States;

D. Serving, or attending upon any court in connection with possible service, as a grand or petit juror in any court of the United States;

E. Participating in or enjoying the benefits of any program or activity receiving Federal financial assistance.

The act further protects those who are:

A. Enrolling in or attending any public school or public college;

B. Participating in or enjoying any benefit, service, privilege, program, facility or activity provided or administered by any State or subdivision thereof;

C. Applying for or enjoying employment, or any perquisite thereof, by any private employer or any agency of any State or subdivision thereof, or joining or using the services or advantages of any labor organization, hiring hall, or employment agency;

D. Serving, or attending upon any court of any State in connection with possible service, as a grand or petit juror;

E. Traveling in or using any facility of interstate commerce, or using any vehicle, terminal, or facility of any common carrier by motor, rail, water, or air;

F. Enjoying the goods, services, facilities, privileges, advantages, or accommodations of any inn, hotel, motel, or other establishment which provides lodging to transient guests, or of any restaurant, cafeteria, lunchroom, lunch counter, soda fountain, or other facility which serves the public and which is principally engaged in selling food or beverages for consumption on the premises, or of any gasoline station, or of any motion picture house, theater, concert hall, sports arena, stadium, or any other place of exhibition or entertainment which serves the public. . .

Traditionally, Title 18, Section 245 has been the statute used to prosecute those who commit "hate crimes." Yet the number of crimes actually prosecuted by the Justice Department stood at 37 in the decade after 1991. The burden of proof for federal prosecutors is high: They must prove that the crime occurred because of the victim's membership in a protected group and because he or she was engaging in the protected activity. In addition, the U.S. attorney general must certify in writing that a prosecution would be in the public interest. In effect, the statute has turned over the prosecution of hate crimes to state and local law enforcement. For this reason, the Hate Crimes Prevention Act was proposed in 1999 to make federal prosecution of hate crimes an easier task; but as of May 2003, the new law had not been passed.

ADL MODEL LEGISLATION

An important basis for modern hate-crimes legislation was a model statute created by the Anti-Defamation League in 1981. Although the Anti-Defamation League was founded to combat anti-Jewish bias, the ADL's model statute uses general language to cover hate crimes against any and all religions, as well as crimes against individuals based on their race, religion, national origin, sexual orientation, or (as of a 1996 amendment) gender. The model statute also criminalizes vandalism against houses of worship, churches, cemeteries, schools, and community centers; creates a cause of action for civil lawsuits aimed at perpetrators of hate crimes; provides for the payment of punitive damages in these civil actions; and provides for the liability of parents for the actions of their minor children. According to the ADL, "Expressions of hate protected by the First Amendment's free speech clause are not criminalized. However, criminal activity motivated by hate is subject to a stiffer sentence."

The "penalty-enhancement" concept that lies at the heart of the ADL model was upheld by the U.S. Supreme Court decision in the case of *Wisconsin v. Mitchell*, which occurred in June 1993. As of early 2001, 43 states and the District of Columbia have enacted laws based on this model legislation (see Appendix I).

THE HATE CRIMES STATISTICS ACT

Originally sponsored by Representative John Conyers (D-Mich.) and Senator Paul Simon (D-Ill.), this federal statute was signed into law by President George H. W. Bush in April 1990 and codified as 28 U.S.C. 534. It requires the U.S. attorney general, head of the Department of Justice, to collect information from law enforcement agencies on the occurrence of crimes that "manifest evidence of prejudice based on race, religion, sexual orientation, or ethnicity," and to publish these statistics each year. The specified crimes include homicide, nonnegligent manslaughter, forcible rape, assault, intimidation, arson, and vandalism of property. The attorney general was given the task of setting the guidelines for collecting the data; at the time of passage, Attorney General Richard Thornburgh delegated this task to the FBI, a Justice Department agency. The FBI publishes its findings each January as *Hate Crimes Statistics*, a subsection of the Uniform Crime Reports (UCR). To assist local law enforcement agencies with the job of determining if a hate crime had occurred within their jurisdictions, and how to report it, the FBI issued a *Training Guide for Hate Crime Data Collection* in 1991. This guide states that a hate crime has occurred when "some evidence" demonstrates that the prejudices "in part" motivated the accused.

The Hate Crimes Statistics Act includes the following language, which outlines the general parameters for data collection to be undertaken by the Department of Justice:

1. The Attorney General shall acquire data, for the calendar year 1990 and each of the succeeding 4 calendar years, about crimes that mani-

fest evidence of prejudice based on race, religion, sexual orientation, or ethnicity, including where appropriate the crimes of murder, non-negligent manslaughter; forcible rape; aggravated assault, simple assault, intimidation; arson; and destruction, damage or vandalism of property.

2. The Attorney General shall establish guidelines for the collection of such data including the necessary evidence and criteria that must be present for a finding of manifest prejudice and procedures for carrying out the purposes of this section.

3. Nothing in this section creates a cause of action or a right to bring an action, including an action based on discrimination due to sexual orientation. As used in this section, the term "sexual orientation" means consensual homosexuality or heterosexuality. This subsection does not limit any existing cause of action or right to bring action, including under the Administrative Procedure Act or the All Writs Act.

4. Data acquired under this section shall be used only for research or statistical purposes and may not contain any information that may reveal the identity of an individual victim of crime.

5. The Attorney General shall publish an annual summary of the data acquired under this section.

The first statistics published under the Hate Crimes Statistics Act appeared in January 1993 and covered the calendar year 1991. At the time, compliance with the act amounted to less than 20 percent of all state and local law enforcement agencies (2,771 agencies in 32 states, out of about 16,000 agencies in all that participated in the Uniform Crime Reports). Although the Hate Crimes Statistics Act expired on December 31, 1994, Louis Freeh, then–FBI director, ordered that the data-collection efforts continue. In the meantime, through the 1990s, states were passing statutes that mandated hate-crimes data collection. In addition, the Justice Department instituted the National Incident Based Reporting System (NIBRS), a more comprehensive crime-reporting system that integrates bias motivation as a factor. The new laws and procedures, as well as the growing awareness of hate crimes as an important law enforcement issue, brought the participation by 1999 to well over 90 percent.

The Hate Crimes Statistics Act represented an attempt by federal lawmakers to provide some clarity to an issue clouded by partisan wrangling and debate. While advocacy groups pushed for tougher laws on bias-motivated crimes, opponents of hate-crime law raised the issues of constitutional freedom of speech and opinion, as well as vagueness of the laws and the additional burden placed on police and prosecutors. Although well-intentioned, the Hate Crimes Statistics Act has been only partially successful in its original goal. Private advocacy groups are still providing their own statistics, which in many cases include bias-motivated "incidents," which have an element of prejudice but do not rise to the level of prosecutable crime. Such statistics often clash with those provided by the Uniform Crime Reports. In addition, local law enforcement agencies may avoid reporting true hate crimes out of fear of damaging community reputation.

By the Violent Crime Control and Law Enforcement Act of 1994, data collection was extended, as of January 1, 1997, to hate crimes against those defined as "disabled."

Further Federal Measures Against Hate Crime

Hate crimes remained a prominent topic of news headlines and public debate in the early 1990s, and as a result further initiatives were undertaken by Congress. As part of the Juvenile Justice and Delinquency Prevention Act of 1992, the states were required to include hate-crimes prevention as part of their plans to combat juvenile delinquency. The Office of Juvenile Justice and Delinquency Prevention (OJJDP), part of the Department of Justice, also was mandated to make a national survey of juvenile hate-crime offenders.

The Hate Crimes Sentencing Enhancement Act was passed as Section 28003 of the Violent Crime Control and Law Enforcement Act of 1994. It affects the guidelines to be followed by the U.S. Sentencing Commission, which is charged with setting penalty levels for those found guilty of federal crimes. The commission must provide an "enhancement" of no less than three offense levels for hate crimes, defined as a crime against persons or property motivated by the victim's actual (or perceived) race, color, religion, national origin, ethnicity, gender, disability, or sexual orientation. The predicate crimes—which must take place on federal property—were specified as murder, nonnegligent manslaughter, forcible rape, aggravated assault, simple assault, intimidation, arson, and destruction, damage, or vandalism of property.

The Violence Against Women Act of 1994 was passed as Title IV of the Violent Crime Control and Law Enforcement Act of 1994 in September 1994. It provides that "all persons within the United States shall have the right to be free from crimes of violence motivated by gender," and sets down criminal penalties for those who commit violent acts after traveling across state lines and while violating a protective order. By Title III, the law also creates a "cause of action," or a basis for a civil lawsuit in which a plaintiff can recover monetary damages: "A person (including a person who acts under color of any statute, ordinance, regulation, custom, or usage of any State) who commits a crime of violence motivated by gender . . . shall be liable to the party injured, in an action for the recovery of compensatory and punitive damages, injunctive and declaratory relief, and such other relief as a court may deem appropriate."

The bill also allocated federal funds for education, crisis centers, hot lines, victim services, and law enforcement training.

CHURCH ARSON PREVENTION ACT

A rash of church burnings during the early 1990s prompted Senator Edward Kennedy (D-Mass.), Senator Lauch Faircloth (R-N.C.), Representative Henry Hyde (R-Ill.), and Representative John Conyers to sponsor the Church Arsons Prevention Act. The law was intended to assist local and federal investigations in cases of vandalism and arson against houses of worship. It was passed on July 3, 1996.

The Church Arson Prevention Act created the National Church Arson Task Force (NCATF), charged specifically with investigating cases of arson against churches. The NCATF coordinates federal prosecutors and local law enforcement agencies in these investigations.

The Church Arson Prevention Act of 1996 enhanced a 1988 statute that made vandalism causing more than $10,000 damage against church property a federal crime. It allowed a sentence of death if a death, kidnapping, or aggravated sexual assault resulted from a violation. For noncapital offenses, it set a statute of limitations of seven years. It also allowed for loan guarantees for rebuilding damaged property.

HATE CRIMES PREVENTION ACT

Since the passage of Title 18, Section 245, lawmakers have introduced new statutes targeted at more specific aspects of bias-motivated crimes, such as church arsons and violence against women. Yet because the original law set a high burden of proof on federal prosecutors, the investigation and prosecution of hate crimes fell in large part to local law enforcement. Through the 1990s, while the UCR documented more than 50,000 hate crimes, the federal government brought only 37 cases under the hate-crimes law codified as 18 U.S.C. 245.

In the late 1990s, lawmakers introduced new bills to remedy what they perceived as an important yet toothless federal law. In 1997, the first Hate Crimes Prevention Act (HCPA) was introduced as H.R. 3081, amending 18 U.S.C. 245, in the 105th Congress. The bill failed to pass, and so it was reintroduced as H.R. 1082 in 1999. The law, slightly amended and renamed the Local Law Enforcement Enhancement Act, and attached as an amendment to the National Defense Authorization Act for fiscal year 2001, was passed by the Senate by a vote of 57 to 42 on June 20, 2000. In the House of Representatives, however, the bill did not emerge for a final roll-call vote, instead becoming the focus of a variety of arcane parliamentary procedures. After the Senate passage, supporters in the House of Representatives forced the House to vote on a nonbinding motion that "instructed" the leaders of the House to accept an identical version to that passed in the Senate. This motion passed by a vote of 232 to 194, with 41 Republicans joining 191 Democrats in support. But a conference committee of House and Senate members voted to kill the motion, ending any hope supporters had of bringing the bill to a House vote.

When and if passed by the House of Representatives, the bill would expand the role of the federal government in hate-crimes prosecution; it would also expand the meaning of "hate crime" to include those committed on the basis of gender, sexual orientation, or disability. It would provide technical, forensic, prosecutorial, or any other form of assistance to state and local law enforcement officials in cases of crimes that are considered hate crimes under state law, or that: (a) constitute a crime of violence; (b) constitute a felony under state law; and (c) are motivated by bias based on race, color, religion, national origin, gender, disability, or sexual orientation. The Local Law Enforcement Enhancement Act authorizes the attorney general to grant up to $100,000 to local law enforcement for hate-crimes investigations; it also authorizes grants to train local law enforcement officers in identifying, investigating, prosecuting, and preventing hate crimes.

The act requires the Justice Department to certify that reasonable cause exists to believe the crime was motivated by bias, and to certify that a federal attorney has determined that a state does not have jurisdiction, has requested the Justice Department to assume jurisdiction, and/or does not object to the Justice Department assuming jurisdiction. The law also includes those crimes in which the state has completed prosecution and which the Justice Department wishes to prosecute.

Opponents argue that the legislation is vague and unconstitutional. Supporters state that it would simply strengthen existing local laws by making federal prosecution a backup to local law enforcement when such action is requested by local prosecutors and investigators.

The new hate crimes bill came under debate in the Senate on January 3, 2001, when it was reintroduced with a concurrent resolution by Texas representative Sheila Jackson-Lee. The resolution expressed "the sense of the Congress regarding the need to pass legislation to increase penalties on perpetrators of hate crimes." Nevertheless, the bill remained stalled, with opponents blocking any effort to bring it to a final floor vote. In 2002, the reintroduced bill was subject to a filibuster (parliamentary delay) in the Senate, a tactic that succeeded in delaying Senate passage in that year. In September 2002, Representative Conyers introduced a rarely used discharge petition. If a simple majority (or 218 members out of the total 435) of members of the House sign such a petition, the Speaker of the House (at the time, Dennis Hastert, R-Ill.) must call a vote. By October 2, 2002, the petition had 165 signatures.

As of May 2003, the renamed Hate Crimes Prevention Act had not yet been passed by the Senate. According to supporters, the HCPA would strengthen the Justice Department's ability to prosecute crimes based on race, color, or national origin but would also allow the federal prosecution of hate crimes based on sexual orientation, gender, or disability. It would permit federal law enforcement to provide assistance to state and local agencies while investigating hate crimes.

STATE LEGISLATION

Since the passage of the post–Civil War statutes, the states have followed the lead of federal legislators in enacting their own civil rights and hate-crimes laws. State laws provide the true focus of the hate-crimes debate, as it is on the state level that the vast majority of hate-crimes laws are prosecuted. Most of these laws increase the sentence of a convicted criminal, or provide a mandatory minimum sentence, if the evidence shows a certain specified crime was motivated "because of" or "by reason of" a certain specified prejudice. Relying on the phrase "because of" allows prosecutors to muster a case regardless of the perpetrator's racist beliefs—simply convincing a jury of racist motive surrounding a single act is sufficient to gain a conviction.

The crimes may vary from state to state (the ADL model statute, on which many state hate-crimes laws are based, covers the crimes of intimidation and harassment). They may include murder, assault, aggravated assault, manslaughter, rape, robbery, kidnapping, arson; they may include misdemeanor offenses such as intimidation, trespassing, menacing, or criminal mischief. The specified prejudices in the various state hate-crimes laws include bias against race, color, religion, national origin, gender, personal appearance, sexual orientation, disability, union membership, age, service in the armed forces, marital status, political views, or position on abortion.

What most legal scholars consider as the original modern state hate-crime statute was passed in 1987 by California and is closely modeled on the federal civil rights law passed in 1968. The California statute reads: "No person, whether or not acting under the color of law, shall by force or threat of force, willfully injure, intimidate, interfere with, oppress, or threaten any other person in the free exercise or enjoyment of any right secured to him or her by the constitutional laws of this state or by the Constitution or the laws of the United States because of the other person's race, color, religion, ancestry, national origin, or sexual orientation."

Legislative Strategies of the States

In their book *Making Hate a Crime*, scholars Valerie Jenness and Ryken Grattet have identified five distinct legal strategies used by the states in their new hate-crimes statutes. These strategies were devised in the 1980s, when many state hate-crimes laws first came into existence. The first harkens back to the earliest form of such federal legislation: criminalizing the "interference" with the exercise of their civil rights, as defined in the federal or state constitutions, because of the victim's real or perceived race, national origin, religion, and so on. The second legal strategy involves creating a freestanding statute that creates an entirely new category of criminal act, such as ethnic intimidation, harassment, or malicious behavior, committed on the basis of prejudice.

"Coattailing" statutes simply add a new hate-crimes dimension to preexisting laws. By this strategy, the ordinary crime of assault, for example, can be doubly prosecuted as a hate crime if there is sufficient evidence to show that it was committed by reason of ethnic or religious prejudice. A parallel strategy is to amend a preexisting statute to reclassify crimes committed on the basis of prejudice. Most states set down categories for crimes (Class 1 misdemeanor, Class 2 misdemeanor, and so on) based on their severity or the circumstances surrounding the crime. These two legal strategies—coattailing and modification—are the easiest to write and enforce, as they do not set down new categories of crime that may or not be struck down by the courts as unconstitutional.

A final and important legal strategy is penalty enhancement, which increases the sentence for certain crimes that have been found to be bias crimes. The penalty enhancement may bring a longer sentencing range on conviction, or it may increase the offense category. The penalty-enhancement strategy was put to the test in the case of *Wisconsin v. Mitchell*, in which a penalty-enhancement statute was brought to the U.S. Supreme Court and upheld in June 1993. The law in question, Wisconsin statute 939.645, first defines hate crimes as those committed "in whole or in part because of the actor's belief or perception regarding the race, religion, color, disability, sexual orientation, national origin or ancestry of that person or the owner or occupant of that property, whether or not the actor's belief or perception was correct."

In general, the penalty enhancement approach has proven to be the most popular method of writing state hate-crimes legislation, along with "coattailing" ethnic intimidation laws. The penalty enhancement strategy, given the favorable decision in *Wisconsin v. Mitchell*, also has passed constitutional muster. Modifying previously existing laws and criminalizing interference with civil rights are the least used options in writing new hate-crime laws.

Summary of State Laws and Regulations Regarding Hate Crimes

The following list summarizes the various forms of hate-crimes laws passed by state legislatures through February 2003.

Age: The following states have criminalized bias-motivated actions inspired by prejudice against the victim's age: District of Columbia, Iowa, Louisiana, and Vermont.

Bias-Motivated Violence and Intimidation: In all, 45 states and the District of Columbia have passed statutes punishing bias-motivated violence and intimidation: Alabama, Alaska, Arizona, California, Colorado, Connecticut, District of Columbia, Delaware, Florida, Georgia, Hawaii, Idaho, Illinois, Iowa, Kansas, Kentucky, Louisiana, Maine, Maryland, Massachusetts, Michigan, Minnesota, Mississippi, Missouri, Montana, Nebraska, Nevada, New Hampshire, New Jersey, New York (limited to aggravated harassment), North Carolina, North Dakota, Ohio, Oklahoma, Oregon, Pennsylvania, Rhode Island, South Dakota, Tennessee, Texas, Utah, Vermont, Virginia, Washington, West Virginia, and Wisconsin.

Civil Action: Thirty states and the District of Columbia have provisions for civil action (lawsuits seeking monetary damages) arising from bias-motivated crimes: Arkansas, California, Colorado, Connecticut, District of Columbia, Florida, Georgia, Idaho, Illinois, Iowa, Louisiana, Maine, Massachusetts, Michigan, Minnesota, Missouri, Nebraska, Nevada, New Jersey, Ohio, Oklahoma, Oregon, Pennsylvania, Rhode Island, South Dakota, Tennessee, Texas, Vermont, Virginia, Washington, and Wisconsin.

Data Collection: Twenty-three states and the District of Columbia have passed statutes mandating the collection of hate-crime statistics by local law enforcement agencies: Arizona, California, Connecticut, District of Columbia, Florida, Idaho, Illinois, Iowa, Kentucky, Louisiana, Maine, Maryland, Massachusetts, Michigan, Minnesota, Nebraska, New Jersey, Oklahoma, Oregon, Pennsylvania, Rhode Island, Texas, Virginia, and Washington.

Gender: The following 25 states and the District of Columbia have passed laws providing criminal penalties for violence motivated by bias against the victim's gender: Arkansas, Arizona, California, Connecticut, District of Columbia, Hawaii, Illinois, Iowa, Louisiana, Maine, Michigan, Minnesota, Mississippi, Missouri, Nebraska, New Hampshire, New Jersey,

New York, North Carolina, North Dakota, Pennsylvania, Rhode Island, Texas, Vermont, Washington, and West Virginia.

Institutional Vandalism: The following states, 42 in all, and the District of Columbia have laws criminalizing institutional vandalism, acts of arson, or other property crimes motivated by bias: Alabama, Arizona, Arkansas, California, Colorado, Connecticut, District of Columbia, Delaware, Florida, Georgia, Hawaii, Idaho, Illinois, Indiana, Kansas, Kentucky, Louisiana, Maine, Maryland, Massachusetts, Michigan, Minnesota, Mississippi, Missouri, Montana, Nebraska, Nevada, New Jersey, New Mexico, New York, North Carolina, Ohio, Oklahoma, Oregon, Pennsylvania, Rhode Island, South Carolina, South Dakota, Tennessee, Texas, Virginia, Washington, and Wisconsin.

Interference with Religious Worship: The following states and the District of Columbia have passed laws criminalizing interference with religious worship: California, District of Columbia, Florida, Idaho, Maryland, Massachusetts, Michigan, Minnesota, Mississippi, Missouri, Nevada, New Mexico, New York, North Carolina, Oklahoma, Rhode Island, South Carolina, South Dakota, Tennessee, Virginia, and West Virginia.

Law Enforcement Training: The following states have passed statutes that mandate training in dealing with hate crimes for law enforcement personnel: Arizona, California, Illinois, Iowa, Kentucky, Louisiana, Massachusetts, Minnesota, Oregon, Rhode Island, and Washington.

Mental or Physical Disability: The following states and the District of Columbia criminalize bias-motivated violence on the basis of disability or handicap: Alabama, Arizona, Alaska, California, Connecticut, District of Columbia, Delaware, Florida, Hawaii, Illinois, Iowa, Kansas, Louisiana, Maine, Massachusetts, Minnesota, Missouri, Nebraska, Nevada, New Hampshire, New Jersey, New York, Oklahoma, Pennsylvania, Rhode Island, Texas, Vermont, Washington, and Wisconsin.

Political Affiliation: The District of Columbia and the following states have passed laws making it a crime to commit violence inspired by political prejudice: District of Columbia, Iowa, Louisiana, and West Virginia.

Race, Religion, or Ethnic Group: Forty-three states and the District of Columbia have passed laws criminalizing crimes committed because of bias against race, religion, or ethnic group: Alabama, Alaska, Arizona, California, Colorado, Connecticut, District of Columbia, Delaware, Florida, Hawaii, Idaho, Illinois, Iowa, Kansas, Kentucky, Louisiana, Maine, Maryland, Massachusetts, Michigan, Minnesota, Mississippi, Missouri, Montana, Nebraska, Nevada, New Hampshire, New Jersey, New York, North Carolina, North Dakota, Ohio, Oklahoma, Oregon, Pennsylvania, Rhode Island, South Dakota, Tennessee, Texas, Vermont, Virginia, Washington, West Virginia, and Wisconsin.

Sexual Orientation: The following 28 states and the District of Columbia specify sexual orientation as a category protected by hate-crimes statutes: Arizona, California, Connecticut, District of Columbia, Delaware, Florida, Hawaii, Illinois, Iowa, Kansas, Kentucky, Louisiana, Maine, Massachusetts, Minnesota, Missouri, Nebraska, Nevada, New Hampshire, New Jersey, New York, Oregon, Pennsylvania, Rhode Island, Tennessee, Texas, Vermont, Washington, and Wisconsin.

COURT CASES

The cases below were decided in a variety of jurisdictions, including the U.S. Supreme Court, federal appeals courts, state supreme courts, and state appeals and criminal courts. Each has some bearing on hate-crimes law, setting a precedent either for the prosecution of crimes or in deciding the constitutionality, on either a state or federal level, of hate-crimes statutes.

The principal questions involved in hate-crimes litigation include the following:

- Do hate-crimes statutes punish opinion, in violation of the First Amendment; are they unconstitutionally vague or overbroad, or do they have a chilling effect on the exercise of free (protected) speech? Are hate-crimes laws an unconstitutional regulation of speech based on its content?
- Do hate-crimes laws punish motive and/or intent rather than conduct?
- Do hate-crimes statutes violate the Fourteenth Amendment and the doctrines of equal protection and due process? Do they lead to arbitrary enforcement, or do they mandate preferential treatment for minority groups?
- Must hate-crimes statutes punish only criminal conduct, motivated by racism, homophobia, anti-Semitism, and so on, and not expression and/or opinion?
- In passing and enforcing hate-crimes laws, do legislators and the courts have a valid motive in maintaining public order and preventing the more serious social injuries that result from hate crimes?

Supreme Court Cases

In general, the broad constitutional issues were decided by the U.S. Supreme Court in the early 1990s, in the cases of *R.A.V. v. St. Paul* and *Wisconsin v. Mitchell*. These decisions set the general constitutional boundaries for hate-crimes legislation in the states, where the vast majority of hate crimes are prosecuted. Later state court decisions refined hate-crimes jurisprudence, setting precedent on more specific issues raised by hate-crimes law.

CHAPLINSKY V. NEW HAMPSHIRE
315 U.S. 568 (1942)

Background

Walter Chaplinsky, a member of the Jehovah's Witnesses, was distributing religious tracts on the streets of Rochester, New Hampshire, in 1940. Several people complained of a disturbance to City Marshal Bowering, telling the marshal that Chaplinsky was denouncing all organized religion as "a racket." Although the marshal allowed Chaplinsky to continue his lawful activities, he later arrested Chaplinsky as disorder began to occur. Chaplinsky then turned on the marshal and addressed him as follows: "You are a God damned racketeer . . . a damned Fascist and the whole government of Rochester are Fascists or agents of Fascists."

Chaplinsky was convicted in the municipal court of Rochester, New Hampshire, for violation of New Hampshire's Chapter 378, §2, which states that "No person shall address any offensive, derisive or annoying word to any other person who is lawfully in any street or other public place, nor call him by any offensive or derisive name, nor make any noise or exclamation in his presence and hearing with intent to deride, offend or annoy him, or to prevent him from pursuing his lawful business or occupation." The conviction was appealed in New Hampshire Superior Court on the grounds that the statute represented an unconstitutional abridgement of free speech, freedom of the press, and freedom of religious worship, in violation of the First and the Fourteenth Amendments to the Constitution. But Chaplinsky was again found guilty, a judgment that was affirmed by the New Hampshire Supreme Court. In early 1942, the case reached the U. S. Supreme Court.

Legal Issues

The New Hampshire statute had been construed by the state courts to apply only to those words which might cause an immediate breach of the peace. Chaplinsky charged that the law was an infringement of speech, of the press, and of freedom of worship. The state of New Hampshire argued that the spoken word per se is not always protected by the constitution, such as in cases of obscenity, slander, and in this case "fighting words." In its opinion, the New Hampshire Supreme Court wrote that "the statute . . . does no more than prohibit the face-to-face words . . . whose speaking constitutes a breach of the peace by the speaker—including 'classical fighting words', words in current use less 'classical' but equally likely to cause violence, and other disorderly words, including profanity, obscenity and threats."

Decision

On March 9, 1942, the Supreme Court handed down its opinion. It first dismissed Chaplinsky's argument that the New Hampshire law impinged on freedom of the press or of religious worship, as it was only Chaplinsky's spoken word that brought the arrest and conviction. The written opinion states that "The spoken, not the written, word is involved. And we cannot conceive that cursing a public officer is the exercise of religion in any sense of the term."

The Court then affirmed the New Hampshire Supreme Court decision, holding that the state statute complied with due process and did not impinge upon constitutionally protected speech. In their opinion, the justices found that "even if the activities of the appellant which preceded the incident could be viewed as religious in character, and therefore entitled to the protection of the Fourteenth Amendment, they would not cloak him with immunity from the legal consequences for concomitant acts committed in violation of a valid criminal statute. . . . There are certain well-defined and narrowly limited classes of speech, the prevention and punishment of which have never been thought to raise any Constitutional problem. These include the lewd and obscene, the profane, libelous, and the insulting or "fighting" words—those which by their very utterance inflict injury or tend to incite an immediate breach of the peace. . . . Argument is unnecessary to demonstrate that the appellations 'damned racketeer' and 'damned Fascist' are epithets likely to provoke the average person to retaliation, and thereby cause a breach of the peace."

Impact

The case of *Chaplinsky v. New Hampshire* would have far-ranging effects, down to the writing and enforcement of hate-crimes laws 50 years later. In effect, the justices held that certain speech, which can be characterized as "fighting words," is not protected by the Constitution on the grounds that it tends to cause a breach of the peace. When writing and litigating hate-crimes laws, legislators and prosecutors would draw on this opinion to support their contention that racist or otherwise biased language is not always protected by the constitution, and that such speech can make up an important element of a hate crime—either as evidence of intent or motive, or as a crime in itself. Ironically, the Supreme Court would never again use the precedent set down in 1942 to support the prohibition or repression of speech.

R.A.V. V. CITY OF ST. PAUL, MINNESOTA 505 U.S. 377 (1992)

Background

On June 21, 1990, Russell Jones, an African-American resident of the predominantly white Dayton's Bluff neighborhood of St. Paul, Minnesota, found a crudely made burning cross in the front yard of his home. A 17-year-old, known in court documents as R. A. V. (Robert Anthony Viktora), was charged with violation of St. Paul's bias assault law, section 292.01. Not certain of an assault conviction in this case, the city prosecutor then amended the charge to the bias disorderly conduct law, or Section 292.02, which specifically mentions cross burning. The ordinance, which had been adopted in 1982 by the St. Paul City Council in reaction to a wave of bias violence and vandalism, provided that:

> *Whoever places on public or private property a symbol, object, appellation, characterization or graffiti including, but not limited to, a burning cross or Nazi swastika, which one knows or has reasonable grounds to know arouses anger, alarm or resentment in others on the basis of race, color, creed, religion or gender commits disorderly conduct and shall be guilty of a misdemeanor.*

Viktora's attorney challenged the city ordinance on the grounds that rather than punishing criminal conduct, it punished constitutionally protected expression. The trial court dismissed the charges on the ground that the ordinance was substantially overbroad and impermissibly content based. The city appealed in turn, and the Minnesota Supreme Court then reversed the lower-court decision. It rejected the overbreadth claim because the phrase "arouses anger, alarm or resentment in others" had been construed in earlier state cases to limit the ordinance's reach to "fighting words" within the meaning of the 1942 Supreme Court decision in *Chaplinsky v. New Hampshire*, in which "fighting words" were defined as a category of expression not protected by the First Amendment. The Minnesota Supreme Court also concluded that the ordinance was not impermissibly content based because it was narrowly tailored to serve a compelling governmental interest in protecting the community against bias-motivated threats to public safety and order. The case was then certified to the U.S. Supreme Court.

The Law of Hate Crime

Legal Issues

Viktora's attorney maintained that his client's conviction under the St. Paul ordinance should be overturned, as the ordinance prohibits speech and expression protected by the First Amendment. Attorneys for St. Paul argued that the law may ban certain expressions, in particular "fighting words," or expressions designed to arouse a violent reaction, and that St. Paul had the right to pass such a law in the interest of protecting the community against a threat to public order. Viktora's attorney responded that although certain speech may be proscribed by the law, the law cannot discriminate in such speech, in other words, it cannot select the expression of certain ideas (such as racism) and not others as crimes that merit punishment.

Decision

In its decision of June 22, 1992, the Supreme Court did not put cross burning in the same criminal category as "fighting words," finding that "The [St. Paul] ordinance is facially invalid under the First Amendment." The opinion read, in part: "A few limited categories of speech, such as obscenity, defamation, and fighting words, may be regulated. . . . However, these categories are not entirely invisible to the Constitution, and government may not regulate them based on hostility, or favoritism, towards a nonproscribable message they contain [e.g., racist opinion]. Thus the regulation of 'fighting words' may not be based on nonproscribable content. It may, however, be underinclusive, addressing some offensive instances and leaving other, equally offensive, ones alone, so long as the selective proscription is not based on content, or there is no realistic possibility that regulation of ideas is afoot." The court found that the ordinance "imposes special prohibitions on those speakers who express views on the disfavored subjects of 'race, color, creed, religion or gender' . . . St. Paul's desire to communicate to minority groups that it does not condone the 'group hatred' of bias motivated speech does not justify selectively silencing speech on the basis of its content." While the First Amendment grants freedom of speech and expression, in a few instances such expression may be regulated by the common interest in public order and morality—a test that this particular ordinance did not meet.

The members of the Supreme Court agreed unanimously on the decision, but a minority of justices disagreed with the legal reasoning given in the Court's opinion. Writing for this minority, Justice Blackmun described "the possibility that this case . . . will be regarded as an aberration—a case where the Court manipulated doctrine to strike down an ordinance whose premise it opposed, namely, that racial threats and verbal assaults are of greater harm than other fighting words. I fear that the Court has been distracted from its proper mission by the temptation to decide the issue over 'politically correct speech' and 'cultural diversity,' neither of which is presented here."

Impact

In *R.A.V. v. St. Paul*, a landmark case in the history of hate-crimes law, the U.S. Supreme Court decided, in effect, that St. Paul had prosecuted Robert Viktora under the wrong law. "Let there be no mistake about our belief that burning a cross in someone's front yard is reprehensible," the opinion concluded. "But St. Paul has sufficient means at its disposal to prevent such behavior without adding the First Amendment to the fire." Although trespassing, vandalism, disorderly conduct, and arson may all be punished by city ordinances, such acts could not, in the future, be punished solely on the basis of their racist content. All similar city ordinances banning racist messages, placards, displays, and the like, were held to be unconstitutional, and those opposing hate-crimes laws were bolstered in their opinion that ordinary laws against criminal behavior would have to be sufficient without referring to racial, ethnic, or religious prejudice. In the future, states and cities seeking to set penalties for "hate crimes," which by definition are those inspired by the perpetrator's dislike of certain groups or certain types of people, would have to write or revise their laws with *R.A.V. v. St. Paul* in mind.

WISCONSIN V. MITCHELL
508 U.S. 476 (1993)

Background

On October 7, 1989, in Kenosha, Wisconsin, several African-American youths gathered after viewing *Mississippi Burning*, a film about the deadly violence that occurred in Mississippi during the 1960s. Angered by a scene in the film in which a white man beats a black boy, and seeing a white youth on the street, the petitioner Todd Mitchell roused his companions: "You all want to f—k somebody up? There goes a white boy; go get him." Mitchell then counted to three and the group ran towards the white youth, beat him unconscious, and stole his shoes. The victim survived the beating but remained in a coma for four days afterward.

Mitchell was convicted of aggravated battery in Kenosha County Circuit Court. The two-year sentence was then enhanced because, as the jury found, Mitchell had intentionally selected the victim based on the victim's race. According to the Wisconsin penalty enhancement formula, such an act carries a maximum punishment of seven years in prison. In this case, the defendant was sentenced to four years.

Mitchell appealed, arguing that Wisconsin's penalty-enhancement statute violated the First Amendment. The Wisconsin Court of Appeals decided against the appeal, but the Wisconsin Supreme Court reversed this decision, holding that the statute punishes "what the legislature has deemed to be offensive thought." The Wisconsin Supreme Court also found that bringing evidence of the defendant's prior speech ("There goes a white boy, go get him") would have a "chilling effect," that is, a fear of prosecution based solely on one's expressed ideas, and that the statute "punishes the subjective mental process." The decision of the Wisconsin Supreme Court was then brought to the U.S. Supreme Court.

Legal Issues

The case of *Wisconsin v. Mitchell* put all state penalty-enhancement statutes, the most commonly prosecuted form of hate-crimes laws, under the legal microscope. Mitchell's attorney argued that Wisconsin's penalty-enhancement law punished bigoted thought and not conduct. The state argued exactly the opposite—that Mitchell's "conduct" of directing his companions to beat the victim was punished, and then enhanced because of his discriminatory motive in committing the assault, and that such conduct had nothing to do with his rights to free expression under the First Amendment. Looming in the background as an important precedent was the decision of the U.S. Supreme Court in the case of *R.A.V. v. St. Paul*, reached a year earlier, in which the Court struck down a city ordinance banning any "symbol, object, appellation, characterization, or graffiti" tending to arouse "anger, alarm or resentment . . . on the basis of race, color, creed, religion, or gender. . ."

By long legal precedent, the "conduct" of assault cannot be considered as "expression" protected by the First Amendment. In addition, the practice of penalty enhancement has been found constitutional, and by state and federal laws a wide range of possible enhancements can be passed on defendants for a wide variety of criminal acts. But the abstract beliefs of a defendant cannot be taken solely into consideration—thus, a white racist found guilty of murder cannot see his penalty enhanced solely because of his bigoted beliefs (*Dawson v. Delaware*, 503 U.S. 159 1992). The Supreme Court now had to decide in what manner such beliefs could be the basis for penalty enhancement.

Decision

In its decision of June 11, 1993, the U.S. Supreme Court reversed the decision of the Wisconsin Supreme Court and held that Mitchell's First Amendment rights were not violated by the application of the penalty-enhancement provision in sentencing him. The opinion read, in part:

> *In determining what sentence to impose, sentencing judges have traditionally considered a wide variety of factors in addition to evidence bearing on guilt, including a defendant's motive for committing the offense. While it is equally true that a sentencing judge may not take into consideration a defendant's abstract beliefs, however obnoxious to most people, the Constitution does not erect a per se barrier to the admission of evidence concerning one's beliefs and associations at sentencing simply because they are protected by the First Amendment.*
>
> *Nothing in R. A. V. v. St. Paul compels a different result here. The [St. Paul, Minnesota] ordinance at issue there was explicitly directed at speech, while the one here is aimed at conduct unprotected by the First Amendment. Moreover, the State's desire to redress what it sees as the greater individual and societal harm inflicted by bias-inspired conduct provides an adequate explanation for the provision over and above mere disagreement with offenders' beliefs or biases.*

The U.S. Supreme Court disagreed with the Wisconsin Supreme Court in finding that the penalty enhancement law had no chilling effect on free speech. "The prospect of a citizen suppressing his bigoted beliefs for fear that evidence of those beliefs will be introduced against him at trial if he commits a serious offense against person or property is too speculative a hypothesis to support this claim. Moreover, the First Amendment permits the admission of previous declarations or statements to establish the elements of a crime or to prove motive or intent, subject to evidentiary rules dealing with relevancy, reliability, and the like."

Impact

The *Wisconsin v. Mitchell* decision gave the states broad legal authority to write and pass penalty-enhancement statutes for criminal conduct inspired by prejudice. While the constitutionality of laws that simply punish thought or expression remain in serious doubt after *R.A.V. v. St. Paul,* the constitutionality of laws enhancing punishment for conduct based on prejudice was recognized. This decision remains a controversial one, and hate-crimes laws are still being challenged on the basis that they violate the First Amendment. Yet nearly every such challenge in state supreme courts to penalty enhancement has been defeated, with the judges citing the U.S. Supreme Court as their authority and *Wisconsin v. Mitchell* as their precedent.

The Law of Hate Crime

BRZONKALA V. MORRISON
120 S. CT. 1740 (2000)

Background

The case of *Brzonkala v. Morrison* began in October 1994, at Virginia Polytechnic University, when student Christy Brzonkala accused two other students, Antonio Morrison and James Crawford, of raping her in a dormitory room. Brzonkala filed a claim under the university's sexual assault policy, and at the subsequent hearing Morrison was found guilty and handed a two-semester suspension (insufficient evidence was found to convict Crawford). Brzonkala then took the case to the U. S. District Court for the Western District of Virginia, seeking damages from Morrison and Crawford under Section 13981 of the Violence Against Women Act of 1994, which allows for victims of gender-motivated violence to sue for compensatory and punitive damages. The defendants moved to dismiss the case on the grounds that Brzonkala had failed to state a claim for damages, and that Section 13981 was an unconstitutional exercise of congressional power under the commerce clause (Article 1, Section 8 of the Constitution) and the enforcement clause (Fourteenth Amendment, Section 5); the district court agreed and dismissed the suit.

This decision was reversed by the U.S. Court of Appeals for the Fourth Circuit, which found that the statute in question was constitutionally legitimate. At a subsequent rehearing, the appeals court reversed itself. The case was granted certiorari by the U.S. Supreme Court on September 28, 1999.

Legal Issues

The case of *Brzonkala v. Morrison* was the test for the constitutionality of civil lawsuits brought by victims of gender-motivated violence. The Supreme Court had to decide whether Section 13981 of the Violence Against Women Act of 1994, specifically its section dealing with redress in civil court, was constitutional under the commerce clause or the enforcement clause. Those arguing for constitutionality held that violence against women deters them from interstate travel and business, and thus interferes with commerce; that violence against women is a growing national problem that has an important economic impact and that calls for federal legislation; and that the commerce clause does not strictly limit such legislation to economic activities. Since not all states have passed laws addressing gender-based violence, women in those states are deprived of their Fourteenth Amendment right to equal protection of the laws, and thus Congress should have the power to pass federal legislation addressing the issue.

Those opposed to the law under which Brzonkala originally sued stated that the commerce clause is indeed limited to economic activities, and that the Violence Against Women Act has nothing to do with interstate commerce. In addition, since the Fourteenth Amendment deals with acts of state governments and public authorities, the acts of private individuals cannot be legislated against by its authority.

Decision

By a 5-4 decision, the U.S. Supreme Court justices held that the commerce clause does not permit the civil redress section of the Violence Against Women Act, as the act regulates criminal and not economic activity, and such activity does not substantially affect interstate commerce. The majority also agreed with the argument that the Fourteenth Amendment deals with discriminatory conduct by state agencies, and that Brzonkala's lawsuit involves private individuals and thus is invalid under the amendment.

The dissenting justices agreed with the argument that Congress had established that crimes against women were having a substantial economic impact (including costs to the public incurred by the criminal justice system). The dissenters also opined that the decision on whether criminal activity has such an impact rests with Congress and not with the Supreme Court.

Impact

With the *Brzonkala v. Morrison* decision, the Supreme Court struck down a key provision of the 1994 Violence Against Women Act, thus invalidating a federal law allowing civil redress for victims of bias-motivated violence. Although the decision was deplored by some women's rights groups, several commentators pointed out that very few such lawsuits had been initiated since the law was passed, and that civil litigation in such cases is usually meaningless, as most defendants have few assets to collect.

APPRENDI V. NEW JERSEY
120 S. CT. 2348 (2000)

Background

On December 22, 1994, the petitioner, Charles C. Apprendi, fired several shots into the home of an African-American family and made a statement, which he later retracted, that he did not want the family in his neighborhood because of their race.

The Law of Hate Crime

Legal Issues

Apprendi was charged under New Jersey law with second-degree possession of a firearm for an unlawful purpose, which carries a prison term of five to 10 years. The charge did not refer to the state's hate crime statute, which provides for an enhanced sentence if a trial judge finds, by a preponderance of the evidence, that the defendant committed the crime with a purpose to intimidate a person or group because of, inter alia, race. After Apprendi pled guilty, the prosecutor filed a motion to enhance the sentence. The court found by a preponderance of the evidence that the shooting was racially motivated and sentenced Apprendi to a 12-year term on the firearms count. In upholding the sentence, the appeals court rejected Apprendi's claim that by the due process clause of the U.S. Constitution, a finding of bias must be proved to a jury rather than decided by a judge. The New Jersey Supreme Court affirmed the lower court's decision.

Decision

On June 26, 2000, the U.S. Supreme Court held that the Constitution requires that any fact that increases the penalty for a crime beyond the prescribed statutory maximum, other than the fact of a prior conviction, must be submitted to a jury, and proved beyond a reasonable doubt.

The Supreme Court opinion read, in part:

(A) The answer to the narrow constitutional question presented—whether Apprendi's sentence was permissible, given that it exceeds the 10-year maximum for the offense charged—was foreshadowed by the holding in Jones v. United States that, with regard to federal law, the Fifth Amendment's due process clause and the Sixth Amendment's notice and jury trial guarantees require that any fact other than prior conviction that increases the maximum penalty for a crime must be charged in an indictment, submitted to a jury, and proved beyond a reasonable doubt. The Fourteenth Amendment commands the same answer when a state statute is involved.

(B) The Fourteenth Amendment right to due process and the Sixth Amendment right to trial by jury, taken together, entitle a criminal defendant to a jury determination that he is guilty of every element of the crime with which he is charged, beyond a reasonable doubt. . .

Impact

The complex decision in the *Apprendi v. New Jersey* case, although only indirectly concerned with hate-crimes law, may have far-reaching implications in the nation's criminal justice system. The case has spawned hundreds of new cases and appeals, based on the initial failure of the courts to submit penalty-enhancement evidence to juries. Defendants in capital cases have asked for additional appeals on this basis, and drug cases have been reopened so that evidence of the amount of controlled substance can be determined by a jury and not by a judge, which was the practice in circuit courts. In general, *Apprendi* means that sentencing schemes in which a state permits a judge to pass a sentence beyond the statutory maximum, based on his own findings of the evidence, are now unconstitutional.

Federal/State/Criminal Court Cases

COMMONWEALTH OF MASSACHUSETTS V. POOR AND TILTON
MASSACHUSETTS COURT OF APPEALS
467 N.E.2d 877 (1984)

Background

On August 30, 1982, Mrs. Regina Campbell, a black woman, moved into an apartment at the Snug Harbor housing project in Quincy, Massachusetts. Bradley Poor, a white male, lived nearby with his wife and children at 30 Taffrail Road. Poor's brother-in-law John Tilton, also white, often stayed with Poor's family, although he was not a resident of the project. On September 9, 1982, around 9:00 P.M., Mrs. Campbell and her children returned home after visiting a relative. She stopped at her back step to talk to a neighbor. As they were talking, an explosion blew out the front living room window. There was no direct evidence of exactly what caused the explosion and fire. Shortly before the explosion, the defendants were observed near the scene and, within a few seconds of the explosion, running away from the smoking window. After an investigation the defendants were arrested and charged with various crimes in connection with the incident.

Legal Issues

The jury in the criminal trial found Poor and Tilton guilty of willfully throwing or placing explosives at or near persons or property and "interference with the civil rights of persons." It was the Commonwealth's theory that the crimes were racially motivated and that the defendants were engaged in a joint enterprise at the time the crimes were committed. During the trial, a Commonwealth witness testified that a few days before the explosion she heard Poor say to Tilton, "Well, why don't they just kill all the n——s." There was no response from Tilton. The judge ruled that the statement was admissible as evidence because it was "relevant as to the knowledge that Tilton might have had as to Mr. Poor's racial attitude" and that it was "material to show what each knew of the other's attitude toward . . . black residents." On appeal, Tilton argued that the admission of the statement against him was an error because Poor's statement had no relevance to the case against him.

Decision

The Massachusetts Court of Appeals noted that out-of-court statements of joint criminal venturers are admissible if made during the pendency of the criminal enterprise and in furtherance of it. The court held that the admission of this evidence was harmless in light of earlier testimony that about an hour before the explosion Tilton was heard to say, "The only way to get these f——g n——s out of here is to burn them out." The court also found that the judge did not err in admitting evidence of an earlier explosion which was relevant to show that the defendant possessed, or had access to, the means to commit the crime. Also, the court held that the defendant was not prejudiced by testimony by a witness that a few days before the bombing she had heard the codefendant, speaking to the defendant, make violent remarks against blacks—the judge's action in permitting the jury to consider this testimony against the defendant could not have prejudiced him in light of earlier testimony about similar remarks made by the defendant.

Impact

The decision in the case of *Massachusetts v. Poor and Tilton* was reached several years before the modern era of federal and state hate-crimes legislation. It set an important precedent, however, in concluding that the racial views and opinions expressed by defendants—even when not made during the commission of a crime—are admissible as evidence supporting a guilty verdict on a civil rights charge.

NEW YORK V. GRUPE
NEW YORK CITY CRIMINAL COURT
532 N.Y.S.2d 815 (1988)

Background

A witness described the defendant, Peter Grupe, striking his victim while shouting ethnic slurs, including, "Is that the best you can do? I'll show you Jew b——d." Grupe was charged with aggravated harassment in the second degree (Penal Law 240.30 [3]) in that he allegedly made the assault while shouting ethnic slurs. Prior to this incident, the New York legislature had rewritten the criminal code to classify bias-motivated harassment as a Class A misdemeanor, punishable by up to one year in jail, while such conduct not motivated by bias remained a noncriminal offense punishable by up to 15 days.

Legal Issues

The relevant statute reads, "A person is guilty of aggravated harassment in the second degree when, with intent to harass, annoy, threaten or alarm another person, he . . . strikes, shoves, kicks, or otherwise subjects another person to physical contact, or attempts or threatens to do the same because of the race, color, religion or national origin of such person." Grupe moved to dismiss the charge on the ground that the statute violated his rights to freedom of speech and equal protection of the laws under the First and Fourteenth Amendments of the U.S. Constitution.

Decision

On August 17, 1988, Grupe's motion was denied. The New York City Criminal Court's opinion stated that "No First Amendment issue is raised since the intent of the statute is to prohibit violence and physical intimidation based upon bigotry. Even if defendant's behavior were considered expressive, violent demonstrations are not protected under the First Amendment, and constitutional guarantees of freedom of speech do not prevent states from punishing 'fighting words,' those by which their very utterance inflict injury or tend to incite an immediate breach of the peace. There is a compelling governmental interest in penalizing bias-related violence which is unrelated to the suppression of free expression, and the statute is narrowly drawn to apply only to those situations involving acts of violence or physical intimidation. . . . Furthermore, there is a rational basis for the Legislature to have concluded that the measure was necessary to redress past discrimination."

Impact

This decision drew on the landmark Supreme Court case of *Chaplinsky v. New Hampshire*, which found that "fighting words," or those intended to elicit a violent reaction, are not necessarily protected by the First Amendment. It paved the way for courts to find that certain expressions of bigotry, racism, and prejudice, like "fighting words," are prima facie evidence that a hate crime has been committed. When such expressions are made in the course of a crime such as a murder or assault, they may serve as grounds for separate hate-crime charges or penalty enhancement on ordinary criminal charges, as set down in the new state statutes and local ordinances. The issue of the constitutionality of such laws and prosecution would eventually be resolved by the U.S. Supreme Court decision in the case of *Wisconsin v. Mitchell.*

STATE OF OHIO V. WYANT
OHIO SUPREME COURT
624 N.E. 2d 722 (1992)

Background

On the evening of June 2, 1989, David Wyant and his relatives were camping in Ohio's Alum Creek State Park. The adjoining campsite had been rented to Jerry White and his girlfriend, Patricia McGowan. White and McGowan are black; everyone in the Wyant party is white. Sometime between 10:30 and 11:45 P.M., White went to park officials to complain of loud music coming from the Wyant campsite. A park official went to site L-16 and asked Wyant to turn off the radio. Wyant complied.

Fifteen or 20 minutes later the radio came on again, and White and McGowan heard racial epithets and threats made in a loud voice by Wyant. Specifically, Wyant was heard to say: "We didn't have this problem until those n———moved in next to us," "I ought to shoot that black motherf———," and "I ought to kick his black a—." White and McGowan complained to park officials and left the park.

Wyant was indicted and convicted on one count of ethnic intimidation, Ohio statute 2927.12, predicated on aggravated menacing, and sentenced to one and one-half years' imprisonment. The court of appeals affirmed the conviction. The case was then appealed to the Ohio Supreme Court.

Legal Issues

The Ohio statute set down enhanced criminal penalties for "aggravated menacing," "menacing," "criminal damaging or endangering," "criminal mischief" when motivated "by reason of the race, color, religion, or national origin of another person or group of persons." Although all these actions are punishable under ordinary criminal statutes, the Wyant case raised the question whether an additional crime or penalty enhancement can be set down for a defendant's motive. In criminal law, motive can be presented as evidence of guilt, but normally is not punishable by itself, as it is considered thought and not conduct. Wyant's attorneys maintained that the statute violated the U.S. Constitution as well as the state constitution, which guarantees the freedom to "speak, write, and publish . . . sentiments on all subjects."

Decision

The Ohio Supreme Court found on August 26, 1992 that R.C. 2927.12 violated both the U.S. and Ohio constitutions. The court reversed the decision of the court of appeals, vacated Wyant's sentence on the conviction for ethnic intimidation, and remanded the case for sentencing on the charge of aggravated menacing. Part of the opinion in the case read: "Once the proscribed act is committed, the government criminalizes the underlying thought by enhancing the penalty based on viewpoint. This is dangerous. If the legislature can enhance a penalty for crimes committed 'by reason of' racial bigotry, why not 'by reason of' opposition to abortion, war, the elderly (or any other political or moral viewpoint)? If the thought or motive behind a crime can be separately punished, the legislative majority can punish virtually any viewpoint which it deems politically undesirable . . . applying these principles, we believe that the government is not free to punish an idea, though it may punish acts motivated by the idea. It may also punish unprotected speech expressing the idea."

Impact

In this case, the Ohio Supreme Court decided that Ohio's penalty enhancement law created a "thought crime," an unconstitutional restriction of speech and opinion. However, in the wake of the U.S. Supreme Court's decision in *Wisconsin v. Mitchell*, the case was vacated by the Supreme Court and remanded to the Ohio Supreme Court for reconsideration. This court would subsequently reverse its earlier decision, keeping alive the constitutional confusion and legal debate over hate-crimes law.

STATE OF OREGON V. SHAWN WAYNE HENDRIX
SUPREME COURT OF OREGON
838 P.2d 566 (1992)

Background

The defendant entered a store with several codefendants, who were in possession of weapons. After the codefendants observed that the store employees spoke little English, they made statements concerning the race and ethnic origins of the employees, and all defendants then proceeded to beat the victims while continuing to make the statements. The defendant was then convicted of first-degree intimidation under Oregon statute 166.165(1)(a)(A), which states that "Two or more persons acting together commit the crime of intimidation in the first degree, if the persons: Intentionally, knowingly, or recklessly cause physical injury to another because of their perception of that person's race, color, religion, national origin or sexual orientation. . ."

Legal Issues

Hendrix appealed the criminal court decision on the grounds of insufficient evidence, claiming that the state had failed to prove beyond a reasonable doubt that he had acted because of his perception of the victims' race or national origin. He also claimed that each defendant must have specific intent to act on prejudiced motive, and that since, according to testimony in the case, he had not made prejudiced statements before the criminal act, he could not be convicted under the statute in question. A state appeals court affirmed the conviction, and the case was appealed to the Oregon Supreme Court.

Decision

The Oregon Supreme Court affirmed the appeals court decision on August 27, 1992. The opinion read that "from [the defendant's conduct], the trier of fact reasonably could find beyond a reasonable doubt that defendant acted because of his perception of the victims' race or national origin." The justices agreed with the defendant that he had to have specific intent, and that such intent must be proven beyond a reasonable doubt. But the court also found that the evidence was sufficient to find that the defendant did indeed have the identical, biased intent of his codefendants in the case.

Impact

This decision upheld Oregon's ethnic intimidation statute, finding that those committing a hate crime in concert with others, although perhaps not found to have prejudiced motives or intent themselves, may be found guilty of committing a bias-motivated crime.

MICHIGAN V. DAVID ALLEN RICHARDS, JR.
MICHIGAN COURT OF APPEALS
509 NW 2d 528 (1993)

Background

On May 7, 1990, Richards confronted and threatened an African-American couple while they were attempting to move out of their apartment. The threats included the following: "black motherf——r"; "black sons of b——s"; "half-breed baby"; "[I'll] whip your black a—"; "[I'll] kill [your] n——r-loving whore." Richards pounded on the victims' door and said that he had a gun with him and had "shot motherf———s before." He also threatened to destroy the couple's property.

The victims made a couple of trips back and forth, and at one point Richards, his girlfriend, and another male approached the victims' vehicle. Richards's male companion had a stick, and the victims decided to drive off after Richards threatened to shoot them. The police arrived shortly thereafter, and Richards continued to shout racial epithets after he saw the police.

On October 2, 1990, a jury convicted Richards of ethnic intimidation (Michigan statutes 750.147b and 28.344(2)). On February 14, 1991, he was sentenced to one to two years of imprisonment. He then appealed the constitutionality of the ethnic intimidation statute.

Legal Issues

The defendant made what would become the standard objections to Michigan's ethnic intimidation statute: that it is overbroad because it sweeps protected speech within its reach; that it has a chilling effect on the speech of others; and that it is vague by not setting reasonably clear guidelines to prevent arbitrary prosecutions.

Decision

In its opinion of November 2, 1993, the Michigan Court of Appeals held that the U.S. Supreme Court's *Wisconsin v. Mitchell* decision disposed of the defendant's constitutional challenge based on the First Amendment. The appeals court judges wrote that "The Supreme Court opined that a defendant could be punished for a discriminatory motive because 'motive plays the same role under the Wisconsin statute as it does under federal and state antidiscrimination laws.'" Furthermore, the court concluded that the Wisconsin statute was aimed at conduct unprotected by the First Amendment.

With respect to Richards's vagueness argument, the court held that "a Michigan statute may be challenged if it is so indefinite that it confers unstructured and unlimited discretion on the trier of fact to determine whether an offense has been committed." In this case, the court found that the statute did not give unlimited discretion: "The statute is satisfied when there is evidence of an underlying predicate criminal act committed because of racial animosity. These elements are very clear and definite."

Impact

This decision took place in the immediate wake of the Supreme Court's *Wisconsin v. Mitchell* opinion and was one among hundreds of state-level cases that cited the Supreme Court in upholding ethnic intimidation statutes and hate-crimes convictions. As in many other such cases, the Michigan court drew a parallel between hate-crimes statutes and antidiscrimination laws, turning aside the argument that hate-crimes laws unconstitutionally punish speech. In the years to come, this argument would become one of the most common justifications for similar decisions across the country.

MISSOURI V. JASON THOMAS VANATTER
MISSOURI SUPREME COURT
869 SW 2d 754 (1994)

Background

On July 9, 1990, Jason Vanatter was arrested and charged with burning a wooden cross on the front porch of the Church of Christ, an African-American church in West Plains, Missouri. The state charged Vanatter with committing the crime of ethnic intimidation "in that defendant knowingly damaged the property of the Church of Christ, West Plains, to wit: the front porch of the Church of Christ located at Washington Avenue, Missouri by burning a wooden cross next to said porch."

Legal Issues

On October 14, 1992, Vanatter filed a motion to dismiss the charge, alleging that the ethnic intimidation statute under which he was charged (Missouri statute 574.093) violated the First Amendment to the U.S. Constitution and Article I, Section 8 of the Missouri Constitution. Relying on the U. S. Supreme Court decision in *R.A.V. v. St. Paul*, the trial court found that Section 574.093 violated the First Amendment and dismissed the ethnic intimidation charge against the defendant on January 22, 1993. The State of Missouri appealed, contending that the statute is constitutional and citing another Supreme Court case, *Wisconsin v. Mitchell*, in support of the statute's constitutionality.

Decision

On January 25, 1994, the Missouri Supreme Court affirmed the original conviction in this case, holding that "Crimes committed because of the perpetrator's hatred of the race, color, religion or national origin of the victim have the obvious tendency to ignite further violence by provoking retaliatory crimes and inciting community unrest. . . . The legislature of this state has determined that the commission of various crimes with a motive relating to the victim's race, color, religion, or national origin should be classified as ethnic intimidation and carry strict penalties." The court agreed that the Missouri statute is more similar to that upheld in *Wisconsin v. Mitchell* as it requires criminal conduct that is subject to criminal sanction and is not afforded First Amendment protection.

Impact

This case brought the two landmark Supreme Court hate-crimes decisions—*R.A.V. v. St. Paul* (which struck down a hate-crimes law) and *Wisconsin v. Mitchell* (which upheld one)—into close contention. The lawyers and justices in the Missouri case had to walk a very fine line in arguing and then deciding whether the defendant's conduct or thought was actually being punished. The final decision cited not only actual arson damage to the property in question but also the state's compelling interest in preventing further outbreaks of violence after a hate crime has been committed. By this time, the *Wisconsin v. Mitchell* decision was gaining precedence in state court decisions regarding hate crimes, which as a result were tending toward uniformity of language and successful prosecution.

STATE OF FLORIDA V. RICHARD STALDER
SUPREME COURT OF FLORIDA
630 SO.2d 1072 (1994)

Background

Herbert Cohen and a friend, Denise Avard, went to Richard Stalder's home on April 14, 1991, to retrieve Avard's earrings. Stalder assaulted Cohen and maligned his Jewish heritage. When Stalder answered the door, he stated, "Hey Jew boy, what do you want?" Cohen replied that he was looking for Avard's earrings. Stalder then started to yell statements to the victim about his Jewish descent, at one point pushing Cohen.

Stalder was charged with violating Section 784.03(1), Florida Statutes (1989) (simple battery) for pushing Cohen, and the penalty was subject to reclassification pursuant to Section 775.085(1) (Florida's hate-crime enhancement statute) from a first-degree misdemeanor to a third-degree felony.

Legal Issues

Stalder contended that Florida's hate-crime enhancement statute is both vague and overbroad and punishes pure thought and expression in violation of the First Amendment of the Constitution. The trial court granted

Stalder's pretrial motion to dismiss the enhancement charge, adopting Stalder's argument that the statute violates the free-speech clause. The state appealed, contending that Section 775.085 is neither unconstitutionally vague nor overbroad—the statute simply enhances punishment for those crimes that are committed because the victim has one of several identified characteristics. It was the State's position that the statute punishes criminal action, not speech, and thus does not implicate the First Amendment.

Decision

On January 27, 1994, the Florida Supreme Court agreed with the state and upheld Stalder's conviction.

Impact

The two sides in this case were litigating not just constitutional issues but also the question of how severe hate-crimes penalty enhancements can be. The outcome was positive for those favoring tough hate-crimes laws. In its decision, the Florida Supreme Court accepted the state's argument that bias motivation can turn an action normally punishable as a misdemeanor into a felony.

DOBBINS V. FLORIDA
SUPREME COURT OF FLORIDA
631 SO. 2d 303 (1994)

Background

An adolescent seeking the acceptance of his peer group, John Daly, who is Jewish, joined the Skinheads, an openly anti-Semitic organization. When his fellow members learned of his Jewish background, Michael Earl Dobbins and several other members beat him. During the beating, Dobbins and others made such statements as "Die, Jew boy." Dobbins was tried and convicted under Florida's battery statute and sentenced under the enhancement provisions of Florida's hate-crime statute, Section 775.085, which provides that "the penalty for any felony or misdemeanor shall be reclassified as provided in this subsection if the commission of such felony or misdemeanor evidences prejudice based on the race, color, ancestry, ethnicity, religion or national origin of the victim."

Legal Issues

Dobbins appealed the verdict and sentence, contending that Florida's hate-crime statute is vague and overbroad and that it applies to speech protected by the First Amendment, as it does not require that the alleged prejudice have any specific relationship to the crime. Dobbins maintained that the language of the statute can be read to apply to a situation in which the defendant commits a race-, color-, or religious-neutral crime, but during the commission of the offense makes a racial slur.

Decision

On February 10,1994, the court found the evidence sufficient to uphold the jury's verdict that Dobbins committed criminal battery and that the commission of the act evidenced prejudice based on Daly's "ancestry, ethnicity, religion or national origin." The opinion read, in part, "the statute requires that it is the commission of the crime that must evidence the prejudice; the fact that racial prejudice may be exhibited during the commission of the crime is itself insufficient. In the present case the jury was required to find that the beating, based on the background and relationship between the participants and the statements made during the beating, evidenced that Daly was the chosen victim because he was Jewish. Had the fight occurred for some other reason (over a woman, because of an unpaid debt, etc.), the mere fact that Daly might have been called a 'Jew boy' could not enhance the offense."

The court also found Florida Statutes Section 775.085 to be constitutional. Although Dobbins contended that the enhancement provision punishes protected speech and opinion, the court found the statute involved in this case sufficiently different from *R.A.V. v. St. Paul* (the hate-crime ordinance overturned by the U.S. Supreme Court), in that Section 775.085 does not punish intolerant opinions but rather acts committed on the basis of such opinions to the injury of others. "We believe that the act of choosing a victim for a crime because of his race or religion is a type of speech that is subject to regulation. . . . In such cases it is not the content of the speech that is prohibited, but such act of discrimination. It does not matter why a woman is treated differently than a man, a black differently than a white, a Catholic differently than a Jew; it matters only that they are."

NEW JERSEY V. VAWTER AND KEARNS
NEW JERSEY SUPREME COURT
136 N.J. 56 (1994)

Background

On May 13, 1991, a person or persons spray painted a Nazi swastika and words appearing to read "Hitler Rules" on a synagogue, Congregation B'nai Israel, in the town of Rumson, New Jersey. On that same night the same person or persons also spray painted a satanic pentagram on the driveway of a Roman Catholic church, the Church of the Nativity, in the neighboring town of Fair Haven.

Stephen Vawter and David Kearns were charged with four counts of putting another in fear of violence by placement of a symbol or graffiti on property, a third-degree offense; four counts of defacement; two counts of third-degree criminal mischief; and two counts of conspiracy to commit the offenses charged in counts one through 10, under New Jersey statutes 2C:33-10 (Section 10) and Section 11, New Jersey's hate-crimes laws.

Section 10 reads as follows: "A person is guilty of a crime of the third degree if he purposely, knowingly or recklessly puts or attempts to put another in fear of bodily violence by placing on public or private property a symbol, an object, a characterization, an appellation or graffiti that exposes another to threats of violence, contempt or hatred on the basis of race, color, creed or religion, including, but not limited to[,] a burning cross or Nazi swastika. A person shall not be guilty of an attempt unless his actions cause a serious and imminent likelihood of causing fear of unlawful bodily violence."

Section 11 provides that "A person is guilty of a crime of the fourth degree if he purposely defaces or damages, without authorization of the owner or tenant, any private premises or property primarily used for religious, educational, residential, memorial, charitable, or cemetery purposes, or for assembly by persons of a particular race, color, creed or religion by placing thereon a symbol, an object, a characterization, an appellation, or graffiti that exposes another to threat of violence, contempt or hatred on the basis of race, color, creed or religion, including, but not limited to, a burning cross or Nazi swastika."

At their trial, the defendants moved to dismiss counts one through eight of the indictment on the ground that Sections 10 and 11 violate their First and Fourteenth Amendment rights under the U.S. Constitution. In denying defendants' motion to dismiss the first eight counts of the indictment, the trial court held that Sections 10 and 11 were violations of their constitutional right to free speech. The state appealed this decision, and the New Jersey Supreme Court then addressed the defendants' constitutional challenge to the New Jersey statutes.

Legal Issues

The basic legal issue at stake was the circumstance under which speech, more specifically, the expression of a threat, can be prosecuted as a criminal act. The state of New Jersey argued that because Sections 10 and 11 regulate only threats of violence, a class of speech that has been found unprotected by the Constitution, the laws fall within the first exception for content discrimination, in which an entire class of speech can be held as illegal.

Decision

On May 26, 1994, the court found that Sections 10 and 11 do not increase the penalty for an underlying offense because of a motive grounded in bias; rather, those sections make criminal the expressions of hate themselves, particularly in view of the fact that New Jersey already had statutes proscribing conduct such as criminal mischief, defacement of property, placing of symbols, arson, and trespass.

Impact

The New Jersey court's decision struck down Sections 10 and 11 of the state's criminal code as regulating expression protected by the First Amendment: "We conclude that sections 10 and 11 are content-based restrictions. In adopting those sections the Legislature was obviously expressing its disagreement with the message conveyed by the conduct that the statutes regulate." The court also found that even if Sections 10 and 11 were construed to proscribe only threats of violence, another problem would arise: the statutes proscribe threats "on the basis of race, color, creed or religion." Under the Supreme Court's ruling in *R.A.V. v. St. Paul*, that limitation makes the statutes viewpoint discriminatory and thus impermissible. Although a statute may prohibit threats, it may not confine the prohibition to threats based on their objectionable content. Because Sections 10 and 11 limit their scope to the topics of race, color, creed, and religion, the statutes were found unconstitutional.

AYERS V. MARYLAND
MARYLAND COURT OF APPEALS
645 A.2d 22 (1994)

Background

On the evening of March 2, 1992, John Randolph Ayers, age 22, and a friend, Sean Riley, age 20, were at Ayers's home, in the Aspen Hill section of Silver Spring, Maryland, assembling a shed in the backyard and drinking beer. They worked on the shed until about 10:30 P.M. Later, they discussed an incident of racial confrontation that had occurred at an area 7-Eleven store several nights earlier, an incident in which Ayers was involved. Ayers and Riley left Ayers's house at 2 A.M. on March 3 to look for black people to beat up. They soon observed two black women walking on Georgia Avenue. They stopped their vehicle and began walking behind the women. After the women began to run, the two men chased them. The women separated.

Riley chased one of the women, Myrtle Guillory; Ayers chased the other, Johnnie Mae McCrae. Guillory testified at the trial that as she ran she looked back, saw Ayers grab McCrae and heard McCrae scream. She testified that as Riley chased her, he yelled repeatedly, "I'm going to kill you, you black b——h." She said Riley grabbed her from behind, but she got away when he was distracted by a passing car. Guillory said she ran toward the home of David Davis, a friend. When Guillory reached Davis's yard, she began screaming for help. She ran up to the porch and began banging on the door. Davis opened the door and Riley fled. McCrae testified that as she ran from Ayers, she fell, and Ayers grabbed her by the back of her coat collar and dragged her into the woods. She said that he began "banging her head" and told her he was going to kill her.

Ayers was found guilty of assault, assault with intent to maim, kidnapping, conspiracy to commit a racially motivated crime, and committing a racially motivated crime in violation of Maryland statute section 470A (b)(3)(i). He was sentenced to 10 years for conspiracy to commit a racially motivated crime against Guillory. He was further sentenced to 10 years for assault with intent to maim McCrae (the assault conviction was merged into the aggravated assault conviction); 30 years for kidnapping McCrae; and 10 years for committing a racially motivated crime against McCrae. The court directed that the sentences run consecutively, for a total of 60 years.

Legal Issues

Ayers appealed his conviction, arguing that Section 470A violates the First and Fourteenth Amendments to the U.S. Constitution because that part of the statute which prohibits harassment of someone because of race, color, religious beliefs or national origin is unconstitutionally vague and overbroad. He also argued that the "harass" prong of the statute is a content-based regulation of speech that cannot be justified by the state, maintaining that the state could better advance its interest in deterring bias-motivated crime by instead enacting a penalty-enhancement statute.

Ayers also contended that the trial court erred in allowing irrelevant and prejudicial evidence (the 7-Eleven incident) to be introduced against him. He argued that the evidence of the February 29 incident at the 7-Eleven store was prejudicial because of the danger of it being considered as indicative of a propensity on his part to commit a racially motivated crime. Ayers claims also that there was legally insufficient evidence to convict him under Section 470A because the only evidence that his acts of March 3 were racially motivated came from his accomplice, Riley. Consequently, Ayers suggested that his conviction violates a longstanding rule that a person may not be convicted upon the uncorroborated testimony of an accomplice.

Ayers also argued that the court abused its discretion in sentencing him to 60 years imprisonment, asserting that the sentence was so oppressive as to constitute cruel and unusual punishment under the Eighth Amendment to the Federal Constitution and Articles 16 and 25 of the Maryland Declaration of Rights.

Decision

In its decision of July 21, 1994, the Maryland Court of Appeals found that Ayers was convicted of committing several distinct crimes in addition to the conviction under Section 470A. Because Ayers did not challenge the evidence that supported those convictions, he was found guilty of not only committing the underlying crimes but also of committing them "because of [the victim's] race." The court concluded that Ayers lacked standing to challenge the statute facially on the basis that the harassment prong of Section 470A is vague and overbroad. In addition, the court held that the evidence of Ayers's participation in the February 29 altercation at the 7-Eleven store (and the racial nature of the incident) was admissible because it was relevant to motive, and that admitting the evidence regarding the 7-Eleven incident did not violate the First Amendment, nor did it violate the rule which generally prohibits the introduction of "other crimes evidence."

The court found that the sentences imposed for the crimes against McCrae—assault with intent to maim, kidnapping, and committing a racially motivated crime—were not grossly disproportionate; it also found that the 10-year sentence for conspiracy to commit a racially motivated crime against Guillory was not grossly disproportionate.

Impact

The decision upheld Maryland's hate-crimes statutes and reinforced the ability of state prosecutors to introduce evidence of bias not directly linked to the crime in question.

PENNSYLVANIA V. DUANE BURLINGAME, TERRY ORNDORFF, AND CLYDE HARRIS
SUPREME COURT OF PENNSYLVANIA
672 A.2d 813 (1996)

Background

On August 30, 1994, Burlingame, Orndorff, and Harris were picketing in front of the Caterpillar heavy-equipment manufacturing plant in York, Pennsylvania, where Caterpillar and the United Auto Workers (UAW) were in the midst of a labor dispute. As workers who had crossed the picket lines were attempting to drive away from the plant at the end of their shift, the defendants allegedly approached the workers' cars, pointed fingers at the workers, and screamed insults, some of which included racial epithets. In addition, one of the defendants, Clyde E. Harris, allegedly spit on a car. The Court of Common Pleas of York County found that the defendants' actions constituted a violation of Pennsylvania Statute 2709(a)(3), which states that "a person commits the crime of harassment when, with intent to harass, annoy or alarm another person, he engages in a course of conduct or repeatedly commits acts which alarm or seriously annoy such other person and which serve no legitimate purpose." They were also charged with ethnic intimidation.

The court also found, however, that since appellees were parties to a labor dispute at the time they engaged in such conduct, the provisions of section 2709(e) required dismissal of the harassment charges. Subsection (e) of the statute was added by the Pennsylvania legislature in 1993 and reads: "This section shall not apply to conduct by a party to a labor dispute . . . or to any constitutionally protected activity." The Commonwealth of Pennsylvania then appealed.

Legal Issues

The appellees argued that since the actions that gave rise to the harassment charges constituted conduct by a party to a labor dispute, the prosecution was barred by the provisions of section 2709(e), and that since ethnic intimidation cannot stand alone as a separate offense, that charge should also be dismissed.

Decision

On March 5, 1996, the Pennsylvania Supreme Court agreed with the defendants in this case. The opinion read, in part: ". . .the Commonwealth contends that the trial court erred in its application of section 2709(e). It argues that the language of section 2709(e) is ambiguous . . . However . . . when the words of a statute are clear and unambiguous, we must give effect to their plain meaning. Section 2709(e) provides, quite simply, that section 2709 of the Crimes Code, which defines the crime of harassment, does not apply to conduct by a party to a labor dispute as that term is defined by the Labor Anti-Injunction Act. Since it is beyond question that Appellees' conduct, however offensive, occurred during a labor dispute to which they were parties, it is shielded from prosecution under the harassment statute and the charges were properly dismissed."

Impact

The Pennsylvania case offers an example of a hate-crimes statute that cannot stand alone. The state supreme court found that an underlying criminal act, enforceable under ordinary statutes, must be committed before a hate crime can be charged and penalty enhancement be applied. In this case, however, the charges were dismissed, as the harassment occurred under circumstances that barred prosecution—therefore the hate-crimes charges also failed.

STATE OF ILLINOIS V. B.C. ET AL. (MINORS)
SUPREME COURT OF ILLINOIS
680 N.E. 2d 1355 (MAY 22, 1997)

Background

The state filed hate-crimes charges against the juvenile defendants, referred to as B.C. and T.C. in court documents, for allegedly committing disorderly conduct on October 14, 1994, by displaying "patently offensive depictions of violence toward African Americans. . . . The alleged depictions consisted of a hand drawing of an eerily smiling, hooded Ku Klux klansman who held an axe-like object from which drops of blood apparently fell. At the klansman's feet lay the prone body of a dark complexioned person. . ."

The defendants were accused of violating Section 12-7.1(a) of the state's criminal code. This hate-crimes statute borrowed from the Anti-Defamation League's model legislation and states, in part, that "A person commits a hate crime when, by reason of the actual or perceived race, color, creed, religion, ancestry, gender, sexual orientation, physical or mental disability, or national origin of another individual or group of individuals, he commits assault, battery, aggravated assault, misdemeanor or theft, criminal trespass to residence, misdemeanor criminal damage to property, criminal trespass to vehicle, criminal trespass to real property, mob action or disorderly conduct. . ." The phrase "actual or perceived" [race, color, and so on] was added to the law in 1994.

At the preliminary hearing, the parties stipulated that James Jeffries—a vice principal at the defendants' school (and listed as the victim on the criminal complaint)—was not an African American, nor did the defendants perceive him to be, but that other unnamed individuals who were African Americans were present at the time of the alleged offense. Also, such unnamed individuals were not identified in the petitions as victims. It was also stipulated that the allegedly patently offensive depictions of violence toward African Americans were confiscated from the respondents. The depictions were subsequently admitted without objection.

The circuit court dismissed the petitions for failure to state an offense, finding that the charges could not be sustained because Jeffries was not actually and was not perceived to be, by defendants, a member of the protected classifications, a necessary element of the offense of hate crime. The state appealed the dismissals. On review, the appellate court reasoned that if the victim of a hate crime was not, or at least thought to be, a member of the targeted group, under the statute, the word *perceived* within the provision would be superfluous. The appellate court affirmed the dismissal of the petitions because Jeffries was not, and was not perceived to be, African American.

The Illinois Supreme Court then heard the state's appeal of these decisions.

Legal Issues

The Illinois Supreme Court had to decide whether Section 12-7.1(a) of the state's Criminal Code requires that the victim of the offense be the individual whose actual or perceived race provided reason for the offense. Alongside this issue was that of First Amendment protection for speech and opinion, in the form of the drawings in question, which the defendants held were constitutionally protected.

The state claimed that the hate-crime statute intends to focus on the accused's motive and conduct, and not on the status or the perceived status of any victim or victims. Further, according to the state, the provision includes no language that suggests that an accused's bias-motivated actions must be directed against even a particular victim in order for a hate crime to occur. The state claims that by inclusion of the phrase "actual or perceived," the legislature intended to focus not on the victim's status, but rather on the defendant's motivation.

The defendants maintained that a person cannot be a "victim" of a hate crime when the offender's improper bias in committing the underlying crime is not directed against that individual or the class to which he belongs. Thus, as applied to this case, James Jeffries cannot be the victim of a hate crime because the racially offensive materials were not directed against either him or his race.

Decision

On May 22, 1997, the court held that under Section 12-7.1(a), the victim of a bias-motivated crime does not have to actually belong to the protected group, either in fact or simply as perceived by the perpetrator. In their opinion, the justices stated that "the plain language of the hate crime statute states that the offense is committed when a person commits one of the underlying predicate offenses 'by reason of the actual or perceived race' . . . the statute includes no expression that the victim or complainant of the underlying offense must be that individual or of that group of individuals . . . In our view, the legislative history supports, instead, a generally more expansive meaning of the statute . . . the primary focus of the statute was intended to be directed towards the biased motivation of the perpetrator, rather than towards the status of the victim of the hate crime statute. . ."

A dissenting opinion held that the drawings in question, although offensive, fall "within that class of expression which the Supreme Court [in *R.A.V. v. St. Paul*] has declared 'government may not regulate based on hostility—or favoritism—towards the underlying message expressed . . . The charge of disorderly conduct also does not pass constitutional scrutiny on the basis that the drawings depict or advocate violence."

Impact

The decision in this case broadened the state's powers to prosecute hate crimes, in that the protected status of the victims would now take second place to the motivations of the accused hate-crime offenders.

CITY OF WICHITA V. EDWARDS
KANSAS COURT OF APPEALS
939 P.2d 942 (1997)

Background

John Edwards and his girlfriend, Terri Smith, were at a Wichita club when Smith and her former roommate, Marie Anderson, met and had a conversation. Anderson asked for and received her house key from Smith, who is white. (Anderson is black.) Edwards, who is white, was wearing a T-shirt with the slogan "White Power" on the front. According to Edwards, Anderson upset Smith by calling her a "Nazi-loving slut" and threatening to expose her cocaine habit. According to Anderson, Edwards shoved her chair, pinning her up against the bar, and said, "You g——n n——r b——h, if you ever talk to Terri again, I'll f——ing kill your ass." Edwards then spat in her face. Anderson described Edwards as very hostile, hateful, and angry. Edwards released her and left the club.

Although Edwards did not recall touching Anderson's chair, he admitted yelling at Anderson and calling her names. Edwards stated that he told Anderson he would "cut her fat n——r legs off" if she did not leave Smith alone. Edwards stated that he did not approach Anderson because she was black, but did so because he wanted to tell her to leave Smith alone. Edwards denied spitting on Anderson. Edwards also acknowledged that he was a skinhead and has the word *skinhead* tattooed on the back of his head.

Legal Issues

Edwards was charged under the Wichita City Code with battery, disorderly conduct, and (under Section 5.01.010) ethnic intimidation. The municipal court found Edwards guilty of all three charges, and he appealed to the district court. Edwards moved to dismiss the ethnic intimidation charge on constitutional grounds, but the court rejected his arguments. The court found that Wichita's ethnic intimidation ordinance was not unconstitutionally vague or overbroad and did not violate the equal protection clause. Edwards was convicted and sentenced on all three charges.

Edwards then appealed to the Kansas Court of Appeals, contending that the ordinance is unconstitutionally overbroad and vague, and also that it violates the equal protection clause of the Fourteenth Amendment to the Constitution.

Decision

On May 23, 1997, the Kansas Court of Appeals upheld the conviction, holding that Section 5.01.010 of the Wichita City Code (the ethnic intimidation ordinance) is not unconstitutionally overbroad when construed to encompass "fighting words." The opinion found that the ordinance "penalizes conduct undertaken by reason of specific motivations or intents." The court also held that the ordinance is not unconstitutionally vague and that it does not violate the equal protection clause.

Impact

The Kansas decision harkened back to *Chaplinsky v. New Hampshire*, in which the U.S. Supreme Court upheld a conviction based on the use of "fighting words" that are not protected by the constitution. The court also found that the Wichita ordinance "distinguishes between types of crimes based on the motivations underlying the crime" and is "related to the State's legitimate interest in protecting its citizens from bias-related crimes."

U.S. v. Machado
United States District Court
Southern District of California
SACR 96-142-AHS (1998)

Background

On Friday, September 20, 1996, 59 Asian-American students at the University of California, Irvine (UC Irvine) received identical e-mail messages, sent from an anonymous source, that read as follows:

Hey Stupid F——er:
As you can see in the name, I hate Asians, including you. If it weren't for asias at UCI, it would be a much more popular campus. You are responsible

*for ALL the crimes that occur on campus. YOU are responsible for the campus being all dirt. YOU ARE RESPONSIBLE. That's why I want you and your stupid a—— comrades to get the f——out of UCI. If you don't I will hunt you down and kill your stupid a——. Do you hear me? I personally will make it my life career to find and kill everyone of you personally. OK??????
That's how determined I am.
Get the f—— out.
MOther F—— (Asian Hater).*

Several of the recipients reported the e-mail message to the UC Irvine Office of Academic Computing (OAC). An investigation of the e-mails showed that the sender had pulled up a list of all people then online at the time, and from that list selected 59 individuals based on their apparently Asian surnames. The user IDs were then entered into the "To:" field and sent to these users. The OAC immediately determined the identity of the sender: Richard Machado, a 19-year old student and naturalized U.S. citizen originally from El Salvador. Still at work in the computer lab at the time, Machado was asked to leave.

According to OAC's Computer and Network Policy, users may not "[use] computers or electronic mail to act abusively toward others or to provoke a violent reaction, such as stalking, acts of bigotry, threats of violence, or other hostile or intimidating 'fighting words.' Such words include those terms widely recognized to victimize or stigmatize individuals on the basis of race, ethnicity, religion, sex, sexual orientation, disability, and other protected characteristics."

The incident was reported to the campus police department, and campus police interviewed Machado on September 28. On meeting with a police officer, Machado admitted sending the e-mails out of frustration over the number of Asian-descended students on the UC Irvine campus (where the Asian-American population made up about half of the student body), over problems with his Asian roommate, and over his belief that Asian students were given preferential treatment.

Based on the suspected violation of the federal statute banning interference with federally protected activities (including attendance at a public educational institution), the Los Angeles FBI office began an investigation of the case on October 3. Machado was indicted by a federal grand jury but failed to respond to a summons to appear before a federal magistrate on November 25. A warrant was issued for his arrest, and Machado was finally apprehended on February 6, 1997, in Nogales, Arizona.

At his trial, which began on November 11, 1997, Machado pleaded not guilty to 10 counts of violation of Title 18, Section 245(b)2(A), Interference with Federally Protected Activities.

The Law of Hate Crime

Legal Issues

The Machado case was a precedent-setting trial of hate crime committed on the Internet. Machado's defense team argued that his e-mail message was nothing more than a common online prank, a flame, in which the sender composes an inflammatory, obscenity-laced message with the intention of aggravating or intimidating the recipient. The defense also argued that the Internet, as a fairly new, open, and often anonymous means of communication, allows the airing of extreme opinions and that such speech, although unpleasant and sometimes racist in nature, should be protected by the First Amendment. The defense argued that the charges against Machado could have a chilling effect on free speech, as it is sometimes conducted on the Internet, and criminalizes thoughts rather than criminal actions. The defense also presented into evidence a questionnaire distributed to the recipients of Machado's e-mail, in which several answered that they had not felt directly threatened by the message, and that only 10 of the 59 recipients considered the threat serious enough to press charges against Machado.

The prosecution in the case argued that any threat against life that can reasonably be taken as serious by the recipient of an e-mail should be punishable just as such a threat would be if uttered in public or sent through the regular mail. The fact that the e-mail had been sent only to recipients with Asian surnames made it a case of civil rights violation based on ethnicity. The prosecution also introduced evidence that Machado, using his roommate's computer, had previously used e-mail to send a threat to a campus newspaper.

Decision

The trial of Richard Machado began on November 4, 1997, in the U.S. District Court, Southern District of California. However, after three days of deliberations, the jury announced that it was deadlocked, 9 to 3, and could not reach a unanimous verdict. A mistrial was declared, but as Machado was considered a flight risk, he was denied bail and detained. A second trial began on January 27, 1998, in which Machado was charged with two counts of federal civil rights violations: sending the e-mail threats based on the ethnicity of the recipients and interfering with their federally protected right to attend a public educational institution. The jury in this case deliberated for a day before reaching a unanimous verdict of guilty on February 13, 1998. As Machado had already spent more than a year in prison, and the sentencing guidelines call for a prison term of a year for his conviction, he was released but fined $1,000, asked to attend racial tolerance counseling, banned from the UC Irvine campus, banned from the use of UC Irvine computers, and barred from any contact with the e-mail recipients.

Impact

The Machado decision was the first to set legal standards for content on the Internet. It followed the first Internet "hate crime" prosecution, in which violating federal civil rights statutes by e-mail put this communication medium on the same legal footing as regular mail or the telephone.

STATE OF WASHINGTON V. DAWSON WASHINGTON COURT OF APPEALS NO. 38411-2-I (1998)

Background

On the evening of November 3, 1995, at about 10 P.M., Corey Baker and Carolyn Crawford were leaving a college party in Bellingham, Washington. As they approached their vehicle, they encountered a group of whites standing in front of it. Baker asked the group if everything was okay. He looked around the front of the vehicle to see if there was a dent, and asked if the car parked in front of it had backed into it. Someone from the group said, "Yeah, there's a problem, n——r."

The group started walking toward Baker. Further racial slurs were directed at Baker. He backed up, put his hands in the air, and said there was no problem. Without seeing what happened, Baker heard and felt a blow from a 40-ounce beer bottle when it hit him in the face, fracturing his cheekbone. Baker ran. His companion, Crawford, ran after him. The group chased her, shouting racial epithets directed at her association with Baker. Other people from the college party responded to the situation and a fight ensued until the police arrived about 10 minutes later.

To police, Crawford pointed out individuals, later identified as Banner Dawson and Jason LaRue, as the instigators of the attack on Baker, and pointed to Dawson as the person who hit Baker with the bottle.

Legal Issues

The state charged Dawson with malicious harassment and a racially motivated assault. Before the trial began, the court, over Dawson's objection, granted the state's motion for an order directing the jail to shave Dawson's head so the state could inspect a tattoo on his scalp. A jury then convicted Dawson on both counts, and he appealed. Dawson contended that evidence of the tattoo was not material to the crimes charged and therefore should not have been admitted as evidence at his trial.

The Law of Hate Crime

Decision

The Washington Court of Appeals affirmed the convictions for a racially motivated assault on January 26, 1998. The opinion stated, in part:

> *In a prosecution for malicious harassment, evidence of expressions or associations of the accused may not be introduced as substantive evidence at trial unless the evidence specifically relates to the crime charged. But in this case the State knew that Dawson had a tattoo on his scalp, and, having collected white supremacist materials in his possession, the State reasonably suspected that Dawson's tattoo might have been an expression of racist sentiments directed against African-Americans. If so, Dawson's tattoo would have specifically related to the crime charged because it would have tended to prove that Dawson had a racial motive in selecting Baker, an African-American, as a victim. The tattoo did not need to be directed personally at the victim, as Dawson argues, to be . . . admissible at trial. The tattoo may have been relevant to prove Dawson assaulted Baker because of his . . . perception of the victim's race.*

Impact

The *Washington v. Dawson* decision touched on the problem of evidence of motive, a sticking point in the prosecution of many hate-crimes cases. Assaults and other crimes are often accompanied by racial epithets, name-calling, and so forth, yet such speech does not necessarily prove that the defendant had a biased motive, or had selected his or her victim on the basis of race, religion, national origin, and so on. Such vagueness in the law is a common objection raised by those who generally oppose hate-crimes statutes, and the investigation of this case, in which a tattoo was used as evidence of biased motive, is sometimes cited in such objections.

MARTINEZ V. TEXAS
TEXAS COURT OF APPEALS
980 S.W. 2d 662 (1998)

Background

On the morning of June 20, 1994, Cindy Harris discovered her two-year old son, Johnny Vasquez, lying dead, face down on the top bunk of her children's bunk bed. The death, due to blunt abdominal trauma, was ruled a homicide by the Bexar County Assistant Medical Examiner, Dr. Jan Garavaglia.

Pablo Martinez was then indicted for capital murder under Texas Penal Code Section 19.03(a)(8) for the murder of a child under six years of age. At the criminal trial, the evidence showed that Martinez lived with Cindy

89

Harris and her three children approximately three to five months prior to Johnny's death. Harris testified that Martinez expressed to her his dislike for Johnny because of the color of Johnny's skin, and that a dark birthmark over one eye was evidence that Johnny's father was African American.

Following the jury's verdict of guilty on the lesser offense of serious bodily injury to a child based on reckless conduct, the trial judge entered a finding that Martinez committed the offense because of bias or prejudice based on sex and race, and enhanced the punishment range to that of a second-degree felony, and so instructed the jury. The jury assessed punishment at the maximum penalty of 20 years' imprisonment and imposed a $10,000 fine.

Legal Issues

Martinez appealed his sentence, arguing that the evidence was insufficient to show that he intentionally selected Johnny as a victim because of a bias or prejudice, and that there was no evidence of a causal connection between his alleged bias and Johnny's fatal injury. In the appeal, the state argued that the record contained sufficient evidence to support the sentence enhancement under the statute.

In their published opinion, the appeals court judges quoted the trial judge as follows: "Well, the jury has found that the Defendant killed this child, caused the death of this child. This child is a male child. The evidence adduced by the Defense has shown relationships with female children not with male children. It's a male child that bared a birthmark and that the Defendant perceived as being of a dark race, or at least accused or called or classified that. So, in looking for a motive of why someone would torment a child for five months, eventually causing the death of that child in the fashion that we have heard in this Court, this Court is of the opinion that this Defendant selected this child in a biased and prejudiced fashion based both on sex and race."

Decision

The Texas Court of Appeals affirmed the trial judgment on July 22, 1998. According to the appeals court, the hate-crime punishment enhancement may be assessed when the assailant acted because of the victim's perceived race or color. Its opinion read, in part: "Although Johnny was not African-American, the State presented sufficient evidence through Cindy Harris' testimony from which a rational trier of fact could have found beyond a reasonable doubt that Martinez was biased against African-American people and that Martinez's pattern of abuse against Johnny was because he associated Johnny with the African-American race."

Further, the court held that the punishment enhancement may be based upon circumstantial evidence of the appellant's bias or prejudice motive, including previous racial epithets directed at the victim. "This evidence provides a sufficient basis from which the trial court could reasonably conclude that this bias or prejudice was the intentional motivation of the crime for which Martinez was convicted. . . . While the evidence does not directly show that Martinez acted out of any bias or prejudice at the time he caused the fatal injury to Johnny, such inference may be reasonably drawn from the proven pattern of abuse based on bias or prejudice."

Impact

The Martinez case extended culpability for a hate crime to those who, even if mistakenly, perceive their victims to be members of protected groups and who act on prejudice against such groups. The circumstantial evidence applied against the defendant would also make it easier to win a conviction on hate-crimes charges, even when the crime itself shows no direct evidence of prejudiced motive through the speech or actions of the defendant.

Tennessee v. Bakenhus
Tennessee Criminal Appeals Court
No. 01C01-9705-CC-00165 (1999)

Background

During the early morning hours of August 4, 1994, James L. Johnson and his family were awakened by a loud noise. Johnson told his wife to call 911, got a gun, and went to investigate. When he opened his front door, Johnson discovered his garage on fire and then noticed someone in a small white car drive by several times. Sometime after daylight, Johnson discovered melted siding and burned shutters. He found broken liquor bottles in the flowerbed and smelled gasoline or diesel fuel. Johnson found a hate letter in his mailbox and noticed eight or 10 small holes in his front gutter, which appeared to be caused by a shotgun blast.

This incident was followed by several more burglaries and arsons in the area. At one point, Robert Smith, a local newspaper photographer, received an anonymous phone call. The caller claimed that "A.F." was responsible for burning a house and that if the "n—— in the area didn't get out of the area, then he was going to kill them all."

Brian Beuscher had been introduced to the defendant, John Jason Bakenhus, in late July 1994 by a mutual friend, Charles Neblett. Beuscher recalled that the defendant, then 21 years old, was attempting to organize a group that would conduct acts of violence against African Americans and Hispanics in return for payment. Beuscher, age 16 at the time, signed an oath and joined the group. Five other members between the ages of 14 and 16 were also recruited by the defendant. Beuscher testified that he, Neblett, and the defendant prepared Molotov cocktails by filling liquor bottles with gasoline and inserting a cloth wick. They also had ski masks and gloves, a shotgun, and a note Beuscher had written at the direction of the defendant: "Dear Johnsons, A.F. wants you to leave our white community! You coons! Coon hunting season is open! A.F."

On August 4, the defendant was stopped in his vehicle, whereupon he consented to a search. Accelerants were discovered. Eventually, the defendant confessed. His statement led to the discovery of pawn tickets, a shotgun, number six and eight shells, and empty cans of spray paint. Police detectives took the defendant's briefcase from the garage of his father's house. It contained organization rules, regulations, oath, and a membership list. There were manuals on bomb making and war devices and a piece of paper listing types of grenades and explosives. Officers photographed a painting of a Nazi swastika on the wall of the defendant's bedroom. The defendant provided investigators with a small notebook containing hand drawings of a hooded Ku Klux Klan member lynching a man.

In his statements to Detective Clifton Smith, the defendant denied having animosity toward African Americans but acknowledged that he despised interracial marriages. Although he initially denied membership in an extremist organization, he inquired whether Detective Smith had found a note in a mailbox, whether anyone had called the newspaper, and whether any graffiti had been found on a roadway or building. Detective Smith reviewed the membership list, contacted and interviewed the members, and finally confronted the defendant, who then admitted his guilt.

Bakenhus was indicted for aggravated arson, two counts of arson, three counts of civil rights intimidation, aggravated burglary, theft of property over $500 and theft of property under $500. The jury returned guilty verdicts on all nine counts. The defendant was convicted for the same acts in federal court.

Legal Issues

In his appeal, the defendant argued, among other defenses, that the trial court erred by admitting a photograph of a swastika and a sketch of a Ku Klux Klan lynching.

Decision

The appeals court affirmed the criminal court decision on January 11, 1999, ruling that ". . .the photograph and sketch are valuable to prove the defendant's intent to intimidate his victims because of their race. While we concede that the exhibits may be offensive and crude, any prejudice is outweighed by their significant probative value as to the charged offense." The criminal trial verdict of guilty was affirmed.

NEW JERSEY V. DOWELL ET AL.
NEW JERSEY SUPERIOR COURT
756 A.2d 1087 (2000)

Background

The Monmouth County Grand Jury indicted the defendants for kidnapping, conspiracy to commit same, aggravated assault and harassment by bias intimidation (New Jersey statutes 2C:12-1(e) and 2C:33-4(d)), terroristic threats, weapons offenses, and aggravated criminal sexual contact.

The victim, E.K. in court documents, was 23 years old at the time of the alleged assault. He is learning disabled, of low I.Q., exceptionally short in stature, deaf in one ear, and speech impaired. He has a pinhole defect in his heart. E.K. and some of the defendants attended special education classes together. Over a three-day period in January 1999, it was alleged that E.K. was kidnapped, forced to drink a mixture of iced tea and alcohol, and taped to a chair. He had his head and eyebrows shaved and was punched about his face and body, forced to drink urine, kiss the shoes of the defendants, lick a drink off the floor, and dress in women's clothing. He was beaten with beads and a curtain rod and had lit cigarettes put out on his chest, ashes flicked into his mouth, and a pillowcase placed over his head. Ultimately he was dumped into a deserted wooded area known as the "pit."

Legal Issues

According to New Jersey law, a defendant may be sentenced to an extended term of imprisonment if "the defendant in committing the crime acted with the purpose to intimidate an individual or group of individuals because of race, color, gender, handicap, religion, sexual orientation or ethnicity." When the New Jersey hate-crimes statutes were amended in 1997 to add gender and handicap as categories, the legislation did not define handicap or declare the legislature's intent.

Decision

In this case of first impression (meaning a statute or legal issue is being visited for the first time), the New Jersey Superior Court held on March 16, 2000, that the word *handicap* is not unconstitutionally vague both as applied or on its face. The superior court quoted the New Jersey Law Against Discrimination (Section 10:5-1), which defines handicap as "suffering from physical disability, infirmity, malformation or disfigurement which is caused by bodily injury, birth defect or illness, which shall include, but is not limited to, lack of physical coordination, blindness, or visual impediment, deafness or hearing impediment, speech impediment, any mental, psychological or neurological condition."

The court also held that a disability, disease, or defect must be of such a nature that a reasonable person in the position of the defendants would be on fair notice that their victim was handicapped: "Giving the state the benefit of the reasonable inferences of the evidence presented to the grand jury, E.K. falls within the definition of "handicap" and the statutes in question are not vague facially or as applied to this case." The defendants' motion to dismiss the indictment was denied.

Impact

The decision in this case gave further impetus to hate-crimes prosecutions on behalf of the disabled, an important recent issue in the debate over hate-crimes law. The decision answered critics who maintain that the definition of *handicapped* or *disabled* is vague and open to a too-broad interpretation by police, prosecutors, and the courts.

CALIFORNIA V. CARR
CALIFORNIA COURT OF APPEAL
81 CAL. APP. 4TH 837 (2000)

Background

On the night of May 19, 1998, David Shostak, who is Jewish, was at his Huntington Beach, California, home with his wife Barbara, their 15-year-old son Jarod, and another son. David Shostak was just about to turn in when he noticed flames in his yard. When he looked outside, he saw a seven-foot cross burning on the side of his house. He sprinted to the cross, knocked it to the ground, and extinguished the flames with his garden hose.

An investigation into the matter led the police to Daniel Carr. A high school senior at the time, he had bragged to friends about burning a cross on "some Jew's lawn." He also responded with glee when shown a newspaper article about the incident. When the police searched his bedroom, they found Nazi paraphernalia and an American flag containing the initials S.W.P., which, according to an expert on racist ideology, stand for Supreme White Power.

Carr told police that on the night in question, he was drinking beer in a park with Derrick Yates and Dick Rutherford, who were friends of Jarod Shostak. At one point, he suggested that they burn a wooden cross he had built. Yates said they should burn it at Jarod's house, because the Shostaks are Jewish. Carr thought that was a good idea, so they retrieved the cross and, while Rutherford and Yates looked on, Carr placed it against the Shostak house and set it on fire. Carr told police he did it to show his "white power beliefs."

Legal Issues

Jarod Shostak invoked his Fifth Amendment privilege—the right not to incriminate oneself with sworn testimony—and refused to testify at the trial. However, the parties stipulated that one week prior to the incident, Jarod suggested to Yates and Rutherford that they should burn the cross at his house because "he was mad at his parents; he didn't like his curfew and other rules." California's Penal Code (§§ 11411, subd. (c)) prohibits only "unauthorized" cross burning. Thus the court had to determine whether Jarod Shotak had "authorized" the cross burning carried out by Carr, Yates, and Rutherford.

Decision

After the criminal trial, Carr was convicted for burning a cross on another person's property without authorization. On appeal, Carr contended the court and prosecutor impermissibly undermined his efforts to show the cross burning was authorized (by Jarod Shostak). He also faulted the court for disallowing the defense that he was intoxicated on the night of the incident. On June 20, 2000, the appeals court judges upheld the conviction, finding no merit in Carr's intoxication defense or in his argument that one person can authorize victimization of another.

Kapadia v. Tally
United States Seventh Circuit Court of Appeals
98-1654 (October 12, 2000)

Background

In November 1993, Amyn Kapadia and Jason Wiederhold burglarized and set fire to the Jewish-affiliated Friends of Refugees of Eastern Europe center in Chicago, Illinois. After a bench trial, the court found both defendants guilty of burglary and arson and set a date for a sentencing hearing. On his way out of the courtroom, Kapadia said to Deputy Joseph Bennett, "You can tell the Judge for me . . . that he's a b——h and f——k the Jews." Kapadia made several more anti-Semitic remarks, and Bennett passed them on to the trial judge before the sentencing hearing; the trial judge then told the deputy to inform both the prosecution and the defense about the remarks. At the sentencing hearing, the prosecution urged the judge to sentence Kapadia to "substantial penitentiary time" based on these remarks.

Kapadia was sentenced by the judge to 14 years in prison, the maximum penalty allowed for the underlying crimes of burglary and arson. The court sentenced Wiederhold to a five-year term of imprisonment, reasoning that his conduct was caused at least in part by his association with "the tumultuous and virulent Mr. Kapadia," and that he was therefore less culpable than Kapadia and could conceivably be reintegrated into society.

Kapadia appealed the sentence, claiming that the sentencing judge had not tied his remarks to his motivation to commit the crime in question, and that the harsh sentence violated his First Amendment free speech rights. The district court held that the harsh sentence was based on Kapadia's "poor rehabilitative potential," based on his evidently virulent anti-Semitism, and denied Kapadia's appeal. The case came before the Illinois Court of Appeals, which affirmed the sentence; the Illinois Supreme Court subsequently declined to hear the case, which then arrived at a federal appeals court.

Legal Issues

The basic debate in the case concerned the grounds for the original maximum sentence—either the sentencing judge had punished the protected beliefs and speech of the defendant or he had acted on the impossibility of rehabilitating the defendant. Kapadia contended that he was punished for his abstract beliefs rather than because of his motive or future dangerousness. He also claimed that the state court found no religious motivation on his part in committing the offense, and that the state court made no specific finding that he selected the property because of the religious affiliation of the owners.

The state contended that the court based the enhancement not on improper considerations but rather on Kapadia's criminal history, and that Kapadia's anti-Semitic statements were tied to his crimes of burglary and arson of a Jewish community center; therefore the court could properly use the statements to enhance his sentence, if for no other reason than because his statements showed he lacked remorse.

In other words, the court considered the deputy's testimony to be evidence of a connection between Kapadia's conduct and the Jewish affiliation of the community center. Implicit in the court's comments is the finding that Kapadia's conduct was tied to his anti-Semitic bias, and that the court wanted the deputy's statement on the record to lend support to that finding. The sentencing judge, after receiving the deputy's statement into evidence, said that he took Kapadia's comments into consideration because he believed Kapadia was less likely to be reformed. He found Kapadia more dangerous because he held anti-Semitic views and attacked a Jewish community center. Because Kapadia's remarks came after his conviction, the sentencing judge was free to conclude that he lacked remorse and was less likely to be rehabilitated.

Decision

The federal appeals court upheld Kapadia's original 14-year sentence. In the published opinion, the judges found that

> Kapadia's acts were motivated by bias against the very group of people he maligned with his hateful invective. He did not burglarize and set fire to a Walmart, for example, or some other business with no particular affiliation, and then utter anti-Semitic slurs . . . the fact that he did not spray his slogans on the walls but rather uttered them after his conviction is irrelevant. The court was free to infer from his post-trial statements that he held the same views at the time of the crime and was motivated by those views in selecting the victim. The First Amendment does not bar consideration of these statements at sentencing when they are indicative of motive and future dangerousness, and we think the sentencing court's comments make plain enough that it was considering the remarks as such. . .
>
> Nothing in the Constitution prevents the sentencing court from factoring a defendant's statements into sentencing when those statements are relevant to the crime or to legitimate sentencing considerations. Because the sentencing court was not punishing Kapadia for his abstract beliefs but rather for his concrete application of those misguided beliefs in criminal activity, we affirm the judgment of the district court.

Impact

By longstanding legal precedent, judges are allowed to take into consideration the chances for rehabilitation in passing sentence on a criminal defendant. The less likely the defendant's ability to reintegrate into society, the longer term he or she is likely to get. This ability can be measured by any number of factors, introduced by the prosecution as well as the defense at trial and in the sentencing phase, and in this case also by factors evidenced by the defendant's own conduct during and after the trial. Free-speech issues in such circumstances become an irrelevant consideration as a result of the decision in this case.

KING V. TEXAS
TEXAS COURT OF APPEALS
NO. 73, 433 (2000)

Background

On June 7, 1998, police officers responded to a call to go to Huff Creek Road in the east Texas town of Jasper. In the road, in front of a church, they discovered the body of an African-American male missing the head, neck, and right arm. The remains of pants and underwear were gathered around the victim's ankles. About a mile and a half up the road, they discovered the head, neck, and arm by a culvert in a driveway.

A trail of smeared blood and drag marks led from the victim's torso to the detached upper portion of the victim's body and continued another mile and a half down Huff Creek Road and a dirt logging road. A wallet found on the logging road contained identification for James Byrd, Jr., a Jasper resident. Along the route, police also found Byrd's dentures, keys, shirt, undershirt, and watch. At the end of the logging road, the trail culminated in an area of matted-down grass, which appeared to be the scene of a fight.

At this site and along the logging road, the police discovered a cigarette lighter engraved with the words *Possum* and *KKK*, a nut driver wrench inscribed with the name *Berry*, three cigarette butts, a can of Fix-a-Flat, a compact disk, a woman's watch, a can of black spray paint, a pack of Marlboro Lights cigarettes, beer bottles, a button from Byrd's shirt, and Byrd's baseball cap.

Shawn Berry, Lawrence Russell Brewer, and John William King were arrested and charged with kidnapping and murder. At the time of their arrests, Texas did not have a hate-crimes statute. The state presented evidence linking all three men to Byrd's kidnapping and murder. DNA testing revealed that blood spatters underneath Berry's truck and on one of the truck's tires matched Byrd's DNA. In the bed of the truck, police noticed a rust stain in a chain pattern and detected blood matching Byrd's on a spare tire. Tire casts taken at the fight scene and in front of the church where Byrd's torso was found were consistent with those taken from the tires on the truck.

Shawn Berry shared an apartment with Brewer and King. Police and FBI agents searched the apartment and confiscated King's drawings and writings as well as clothing and shoes of each of the three roommates. DNA analysis revealed that the jeans and boots that Berry had been wearing on the night of the murder were stained with blood matching Byrd's DNA.

At the criminal trial, the state presented evidence of King's racial animosity, particularly toward African Americans. Several witnesses testified about how King refused to go to the home of an African American and would leave a party if an African American arrived. In prison, King was known as the "exalted cyclops" of the Confederate Knights of America (CKA), a white supremacist gang. Among the tattoos covering his body were a woodpecker in a Ku Klux Klansman's uniform making an obscene gesture; a patch incorporating "KKK," a swastika, and "Aryan Pride"; and a black man with a noose around his neck, hanging from a tree. King had on occasion displayed these tattoos to people and had been heard to remark, "See my little n——r hanging from a tree?"

A gang expert reviewed the writings that were seized from the apartment and testified that King used persuasive language to try to convince others to join in his racist beliefs. The writings revealed that King intended to start a chapter of the CKA in Jasper and was planning for "something big" to happen on July 4, 1998. The expert explained that to gain credibility, King would need to do something public. He testified that leaving Byrd's body in the street in front of a church—as opposed to hiding it in one of the many wooded areas around town—demonstrated that the crime was designed to strike terror in the community.

King was convicted of capital murder on February 25, 1999, and the trial judge sentenced him to death. In Texas, direct appeal in capital cases is automatic; on this appeal, King raised eight points of error.

Legal Issues

Evidence of the defendant's racial animosity was introduced as motive in the case, even though Texas had no hate-crimes statute at the time. Rather than combatting the introduction of such evidence, the defendant argued against the kidnapping conviction on technical grounds holding that "there was no evidence presented which would permit the jury to believe that prior to his being dragged to his death, the deceased was moved 'from one place to another.'" Although the defendant did not dispute that a fight occurred and that Byrd was chained to a truck and dragged to his death, he contended that this evidence failed to demonstrate that force was used to chain Byrd to the truck. He was guilty of "nothing more than a false imprisonment, in that the actor or actors would not let the victim go" and contended that no kidnapping occurred because Byrd "went along voluntarily." King's lawyers also suggested that no kidnapping occurred when Byrd was chained and dragged because he initially accepted a ride to his house in the pickup.

Decision

The court found that the act of chaining Byrd to the truck and dragging him for a mile and a half was, by itself, a kidnapping under the law, and that "dragging a chained man from a truck also constitutes the use of deadly force to restrain that person and prevent his liberation." The court found that DNA and other circumstantial evidence was sufficient for a jury to find beyond a reasonable doubt that the appellant was guilty of the criminal charges. In addition, according to the opinion, "the extensive evidence of appellant's hatred for African-Americans, including his graphic tattoos and drawings, is evidence that appellant had a motive to kill Byrd because of his race."

Impact

The James Byrd case became national news as the topic of hate crimes entered into the presidential election year of 2000. The lack of effective hate-crimes law in Texas became an important issue for opponents of George W. Bush, then Texas governor and a presidential candidate, who through the campaign voiced his opposition to such statutes. The killers of James Byrd, Bush maintained, would suffer the maximum penalty under the law—the death penalty—and for this reason he considered hate-crimes statutes an unnecessary complication and elaboration of criminal law. After extensive lobbying by groups favoring hate-crimes laws, however, and the generally negative publicity that came to Texas after the Byrd case, the Texas legislature passed a new hate-crimes statute in the spring of 2001.

U.S. V. NELSON
U.S. SECOND CIRCUIT COURT OF APPEALS
NOS. 98-1231 AND 98-1437 (2002)

Background

The Crown Heights disturbances in Brooklyn, New York, began on August 19, 1991, when two African-American children were struck by a station wagon driven by a Jewish man. An angry crowd soon gathered at the scene of the accident; members of the crowd began to attack the driver. An ambulance (readily identifiable as originating from a local Jewish hospital) arrived on the scene to aid the driver, then left after being warned off by police officers. Soon afterward, two New York City ambulances arrived to assist the children, who were both taken to the hospital, where one of them, Gavin Cato, later died.

Complaining about perceived preferential treatment for Jews, including the appearance of the Jewish ambulance at the scene, the crowd that had gathered at the scene of the accident grew unruly. An African-American man later identified as Charles Price roused his listeners to violence. Confrontations between blacks and Jews began taking place, a result of years of rising tensions between these two communities in the Brooklyn neighborhood. The riots resulted in a mob attack on a visiting Australian Hasidic Jew, Yankel Rosenbaum, who was beaten and then stabbed. Rosenbaum later died of his injuries.

On August 27, 1991, a 16-year-old African American, Lemrick Nelson, was charged with murdering Rosenbaum. He was tried in a state court and acquitted of the charge on October 29, 1992. The acquittal brought a public uproar, with many city and state officials charging that the jury had been biased in favor of the defendant. The FBI then undertook an investigation to determine if Nelson had violated a federal civil rights statute, Title 18, Section 245 (b)(2)(B) (Interference with Federally Protected Activities). The investigation resulted in the August 11, 1994, indictment of Nelson for the violation of Rosenbaum's civil rights. On August 7, 1996, a second indictment was handed down against Charles Price for violation of the same statute, and for aiding and abetting Nelson's violation of the statute. The indictment read, in part: "The defendants by force and threat of force did willfully injure, intimidate, and interfere with, and attempt to injure, intimidate and interfere with, Yankel Rosenbaum, an orthodox Jew, because of his religion and because he was enjoying facilities provided and administered by a subdivision of the State of New York, namely, the public streets provided and administered by the City of New York, and bodily injury to and the death of Yankel Rosenbaum did result."

Although the principle of double jeopardy would normally bar another trial for Nelson for the murder, the law allows prosecution of the same defendant on the same charge in federal court following the conclusion of the trial, based on the same evidence, in a state court. Price and Nelson were ultimately both found guilty of violating Title 18, Section 245, after four days of jury deliberations. Nelson was sentenced to 235 months in prison, Price to 260 months in prison.

Legal Issues

The evidence presented in the federal district court case showed that Price had encouraged Nelson (and others) to attack Rosenbaum, not only to avenge the death of Gavin Cato but also because Rosenbaum was Jewish (Rosenbaum was unrelated to the driver of the car that struck Cato). However, the empanelment of the jury was brought into question and became the basis for the appeal of the conviction in the Second Circuit Court of Appeals.

During the voir dire (pretrial examination) of potential jurors, the government used five out of nine peremptory challenges to strike African Americans from the jury pool. This represented 55 percent of the challenges allowed, even though African Americans represented 30 percent of the jury pool. In addition, a Jewish candidate for the jury (juror 108) admitted during the voir dire process that he had followed the first trial and was not sure he could be objective in the federal trial. Despite this admission, and although he was challenged for cause by the defense attorneys, the District Court judge, David Trager, insisted that this particular candidate be allowed to sit on the jury, stating during the proceedings that

> *I will not allow this case to go to the jury without 108 as being a member of that jury, and how that will be achieved I don't know. It may well be just by people falling out. It may well happen, in which event I propose never to make any findings on this issue, and if I can I would seal the whole discussion because I see it serving no one's interest. I am not sure I can get away with that. I don't know if the press will allow it, but I don't think it would serve the public's interest to have this discussion go on the record, and especially, if I don't make any findings and I hope that I will not have to make any findings.*

To reach an agreement and bring juror 108 onto the jury panel, Judge Trager agreed to accept an African-American candidate to the jury as well. Finally, when an African-American juror was excused from service due to illness, the court moved a white juror from the main panel to the alternate jury, and then filled the two open seats with alternate jurors selected out of order: one African-American and one Jewish candidate. Defense counsel as well as the defendants agreed to these decisions on the record.

In their arguments for overturning the district court conviction, however, the defendants argued that Section 245(b)(2)(B) is an unconstitutional law, because it reaches conduct that lies beyond congressional powers of regulation; that the evidence presented at the trial was insufficient to prove their biased intent under the same law; and that the extraordinary efforts made by the court to empanel a racially and religiously mixed jury was unconstitutional and should bring a reversal on appeal. Judge Trager was charged with mishandling the jury selection in order to obtain a panel prejudicial to the defendants. In his public statements following the trial, Trager stated that in his opinion the jury fairly represented New York's mixed religious and racial communities.

Decision

On January 7, 2002, the Second Circuit Court of Appeals reached a two-part decision. First, the court upheld the convictions of Price and Nelson under Section 245(b)(2)(B), which was found to be a constitutional law that fell within Congress's authority to enact statutes prohibiting acts of violence motivated by the victim's race or religion, under the Thirteenth Amendment's banning of slavery and the "badges and incidents of slavery." The court also found that Nelson and Price had acted because of their prejudice against Rosenbaum's religion, and that Rosenbaum's use of a public street at the time of the murder clearly and unambiguously falls within the meaning of "public facility" in the statute prohibiting bias-motivated interference with Rosenbaum's use of that facility.

The court also found, however, that Judge Trager's actions in the matter of jury selection had been improper; specifically, allowing juror 108 to sit on the jury despite his admitted lack of objectivity during the voir dire process. The court also found that the defendants' acceptance of juror 108 before the trial did not constitute a waiver of their rights to a proper jury selection. The case was remanded for a retrial.

Impact

The Crown Heights riots turned from a federal civil rights and hate-crimes case to a decision on the process of jury selection. In principle, the selection of jurors is a strictly defined procedure in which judges and attorneys strive to obtain a panel completely objective and unbiased, and in this way ensure a fair verdict in the case. Each side has a limited number of peremptory challenges, in which a juror can be barred from service for no particular cause. The Supreme Court has determined that using peremptory challenges to reject jurors based on their race or gender violates the Fourteenth Amendment, which guarantees equal protection of the laws. The Second Circuit found that Judge Trager erred in allowing an admittedly biased individual to sit on the jury, although his goal of seating a representative cross-section of the community might have been defensible. The problem remains of finding a truly neutral jury within communities that are politically, racially, or religiously homogenous, and therefore possibly biased for or against the defendant.

CHAPTER 3

―――――――

CHRONOLOGY

This chronology presents historical background to the modern hate-crimes debate; significant hate-crime incidents of the past and present; important criminal cases, appeals, and Supreme Court decisions in cases related to hate crimes; and important federal legislation dating to 1866. By the reckoning of many historians of the era, this year marks the dawn of the modern civil rights struggle on the part of African-American organizations and of black leaders such as Martin Luther King, Jr., a struggle that ultimately resulted in the passage of new civil rights legislation and hate-crimes statutes.

1649

■ The colony of Maryland, founded by Catholics, passes the Act of Toleration, extending religious freedom to all those who profess to believe in Jesus Christ and the Trinity. All others are subject to arrest, imprisonment, and execution.

1755

■ Several thousand Acadians, or French-speaking Catholics, are driven away by the government of the British colony of Canada. They flee to other colonies in the Americas, from Massachusetts to the Spanish-controlled region around New Orleans, where they are known as Cajuns and where many join militias fighting against the British.

1762

■ In the port of New Orleans, controlled by the kingdom of Spain, the Spanish governor orders all English, Protestants, and Jews to be driven out of the city.

Chronology

1768

- A wave of prejudice against Baptists sweeps through England's North American colonies and will continue for six years, a period known in American religious history as the Great Persecution. Baptists are assaulted; they are jailed for writing and distributing religious tracts; their homes and shops are burned; and they are driven from cities where the majority Anglican population despises them as political and spiritual troublemakers.

1776

- Suspecting the loyalty of blacks to the American Revolution, the Commonwealth of Virginia forcibly relocates all black males over the age of 13 to the interior, well away from British forces along the seacoast.

1780

- By the constitution of Massachusetts, all Christians are granted equal protection of the laws, but Catholics are required to repudiate the authority of the pope if they wish to hold public office.

1819

- The first federal immigration statute is passed, regulating the number of passengers that can be transported on ships arriving from foreign ports.

1822

- The first recorded arson of an African-American church takes place in South Carolina, the scene in the same year of a slave revolt led by Denmark Vesey.

1828

- Abolitionist speaker Benjamin Lundy is attacked and beaten in the streets of Baltimore, Maryland.

1834

- Anti-immigrant violence and mob battles between Protestants and Catholics and between whites and blacks, flare in the eastern cities of the United States and continue for several years. In Philadelphia, a mob of several hundred whites attacks a crowd of African Americans, destroys homes in black neighborhoods, and burns down two churches.

1835

- In Washington, D.C., abolitionist Reuben Campbell is nearly lynched by a proslavery mob, which then runs amok through the city's African-American neighborhoods. Black homes, shops, churches, and schools are burned.

1844

- A mob invades an Irish neighborhood of Philadelphia, killing the residents, looting homes, and burning several Catholic churches to the ground.

1863

- *June:* Riots erupt in New York City during a Union army conscription drive. Suspected of replacing white workers, blacks are hunted down, assaulted, burned, and lynched.

1866

- Congress passes the Civil Rights Act and the Freedmen's Bureau Act, granting equal rights to black citizens and freed slaves, and establishing the Freedmen's Bureau to provide education, health services, and job training to former slaves.
- A pro-Confederate organization known as the Ku Klux Klan is formed by Confederate veterans in Pulaski, Tennessee. Over the next several years, the Klan will spread to South Carolina, Florida, Mississippi, Georgia, Louisiana, and Alabama, its members raiding, killing, and torturing free blacks and attacking all symbols and institutions of Reconstruction imposed by the federal government on the defeated Confederacy.
- *April 30:* In Memphis, Tennessee, whites riot and kill 46 black citizens over three days of fighting.

1868

- *July 9:* The Fourteenth Amendment to the U.S. Constitution, holding that all blacks born or naturalized in the United States are citizens with the right of due process and equal protection of the law, is ratified.

1870

- *February 3:* The Fifteenth Amendment to the U.S. Constitution, holding that black citizens cannot be denied the vote on account of their race, is ratified.

Chronology

1871

- During a wave of anti-immigrant violence, a Los Angeles mob attacks a Chinese neighborhood, lynching 22 residents.

1875

- By the Civil Rights Act passed by Congress in this year, discrimination against blacks is outlawed in public places such as theaters, hotels, and public conveyances.

1876

- New Hampshire becomes the last state to end the requirement that its governor and legislators be Protestants.

1881

- Eleven Italian Americans are randomly selected for arrest after the murder of the New Orleans police superintendent; after being found not guilty, they are lynched by a mob.

1882

- By the first of several "Exclusion Acts," immigration from China is suspended for a period of 10 years. In 1902, the Chinese Exclusion Act will be amended to become a permanent ban, not to be repealed until 1943.

1887

- By the Edmunds-Tucker Act, Congress disenfranchises Mormons, bars their church, and confiscates their property.

1896

- The Supreme Court decision in *Plessy v. Ferguson* upholds a Louisiana state law mandating "separate but equal" railroad accommodations for whites and blacks.

1906

- Accused of assaulting and killing a white bartender, 167 African-American soldiers posted near Brownsville, Texas, are dishonorably discharged from the U.S. Army.

1909

- Mobs attack Greek Americans in the streets of Omaha, Nebraska, after rumors accuse a Greek man of killing a policeman.

1915

- After the 1913 murder of Mary Phagan, a young factory worker in Atlanta, Georgia, Leo Frank, the Jewish factory owner, is found guilty of the murder. After the governor commutes a death sentence passed on Frank, a mob kidnaps Frank from his prison cell and hangs him.

1919

- Race riots erupt in Chicago, Omaha, and across the Midwest and Northeast, pitting whites against blacks, immigrants, and suspected socialists and communists, resulting in hundreds of deaths and thousands of injuries.

1921

- By the Emergency Quota Act, total immigration from any European country into the United States is limited to 3 percent of the foreign-born population already in the country, as determined by the census of 1910.

1931

- *March 25:* In Paint Rock, Alabama, nine African-American men are arrested on assault and rape charges in what will become known as the Scottsboro case. Eight will be sentenced to death; in the next year the Supreme Court will reverse the convictions. Retrials and legal proceedings drag on until Alabama governor George Wallace officially pardons Clarence Norris, one of the original defendants, in 1976.

1939

- The SS *St. Louis,* a passenger steamship holding several hundred Jewish refugees from Nazi Germany, is turned away from the United States and forced back to Europe, where many passengers will be imprisoned and murdered by the Nazi regime.

1942

- During the "zoot suit riots" in Los Angeles, soldiers, police, and ordinary citizens attack Mexican-American and black citizens throughout the city.

Chronology

1948

■ By an executive order, President Harry Truman bars all segregation of African Americans in the U.S. military.

1954

■ In the Supreme Court decision in *Brown v. Board of Education*, the court strikes down the practice of "separate but equal" educational facilities for African Americans, beginning the era of school desegregation.

1955

■ *May 7:* Reverend George Lee, a member of the National Association for the Advancement of Colored People (NAACP), is murdered in Belzoni, Mississippi.
■ *August 28:* A 14-year-old African-American boy, Emmett Till, is kidnapped and murdered near Money, Mississippi, after allegedly whistling at a white woman. Men brought to trial for the murder are acquitted.
■ *October 22:* During a spree of violence directed at the African-American community of Mayflower, Texas, a 16-year-old African American is killed and two others are wounded in a local café.

1956

■ *January 30:* Rev. Martin Luther King's home in Montgomery, Alabama, is bombed.
■ *February 3:* Rioting breaks out at the University of Alabama after a black woman, Autherine Lucy, attempts to attend classes. Lucy will be suspended and then expelled from the university.

1957

■ *January 23:* A black truck driver, Willie Edwards, is kidnapped and forced to jump from a bridge over the Alabama River near Montgomery Alabama, by a group of Klansmen. The death is officially considered an accident until 1976, when one of the Klansmen confesses.

1958

■ *August 24:* Two schools scheduled to be integrated in Deep Creek, North Carolina, are burned by an arsonist.
■ *October 12:* A bomb explodes at an Atlanta, Georgia, synagogue known as the Temple, during a wave of bombings at southern synagogues,

including those in Birmingham, Alabama; Miami, Florida; and Jacksonville, Florida.

1959

- *April 25:* Accused of raping a white woman, truck driver Mack Parker is taken from his jail cell and lynched by a mob in Poplarville, Mississippi.

1960

- *January:* A wave of vandalism against synagogues sweeps the nation, with incidents in New York, Chicago, Boston, and other cities.
- *January 28:* A Kansas City, Missouri, synagogue is bombed, an incident police later link to local neo-Nazi youths.
- *April 23:* A civil rights worker, William Moore, is murdered in Alabama, while marching alone from Tennessee to Mississippi.
- *August 27:* A riot erupts between blacks and Ku Klux Klan members in Jacksonville, Florida, resulting in dozens of injuries and more than 100 arrests.
- *November 15:* White and black citizens clash in New Orleans, Louisiana, over a period of three days.

1961

- *January 11:* A rowdy group of white students attack a desegregated dormitory at the University of Georgia in Athens over the admittance of an African-American woman.
- *May 14:* "Freedom riders," demanding desegregated buses and other public facilities, are attacked and beaten by white mobs in Anniston and Birmingham, Alabama. Such attacks will continue through the spring and summer throughout the South.
- *September 25:* E. H. Hurst, a white state legislator, shoots and kills Herbert Lee, a black civil rights demonstrator, in Liberty, Mississippi.

1962

- *January 16:* Black churches are firebombed in Birmingham, Alabama.
- *April 9:* In Taylorsville, Mississippi, a white police officer shoots and kills Roman Ducksworth, a black soldier, after Ducksworth refuses to give up his seat on a segregated bus.
- *August 31:* White citizens open fire on the homes of black citizens in Lee County, Georgia, during a campaign to register black voters.

Chronology

1963

- *June 12:* Black civil rights leader Medgar Evers is shot and killed in his driveway in Jackson, Mississippi. A Ku Klux Klan member, Byron De La Beckwith, is later charged with the murder, but two hung juries bring about his release. In 1994, Beckwith will be tried and convicted for the murder and sentenced to life in prison.
- *August 10:* A black youth is killed by two whites outside a bar in Jersey City, New Jersey.
- *September 15:* The Sixteenth Street Baptist Church in Birmingham, Alabama, is bombed, resulting in the deaths of four black girls.
- *November 19:* A desegregated college dormitory is bombed in Tuscaloosa, Alabama.
- *December 22:* A fire breaks out at the Roanoke Baptist Church in Hot Springs, Arkansas.

1964

- *May 2:* Two black youths, Henry Dee and Charlie Moore, are kidnapped and murdered by members of the Ku Klux Klan in Meadville, Mississippi.
- *June 16:* Klan members attack black worshippers at the Mt. Zion Church in Philadelphia, Mississippi, and then destroy the church.
- *June 21:* Three white civil rights workers, Michael Schwerner, James Chaney, and Andrew Goodman, are abducted and murdered by members of the Ku Klux Klan in Philadelphia, Mississippi.
- *July 11:* Members of the Ku Klux Klan attack a group of black soldiers in Colbert, Georgia, killing Lemuel Penn, a black officer.
- *September 7:* Herbert Oarsby, a black youth, is kidnapped and murdered in Pickens, Mississippi.

1965

- *March 9:* Three black ministers are beaten by a group of whites in Selma, Alabama, resulting in the death of Reverend James Reeb.
- *March 25:* A northern civil rights worker, Viola Liuzzo, is shot and killed by members of the Ku Klux Klan in Lowndesboro, Alabama. The case is solved by a white FBI informant and will bring the FBI into more active investigation and prosecution of bias crimes in the South.
- *August 20:* A priest is wounded and a white seminary student, Jonathan Daniels, is murdered by a member of the Klan in Haynesville, Alabama.

1966

- *January 3:* A black civil rights worker, Samuel Yonge, is murdered in Tuskegee, Alabama, by a white citizen who objects to Yonge's using a whites-only public restroom.

- *January 10:* Klan members bomb the home of Vernon Dahmer, a black civil rights activist, resulting in Dahmer's death.

1968

- *January 20:* Black students stab and wound a white student at South High School in Philadelphia, resulting in a student riot and a dozen further injuries.
- *January–March:* Seventeen white-owned businesses are burned in a largely black area of Gainesville, Florida. The arson wave ends with the arrest of six suspects on March 13.
- *April 4:* African-American civil rights leader Martin Luther King is assassinated on the eve of a protest rally in Memphis, Tennessee. The killing brings a nationwide wave of rioting that leaves about 50 people dead.
- *April 19:* A group of eight black youths are assaulted by a white gang in Boston; one is stabbed to death.
- *April 22:* Two white soldiers are attacked and beaten by a group of black and Hispanic men in San Antonio, Texas. The incident is followed by a huge melee in which eight more people are injured.
- *August 4:* A white gunman opens fire from his home on a group of black pedestrians, sparking a wave of rioting and arson in York, Pennsylvania.
- *August 8:* A white youth is murdered in Woodside, New York. Six black men are charged in the crime, carried out in retaliation for the earlier beating of a black youth by a white truck driver.

1969

- The Anti-Defamation League of B'nai B'rith (ADL) is founded to combat anti-Semitic violence and prejudice. The ADL will become a leading organization in tracking hate groups and hate crimes and in the effort to enact new hate-crimes legislation.
- *March 31:* A white mob runs amok through a black neighborhood in Cairo, Illinois, sparking a night and day of random shootings, arson, and violence.
- *April 11:* White students are assaulted by a gang of black youths on the campus of the University of Florida in Gainesville.
- *April 25:* Snipers shoot and injure black youths in St. Louis, Missouri, bringing about two weeks of violence between white and black gangs roaming the city streets.
- *May 16:* Fighting erupts at Fenger High School in Chicago, Illinois, after a group of black youths commit random assaults against white students.

1970

- *April 25:* A wave of bombings and arson strikes Seattle, Washington, after the killing of a black man, Larry Ward, by the Seattle police.

- *June 21:* In Pittsburgh, Pennsylvania, a white sniper shoots and kills a black youth, Ernest Caldwell, by firing shots into Caldwell's house from the street. The murder sparks several days of rioting.
- *June 27:* As tensions between blacks and Jews rise in a Brooklyn, New York, neighborhood, a black girl is accidentally run down by a Jewish truck driver, sparking an assault on Hasidic Jews by a group of black men.
- *August 17:* One police officer is killed and seven others are wounded after a bomb goes off in an abandoned house in Omaha, Nebraska. Six Black Panthers are later charged with murder.
- *October 10:* A gang of Puerto Rican youths attack a synagogue during Yom Kippur services in Brooklyn, causing a brawl between Jews and Puerto Ricans in the street.

1971

- The Southern Poverty Law Center (SPLC) is founded in Montgomery, Alabama, by civil rights attorney Morris Dees. In 1980, the SPLC will establish the Klanwatch Project to gather information on the Klan and other hate groups and to combat hate crimes and bias-motivated violence through civil litigation.
- *May 26:* A white sniper shoots and kills a black student, Jo Etta Collier, shortly after her high school graduation ceremony in Drew, Mississippi.
- *August 30:* During a bitter public controversy over school desegregation and busing, 10 school buses are destroyed in Pontiac, Michigan. Robert Miles, a "grand dragon" of the Ku Klux Klan, will be charged and convicted of masterminding the arson.
- *September 9:* A white youth kills a black student, Willie Ray Collier, at a Lubbock, Texas, high school. Two days of rioting and arson follow the shooting.

1972

- *January 28:* Two white police officers, Gregory Foster and Rocco Laurie, are shot and killed by black militants in New York City.
- *December 31:* A black sniper, Mark Essex, opens fire on a group of police officers in New Orleans, Louisiana, killing one and wounding two. Essex escapes arrest and continues a one-man rampage on January 7, 1973.

1973

- The National Gay and Lesbian Task Force (NGLTF) is founded in Washington, D.C., to represent the interests of homosexuals. The NGLTF will create the Anti-Violence Project in 1982 to combat bias-motivated violence against gays and lesbians.

- *January 7:* In New Orleans, Mark Essex opens fire on white guests of a Howard Johnson motel. Seven people are killed before Essex is brought down by police. Essex was responsible for a sniping incident on December 31, 1972, when a white police cadet was killed, and for setting fire to two downtown warehouses on January 1, a deed that sparked a five-day downtown fire.
- *January 21:* Wesley Bad Heart Bull, a Native American, is murdered by a white man at a gas station in Buffalo Gap, South Dakota.
- *June 2:* A riot breaks out in Brooklyn after an African-American doctor is attacked by a group of Hasidic Jews.
- *October 2:* A white motorist, Evelyn Walker, is dragged from her car and burned to death by black youths in Boston, Massachusetts.
- *November 26:* A black minister, Reverend Edward Pace, is murdered at his home in Gadsden, Alabama, by a member of the Ku Klux Klan.
- *November 27:* Five white high school students are shot and wounded by a black sniper in Pontiac, Michigan.

1974

- *April 19:* A white store owner, Frank Carlson, is murdered by an African-American man in San Francisco. The killing is attributed to the Death Angels, a group of Black Muslim vigilantes blamed for nearly 100 murders in California.
- *November 30:* Five African-American fisherman are drowned near Pensacola, Florida, after their boat is sabotaged by a local white shop owner.

1975

- *July 28:* A black teenager, Obie Wynn, is shot and killed by a white bar owner in Detroit, Michigan. A race riot erupts after the bar owner's arrest, leading to the racially motivated murder of a white motorist, Marian Pyszko.
- *August 14:* A white motorist is dragged from his truck and beaten and stabbed by a group of Hispanic men, leading to a confrontation with police in which five people are injured.
- *September 14:* Richard Morales, a Hispanic prisoner, is shot and killed by the police chief of Castroville, Texas.

1976

- *June 15:* During a heavy thunderstorm in Boston, Massachusetts, white motorists are diverted through a black neighborhood, touching off confrontations and violence during which Phyllis Anderson, a white woman, is shot and killed by black youths.

- *September 8:* White youths rampage through Washington Square Park in New York City, killing one African-American victim and wounding 13 others.

1977

- *February 14:* A suspended worker linked to white supremacist groups, Fred Cowan, kills five people after a confrontation with a Jewish supervisor.
- *August 7:* An interracial couple, Alphonse Manning and Toni Schwenn, are murdered by a sniper in Madison, Wisconsin.
- *November 18:* Four African-American churches are firebombed in Wilkes County, Georgia.

1978

- California passes the first modern hate-crimes law, a penalty-enhancement measure that punishes murders motivated by bias against race, religion, color, or national origin.
- *August 4:* Paul Corbett, his wife, and his daughter are killed by a black racist group known as the Mau Mau in Barrington Hills, Illinois. The same group will be blamed for several similar murders in the Chicago area that take place during the year.

1979

- The Center for Democratic Renewal, formerly the National Anti-Klan Network, is established in Atlanta to monitor hate groups, particularly the Ku Klux Klan and its associated organizations, across the country.
- *June 4:* Loyal Bailey, a witness for the prosecution in a Ku Klux Klan trial in Birmingham, Alabama, is murdered by a member of the Klan.
- *July 22:* An African American, Harold McIver, is shot and killed in a restaurant by a sniper in Doraville, Georgia.
- *October 21:* An interracial couple, Jessie Taylor and Marion Bresette, are shot and killed in Oklahoma City.

1980

- The New York City Police Department establishes a task force to deal with a series of arsons and vandalism incidents at city synagogues. The task force will develop into the Bias Incident Investigation Unit, or Bias Unit, charged with investigating crimes for possible bias motivation and prosecution under hate-crimes statutes.
- *January 20:* In Idabel, Oklahoma, a young African American is murdered near a whites-only club. The killing touches off riots and vandalism.

- *April 8:* Race riots erupt in Wrightsville, Georgia, during an anti-Klan demonstration conducted by African Americans.
- *May 3:* A white mob attacks and kills an African American, William Kelly, in the Charlestown neighborhood of Boston.
- *June 8:* A sniper kills two African Americans, Darrell Land and Dante Brown, in Cincinnati.
- *August 20:* White racist Joseph Franklin shoots and kills two African Americans, David Martin and Ted Fields.
- *September 24:* An African-American man, Joseph McCoy, is shot and killed in Niagara Falls, New York. The murder is linked to racial killings during the two previous days in Buffalo and is eventually attributed to Joe Christopher, dubbed the ".22-caliber killer."
- *November 8:* In Algiers, Louisiana, a white police officer, Gregory Neupert, is shot and killed while patrolling a housing project. While searching for the assailant, police officers kill four local African-American residents.

1981

- The Anti-Defamation League formulates a model statute for use by states seeking to pass hate-crimes laws. The statute proposes a penalty-enhancement scheme in which those found guilty of bias-motivated crimes would be given a longer jail term.
- *January 1:* A racist serial killer, Joe Christopher, stabs and wounds two African Americans, Larry Little and Calvin Crippen, in Buffalo, New York. The incident follows several similar attacks by Christopher in upstate New York.
- *March 21:* An African-American youth, Michael Donald, is kidnapped in Mobile, Alabama, driven to the next county, and hanged from a tree. Two members of the Ku Klux Klan will later be charged and convicted of murder.
- *December:* An African-American soldier, Lynn Jackson, appears to have been lynched in Walton County, Georgia, but the death is later ruled a suicide.

1982

- *March 13:* An African American, William Atkinson, is chased by a mob of white men before being hit and killed by a passing train.
- *June 19:* In Detroit, Michigan, a Chinese American named Vincent Chin is beaten to death by a father and a son who mistake him for a Japanese, and who fear Japanese economic domination of the United States. The murderers are tried, found guilty, and sentence to three years of probation.

Chronology

1983

- *January 12:* In Memphis, Tennessee, members of a black cult abduct two white police officers and torture one of them to death. On the following day, a shootout results in the death of the cult's leader, Lindbergh Sanders.
- *July 28:* Seeking to destroy the records of Project Klanwatch to be used in a pending lawsuit, arsonists attack the headquarters of the Southern Poverty Law Center in Montgomery, Alabama.
- *September 1:* A sniper opens fire on Jewish students in New York City, killing a bystander named Lucille Rivera.

1984

- The National Institute Against Prejudice and Violence is founded in Baltimore. The organization's intent is to gather and disseminate information on interethnic violence and to inform victims of hate crimes of their remedies under the law.
- *March 15:* Rioting takes place in Miami, Florida, after a police officer is acquitted of the charge of murdering a black prisoner, Nevell Johnson.
- *June 18:* Alan Berg, a Jewish talk radio host, is murdered by members of the Order, a neo-Nazi group, in Denver, Colorado.
- *August 22:* In the case of *Massachusetts v. Poor and Tilton*, a state appeals court finds that racist comments are admissible as evidence if made in furtherance of a criminal act and may support a conviction on civil rights charges.
- *October 31:* Bombs explode at the Mapleton Park Hebrew Institute in Brooklyn, New York.

1985

- *March 21:* Congressional hearings begin on the Hate Crimes Statistics Act, which will be passed in 1990 and mandate collection of hate-crimes data by the Department of Justice.
- *April 15:* Members of the neo-Nazi Bruder Schweigen murder Jimmie Linegar, a Missouri state trooper, at Ridgedale, Missouri.
- *June 7:* Two African Americans, Walter Jones and Louis Wright, are murdered and their bodies left along a rural road near Panama City in the Florida Panhandle.
- *October 31:* An African-American woman, Joyce Sinclair, is raped and murdered by a member of the Ku Klux Klan in Robeson County, North Carolina.
- *November 20:* In Philadelphia, a mob of several hundred whites confronts a black family and forces them out of their home.

- *December 24:* David Rice, a Seattle white supremacist, murders a family of four, believing them to be Jews and Communists.

1986

- *March 16:* Fred Finch, a civil rights leader, and his wife are stabbed to death in their Dallas home.
- *April 29:* A one-man campaign against his black neighbors conducted by Carl Rosendahl, a Kansas City, Missouri, white supremacist, culminates in a bombing in the family's back yard.
- *September 29:* During a tense conflict between the white supremacist group Aryan Nations and their opponents in the Idaho town of Coeur d'Alene, a series of bombs explodes in the city center.
- *December 26:* In the Howard Beach neighborhood of Queens, New York, a black youth who is being chased by a white mob runs onto a highway and is struck and killed.

1987

- *November 11:* Jewish stores are vandalized in Chicago in imitation of and on the anniversary of Kristallnacht, when in 1938 Jewish-owned stores were burned and looted in Nazi Germany.
- *November 28:* In Wappingers Falls, New York, Tawana Brawley, a young African-American girl, is found beaten and tied up in garbage bags. Brawley claims that six white men had raped and beat her, but she will not identify the assailants and is ultimately accused of staging a hoax.

1988

- Congress passes 18 U.S.C. 247, providing federal jurisdiction in cases of religious vandalism in which the damages exceed $10,000.
- *March 26:* In Lumberton, North Carolina, Julian Pierce, a Native American, is murdered by two white gunmen during Pierce's campaign for county judge.
- *May 5:* David Price, a black teenager, is shot and killed by white assailants during a confrontation in Louisville, Kentucky.
- *August 17:* In the case of *New York v. Grupe*, a criminal court convicts a defendant on an enhanced misdemeanor charge for making bigoted comments during an assault.
- *November 13:* Mulugeta Seraw, an Ethiopian immigrant, is beaten to death by white skinheads on a Portland, Oregon, street. The murder will

bring about a civil lawsuit by the Southern Poverty Law Center against the White Aryan Resistance.

1989

- *May 29:* In an Ohio state park, a white man named David Wyant utters threats and racial insults at African Americans who occupy a neighboring campsite. On the basis of this, he will be convicted in the case of *Ohio v. Wyant* of ethnic intimidation and sentenced to 18 months in prison. The decision will be appealed and overturned by the Ohio Supreme Court on constitutional grounds.
- *June 24:* Max Kowalski, a Jewish resident of Brighton Beach, in Brooklyn, New York, is stabbed to death by a neighbor during an argument over the appearance of a swastika on Kowalski's apartment door.
- *August 23:* In Bensonhurst, Brooklyn, an African-American teenager, Yusuf Hawkins, is beaten and shot to death by a gang of white men.

1990

- *April 23:* President George H. W. Bush signs the Hate Crimes Statistics Act, mandating collection of statistics by the Department of Justice on crimes that "manifest prejudice based on race, religion, sexual orientation, or ethnicity."
- *June 20:* Congressional hearings begin on the Violence Against Women Act.
- *October 22:* The jury finds against White Aryan Resistance in the civil suit brought by the Southern Poverty Law Center over the death of Mulugeta Seraw in 1988, awarding more than $10 million to Seraw's family.

1991

- *January:* During and after the first Persian Gulf War, the ground phase of which ends in January, a sharp increase in hate-crime incidents against Arab Americans is reported. Anti-Arab hate crimes occur in Los Angeles, Cincinnati, Baltimore, New York, San Francisco, Detroit, and Tulsa.
- *August 19:* A riot breaks out in Crown Heights, a Brooklyn neighborhood, after a vehicle driven by a Jewish man strikes two African-American children, one of whom—Gavin Cato—will die of his injuries. Roused to violence by Charles Price and others, 16-year-old Lemrick Nelson will fatally stab an Orthodox Jew, Yankel Rosenbaum. Price and Nelson will be tried and convicted in federal court with a violation of Title 18, Section 245, the federal civil rights statute, but the case will be remanded

after an appeals court finds, in January 2002, that the judge in the federal trial improperly interfered with the jury selection.

1992

- *April 29:* Rioting erupts in Los Angeles after the acquittal of police accused of beating Rodney King, an African-American motorist, during a traffic stop. The riots will last for three days and result in more than 50 deaths.
- *June 22:* In the case of *R.A.V. v. St. Paul*, the U.S. Supreme Court overturns a St. Paul, Minnesota, city ordinance banning, among other symbols, burning crosses, a common method of ethnic intimidation.
- *August 26:* In the case of *Ohio v. Wyant*, the Ohio Supreme Court finds that the state's ethnic intimidation law violates the Ohio and U.S. constitutions, as the statute punishes protected forms of speech.

1993

- *June 11:* In the case of *Wisconsin v. Mitchell*, the U.S. Supreme Court upholds the sentence passed on defendant Todd Mitchell under Wisconsin's hate-crimes penalty-enhancement statute. The decision gives broad legal authority for penalty-enhancement laws, the primary statutory tool of hate-crimes prosecution.
- *July 1:* In the case of *Vermont v. Ladue*, the Vermont Supreme Court upholds a hate-crimes conviction for aggravated assault motivated by perception of the victim's sexual orientation.
- *October 2:* A group calling itself the Aryan Liberation Front claims responsibility for bombing the Japanese American Citizens League office in Sacramento, California.
- *November 2:* In the case of *Michigan v. Richards*, a state ethnic intimidation law is challenged on the grounds of vagueness, overbreadth, and its chilling effect on ordinary free speech; the Michigan Supreme Court upholds the statute.
- *December 23:* In Wyckoff, New Jersey, vandals steal a banner, erected by the New Jersey Chapter of American Atheists, celebrating the winter solstice. The incident will be investigated by the state police as a bias crime motivated by prejudice against atheists.

1994

- The Federal Violence Against Women Act of 1994 allows individuals to file federal lawsuits in cases of gender-based violence.
- The Violent Crime Control and Law Enforcement Act of 1994 is passed. By Section 280003, the law directs the U.S. Sentencing Commission to

increase "offense levels" for hate crimes. Hate crime is defined as "a crime in which the defendant intentionally selects a victim, or in the case of a property crime, the property that is the object of the crime, because of the actual or perceived race, color, religion, national origin, ethnicity, gender, disability, or sexual orientation of any person." In this way, the federal government follows the examples of states that have already passed penalty-enhancement laws.

- **January 19:** In the case of *Iowa v. McKnight*, the Iowa Supreme Court upholds a conviction for "infringement of individual rights" and finds that a state hate-crimes statute does not violate a defendant's First Amendment rights.
- **February 10:** The Supreme Court of Florida, in *Dobbins v. Florida*, finds that the state hate-crimes law applies strictly to criminal conduct, and not opinion or speech, based on prejudice. Along with the Supreme Court decisions in *R.A.V. v. St. Paul* and in *Wisconsin v. Mitchell*, this decision helps to clarify the nature and enforceability of hate-crimes law.
- **May 26:** In the case of *New Jersey v. Vawter and Kearns*, the New Jersey Supreme Court finds that, although ordinary threats of violence may be punished, a statute prohibiting threats motivated by prejudice is unconstitutional, on the basis that the law discriminates against protected opinion.
- **July 21:** In *Ayers v. Maryland*, a Maryland statute prohibiting bias-motivated harassment is challenged but upheld by the Maryland Supreme Court, which also allows incidents not related to the crime to be introduced as evidence in order to show prejudiced motive.

1995

- **January 1:** The Bluff Road United Methodist Church in Columbia, South Carolina, is firebombed, the first of approximately 40 African-American churches to suffer arson attacks in the following 18 months. The Department of Justice will investigate 658 cases of suspicious fires and bombings from this date until August 18, 1998.
- **June 18:** Thanh Mai, a Vietnamese American, dies during an assault by three white men uttering racial epithets in an Alpine Township, Michigan, nightclub. One of the men, Michael Hallman, is charged and convicted of manslaughter, but prosecutors decline to bring hate-crimes charges.
- **November 1:** An amendment of sentencing guidelines takes effect, announced by the U.S. Sentencing Commission. The amendment increases sentences for those found guilty of hate crimes.

1996

- **March 5:** In *Pennsylvania v. Burlingame et al.*, a charge of harassment is overturned on the grounds that the act took place among parties to a labor dispute, a situation which by state law shielded the defendants from the charges. Later hate-crimes statutes will include "membership in a labor union" as a protected status.

- **September 20:** Richard Machado, an undergraduate at the University of California, Irvine, circulates an e-mail to 59 Asian-American students in which he threatens to kill them. Machado becomes the first person prosecuted for hate crime committed via the Internet.

1997

- **February 10:** Lemrick Nelson and Charles Price are convicted of violating a federal civil rights statute (Title 18, Section 245) in the murder of Yankel Rosenbaum during the Crown Heights, Brooklyn, riot of August 19, 1991. Nelson will be sentenced to 235 months in prison, and Price to 260 months in prison. The convictions will later be overturned on appeal due to jury tampering by the judge.
- **February 23:** A police raid in southern Illinois uncovers a cache of bombs, weapons, and hand grenades and a plot by the neo-Nazi group New Order to bomb the Southern Poverty Law Center in Montgomery, Alabama, as well as the Simon Wiesenthal Center in New York.
- **April 26:** In Dallas, Donald Ray Anderson walks into the courtyard of the Baruch Ha Shem synagogue and fires a semiautomatic rifle into the air, then into the walls of the synagogue. He will be charged and convicted under state statutes of aggravated assault and deadly conduct, and then under the federal statute (Title 18, Section 247) prohibiting "damage to religious property and obstruction of the free exercise of religious beliefs."
- **April 27:** In Fort Lauderdale, Florida, Steven Goedersis is beaten to death for his alleged homosexuality.
- **June 7:** James Byrd, Jr., a 49-year-old African American, is chained to the back of a pickup truck and dragged to death in Jasper, Texas. On February 23, 1999, a jury convicts John William King of the murder and he is sentenced to death.
- **July 1:** Two African-American churches, the Tate Chapel African Methodist Episcopal Church and the St. Joseph Baptist Church, are vandalized and burned in Mobile, Alabama. The burnings prompt an investigation by the newly organized National Church Arson Task Force.
- **July 23:** In the case of *Montana v. Nye*, a hate-crimes conviction is upheld for the act of placing provocative bumper stickers on road signs, in mailboxes, and on private property.
- **October 6:** Matthew Shepard, a 21-year-old University of Wyoming student, is beaten, tied to a fencepost, tortured, and left for dead outside Laramie, Wyoming, by two men he met in a Laramie bar. He remains in a coma for six days before dying on October 12. On October 15, the U.S. House of Representatives passes a resolution condemning the murder.

Chronology

- *November 3:* Alan Odom, Brandy Boone, and Kenneth Cumbie are found guilty of violating federal statutes in the arson and vandalism of the Tate and St. Joseph churches in Mobile, Alabama.

1998

- *January 26:* In the case of *Washington v. Dawson*, the Washington Court of Appeals allows the introduction of a tattoo as evidence to show that the defendant committed a racially motivated harassment and assault.
- *February 13:* Richard Machado is convicted of violating the federal statute prohibiting interference with "federally protected activities," (U.S. Code Title 18, Section 245(b)2(A)), in this case attendance at a public educational institution. Machado had been indicted for sending threatening e-mails to Asian-American students at the University of California, Irvine.
- *July 22:* In *Martinez v. Texas*, the Texas Court of Appeals upholds a hate-crimes conviction, finding that the defendant intentionally selected his victim, a two-year-old child, on the basis of the child's perceived race, even though the defendant was mistaken in his perception.

1999

- *January 20:* Two white and two black students at a Pontiac, Michigan, high school are suspended after a fight allegedly incited by racial slurs.
- *February 19:* Billy Jack Gaither is murdered with an axe and his body burned in Sylacauga, Alabama. Steven Mullins and Charles Butler, Jr., are charged with the crime and confess to plotting the crime after Gaither allegedly made a pass at them.
- *February 24:* In Fort Lauderdale, Florida, a skinhead shoots and kills Jody-Gaye Bailey, an African American, while Bailey is stopped at a red light accompanied by her white boyfriend.
- *March 1:* A homeless gay man is murdered and decapitated in Richmond, Virginia's James River Park. The severed head is left on a footbridge.
- *April 3:* Ashley Mance, a six-year-old black boy, is killed by a shot fired by Jessy J. Roten, who fired a semiautomatic weapon into Mance's home from an alley. Roten is charged with first-degree premeditated murder.
- *April 5:* Naoki Kamijima, a 48-year-old Japanese-American shop owner, is shot to death in Crystal Lake, Illinois, by a gunman who had been roaming the neighborhood and questioning store employees about their ethnic background.
- *May 16:* James Langenbach swerves his car into two young black bicyclists in Kenosha, Wisconsin. Langenbach is charged with attempted murder while armed with a dangerous weapon.

- *June/July 1999:* Three Sacramento, California–area synagogues are fire-bombed.
- *July 4–6:* Benjamin Smith murders college basketball coach Ricky Byrd-song and later wounds six orthodox Jews in Chicago, then travels to Bloom-ington, Indiana, where he murders Won-Joon Yoon, a Korean American.
- *August 10:* Buford O. Furrow kills Joseph Ileto, a Filipino-American postal worker, and wounds five people at a Jewish community center in Los Angeles.
- *September 15:* Larry Ashbrook invades the Wedgwood Baptist Church in Fort Worth, Texas, and opens fire on the congregation, killing seven people and wounding seven others.
- *October 29:* Three men invade an Indianapolis, Indiana, apartment shared by two men they believed were homosexuals. They taunt and torture the men for 30 minutes, then set fire to the building. Later, they return to put the fire out.
- *October 31:* In Inverness, Florida, Richard Burzynski drives his car into a group of people dressed up for Halloween, shouting anti-gay epithets and killing 17-year-old Allison Decratel.

2000

- *January 28:* Two African girls are assaulted by three high-school students in a Boston subway car after being seen holding hands, a custom of their native country.
- *February 6:* A University of Arizona student is assaulted while sitting in a café in Tucson, Arizona. The attack inspires a campus rally against hate crimes that takes place a few days later.
- *March 1:* An African American goes on a shooting rampage in Wilkins-burg, Pennsylvania, killing three white men and wounding two others.
- *March 16:* In the case of *New Jersey v. Dowell et al.*, a New Jersey Superior Court upholds a conviction for harassment by bias intimidation, in the case of several defendants who kidnapped and assaulted a mentally and physically disabled person. The category of "handicapped" had been added to the New Jersey hate-crimes statute as a protected status in 1997.
- *April 29:* Richard Baumhammers, a 34-year-old lawyer, murders five people in and around Pittsburgh, including his Jewish neighbor, Anita Gordon; two Asian Americans at a Chinese restaurant; an African American at a karate school; and a grocery store owner from India.
- *May 17:* Thomas Blanton, Jr., and Bobby Frank Cherry are charged with the 1963 firebombing of the Sixteenth Street Baptist Church in Birming-ham, Alabama.

Chronology

- *June 20:* In the case of *California v. Carr*, a cross burning is defended on the grounds that it was authorized by a 15-year-old member of the victimized family (by the letter of California law, only unauthorized cross burnings are prohibited). An appeals court finds that such actions cannot legally be authorized.
- *June 26:* In the case of *Apprendi v. New Jersey*, a defendant argues that a finding of biased motive must be reached by a jury beyond a reasonable doubt, and an enhanced penalty (for biased motive) cannot be passed after the defendant enters a guilty plea (thus precluding a jury trial). The U.S. Supreme Court agrees, finding that the due process clause of the Fourteenth Amendment holds that any fact that increases the penalty for a crime beyond the statutory maximum must be submitted to a jury.
- *October 18:* In *King v. Texas*, an appeal of convictions in the James Byrd, Jr., dragging murder, a Texas court rules that evidence of defendant's hatred of African Americans, including tattoos and drawings found at the defendant's home, is sufficient to show biased motive.

2001

- *January 8:* David Lee Troutman shoots and kills an African-American man, Robert Spencer, at a grocery store in Lake County, Florida, a crime police concluded was racially motivated.
- *February 25:* In Anchorage, Alaska, three white teenagers are arrested after police seize a videotape showing a series of paintball-gun attacks on the city's Native Americans.
- *March 16:* Two Muslim men are attacked by two white men wielding baseball bats outside the Northern Nevada Muslim Community Center in Sparks, Nevada.
- *April 27:* Two Jewish men are attacked and beaten by a San Francisco attorney, Don Henning, who takes them for Palestinians.
- *May 25:* Two teenagers throw rocks, hurl antihomosexual epithets, and set the tents of gay campers on fire at Polihale State Park in Hawaii.
- *July 4:* Two white supremacists stab five African-American youths during a Fourth of July celebration in Waco, Texas.
- *July 29:* Willie Houston is shot and killed after being mistaken for a homosexual in Nashville, Tennessee. The perpetrator, Lewis Davidson, is charged under a hate-crime statute that covers violence based on perceived sexual orientation.
- *September 13:* Two days after the terrorist attacks of September 11, 2001, a Sikh gas station owner, Balbir Singh Sodhi, is shot and killed in Mesa, Arizona. The assailant then drives to another gas station, where he fires shots at a Lebanese American. On the same day, a mosque is firebombed

in Denton, Texas. Throughout the country, many more such reports of similar murders, assaults, firebombings, vandalism, and threats directed at Arab Americans and south Asians are recorded.

- *October 20:* A Tulsa doctor, Stanley Grogg, is charged with a hate-crime misdemeanor after assaulting an Afghani taxicab driver while touring downtown San Diego.
- *November 7:* A fight erupts at a Boston high school over head scarves worn by young Somali students, and police investigate the incident as a possible hate crime.

2002

- *January 7:* In *U.S. v. Nelson*, a case arising from the Crown Heights riots in Brooklyn, New York, a federal appeals court upholds a conviction of racially motivated violence but then remands the case on the basis that the judge improperly interfered with the selection of jurors in an effort to reach a racially balanced jury.
- *February 8:* The home of a lesbian couple is set ablaze in Missoula, Montana. One of the victims, Carla Grayson, is publicly known as a party to a lawsuit over the denial of same-sex benefits by her employer, the University of Montana.
- *April 8:* An Iranian man is attacked and beaten after offering assistance to a tow-truck driver on the Washington, D.C., Beltway in northern Virginia.
- *June 6:* A gang of men attack two gay men outside a bar in Riverside, California. One of the victims, Jeffery Owens, dies of his injuries.
- *October 16:* Three men kill a 20-year-old white bystander who taunts the men during a melee outside a pool hall in North Phoenix, Arizona. Two of the suspects belong to the National Alliance, a neo-Nazi group; police suspect the motive for the murder was a difference of political opinion.

2003

- *January 19:* Four men go on a shooting spree in a largely African-American neighborhood in Portland, Oregon. Later in the month, a grand jury indicts the four suspects on ethnic intimidation charges.
- *January 24:* In Medford, Oregon, three National Guard members recently returned from peacekeeping duty in the Sinai Peninsula assault a motel owner whom they believe to be an Arab American.
- *January 31:* Anonymous hate letters are sent to African-American churches in Missouri and Kansas during preparations for the Martin Luther King, Jr., birthday observance.

Chronology

- *February 3:* Vandals paint anti-Semitic graffiti and swastikas on the walls of Temple Beth El, a synagogue in Boca Raton, Florida, the second such incident since the beginning of the year.
- *April 5:* Two teenagers videotape their confrontation with a gay man on a New York City subway car and are arrested by the police. Antiviolence groups demand that the police classify the incident as a hate crime.
- *April 7:* In the case of *Virginia v. Black*, the Supreme Court rules 6 to 3 that cross burnings are not necessarily a form of First Amendment–protected speech and that the states can outlaw cross burnings carried out with the intent to intimidate. The ruling upholds a Virginia law passed in 1952 and used to prosecute two separate cross-burnings (one done on private property with the owner's permission) in 1998.
- *April 19:* At the University of California Los Angeles Medical Center interfaith chapel, Muslim prayer rugs are defiled with pig's blood, and the FBI quickly opens an investigation into the incident as a hate crime.
- *May 19:* Avtar Singh, a 52-year-old Sikh who wears a turban and is a truck driver, is shot by two young white men, according to police, in Phoenix. Singh had parked his 18-wheeler and was waiting for his son to pick him up when the men yelled "Go back to where you belong!" and then shot.

CHAPTER 4

BIOGRAPHICAL LISTING

Joseph Biden, a Delaware native and five-term U.S. senator from Delaware who has been a prominent supporter of new federal hate-crime measures, particularly in the field of gender-based bias crimes. A native of Pennsylvania, he grew up in Delaware and graduated from the Syracuse College of Law in 1968. He was first elected to the Senate in 1972, at the age of 29, and has since won re-election four times. In the 1980s, he became chairman of the Senate Judiciary Committee. He helped to draft the Violent Crime Control and Law Enforcement Act of 1994 and the original Violence Against Women Act, which passed in the same year. Biden wrote and sponsored a second Violence Against Women Act in 1998, a comprehensive measure to address gender-based hate crimes with new federal statutes and federal money for policing, hot lines, and community organizations such as battered women's shelters. The second Violence Against Women Act was passed and signed into law in 2000.

Sam Bowers, Imperial Wizard of the White Knights of the Ku Klux Klan, who played a prominent role in Klan activities in Mississippi during the 1960s civil-rights struggle. The owner of a vending machine business in Laurel, Mississippi, Bowers founded the White Knights in 1963 in order to turn back the tide of civil rights protests then reaching its peak in Mississippi and throughout the South. Within a few months, membership had risen to more than 10,000, with an especially large "klavern" (chapter) growing in Meridian, Mississippi, where young students were arriving to carry out a voter registration drive. Determined to stop them, Bowers ordered the murder of Michael Schwerner, a 24-year-old New Yorker who was employed by the Congress of Racial Equality (CORE). In 1966, Bowers also arranged the murder of Vernon Dahmer, a businessman whom Bowers believed too sympathetic to blacks (Dahmer had allowed black voters to pay a $2 poll tax at his store in Hattiesburg, Mississippi, thereby encouraging them to vote.) Bowers was convicted of conspiracy in the Schwerner murder in 1967 and, in 1998, of the firebombing death of Vernon Dahmer, a conviction that brought him a life sentence.

Ricky Byrdsong, college basketball coach and corporate executive whose death at the hands of white supremacist Benjamin Smith became one of the nation's most notorious hate-crime murders. Byrdsong was born in Atlanta and graduated from Iowa State University in 1978. He served as a basketball coach at the University of Detroit, Mercy, and, in 1993, as head basketball coach at Northwestern University. He left this position in 1999, when he became vice president of community affairs for the Aon Corporation. On July 3, 1999, while talking with two of his children outside of his home in suburban Chicago, Byrdsong was shot and killed by Benjamin Smith, who had just begun a rampage that would continue with shootings in Springfield, Decatur, and Urbana, Illinois, and end with Smith's suicide in Bloomington, Indiana.

Floyd Cochran, repentant racist and former Ku Klux Klan member from upstate New York. Cochran joined the Ku Klux Klan while still a youth in New York, then moved to the Pacific Northwest, home to many racist, neo-Nazi, and white separatist movements. Cochran became prominent in the Aryan Nations, a white supremacist organization that throughout the 1990s advocated acts of violence against African Americans and Jews. In 1992, Cochran turned against the group out of revulsion for its advocacy of violence against the disabled. He soon renounced the racism he had once avowed and became a prominent spokesman against the far right. Since that time he has toured the country denouncing Aryan Nations and the neo-Nazi movement.

John Conyers, Democratic representative from Michigan, credited by many with the coining of the term *hate crimes* and a prominent sponsor of federal hate-crimes legislation throughout his career as a legislator. Re-elected in November 2000 with 93 percent of the vote in Michigan's Fourteenth Congressional District, Conyers is one of the founders of the Congressional Black Caucus. He wrote the legislation establishing the national Martin Luther King holiday in 1983 and was one of the authors of legislation raising the Environmental Protection Agency to cabinet-level status. Conyers sponsored the Violence Against Women Act in 1998 and wrote the Church Arsons Prevention Act, two key federal hate-crime bills, and remains a strong advocate of the Hate Crimes Prevention Act, the latest hate-crime bill, which remained stalled and unpassed in early 2003.

Abraham Cooper, rabbi and dean of the Simon Wiesenthal Center, which he helped to found in 1977. Since that time, Cooper has been active in combating anti-Semitic and other hate groups worldwide. He coordinates the Simon Wiesenthal Center's efforts to combat anti-Semitic and racist hate crimes and hate propaganda. He lectures around the world on the history, the manifestations, and the consequences of anti-Semitism. In particular, Cooper has actively combated Holocaust denial, the movement that denies the existence of the World War II genocide committed by Nazi Germany against the Jews and other groups.

Morris Dees, founder and chairman of the Southern Poverty Law Center. Born in 1936 in rural Alabama, Dees grew up in a family that held traditional white southern viewpoints regarding separation of the races and the Civil Rights movement. After graduating from the University of Alabama law school, however, he undertook several lawsuits against segregation in academia and in Alabama's public facilities. In 1971, he cofounded the Southern Poverty Law Center with Joseph Levin and Julian Bond. Since its founding, this organization has taken the lead in pro–civil rights legal action in the South and throughout the country. One of Dees's best-known battles was undertaken against the hate group White Aryan Resistance and its founder, Tom Metzger, who were effectively bankrupted by a civil action brought by Dees after the murder of an Ethiopian student by racist skinheads in Portland, Oregon.

David Duke, Louisiana politician closely associated with white supremacist organizations, particularly the Ku Klux Klan. Duke founded the White Student Alliance while a student at Louisiana State University. He graduated in 1974 with a degree in history and then formed the Louisiana Knights of the Ku Klux Klan, which he sought to turn into a more politically effective, media-savvy organization. In the same year, Duke became a national director of the Knights of the Ku Klux Klan. In 1975, he ran for the Louisiana senate but lost with one-third of the vote. In 1979, he ran again for the state senate from Metairie but lost again. In the same year, he was tried and convicted of incitement to riot after a Klan rally in New Orleans, after which he cut his ties to the Klan and formed the National Association for the Advancement of White People (NAAWP). During a campaign for president in 1988, Duke ran on the issues of affirmative action, civil rights, and immigration, and he remained a staunch opponent of hate-crimes legislation of any sort. His presidential bid failed with 47,000 votes, but Duke won a Louisiana House of Representatives seat in 1989. After a failed bid for Louisiana governor in 1991, Duke entered the Republican Party presidential primary in 1992, winning only 11 percent in his best state, Mississippi. Duke currently serves as chairman of the Republican Party Executive Committee in Louisiana's St. Tammany Parish.

Abby Ferber, widely published scholar of the far right and hate groups, author of *Hate Crime in America: What Do We Know?* and *White Man Falling: Race, Gender, and White Supremacy.* Ferber is director of Women's Studies at the University of Colorado at Colorado Springs, and teaches on the subjects of race and gender. She conducts workshops on hate crime and the far right, and served as a panelist for the American Sociological Association's 1999 Press and Congressional Briefings on hate crime in the United States.

David Goldman, founder of Hate Watch, a prominent World Wide Web site dedicated to researching and exposing far-right organizations, particularly those employing the Internet. The group originated with a web page entitled "A Guide to Hate Groups on the Internet," which Goldman originally created simply as an exercise in web page design. The site earned several accolades, and in March 1996, Goldman launched Hate-Watch as an outgrowth of his work investigating far-right organizations on the Internet. Since that time he has often appeared in national and international print and broadcast media as a specialist on the topic.

Matthew Hale, prominent white supremacist and head of the racist organization known as the World Church of the Creator, based in East Peoria, Illinois. In 1996, Hale took over the moribund organization, which stands for the advancement of the white race and had been founded in 1973 by a Florida state legislator and Ukrainian immigrant named Ben Klassen. Assuming the title of Pontifex Maximus, Hale moved the group to East Peoria, headquarters of the Caterpillar Corporation and a town hit hard by labor strife and unemployment. Hale made the World Church of the Creator one of the most prominent racist organizations to appear on the Internet, a medium that attracted most of its new members. But his application for a law license was turned down in the early summer of 1999, on the grounds that Hale's beliefs and character made him unfit for a law license. Hale's very public campaign for an Illinois law license gained him national media notoriety, and his rejection may have inspired one of his more dedicated members, Benjamin Smith, to carry out a shooting rampage through Illinois and Indiana on the July 4 weekend of that year.

Gregory Herek, prominent author and academic researcher on the subject of antihomosexual violence and prejudice. Holding a doctorate in social psychology from the University of California, Davis, Herek currently is a psychology professor at the same institution. He has become an internationally recognized expert on the subject of antigay violence, having published a number of articles and books on the topic since 1992, when he edited a seminal volume on the topic entitled *Hate Crimes: Confronting Violence Against Lesbian and Gay Men.* In 1997, Herek participated in the White House Conference on Hate Crimes; at this time he also participated actively in the debate over the admittance of homosexuals into the armed forces. Herek has also achieved prominence in the field of AIDS-related prejudice.

James Jacobs, author and leading opponent of hate-crimes legislation. As the director of the Center for Research in Crime and Justice at New York University Law School, Jacobs lectures and writes actively on the constitutional problems and social dangers of laws that treat prejudice as a basis for criminal prosecution. With Kimberly Potter, Jacobs coauthored *Hate Crimes: Criminal Law and Identity Politics,* an effective and eloquent summary of the anti–hate crimes legal position.

Jack Levin, specialist in the study of prejudice and hate crimes. Levin is director of the Brudnick Center on Conflict and Violence at Northeastern University in Boston. He has written more than 150 articles and more than 20 books, including *Hate Crimes: The Rising Tide of Bigotry and Bloodshed,* one of the most widely circulated publications in the hate-crimes debate.

Karen Narasaki, executive director of the National Asian Pacific American Legal Consortium (NAPALC). A graduate of Yale University and the University of California at Los Angeles School of Law, she was the Washington, D.C., representative for the Japanese American Citizens League before joining NAPALC. She is a prominent spokesperson on the matter of anti-Asian hate violence.

William L. Pierce, a leader in the American neo-Nazi movement, mainly as the author of the book *The Turner Diaries.* A prominent member of George Lincoln Rockwell's American Nazi Party, Pierce was a fanatical anti-Semite and a determined foe of the federal government, which he saw as dominated by Jewish interests. Leader of his own neo-Nazi organization known as the National Alliance, and the founder of the anti-Semitic Cosmotheist Church, Pierce wrote *The Turner Diaries* in 1978 under the pseudonym of Andrew Macdonald. The book describes a neo-Nazi underground group that mounts a coup against the U.S. government and eventually comes to dominate world government. *The Turner Diaries* in turn inspired Robert Matthews, founder of The Order, a group that carried out threats and violence against individuals as well as government institutions. Pierce died in 2002.

William Rehnquist, chief justice of the U.S. Supreme Court for the Court's two important decisions regarding hate crimes laws. Rehnquist was born in Milwaukee in 1924. He served in the U.S. Army Air Corps during World War II, then graduated first in his class from Stanford University law school in 1952. He worked as a clerk to Supreme Court justice Robert Jackson; through the 1960s he remained a staunch political conservative, generally opposed to school integration and other new civil rights measures on the grounds that the Constitution decrees a limited role for the federal government. Rehnquist was appointed to the Supreme Court in 1971, becoming a standard-bearer for states' rights and conservative positions on racial discrimination and equal opportunity cases. He was appointed chief justice in 1986. Writing in support of the court's 1993 decision in *Wisconsin v. Mitchell*, Rehnquist stated that "the First Amendment ... does not prohibit the evidentiary use of speech to establish the elements of a crime or to prove motive or intent." With this decision, the Rehnquist court determined that the penalty-enhancement hate-crimes laws enacted by Wisconsin and other states should not be struck down on First Amendment grounds.

Michael Schwerner, civil rights worker whose murder in 1964 touched off a widespread public outcry for enhanced federal civil rights measures, a direct precursor to modern hate-crimes legislation. Aged 24 at the time, Schwerner was a New York City native who was hired as a field worker by the Congress of Racial Equality (CORE). He worked in Meridian, Mississippi, to organize a community center and to carry out voter registration among African Americans. On June 21, while driving with James Chaney and Andrew Goodman in rural Neshoba County, Schwerner was pulled over by Sheriff's Deputy Cecil Price, who then turned over the three men to Ku Klux Klan members. Determined to make an example of Schwerner and to discourage any other northern civil rights workers who might be inclined to work in Mississippi, Klan leader Sam Bowers ordered a summary execution, and Schwerner, Chaney, and Goodman were murdered the same night. Media coverage of the crime inspired the FBI to take a direct role in the case, the first time J. Edgar Hoover's FBI made a concerted effort to solve a civil rights case.

Benjamin Smith, a white supremacist who carried out a series of bias-motivated shootings over the weekend of July 4, 1999. A 21-year-old college student at the University of Indiana, Smith had since June 1998 been a committed member of the World Church of the Creator, a white supremacist group based in East Peoria, Illinois. Well known on the Indiana campus for his racist views, he left the university in the spring of 1999 and moved to Chicago, where he was arrested in suburban Wilmette in April for distributing anti-Semitic literature. On July 3, armed with two loaded pistols and driving a blue Ford Taurus, Smith began his shooting spree in Rogers Park, an orthodox Jewish neighborhood of northwest Chicago, then proceeded to the predominantly Jewish suburb of Skokie, where he killed former Northwestern University head basketball coach Ricky Byrdsong. That afternoon, Smith continued the rampage in Springfield, Decatur, and Urbana. On the next day, Smith shot and killed a Korean student in Bloomington, Indiana, then committed suicide when confronted by police. In all, two people were killed and eight wounded in what became one of the nation's most notorious hate-crime sprees.

Kenneth Stern, attorney, member of the American Jewish Committee, and leading spokesman on the topic of anti-Semitic prejudice, Holocaust denial, and anti-Semitic violence. Stern's 1993 book *Holocaust Denial* was one of the first works to describe in detail the methods and philosophies of those who hold the opinion that the Holocaust never took place and is nothing more than cleverly orchestrated propaganda. Stern participated in the 1997 White House Conference on Hate Crimes as a presenter.

Lu-In Wang, legal expert on the topic of hate crimes law and the author in 1994 of *Hate Crimes Law*, a groundbreaking textbook on the subject that is updated annually. An associate professor at the University of Pittsburgh School of Law, Wang has expanded her legal research into a multidisciplinary approach to racism and discrimination, investigating the social and psychological factors that lead to the commission of hate crimes. Her articles have appeared in a variety of law and academic journals.

CHAPTER 5

GLOSSARY

advocacy   Defending or supporting a cause, legal position, group, philosophy, individual, etc.

aggravated assault   An attack against an individual for the purpose of inflicting serious injury, often with the use of a weapon or other means likely to produce death or severe harm.

anti-Semitism   Prejudice against Jews and the Jewish religion.

assault   A verbal or physical attack by one individual against another, or simply a threat to carry out the same.

bias   A negative opinion held against a group or individual on the basis of race, color, religion, national origin, etc. The generally recognized forms of bias, for the purpose of legislation and criminal prosecution, are racial bias, ethnic bias, religious bias, sexual orientation bias, and disability bias.

bias indicators   Facts or circumstances surrounding a criminal act that suggest the act was perpetrated on the basis of prejudice against the victim's race, color, religion, national origin, etc.

bias motive   Prejudice or hatred against a group or individual (based on race, color, religion, national origin, etc.) that plays a role in the commission of a crime carried out against that group or individual.

bipartisan   Characterized by support across the two major political groups or viewpoints, generally Democrat/Republican and liberal/conservative.

chilling effect   The consequence of limiting or inhibiting free speech caused by a proposed law or court verdict.

complaint   A written accusation of a criminal act, filed by a prosecuting attorney in order to initiate legal action against an individual.

discrimination   Prejudicial treatment of an individual based on the individual's membership in a group, whether it be religious, ethnic, socioeconomic, cultural, or nationality.

fighting words   Speech that deliberately provokes violent or criminal acts, held by legal precedent not to be protected by the free-speech provisions of the First Amendment.

135

freestanding statute A hate-crimes law that creates and defines an entirely new category of criminal act, such as ethnic intimidation, related to the biased motivation of the perpetrator.

hate crime An act of violence, trespassing, intimidation, and/or vandalism perpetrated against a person or group on the basis of prejudice or hatred towards the actual or perceived race, color, religion, national origin, gender, disability, or sexual orientation of the victim.

hate speech Spoken words or printed text that is motivated by bias, prejudice, or hatred against a group or individual based on that group or individual's actual or perceived race, color, religion, national origin, etc.

homicide The killing of one person by another.

institutional violence Criminal acts such as arson, trespassing, or vandalism carried out against property such as churches, synagogues, cemeteries, schools, and/or monuments.

juvenile A person not yet of adult age and, by general legal definition, between 10 and 16 years old.

Ku Klux Klan (KKK) Organization founded in Pulaski, Tennessee, after the Civil War for the purpose of protecting and furthering southern traditions such as the separation of the races.

libel A malicious or false statement made in written form against an individual group.

lynching The killing of an individual outside of the legal system for suspected criminal acts, or on the basis of the individual's race, group affiliation, or other characteristic.

mens rea Mental state, or intent; in law, *mens rea* usually denotes the motivation of someone accused of a crime. Most hate crime law requires prosecutors and juries to decide on the state of mind of the accused, in terms of bias towards a group or individual based on certain identified characteristics, such as race, religion, national origin, etc.

misogyny The aversion to the opposite sex, most often used to denote sexism by men against women (the aversion of women to men is known more specifically as misandry).

model statute A legislative act, such as a criminal statute, composed to serve as a template to be adopted by lawmaking bodies and adapted to local problems and concerns.

neo-Nazi An individual who subscribes to the beliefs and practices of Adolf Hitler and Nazi Germany.

nolo contendere A plea entered by an individual on trial in which the accused does not admit guilt but agrees to a sentence or punishment commensurate with the crime.

nongovernmental organization (NGO) A group formed to address specific issues or concerns, such as racial prejudice, outside the apparatus of public agencies.

Glossary

nonresponding agency   A law enforcement agency that does not comply with requirements to make a hate-crimes report to either federal or state agencies authorized to collect such data.

overall crime rate   A number expressing the total number of crimes as a percentage of the overall population figure.

participating agencies (reporting agencies)   Law enforcement agencies that comply with requirements to carry out a hate-crimes report covering their jurisdictions.

penalty enhancement   An increase in a convicted criminal's sentence, sometimes based on the finding that the crime was motivated by prejudice or bias against the victim's race, color, religion, national origin, etc.

post-traumatic stress disorder   A physical reaction to a traumatic event, such as a witnessed death or a violent encounter, that manifests as anxiety, depression, insomnia, and/or flashbacks.

prejudice   Opinions or views of an individual or group, usually negative, based on misperceptions of or bias against the group.

prevalence   The number of certain crimes, such as hate-crime assaults, that take place in a reporting jurisdiction.

primary prevention   An effort to prevent future social problems and criminal acts through education, public programs, etc.

property crimes   Generally defined as burglary, theft, arson, and/or vandalism, crimes that directly harm material objects rather than human victims.

protected status   A legal categorization of members of a certain group, such as African Americans, who thereby enjoy the protection of the law against discrimination and bias-motivated actions.

punitive damages   Monetary award granted via a civil trial to the victim of an illegal act.

qualitative data   Information gathered from interviews and questions, generally not statistically based or scientifically analyzed.

quantitative data   Information and/or data collected through a strictly defined method, in which those questioned are given carefully structured responses from which to choose.

racial profiling   The selection of members of a certain ethnic group for closer scrutiny by police or other authority figures.

racialism   Claims or views about natural differences in ability or intelligence between members of an ethnic group or nationality.

racism   The doctrine that certain ethnic groups are as a rule inferior or superior to others based on perceived characteristics among members of that group.

reverse racism   Racism or discrimination directed against the members of a majority ethnic, religious, or socioeconomic group or nationality.

robbery The commission of theft through the use of intimidation, threats, or bodily harm.

secondary prevention An attempt to head off such problems as violence, bigotry, and hate crimes among a population considered at risk for such problems.

sentencing guidelines Uniform penalties set down by a state or federal law for the commission of certain crimes.

sexism The view that holds one sex to be superior to the other, either in intellectual or physical capacity.

skinheads A group characterized by shaven heads, which in some (but not all) cases stands as an emblem of certain beliefs, such as racism or white supremacy.

slander A malicious or false characterization or accusation made against an individual or group, legally defined as an oral (not written) statement.

synagogue A Jewish house of worship, ritual, and prayer.

tertiary prevention An attempt to resolve a threat or problem once it has begun to take place.

Uniform Crime Reports (UCR) Annual statistical surveys on the incidence of crime that are gathered and published by the FBI.

violent crimes Generally defined as murder, forcible rape, robbery, assault, and/or aggravated assault.

white supremacist Someone who believes that white (European-descended) people should hold a dominant place over people of other ethnicities, such as black or Asian.

zero report A report of an agency, such as a police department or prosecutor's office, that indicates that no hate crimes have been committed within a particular jurisdiction during a stated time period.

PART II

GUIDE TO FURTHER RESEARCH

CHAPTER 6

HOW TO RESEARCH
HATE CRIMES

The researcher of hate crimes and hate-crime law is faced with a very diverse, unfocused, and often opinionated field of source material, including books, newspaper and magazine articles, court cases, legal tracts, web sites, and printed and electronic sources offering conflicting statistics. Although the heyday of hate-crimes legislation took place in the early 1990s, and the topic has subsided as a focus of public interest in more recent years, a new federal statute on hate crimes—the Hate Crimes Prevention Act—was reintroduced in the House of Representatives in January 2003. A highly partisan debate over amending or writing new hate-crimes law on the federal level will likely continue.

The student should at all times be aware of the two fundamentally opposed positions on the issue of hate-crimes law: the stand of those, generally but not always identified as political conservatives, who see such laws as an unconstitutional abridgement of free speech and opinion, and the position of those, generally identified as political liberals, who view hate crimes as worthy of more severe punishment by reason of the greater threat they pose to the community at large, and as a redress of historical discrimination. In most cases, those who take a stand one way or another on the subject continue to use these positions as the basis of their argument.

TIPS FOR RESEARCHING
HATE CRIMES

- **Define the topic and the question at issue:** The researcher should develop a very specific issue or question before proceeding into the thicket of research materials and before proceeding to original work. The subject of hate crimes and hate-crimes law gives rise to a variety of secondary subjects: the proper role of the federal government in making criminal law; the history of racism and discrimination; procedures of the modern criminal justice system; the origins and ongoing effect of civil rights legislation; courtroom procedure; the victims' rights movement; the rise of hate groups; the socioeconomic condition of certain minority groups; the role of the media, the Internet, and talk radio; the influence of advocacy groups, and so on. The researcher will soon note that many articles and books on hate crimes suffer from a lack of focus and float interminably from one of these topics to the next, greatly weakening whatever original point the author wished to make.

- **Develop a grounding in the recent history of hate crimes law:** The researcher should first and foremost get a handle on the legislative background, most importantly the federal statutes that have been proposed and written since the Hate Crimes Statistics Act of 1990 (the Hate Crimes Sentencing Act, the Violence Against Women Act, the Church Arsons Prevention Act, and the proposed Hate Crimes Prevention Act). A good source for this review is the web document "Hate Crimes Laws," produced by the Anti-Defamation League and available at http://www. adl.org/99hatecrime/federal.asp. Without a basic knowledge of these laws, the available texts on hate crimes, and especially legal scholarship, can become confusing, as specialized authors in the field tend to assume this knowledge on the part of their readers. Researchers can also help themselves by reviewing a few good texts on the history of the civil rights struggle of the 1950s and 1960s, which turned out to be a precursor to the hate-crimes debates of the 1980s and 1990s.

- **Beware of statistics:** Authors on hate crimes make free use of statistics gleaned from a variety of sources, quite often unattributed, and the researcher will soon note the numbers changing and conflicting. In fact, there are several different ways of counting hate crimes, and law enforcement agencies use their own guidelines when police have to make the decision whether to designate a criminal act as bias motivated. The most important difference to keep in mind is the occurrence of hate crimes actually prosecuted by law enforcement and hate incidents reported by victims, which do not always signify a police investigation or a public prosecutor's case. Advocacy sites with hot lines available to the public, for example, will often publish the total number of reports and contacts as hate incidents. The most widely quoted statistical set on hate crimes remains the Hate Crimes section of the FBI's Uniform Crime Reports (UCR), although the UCR is also open to doubt and interpretation.

- **Know the source:** When delving into the World Wide Web and the Internet, the researcher should be aware of the political stand taken by the source he or she is using. Favoring or opposing hate-crimes law is an all-or-nothing proposition to most of these sources, and the articles, statistics, even photographs and graphics selected are put to use to support this stand. To strengthen their impact on the public, web sources will often dress themselves in a deceptive cloak of neutrality, down to the name the organization has selected for itself. As much as possible, the researcher should investigate the background of authors, the history of organizations, the political viewpoint of periodicals and, in some cases, of book publishers.

BIBLIOGRAPHIC RESOURCES

The researcher of hate crimes should begin with public or university libraries. (Bookstores will have a limited number of titles on hand on this very specific topic, although any book in print can usually be ordered.) A good academic library is the most useful research source of all, as the library will hold not only books and periodicals but also a variety of bibliographic resources such as catalogues, indexes, and bibliographies that can point the student in a very specific direction.

INTERNET RESEARCH

The Internet is a global network of computer servers that share TCP/IP, a common protocol that allows the servers to communicate with each other. Most universities, public libraries, and government agencies have a presence on the Internet as well as a direct connection to it, either through their own servers or through an Internet service provider (ISP).

A variety of activities have been carried out on the Internet since its inception and early growth in the 1960s and 1970s. Discussion groups known as listservs allow members to post and reply to messages on a given topic. By a procedure known as telnetting, a researcher can log onto a distant system and use it as if present at the remote site. By FTP (file transfer protocol), large files can be downloaded from remote sites. By far the largest and most active system present on the Internet is the World Wide Web.

The World Wide Web is made up of millions of pages and sites, all sharing a common programming language known as hypertext markup language (HTML). The language was created to provide direct electronic links to other sites, by far the web's most valuable feature. Through the web, federal agencies such as the Department of Justice, federal and state courts, nongovernmental public-interest agencies, private corporations, and so on can be accessed and investigated to some extent by a researcher seeking information that may be difficult to find in traditional print media such as books, magazines, and reports.

Hate Crimes

Searching the Internet through the World Wide Web can be quite helpful or quite frustrating. A query for "hate crimes" on Google, a relatively comprehensive Internet search engine, on March 13, 2002, returned a grand total of 239,000 results. A thorough researcher might have the time to open and examine a few hundred web sites of interest to the topic at hand. The researcher must bring a critical eye to the content of these sites, as the creations of the World Wide Web range in quality from vital and comprehensive to useless, but there are several useful criteria when looking at a web page. Consider the author or organization that has created the web page. Points of view can be either expressed or hidden by proper names and acronyms. Researchers always must carefully examine any material presented for bias. The most important consideration is the relative expertise held by members of the group in the subject they purport to describe and analyze.

Generally, authoritative web sites will carry plentiful links to other sites (of varying viewpoints); the links will operate properly (demonstrating that the URLs in use are still valid). A wider range of resources given—books, articles, reports, other web pages, and so on—marks the site as broadly useful rather than narrowly focused. Within the documents on the site, reference notes should be provided, with or without Internet links, and these sources should be easily verified.

Good web sites are updated frequently (the Last Updated date is frequently visible). Contact information will be provided: name, physical address or post office box number, phone number, e-mail address. Sponsorship of the site should be given, whether by governmental or nongovernmental organizations, academic institutions, or corporations. Advertising should be kept to a minimum.

Although a subjective consideration, the appearance and overall design of the web page is also a clue to validity. Links within the site should be logical and intuitive. Graphics should serve a useful function, rather than being presented as an end in themselves. A good design reflects careful programming, which in turn signifies a large investment in time and money by the individual or organization that created the page.

Viewing World Wide Web pages requires a software program known as a browser. On instructions from the user, the browser reads the computer code stored on web pages and presents it as text, graphics, photographs, and so on. The two most commonly used browsers are Netscape and Internet Explorer, the latter a product of the Microsoft Corporation.

WEB SITES OF INTEREST

"Hate in America: What Do We Know?"
   URL: http://www.publiceye.org/hate/Hate99ASA_toc.htm

Ten essays on the history and prevalence of hate crimes and hate groups collected from a press conference sponsored by the American Sociological Association on August 6, 1999. Includes "Hate Crime Statistics: Six-Year Comparisons," a breakdown of hate crimes according to race, ethnicity/national origin/religion, sexual orientation, disability, and multiple bias, as distilled from the FBI's Uniform Crime Reporting (UCR) program.

Lambda GLBT Community Services
URL: http://hate-crime.website-works.com
Title: Hate-Crime.Net. Site intended to serve as a resource for victims of hate crimes. Includes pages for reporting hate crimes, news, volunteer work, discussion forum.

Matthew Shepard
URL: http://www.mattshepard.org
Dedicated to Matthew Shepard, a gay college student who was beaten to death outside Laramie, Wyoming.

National Criminal Justice Reference Service
URL: http://www.ncjrs.org/hate_crimes/hate_crimes.html
A site operated by the crime information service of the U.S. Department of Justice, giving summaries of hate-crimes statistics, information on grants and funding, Justice Department programs, legislation, links to hate-crimes websites as well as relevant Department of Justice sites, and a large database of useful article abstracts.

University of California at Davis Psychology Department
URL: http://psychology.ucdavis.edu/rainbow/html/hate_crimes.html
Title: Stop Hate Crimes. Information, articles, and links to current news and articles on hate crimes. Links to books and articles on the subject by Dr. Gregory Herek.

SEARCH ENGINES

Search engines require the user to enter a word or phrase that will return links to hopefully pertinent and useful sites. Surrounding a phrase with quotation marks assures that only the specific phrase—not its components—will be used by the search engine. Entering "hate crimes," as mentioned above, however, returns more sites than the user could ever hope to visit. Therefore, the search has to be further narrowed by adding words—places, dates, people, court cases, and so on. To accomplish this, the user enters modifying phrases after the word AND (capital letters), thus instructing the search engine to return all sites that include both phrases. For instance:

"Hate crimes" AND "federal statutes"
"hate crimes" AND "FBI statistics"
"Clinton Administration" AND "Hate Crime laws"

Seeking the web page of a certain organization can be accomplished by specifying "Home page" after the name of the organization.

"Anti-Defamation League" AND "home page"

Anyone using search engines on the Internet should be aware that prominent listings can be purchased by web page creators, and that organizations that operate search engines can feature (or filter out) certain sites according to their own criteria. Following are some of the most useful search engines now operating on the World Wide Web.

AllTheWeb.com or FAST Search (http://www.alltheweb.com) One of the largest indexes on the World Wide Web, with large multimedia and mobile/wireless web indexes first created in 1999.

Alta Vista (www.altavista.com) One of the original crawler search engines, Alta Vista allows users to build very specific searches with the Advanced Query mode. A Refine feature helps the researcher narrow the search and the user can translate text to or from several foreign languages.

AOL Search (http://search.aol.com) For America Online members, allowing them to search the web as well as providing "priority content" that can only be accessed through an AOL subscription.

Ask Jeeves (http://www.askjeeves.com) A search engine in which the user employs natural language to get responses to very specific requests. The response comes in the form of a list of sites that provide relevant information on a subject phrase recognized by the engine.

Direct Hit (http://www.directhit.com) A search engine that returns results based on the number of times users click to the listed sites (both through this site and through partner sites, including Ask Jeeves and HotBot). Thus Direct Hit is a kind of World Wide Web popularity contest that will reveal what sites have been attracting the highest current interest on a particular subject.

Google (www.google.com) A vast searchable database of web pages has made Google one of the most useful Internet search engines in existence. The Advanced Search feature allows users to specify language, file format, date of the web pages, domains, and placement of the phrase searched for on the page. Users can also browse recent news stories on the topic. The user can have foreign language pages translated and also set the maximum number of results.

HotBot (http://www.hotbot.com) A site that draws on results from other sites, including Direct Hit and Inktomi. This engine is now run by Lycos, a company that maintains another search engine under its own name.

Lycos (http://www.lycos.com) Lycos started out as a crawler service and then was transformed into a directory, in which users search through indexes created by web programmers.

Open Directory (http://dmoz.org) A search engine launched in 1998 and maintained by volunteers, whose catalogues and directories are made freely available to other sites such as Google, Lycos, and HotBot.

Yahoo (http://www.yahoo.com) The oldest and most popular web search engine, Yahoo draws on a team of editors who constantly update and streamline its directories. Although drawing on a smaller database than Google, Yahoo provides users with an organized subject index, somewhat more useful than simply searching keywords, and provides users the alternative of seeing results provided by Google.

Legal Search Engines

There are two important search engines devoted to the subject of law, court cases, statutes, and the like: FindLaw (www.findlaw.com) and WashLaw WEB (www.washlaw.edu). The two major legal databases in current use are Westlaw and LexisNexis, both of which are expanding with a variety of non-legal resources. Loislaw, a division of Aspen Publishers, Inc., has created another subscription website for electronic legal research.

Westlaw and LexisNexis are fee-based subscription services that allow users to search a constantly updated collection of state and federal statutes, cases, regulations, public records, corporate information, and international law databases. The LexisNexis database is located at www.lexis.com; Westlaw resides at www.westlaw.com. A researcher may be able to access these databases through a subscription held by a public, academic, or law library.

Westlaw

Westlaw is a product of West Group, a company formed by the merger of West Publishing and Thomson Legal Publishing. This resource organizes a wide variety of information under the heading of each state. For the state of Florida, for example, Westlaw offers the following (among many more databases) that may be useful for those researching hate crimes:

FL-CS: Florida Cases. Documents from the appellate courts of Florida, including decisions and orders published in the *Southern Reporter*. This database includes "quick opinions," which are made available online before they appear in print.

FL-CS-ALL: Cases from state courts, federal district courts within Florida, and the Eleventh Circuit (federal appeals).

FL-AG: Florida Attorney General Opinions. This section includes opinion letters released by the Florida Attorney General's office. As in the Florida Administrative Code, this section can be searched by several different criteria.

FL-ST-ANN: Florida Statutes—Annotated. Court rules and statutes, including the complete set of updated and revised statutes and the Florida constitution. Also includes state court rules and federal district and bankruptcy court rules as they appear in West Publishing's *Florida Rules of Court.*

FL-LEGIS: Florida Legislative Service—Current. Documents (chapters or resolutions) passed by the state legislature, not including special acts or general acts of local application.

FL-BILLTXT: Florida—State Bill Text—Full Text. This database contains the full text (including all available amended versions) of all legislative initiatives, including pending and recently passed bills, beginning with the most recent legislative session.

FL-BILLTRAK: Florida Bill Tracking—Summaries. Status information on all pending and recently passed bills and legislative initiatives, from the introduction of the bill to most recent action.

WSB-FL: Westlaw State Bulletins—Florida. Documents prepared by the West Group that summarize recent legal developments, such as recent important court decisions, in Florida law.

FLCJ-CS. A case law database dealing exclusively with criminal justice cases.

Florida Newspapers. Contents of the *Miami Herald, Orlando Sentinel, Palm Beach Post, St. Petersburg Times,* and *Fort Lauderdale Sun Sentinel* from 1988 or 1989 to the present.

PAPERSFL. A database allowing researchers to search all of the above newspapers at once.

COURT CASES

Federal and state courts are the final arbiter of hate-crimes laws, as it is within these venues that the constitutionality of these statutes are finally decided. Court decisions are indexed according to a standard format, in which the title represents *Plaintiff v. Defendant,* or *Appellant v. Appellee,* then gives the volume number of the reporting publication, the starting page of the case, the venue (federal or state court), and finally the year.

A sample would be the case of *R.A.V. v. City of St. Paul, Minnesota,* 505 U.S. 377 (1992). The case can be found in the 505th volume of the *Supreme Court Reporter* (the publication is simply designated as "U.S."), starting on page 377 (the case was decided in 1992).

Many state supreme courts and appeals courts publish their full decisions online, and nearly all provide an index to the printed reporting source. There are also several useful private online sources of case law, used by legal scholars and researchers who can now avoid the laborious task of searching the volumes owned by law libraries. These online sources include the Legal Information Institute, which publishes all Supreme Court decisions since 1990, plus more than 600 "historic decisions" at http://supct.law.cornell.edu/supct.

THOMAS

The once-frustrating and time-consuming process of tracking current and recent legislative action by the U.S. Congress has been considerably eased by the creation of THOMAS, a World Wide Web site (at http://thomas.loc.gov) devoted to federal legislative information. THOMAS has the *Congressional Record* and the full text of legislation available from 1989 to the present. In addition, the THOMAS page known as *Congressional Documents and Debates 1774–1873* offers a record of congressional proceedings from the legislature's first century.

The THOMAS homepage has two principal links to be used by researchers: Bill Text and Bill Summary and Status. The searcher must specify the Congress by number (congressional sessions last two years and are consecutively numbered; the 2003–2004 session is thus known as the 108th Congress). By default, the links go to the Congress currently in session. The Bill Text link can return bills dating back to the 101st Congress, or 1989–90. The Bill Summary and Status link can return bills dating back to the 93rd Congress, or 1973–74.

The Bill Text link can be searched by two different criteria: Word/Phrase or Bill Number. Entering the bill number will return the current and all past versions of the bill in question. Using a Word/Phrase search will return all the bills relating to that subject. In March 2002, carrying out the search on hate crimes for the 107th Congress brought 22 results: original bills, amendments, and resolutions, along with their history.

Bill Summary and Status presents related information: how the bill originated, who is sponsoring it, its status in committee, amendments attached to it, scheduled votes, and so on, prepared by an organization known as the Congressional Research Service. In Bill Summary and Status, the researcher has several ways to search: Word/Phrase, Subject Term, Bill/Amendment Number, Stage in Legislative Process, Date of Introduction, Sponsor/Cosponsor, and Committee. This link will not allow the researcher to read the full text of the bill, however; that is the work performed by the Bill Text search. The Bill Summary and Status information includes the following:

Titles

Bill Status (with links to the online *Congressional Record* and information on votes)

Committees

Related House Committee Documents

Amendments

Related Bill Details

Subjects (CRS index terms)

Cosponsors

CRS Summary

Researchers looking for legislative texts and documents prior to 1989 and that are not available on the THOMAS site must locate a Federal Depository Library. There are approximately 1,350 of them in the United States and U.S. possessions, and at least one in each congressional district; a list can be accessed and searched at http://www.gpo.gov/su_docs/locators/findlibs/index.html.

ONLINE BOOK CATALOGS

Retail book catalogs available online include Barnesandnoble.com and Amazon.com. These sites can prove quite useful to the researcher, as they give not only title and publication information but, in many cases, selected reviews by readers and critics as well as text extracts and tables of contents. Tracking down out-of-print books is also possible, as the sites offer links to associated sites that specialize in out-of-print and hard to find books.

The most comprehensive library online catalog is that of the Library of Congress, available at http://lcweb.loc.gov. This site offers useful guides and indexes for researchers, links to other library catalogs, access to foreign collections, interlibrary loan services, and a special section on law research.

Yahoo also offers a library listing at http://dir.yahoo.com/Reference/Libraries. Most usefully for the hate-crimes researcher, this page includes links to law libraries and government document collections. Most public libraries offer their catalogs online as well, free for research, and their books can often be ordered for borrowing through the interlibrary loan system.

The catalogs can usually be searched by author, title, subject category, or keyword. Entering the words "hate crime" (with quotation marks) will return all titles or (sometimes) book descriptions with that exact phrase included. For a comprehensive search, the researcher is better advised to use a subject heading. Relevant subject headings for the topic include:

• hate crimes
• hate speech

- prejudice
- racism
- legislation
- bias
- bias crimes

ONLINE DATABASES

There are many useful online information databases, which can often be accessed free at subscribing public or university libraries. These databases offer indexes of books, periodicals, audiovisual materials, dissertations, government documents, law cases, online federal and state statutes, and the like, as well as indexes to reference works such as bibliographies, encyclopedias, and dictionaries (which in many cases can be accessed online as well through a direct link provided by the database). Among the most comprehensive are InfoTrac and Wilson SelectPlus. The LexisNexis database is an immense online research tool, grouped into topical and state-specific libraries and subdivided into files that may be searched by keyword, author, title, date, and subject. The researcher may browse or search databases specific to a single state, as in Westlaw. Many newspapers and magazines also offer online databases and indexes through their own websites.

In many cases, the database will also offer a full-text version or a one-paragraph abstract of a book or article, giving the researcher a clear idea of the subject covered within the work and the author's approach to the topic and point of view. For the hate crimes researcher, material from the late 1980s and early 1990s will generally cover the first period of hate-crimes legislation, when the debate over the constitutionality of hate crimes was running hot; the late 1990s and the years 2000–02 will bring materials related to the further refinement of hate-crime laws to cover protected statuses of gender, sexual orientation, and disability. Older works can be useful when researching civil rights legislation, the legal precursor to modern hate-crimes law, or the general subjects of racism, prejudice, and bigotry.

GOVERNMENT AGENCIES AND STATISTICS

One of the most useful web sites to any researcher of crime and the criminal justice system is the Bureau of Justice Statistics page at http://www.ojp.usdoj.gov/bjs. This site publishes statistics on crime, crime victims, criminal offenders, law enforcement (federal, state, local, and campus), courts and sentencing, corrections (probation, jails, and capital punishment), and the federal justice system.

Hate Crimes

The traditional federal crime report consisted of a tally of offenses and arrests for certain types of crimes, published in the FBI's annual Uniform Crime Report (UCR). This system is being updated and improved by the National Incident-Based Reporting System (NIBRS), an FBI program that collects more details on more categories of crime, including concurrent offenses, weapons, injury, location, property loss and characteristics of the victims, offenders and arrestees. As of 2001, more than 3,725 agencies in 21 states were submitting NIBRS data. The NIBRS also captures a wide range of information on hate crimes, and the Bureau of Justice Statistics published these findings in *Hate Crimes Reported in NIBRS, 1997–1999* (publication number NCJ 186765), available through the site.

Another important publication is the *Sourcebook of Criminal Justice Statistics*, available online at http://www.albany.edu/sourcebook/index.html. This reference collects information from more than 100 sources into more than 600 tables, most recently from the year 2000 (the 28th edition of the *Sourcebook*). The tables include "Bias-Motivated (Hate) Crimes Known to Police, by Offense, United States," "Bias Motivations in Hate Crimes Known to Police, United States, 2000," and "Race of Suspected Offender in Bias-Motivated (Hate) Crimes Known to Police, By Type of Bias Motivation, United States, 2000."

CHAPTER 7

━━━━━━━━━━

ANNOTATED BIBLIOGRAPHY

The following chapter represents a sample of available printed, audiovisual, and online materials dealing with hate crimes. The material is broken down into the following general categories:

General Works on Racism, Prejudice, and Bigotry
Modern Racist and Hate Groups
History of Hate Violence
Legal and Constitutional Aspects of Hate-Crime Legislation
Criminology, Law Enforcement, and Research
Anti-Homosexual Bias Crime
Current Hate Crime Journalism

These categories are further divided into books, periodicals, reports, Internet documents, and videos, where applicable. Most of the articles and books selected are for the general reader, although there is a good sampling of academic scholarship on the psychology of prejudice and hate-crimes perpetrators as well as legal papers on the constitutionality and historical precedents of modern hate-crimes law. Many of the articles listed are also available online from subscription databases such as InfoTrac and LexisNexis and on the web sites operated by the periodicals themselves, which can often be accessed free of charge at public or university libraries.

GENERAL WORKS ON RACISM, PREJUDICE, AND BIGOTRY

BOOKS

Allport, Gordon. *The Nature of Prejudice.* Menlo Park, Calif.: Addison Wesley, 1979. The author, a pioneering psychologist in the field of religious belief and prejudice, offers a long and detailed exploration of the sources of bigotry and discrimination within the human personality, and why such characteristics often erupt into violence. A seminal publication, the book was adopted as a handbook by the civil rights leaders of the 1960s.

Baird, Robert M., and Stuart E. Rosenbaum, eds. *Bigotry, Prejudice & Hatred: Definitions, Causes and Solutions.* Buffalo, N.Y.: Prometheus Books, 1992. A collection of essays on the modern phenomenon of bigotry, bias-motivated violence, Internet hate sites, school shootings, gay bashings, and the burning of churches and synagogues. Authors include John Dewey, Michael Musto, Cornel West, Gordon Allport, Jean-Paul Sartre, and Tony Kushner.

Bowling, Benjamin. *Violent Racism: Victimisation, Policing and Social Context.* Clarendon Studies in Criminology series. New York: Oxford University Press, 1998. This book documents the daily abuse, assaults, and intimidation that are suffered by black and Asian people in Great Britain, using information obtained in an East London case study. Part I contains four chapters that review literature on violent racism and policing in the recent period. Part II consists of a study of violent racism and the police response to it, preceded by an introduction to the geographical, demographic, social, and economic characteristics of East London. The concluding chapter considers the extent to which policy and practice of the late 1980s and early 1990s achieved the various objectives stated by the organizations that began to respond systematically to violent racism in 1981.

Dray, Philip. *At the Hands of Persons Unknown: The Lynching of Black America.* New York: Random House, 2002. A study of the history of lynching of African Americans, finding that lynching was far from rare. The author maintains that lynching was an important element of systematic discrimination against African Americans, particularly in the South, and was used purposefully as a weapon of terror with widespread sanction in the greater community. The author also documents the gradual end of lynching in the mid-20th century as black servicemen returned home from World War II to set an example of racial pride, patriotism, and heroism, and as dedicated individuals and organizations pressured state and federal legislatures to take more effective action against violations of civil rights.

Ferber, Abby L. *White Man Falling: Race, Gender and White Supremacy.* Lanham, Md.: Rowman & Littlefield, 1998. The author, the director of Women's Studies at the University of Colorado at Colorado Springs, is a widely recognized expert on far right political movements and organized hate groups. She offers a history of the concept of race and background on the white supremacist movement in the United States, and reaches the conclusion that gender issues—particularly the reassertion of their traditional power and authority by men—lie at the heart of contemporary racism.

Annotated Bibliography

Frederickson, George M. *Racism: A Short History*. Princeton, N.J.: Princeton University Press, 2002. The author finds the origins of modern racism in medieval Europe's treatment of Jews, whose refusal to convert to Christianity was considered a basic character flaw, and in the Enlightenment's more scientific classification of nationalities. This racism reached the level of official policy in the 19th century, when nations put in place strict immigration policies to keep their own populations racially "pure," but was finally discredited among the mainstream by the actions of Nazi Germany in the Holocaust.

Hall, Patricia Wong, and Victor M. Hwang. *Anti-Asian Violence in North America: Asian American and Asian Canadian Reflections on Hate, Healing, and Resistance*. Walnut Creek, Calif.: AltaMira, 2001. A wide spectrum of Asian-American and Asian-Canadian contributors—attorneys, students, businesspeople, and activists—discuss the impact of bias crime and racism on themselves and on their communities. The writers cover racism and hate crimes as well as other aspects of the race problem, including Internet-based racism, police bigotry, economic and legal barriers, and immigration issues. They also offer possible solutions and strategies to assist victims, prosecute offenders, and combat ingrained prejudice.

Hemphill, Paul. *The Ballad of Little River: A Tale of Race and Restless Youth in the Rural South*. New York: Free Press, 2000. The author investigates a series of violent crimes, which may or may not have been motivated by race prejudice, and the burning of a black church by five white youths in the poor, isolated hamlet of Little River, Alabama, offering as he does so an in-depth look at race relations in the rural South.

Kaplan, Jeffrey, and Tore Bjorgo, eds. *Nation and Race: The Developing Euro-American Racist Subculture*. Boston: Northeastern University Press, 1998. A description of what the author terms a Euro-American racist subculture, given through a series of essays by experts in sociology, history, and political science.

Kelly, Robert J., and Jess Maghan, eds. *Hate Crime: The Global Politics of Polarization*. Carbondale: Southern Illinois University Press, 1998. A series of essays on hate crimes, on the nature of hate, and the psychological and philosophical underpinnings of racial bias as it is experienced around the world from the United States to the Middle East to Africa and India. The book includes a chapter by Robert Kelly entitled "Black Rage, Murder, Racism, and Madness: The Metamorphosis of Colin Ferguson," a case relevant to the discussion of hate crimes. The author discusses the question of whether Ferguson, who committed a mass murder of white commuters on the Long Island Rail Road, was a deranged man who happened to be black, or an individual whose violence was precipitated by racism, either real or imagined.

Kleg, M. *Hate, Prejudice and Racism.* SUNY Series: Theory, Research, and Practice in Social Education. Albany: SUNY Press, 1993. This book provides a comprehensive overview of the problems caused by prejudiced attitudes, racist beliefs, and acts of discrimination, including racial jokes and ethnic slurs, overt discrimination, and racially motivated violence. The book analyzes hate, prejudice, and violence in the past and the present, the foundation of race as a scientific concept, and the foundation of racism (which views race as a social concept). The author also addresses the meaning of ethnicity and ethnic groups, attitudes, stereotyping, and the manifestations of hate prejudice ranging from discrimination to aggression and scapegoating.

Kotlowitz, Alex. *The Other Side of the River: A Story of Two Towns, A Death, and America's Dilemma.* New York: Doubleday, 1998. The story of a black teenager's death in the St. Joseph River, an event that was either an accident or a bias-motivated murder and that polarized the two communities of Benton Harbor and St. Joseph, Michigan.

Levin, Jack. *The Violence of Hate: Confronting Racism, Anti-Semitism, and Other Forms of Bigotry.* Boston: Allyn & Bacon, 2001. The author analyzes the psychological makeup of racists and bigots and explores the various social factors, including what he terms "the tacit approval of ordinary, even decent people" that bring about hate crimes. The book includes an appendix of antihate websites.

Levin, Jack, and Jack McDevitt. *Hate Crimes: The Rising Tide of Bigotry and Bloodshed.* New York: Plenum Press, 1993. The authors discuss the growth of hate crimes in the 1980s and early 1990s and argue that stereotypes that appear in the popular media contribute to such crimes. They advocate special bias-crime units within police departments and rehabilitation programs for "thrill-seeking" hate-crimes perpetrators.

Minow, Martha. *Breaking the Cycles of Hatred: Memory, Law and Repair.* Princeton, N.J.: Princeton University Press, 2002. A book of essays and lectures exploring cycles of violence, in which one act brings about another, setting off a self-perpetuating cycle of vengeance that can occur among families, ethnic groups, and nations. Minow explores innovative legal and political solutions to this phenomenon, arguing, for example, that civil rather than criminal actions against hate groups and bias crimes will prove most effective in preventing such incidents.

Pincus, Fred L., and Howard J. Ehrlich. *Race and Ethnic Conflict: Contending Views on Prejudice, Discrimination, and Ethnoviolence.* Denver, Colo.: Westview Press, 1994. A compilation of essays and journal articles, offering a wide spectrum of opposing viewpoints on the matters of modern race relations, the nature of prejudice, discrimination in public places and the workplace, group conflict, immigration controversies, public policy, and bias crimes.

Annotated Bibliography

Pinkney, Alphonso. *Lest We Forget: White Hate Crimes—Howard Beach and Other Racial Atrocities.* Chicago: Third World Press, 1994. A description of hate crimes in the news, including the Howard Beach incident in New York City.

Rothenberg, Paula, ed. *Race, Class, and Gender in the U.S.: An Integrated Study.* New York: St. Martin's Press, 1992. Essays on the issues of race, class, and gender, including a chapter entitled "Hate Violence" by Carole Sheffield.

Russell, Diana E. H., and Roberta A. Harmes, eds. *Femicide in Global Perspective.* New York: Teachers College Press, 2001. A series of articles by the editors and others defining and discussing "femicide" (the murder of women) and recounting the incidence of hate crimes against women in Africa, Asia, and North America.

Singular, Stephen. *The Uncivil War: The Rise of Hate, Violence, and Terrorism in America.* Beverly Hills, Calif.: New Millennium Press, 2001. The author draws on prominent incidents of violence, such as the Columbine school shootings in Colorado and the assassination of radio talk-show host Alan Berg, to argue that the United States is suffering an upsurge in hate violence, and that such actions have moved from the fringes of society into mainstream institutions such as schools, churches, and media outlets.

Temple-Raston, Dina. *A Death in Texas: A Story of Race, Murder, and a Small Town's Struggle for Redemption.* New York: Henry Holt, 2002. A book describing the 1998 dragging murder of an African American, James Byrd, Jr., by three white men in the East Texas community of Jasper. The author ponders the nature of small-town racism and describes the effect that the brutal crime and the subsequent nationwide attention and media publicity had on the community.

PERIODICALS

Abramovsky, Abraham. "Bias Crime: A Call for Alternative Responses." *Fordham Urban Law Journal,* vol. 19, 1992, p. 875. The author sees an urgent need for new and innovative responses for what he sees as a rising tide of bias crime, describing the root cause of the problem as a failure of the educational system to teach tolerance and understanding among different ethnic groups. As a model, he offers the efforts of the Canadian government and the effects of Canada's Multiculturalism Act.

Anonymous. "Faking the Hate: Faked Hate Crimes on College Campuses." *US News and World Report,* vol. 128, no. 22, June 5, 2000. Discusses hoax hate crimes and the possible motivation of perpetrators in proving the pervasiveness of racism and sexism on campus.

Anonymous. "Racial Violence Against Asian Americans." *Harvard Law Review*, vol. 106, no. 8, 1993, pp. 339–347. The article discusses common stereotypes regarding Asian Americans, including the fear of economic competition which in many cases has given rise to bias crimes against them.

Anonymous. Untitled. *America*, vol. 184, no. 19, June 4–11, 2001, p. 3. This editorial characterizes hate crimes as "an affront to the national conscience." The editorial discusses hate crimes against Asian Americans in the wake of recent immigration; the reaction of law enforcement to hate-crime complaints on the part of Asian Americans, and the prevention of hate crimes through education.

Burnette Davis, Alice J. "Simply Because We Are Black; The Message of the Illinois Shooting: Race Matters." *Sojourners*, September/October 1999, pp. 10–11. In the wake of Benjamin Smith's racially inspired killings in Illinois and Indiana in July 1999, the writer contends that African Americans are strangers, "others," in their own land; and that because of this otherness, African Americans are brought together in ways that non-blacks do not understand.

Burns, Robert E. "Hate Makes Waste." *U.S. Catholic*, March 1999, p. 2. The writer contends that society must bear some responsibility for instilling in individuals the type of loathing witnessed in hate crimes, and that the murder of Matthew Shepard, a 21-year-old college student from Wyoming, and the death of a Texas man at the hands of a group of white racists, should prompt an examination of society in general.

Corelli, Rae. "A Tolerant Nation's Hidden Shame." *Maclean's*, August 14, 1995, pp. 40–43. An article on hate crimes in Canada, where, according to a confidential study commissioned by the federal justice department, as many as 9,000 hate-inspired crimes may take place annually. The article describes several examples of hate crimes and discusses the reluctance of many victims to report the crimes.

Craig, Kellina M. "Retaliation, Fear, or Rage: An Investigation of African American and White Reactions to Racist Hate Crimes." *Journal of Interpersonal Violence*, vol. 14, no. 2, June 1999, pp. 138–51. The author describes and analyzes an experiment in the varying responses to hate crimes viewed by white and African-American subjects. The experiment is designed to study the question of whether hate crimes are more harmful by provoking more emotional and violent reactions among those who witness or hear about them—an important justification for hate-crime laws among supporters.

Czajkoski, Eugene H. "Criminalizing Hate: An Empirical Assessment." *Federal Probation*, vol. 22, no. 2, 1992, pp. 36–38. The author describes several hate-motivated crimes carried out in Florida and considers the possible motivations for such incidents.

Annotated Bibliography

DeAngelis, Tori. "Understanding and Preventing Hate Crime." *Monitor on Psychology*, vol. 32, no. 10, November 2001. In the wake of the September 11, 2001, terrorist attacks and the subsequent random violence committed against Arab Americans, the author describes efforts of researchers to understand hate crimes and their perpetrators, as well as the phenomenon of ethnic stereotyping, and why some people "turn their ethnic discomfort into drastic action."

Decter, Midge. "The ADL vs. the 'Religious Right'" *Commentary*, September 1994. A criticism of the ADL's 1993 study of the religious right, in which the author accuses the ADL of religious intolerance, defends religious conservatives against what she believes are media distortions, and argues that religious conservatives do not promote or condone anti-Semitism or any other form of bigotry.

Fiske, Susan T. "What We Know Now About Bias and Intergroup Conflict, the Problem of the Century." *Current Directions in Psychological Science*, vol. 11, no. 4, August 2002, pp. 123–28. An overview of psychological studies of prejudice, which is found to be a subtle condition in most individuals, but in extreme cases arises from economic and cultural conflict. The author finds that education and economic opportunity relieve both degrees of prejudice.

Fleischer, Jeff. "Hate Wave?" *Black Issues in Higher Education*, August 5, 1999, pp. 14–15. Description of a memorial service in Bloomington, Indiana, where more than 2,700 people attended a candlelit vigil for Indiana University doctoral student Won Joon Yoon, who was murdered in a racially motivated attack by former Indiana University student Benjamin Smith.

Fumento, Michael. "USA Today's Arson Artistry." *The American Spectator*, December 1996, pp. 28–33. The author criticizes the work of journalist Gary Fields and *USA Today* in creating the false impression of an epidemic of church burnings.

Goldberg, J. J. "Scaring the Jews." *The New Republic*, May 17, 1993, p. 22. Considering the use and misuse of statistics and polling data, the author maintains that anti-Semitism is not increasing and that hostility towards Jews has actually been on the wane.

Green, Donald P., Laurence H. McFalls, and Jennifer K. Smith. "Hate Crime: An Emergent Research Agenda." *Annual Review of Sociology*, vol. 27, 2001, pp. 479–504. A study of the literature of hate crimes and in the data collection by researchers attempting to measure and spot trends in hate crimes. The authors advocate more systematic and consistent methods of collecting data and new research on the link between economic, social, and political trends to ethnic conflict.

Horowitz, Craig. "The New Anti-Semitism." *New York*, vol. 26, no. 2, January 11, 1993, pp. 20–28. The author describes a rash of hate crimes in

New York City that culminated in the Crown Heights riots, as well as identifying new and more virulent forms of anti-Semitism that he believes find wide acceptance through dissemination in the popular media.

Isaac, Jeffrey C. "Responding to Hate: Bloomington United." *Dissent*, Winter 2000, pp. 9–11. The writer describes his community's response to anti-Semitic and racist literature being circulated in the college town of Bloomington, Indiana.

Jordan, June. "The Hunters and the Hunted." *The Progressive*, October 1999, pp. 17–19. Discusses the August 10, 1999, attack by Buford O. Furrow, Jr., on a Jewish community center in Los Angeles, where five Jews were wounded, and the murder of Filipino postal worker Joseph Santos Ileto. The writer examines other recent hate crimes and the Old Testament justification used by perpetrators of such atrocities.

Kifner, John. "Gunman and 7 Others are Killed as Blaze Guts a Store in Harlem." *New York Times*, December 9, 1995, p. 1. News description of the Freddy's Fashion Mart arson in New York City, a crime that police concluded arose from anti-white and anti-Jewish bigotry.

MacGinty, Roger. "Hate Crimes in Deeply Divided Societies: The Case of Northern Ireland." *New Political Science*, vol. 22, no. 1, March 2000, pp. 49–60. The author demonstrates the ways in which hate crime is "masked" or submerged in societies in conflict, using the example of Northern Ireland and its divided Protestant and Catholic populations. In such societies, paramilitary groups may mask hate crimes with political justification; in addition, the populations at odds may be physically segregated, lessening the opportunity for bias crimes.

Manatt, Richard W. "Hate Crimes: Bigotry, Harassment, Vandalism and Violence on Campus." *International Journal of Educational Reform*, October, 1994, pp. 481–90. The author categorizes a variety of hate crimes, describes hate crime and bias incidents in educational institutions from primary school through the universities, and considers the effect of peer groups in bringing these incidents about.

Medoff, Marshall H. "Allocation of Time and Hateful Behavior: A Theoretical and Positive Analysis of Hate and Hate Crimes." *The American Journal of Economics and Sociology*, October 1999, pp. 959–73. A rational-choice economic approach to analyze hateful behavior, predicting that hateful activity decreases with increases in (i) the market wage rate, (ii) the value of time, (iii) age, and (iv) law enforcement activity. The theory is tested on U.S. state hate-crime data, and the results provide convincing support for the model.

Mock, Karen R. "Update '98." *Canadian Social Studies*, Summer 1998, p. 116. Presents a report on how racism and hate crimes are being combated in Canada. Hate group activity and incidents of racism and anti-Semitism peaked in Canada in 1995. However, increased policing services and training, community education, and legislation led to a decrease in reported incidents during 1996.

Patrick, Deval L. "The Rise in Hate Crime." *Vital Speeches of the Day*, October 15, 1994, pp. 13–16. In a speech given to the Organization of Chinese Americans in Los Angeles, the assistant attorney general, Civil Rights Division of the U.S. Department of Justice, discusses hate crimes in America, in particular those directed against Asian Americans.

Petrosino, Carolyn. "Connecting the Past to the Future: Hate Crime in America." *Journal of Contemporary Criminal Justice*, vol. 15, no. 1, February 1999, pp. 22–47. The author explores bias crimes from the earliest colonial period through the 19th century, arguing that racism and hate crimes have been endemic in the United States, that hate crimes will increase in number and severity in the future, and that the problem may lessen with increased exposure in the media and in political debate.

Prochnau, Bill. "The Twisted Tale of a Human Slaughter/Tragedy in Seattle: A Young Itinerant, His 'Friends' in Outer Space—And Brutal Slaying of the Goldmark Family." *Washington Post*, May 13 and 14, 1986, p. Cl. Investigative report on a bias-motivated murder of a Seattle family, in which killer David Lewis Rice acted on the mistaken belief that the victims were Jewish.

Prutzman, Priscilla. "Bias-Related Incidents, Hate Crimes, and Conflict Resolution." *Education and Urban Society*, November 1994, pp. 71–81. The author reports on classroom conflict-resolution programs created by an organization known as the Children's Creative Response to Conflict and discusses the subject of bias incidents that occur in school.

Pruzan, Adam. "What Is a Hate Crime?" *The American Enterprise*, January/February 2000, p. 10. The author believes that coverage in the *New York Times* of a gun attack at the North Valley Jewish Community Center in Los Angeles, California, and of the murder of seven people at a Baptist church in Fort Worth, Texas, was indicative of a remarkable resurgence in "genteel prejudice." The author points out that the California incident received more prominent coverage than the Fort Worth incident, and that the former was labeled a hate crime but the latter was not.

Quist, Ryan M., and Douglas M. Wiegand. "Attributions of Hate: The Media's Causal Attributions of a Homophobic Murder." *American Behavioral Scientist*, vol. 46, no. 1, January 2002, pp. 93–107. An analysis of the different attributions given to the murder of Matthew Shepard by media sources of different political orientation. The authors find that conservative sources tended to downplay situational factors, such as the political climate; tend to disfavor the entire concept of "hate crime"; and tend toward describing homosexuality as a controllable condition—something of a provocation on Shepard's part.

Rosenblatt, Roger. "Their Finest Minute." *New York Times Magazine*, July 3, 1994, p. 22. A report on a demonstration that took place in Billings, Montana, while that city was undergoing a series of racially motivated assaults and vandalism.

Rutledge, Bruce. "Hate Crimes: Arab Americans Feel the Heat of Bigotry." *Human Rights*, vol. 18, no. 1, p. 30. The author relates common negative stereotypes of Arab Americans, the portrayal of Arabs in the media, and the efforts of Arab Americans to combat prejudice and bias-motivated violence in the wake of ongoing terrorism and conflict in the Middle East.

Sanders, Jon. "Hoax Crimes: Faked Hate Crimes on College Campuses." *National Review*, September 14, 1998, p. 38. Part of a special section on American education, describing a new trend on college campuses of students and faculty members creating fictitious racist and antigay incidents to show they are a possibility on campus. Examples of such fake crimes are cited at Duke University, Eastern New Mexico University, the University of Georgia, and Guilford College, North Carolina.

Solomon, Charlene Marmer. "Keeping Hate Out of the Workplace." *Personnel Journal*, July 1992, pp. 30–37. An article covering bigotry and bias-motivated crimes in the workplace. The author discusses steps employers can take to prevent and/or limit racial incidents, starting with eliminating discrimination in the hiring process.

Stanfield, Rochelle. "The New Faces of Hate." *National Journal*, June 18, 1994, pp. 1460–63. An article discussing modern forms of bigotry and intolerance, affecting a wide spectrum of minorities and as practiced by a variety of citizens and religious groups.

Steyn, Mark. "Vandals in the Churchyard." *The American Spectator*, vol. 33, number 4, May 2000, pp. 52–54. The author believes that hate crimes against religions, including Christianity and Catholicism, are seldom reported, and describes attacks on a dozen Brooklyn Catholic churches and an Episcopal church. The author asserts that false reports of church burnings were exploited by a news media interested in playing up racial hatred, while the recent and genuine attacks only demonstrate antireligious hatred, in which the media take little interest.

Torres, Sam. "Hate Crimes Against African-Americans: The Extent of the Problem." *Journal of Contemporary Criminal Justice*, vol. 15, no. 1, February 1999, pp. 48–63. An article that details the incidence of hate crimes against African Americans, using data gleaned from the FBI's Uniform Crime Reports. The author explores the possible reasons for a steady rise in hate crimes against African Americans and describes several possible methods of reducing such crime.

Turpin-Petrosian, Carolyn. "Hateful Sirens . . . Who Hears Their Song? An Examination of Student Attitudes Toward Hate Groups and Affiliation

Potential." *Journal of Social Issues*, vol. 58, no. 2, Summer 2002, pp. 281–301. From a survey of high school and university students, the author explores why young people affiliate themselves with hate groups, finding that although individuals are responsible for the majority of hate crimes, organized hate groups play an important part by attracting disaffected students and giving them a sense of belonging and an outlet for personal frustrations.

Witkin, Gordon, and Jeannye Thornton. "Pride and Prejudice." *U.S. News and World Report*, July 15, 1996, pp. 74–77. A survey of hate crimes statistics, the prevalence of juveniles in hate-crimes police reports, and the appearance of hate groups on the Internet.

Wolfe, Kathi. "Bashing the Disabled: The New Hate Crime." *The Progressive*, November 1995, pp. 24–27. An analysis of the hostility and the hate crimes being perpetrated against the disabled. The author writes that according to disability-community leaders, the backlash against the disabled is being fueled by resentment of the Americans with Disabilities Act (1990).

REPORTS

"1998–2000 Report on Hate Crimes and Discrimination Against Arab-Americans." Washington, D.C.: American-Arab Anti-Discrimination Committee, 2001. In the main, this 77-page report covers discrimination against Arab Americans in education and in employment as well as defamation, hostile public opinion, and media bias. The first section, Legal Issues, details hate crimes committed against Arab Americans.

Ferrante, J, G. Olden, R. Kapler, P. Lawrence, and L. Moran. "A Policymaker's Guide to Hate Crimes." Washington, D.C.: U.S. Department of Justice, Office of Justice Programs, 1999. Information for law enforcement and public officials on community responses to hate crimes, focusing on specific organizations and their cooperative efforts with community leaders to deal with hate-crimes issues as they develop. This report also includes a state-by-state listing of initiatives undertaken by public and nonprofit groups and the resources offered by each group. Also available online at http://www.ncjrs.org/txtfiles1/bja/162304.txt

"Hate Crime Statistics." Washington, D.C.: Federal Bureau of Investigation, annual. Available online. URL: http://www.fbi.gov/ucr/hatecrime.pdf. An annual survey of hate crimes throughout the United States, giving a detailed breakdown by type of bias motivation, race of offenders and victims, and type of incident. This report is the outcome of the original Hate Crimes Statistics Act and has become the standard source for journalists, criminologists, and academics for national hate-crimes statistics and trends.

"Hate Crimes: ADL Blueprint for Action" New York: Anti-Defamation League, 1997. Prepared for the 1997 White House Conference on Hate

Crimes, this report provides hate crimes prevention and response strategies such as penalty enhancement laws, training for law enforcement and the military, security for community institutions, and community antibias awareness initiatives. The ADL report also provides year-by-year information from the *ADL Audit of Anti-Semitic Incidents*, ADL resources on hate violence counteraction, and state hate crime statutory provisions.

"Hate Motivated Crime and Violence: Information for Schools, Communities, and Families." Washington, D.C.: National Education Association, 1997. Recommendations by the NEA to combat hate crimes in schools, including a general procedure to be followed when hate crime incidents occur, strategies for prevention and suppression of hate crimes, recommendations for new curriculum topics, and a sample hate-crimes survey for use in affected schools.

"High Tech Hate: Extremist Use of the Internet." New York: Anti-Defamation League, 1997. A report describing the proliferation of racist and hate groups on the Internet, the methods used to bring their message to a wider public, and the role of such sites in encouraging incidents of hate crime.

Joge, Carmen T. "The Mainstreaming of Hate: A Report on Latinos and Harassment, Hate Violence, and Law Enforcement Abuse in the '90s." Washington, D.C.: National Council of La Raza, 1999. A report on hate crimes, church burnings, and police abuse directed against the Hispanic population in the United States.

WEB DOCUMENTS

American Psychological Association. "Hate Crimes Today: An Age-Old Foe in Modern Dress" Part of the series entitled Clarifying the Debate: Psychology Examines the Issues. Available online. URL: http://www/apa.org/pubinfo/hate. Downloaded on February 7, 2003. A study of the hate-crimes phenomenon through psychological analysis. The paper offers an overview of the topic, hate-crime statistics, trends in hate crime in the 1990s, the question of the effect of economic and social conditions on the phenomenon, and general profiles of hate-crime offenders that serve to create a general theory of their motivation.

Anti-Defamation League. "Audit of Anti-Semitic Incidents." Available online. URL: http://www.adl.org/1999_Audit/Executive_Summary.asp. Downloaded on February 7, 2003. A survey of anti-Semitic violence and incidents, published annually since 1979, and currently including a count of harassment and assault, campus incidents, vandalism, a regional breakdown, charts and graphs, and a summary of federal law and initiatives dealing with anti-Semitic hate crime. The audit represents a primary resource for those monitoring trends in anti-Semitism in the United States.

———. "Hate Crime Laws." Available online. URL: http://www.adl.org/ 99hatecrime/intro.asp. Downloaded on February 7, 2003. A comprehensive series of pages on hate-crimes legislation written for a general audience, including current status of federal legislation, hate crimes laws state by state, the test of the ADL's model legislation, and position statements on constitutionality and effectiveness of various forms of hate-crime legislation.

———. "A Parent's Guide to Hate on the Internet." Available online. URL: http://www.adl.org/issue_education/parents_guide_hate_net.asp. Downloaded on February 7, 2003. This report describes the various ways young Internet users can be confronted with racism and antireligious bigotry online and offers strategies for parents dealing with the phenomenon.

"Hate Crimes" (Special Reports). WashingtonPost.com. Available online. URL: http://www.washingtonpost.com/wp.dyn/nation/specials/ socialpolicy/hatecrimes. Downloaded on February 7, 2003. Site published by the *Washington Post*, providing links to the newspaper's articles on hate crime, as well as information resources. The site also groups articles dedicated to prominent hate-crime topics, including the cases of murder victims Matthew Shepard and James Byrd, Jr., and shootings at the Los Angeles Jewish Community Center.

U.S. Department of Education. "Preventing Youth Hate Crime." Available online. URL: http://www.ed.gov/pubs/HateCrime/start.html. Downloaded on February 7, 2003. A brochure prepared to assist schools in confronting and eliminating bias-motivated harassment, violence, and intimidation. The document reviews the applicable federal laws; gives examples of effective school- and community-based programs; and includes classroom activities, useful organizations, and a bibliography.

U.S. Department of Education. "Protecting Students from Harassment and Hate Crime: A Guide for Schools." Available online. URL: http:// usinfo.state.gov/usa/race/hate/homepage.htm. Downloaded on February 7, 2003. A publication prepared for use by public schools, giving the DOE's approach to the hate crime issue and guidance on writing and implementing policies on bias-motivated incidents. The document includes formal complaint/grievance procedures, suggestions on developing a written antiharassment policy, samples of school policies, reference materials, sources of technical assistance, and a bibliography.

VIDEOS

Anti-Semitism on the College Campus. Anti-Defamation League, 1993. An examination of anti-Semitic incidents on campus and the reaction against such events on the part of students and educators.

Brotherhood of Hate. First Run/Icarus Films, 2000. Directed by Pamela Yates. A video describing the Kehoe family of Coleville, Washington, and Chevie Kehoe, a white supremacist who aspired to build a whites-only settlement in the Pacific Northwest. During a nationwide rampage of theft and murder, Kehoe committed a triple homicide outside of rural Russellville, Arkansas. The video follows the investigation of the murder and the trail followed by Deputy Sheriff Aaron Duvall across the country to an isolated pocket of virulent anti-Semitism and racial prejudice.

Crimes of Hate. Anti-Defamation League, 1998. A documentary overview of the phenomenon of hate crimes, divided into segments on racism, anti-Semitism, and gay bashing, and the methods used to combat them by law enforcement and other public officials.

Learning to Hate. Anti-Defamation League, 1997. The origins of bigotry in childhood experiences within the family as well as the surrounding cultural environment, which sometimes breeds mistrust and fear of outsiders and those who look, sound, and act different. The film compares and contrasts anti-Semitic and antigay discrimination in several locales.

Natives: Immigrant Bashing on the Border. Filmmakers Library, 1993. A documentary look at white/Hispanic conflict and American xenophobia along California's Mexican border, the problems of illegal immigration and undocumented aliens, and a sometimes violent clash of cultures. Shot in black and white, the film follows the activities of groups organized to combat illegal aliens and draws a sharp contrast between support of liberty and the often antidemocratic values espoused for illegal aliens.

Not in Our Town. The Working Group, 1995. A documentary shot in Billings, Montana, during a wave of violence directed against Jews, blacks, and Native Americans, and the efforts of local citizens to combat the hate-crime wave. A follow-up video, *Not in Our Town II*, was produced in 1996, revisiting Billings to examine the effects of the earlier conflicts and to survey reaction against bias-motivated violence in other communities.

Who Killed Vincent Chin? Filmakers Library, 1990. A study of the killing of a young Chinese American and the anti-Asian prejudice that inspired this hate crime.

MODERN RACIST AND HATE GROUPS

BOOKS

Alibrandi, Tom, and Bill Wassmuth. *Hate Is My Neighbor.* Boise: University of Idaho Press, 2002. A book describing the often violent combat between the white supremacist group Aryan Nations and its opponents in the Coeur d'Alene region of northern Idaho.

Barkun, Michael. *Religion and the Racist Right: The Origins of the Christian Identity Movement.* Chapel Hill: University of North Carolina Press, 1994. A political science professor at Syracuse University, Barkun examines the roots and beliefs of the Christian Identity movement, an anti-Semitic, white supremacist ideology that holds that whites are the descendants of the biblical Israelites, that Jews are the descendants of Satan, and that the world is about to experience an apocalyptic battle between Aryans and Jews.

Blee, Kathleen M. *Inside Organized Racism: Women in the Hate Movement.* Berkeley: University of California Press, 2002. The author interviews women in skinhead, Ku Klux Klan, neo-Nazi, Christian Identity, and anti-Semitic groups to discover their backgrounds and motivations. Through these interviews and brief life histories, the book reveals certain common threads running through female members of American hate groups and then offers five suggestions for confronting and dealing with their point of view.

Daniels, Jessie. *White Lies: Race, Class, Gender & Sexuality in White Supremacist Discourse.* New York: Routledge, 1996. The author analyzes several hundred white supremacist books and publications and theorizes that white supremacist thinking lies uncomfortably close to historic (and contemporary) core values of American society.

Dees, Morris, and Steve Fiffer. *Hate on Trial: The Case Against America's Most Dangerous Neo-Nazi.* New York: Villard Books, 1993. A description of the trial of Tom Metzger and his followers for conspiracy in the murder of an Ethiopian student in Portland, Oregon, written by the Southern Poverty Law Center attorney who brought the civil suit against Metzger and his organization, White Aryan Resistance.

Dinnerstein, Leonard. *Anti-Semitism in America.* New York: Oxford University Press, 1994. A scholarly history of American anti-Semitism, from the colonial era to the late 20th century. The author relates the most virulent periods of anti-Semitism to times of economic or social stress, particularly wartime, and traces the history—in some cases back to medieval Europe—of various conspiracy theories surrounding the Jews.

Dobratz, Betty A., and Stephanie L. Shanks-Meile. *The White Separatist Movement in the United States: White Power, White Pride.* Baltimore, Md.: Johns Hopkins University Press, 2000. Through interviewing more than 100 members of white separatist groups, and doing extensive field research on the phenomenon, the authors explore the nature of white power groups and white separatism in an attempt to set aside the preconception that the members of such groups come from a single stratum of American society.

Ezekial, Raphael. *The Racist Mind: Portraits of American Neo-Nazis and Klansmen*. New York: Penguin, 1996. The author attends rallies of the Ku Klux Klan and Aryan Nations, interviews leaders and members of racist groups, and explores the family and social backgrounds of the joiners.

Flynn, Kevin, and Gary Gerhardt. *The Silent Brotherhood: Inside America's Racist Underground*. New York: Free Press, 1989. A book describing the violent white supremacist group known as the Order, implicated in armed robberies as well as notorious hate crimes and race murders. The Order's ultimate goals, according to the authors and the Order's own writings, were to save the white race from a conspiracy to destroy it and to establish a white homeland in the mountains of the West. The book culminates with the showdown between federal authorities and Robert Matthews, the founder of the group.

Kaplan, Jeffrey, ed. *Encyclopedia of White Power: A Sourcebook on the Radical Racist Right*. Walnut Creek, Calif.: Altamira Press, 2000. Within more than 100 entries, contributors aspire to an unbiased and comprehensive description of racist groups and movements in Europe and the United States, breaking them down into eight major categories. Many of the contributors are former members of these organizations, and the book includes quotations of primary source documents, cross-references, and useful bibliographies.

Lee, Martin A. *The Beast Reawakens: Fascism's Resurgence from Hitler's Spymasters to Today's Neo-Nazi Groups and Right-Wing Extremists*. New York: Routledge, 1999. The author describes how fascism survived its defeat in World War II and how right-wing nationalist movements that emerged after the fall of communism in the 1990s brought about a fascist revival in Germany and eastern Europe. The book draws parallels between these movements and the militia and white power groups that have developed in the United States, finding a common thread of philosophy and hate-motivated violence among far-right groups on two continents.

Martinez, Thomas, with John Guinther. *Brotherhood of Murder*. New York: McGraw-Hill, 1988. An insider's close look at his own background as a racist and his association with the Order, a violent white supremacist group. After changing his ways, the author helped the FBI track Robert Matthews, the leader of the Order, who was betrayed by other members and killed in a fiery shootout with the authorities.

Novick, M. *White Lies, White Power: The Fight Against White Supremacy and Reactionary Violence*. Monroe, Mo.: Common Courage Press, 1995. A book detailing the sources of racism in the policies followed by mainstream political and economic institutions. The author maintains that the Ku Klux Klan and other white power groups are the product of

Annotated Bibliography

values that originated with the colonization of North America by European nations.

Phillips, John W. *Sign of the Cross: The Prosecutor's True Story of a Landmark Trial Against the Klan.* Louisville, Ky.: Westminster John Knox Press, 2000. Prosecutor Phillips recounts a long struggle conducted by his office and law enforcement against activities of the Ku Klux Klan in southern California.

Ridgeway, James. *Blood in the Face: The Ku Klux Klan, Aryan Nations, Nazi Skinheads, and the Rise of a New White Culture.* New York: Thunder's Mouth Press, 1995. A study of the rise of white supremacist movements and groups, updated to include the Oklahoma City bombing and the militia movement of the mid-1990s and their connection to such groups.

Schwartz, A. M., ed. *Danger: Extremism—The Major Vehicles and Voices on America's Far-Right Fringe.* New York: Anti-Defamation League of B'nai B'rith, 1996. A book that describes the radical right and extremist political rhetoric of the 1990s. The author describes the activities of skinheads, the Ku Klux Klan, and specific individuals such as David Duke, as well as the marketing of extremist materials on the Internet. The role of law enforcement agencies and the work of the Anti-Defamation League (ADL) in the struggle against extremism is addressed, and extremist activities of specific individuals and organizations are detailed. Appendixes contain additional information on the use of the Internet by extremists, a list of extreme right publications, and a glossary of Ku Klux Klan terminology.

Stern, K. S. *A Force Upon the Plain: The American Militia Movement and the Politics of Hate.* New York: Simon and Schuster, 1996. A noted expert on hate groups, the author explores the dimensions of the modern militia movement, interviews leading paramilitary organizers, and speculates about its influence on actions such as the bombing of the Alfred P. Murrah federal building in Oklahoma City.

Suall, Irwin. *Skinhead International: A Worldwide Survey of Neo-Nazi Skinheads.* New York: Anti-Defamation League of B'nai B'rith, 1995. A short and statistic-laden survey of the racist skinhead movement as it stood in the mid-1990s.

Weller, Worth H., and Brad Thompson. *Under the Hood: Unmasking the Modern Ku Klux Klan.* North Manchester, Ind.: DeWitt Books, 1998. A journalist's account of the rise of the American Knights of the Ku Klux Klan, an organization that flourished in Indiana in the late 1990s.

PERIODICALS

Blazak, Randy. "White Boys to Terrorist Men: Target Recruitment of Nazi Skinheads." *American Behavioral Scientist.* vol. 44, no. 6, 2001, pp. 982–1000.

169

The article states that hate group activity is increasing in the United States, even though the rate of hate crimes may be on the decline, and describes the increased recruitment of skinheads among disaffected juveniles through hate group web sites.

Clarke, Floyd. "Hate Violence in the United States." *FBI Law Enforcement Bulletin*, vol. 60, no. 1, January 1991, pp. 11–18. The author gives a general background on the ideology and modern methods of hate groups and explains the FBI's programs against hate crimes, including the FBI Civil Rights Program and the Domestic Counter-Terrorism Program.

Cloud, John. "Is Hate on the Rise?" *Time*, July 19, 1999, p. 33. Article describing the fear of many law enforcement agencies that hate-motivated violence is on the rise, in part because these groups are using powerful new tools like the Internet and the art of media management to attract a new breed of racist.

Green, D. P., and A. Rich. "White Supremacist Activity and Crossburnings in North Carolina." *Journal of Quantitative Criminology*, vol. 14, no. 3, September 1998, pp. 263–82. The author examines cross burning in North Carolina with respect to whether it increases in areas where white supremacist organizations such as the Christian Knights of the Ku Klux Klan have held rallies or demonstrations. The data, taken from Klanwatch and North Carolinians Against Racial and Religious Violence, covered cross burnings and white supremacist activities in 100 North Carolina counties annually from 1987 through 1993. It was found that none of the suspected cross burners had apparent ties to white supremacist groups. The author concludes that such white supremacist rallies encourage fellow travelers to engage in this form of racial intimidation.

Henry, Sarah. "Marketing Hate." *Los Angeles Times Magazine*, December 12, 1993, p. 18. An exposé of the recruiting practices and dogma of the Church of the Creator, an avowedly racist institution that has, in the author's opinion, inspired a wave of hate crimes.

Janofsky, Michael. "Review at Fort Bragg Finds Few Supremacists." *New York Times*, December 13, 1995, p. B12. After bias-motivated crimes were committed at the large North Carolina military base, the U.S. Army conducted a review and investigation and concluded that the base was not experiencing an upsurge in white supremacist or neo-Nazi activity.

Jasper, William F. "The Rise of the Citizen Militias." *The New American*, February 6, 1995, pp. 4–29. The author defends militias and their members, maintaining that such organizations do not promote violence or racism but instead are an understandable response to an increasingly oppressive federal government.

Annotated Bibliography

Langer, Elinor. "The American Neo-Nazi Movement Today." *The Nation*, July 16/23, 1990, pp. 82–108. At the time of writing, this article provided a thorough and detailed description of the neo-Nazi movement, giving names and backgrounds of the leaders and their recent activities.

Loggins, K., and S. Thomas. "Menace Returns: Mark of the Beast." *Southern Exposure*, vol. 8, no. 2, summer 1980, pp. 2–6. The authors describe the resurgent Ku Klux Klan of the late 1970s, when Klan membership and Klan-related violence rose sharply after a long period of dormancy. A new and more media-savvy version of the Klan was led by leaders expert at generating publicity and manipulating the media in promoting the Klan as a family-oriented, civil rights organization committed to justice for whites.

Mullins, W. C. "Hate Crime and the Far Right: Unconventional Terrorism." In *Political Crime in Contemporary America: A Critical Approach*, Kenneth D. Tunnell, ed., New York: Garland Publishing, 1993, pp. 121–69. The author examines hate crimes with respect to the government's response, the nature and methods of hate organizations, and the recruitment of youth by these organizations. The author describes domestic terrorism as originating in far-right movements, in contrast to international terrorism, which he sees as predominantly left-wing in origin. The chapter covers the Aryan Nations; the Christian Defense League; the Christian Patriots Defense League; The Covenant, the Sword, and the Arm of the Lord; the Ku Klux Klan; the National Socialist Liberation Front; the National Socialist Party of America/American Nazi Party; the New Order/National Socialist White People's Party; the Order; Posse Comitatus; and Skinheads.

Van Biema, David. "When White Makes Right." *Time*, August 9, 1993, pp. 40–43. An in-depth story on the skinhead phenomenon, giving the background of these groups and detailing the miscellaneous assaults and vandalism they carry out.

Wood, Christopher. "Crimes of Hate: Murder Charges Revive the B.C. Racism Debate." *Maclean's*, May 4, 1998, pp. 26–27. This article covers the murder of the Guru Nanak Sikh temple employee Nirmal Singh Gill in British Columbia. All four men accused of the crime were active in local white power groups and had connections with the Heritage Front, Aryan Nations, and a militantly racist skinhead organization known as the Northern Hammerskins. The writer discusses the growth of racial hatred in the province and efforts being made to combat it.

Ziady, Helen. "Women in Hate Groups." *Ms.*, March/April 1991, pp. 20–28. Article discussing the participation of women in neo-Nazi, white supremacist, and other assorted hate groups.

REPORTS

Bond, Julian, and Morris Dees. "The Ku Klux Klan: A History of Racism and Violence, Special Report, Fourth Edition." Montgomery, Ala.: Southern Poverty Law Center, 1991. A report on the history of the Klan, the motivations of its members, the characteristics of its victims, media treatment of the Klan, the white supremacist movement, and current Klan and hate group activities. The authors describe efforts by the SPLC and other organizations to combat the Klan in the courts.

Bullard, S., ed. *Ku Klux Klan: A History of Racism and Violence*, 3rd ed. Montgomery, Ala.: Southern Poverty Law Center, 1988. This 60-page report traces the history of the Ku Klux Klan and updates the activities of the Klan and other white supremacist groups. Articles in the report examine the development of bigotry in children and adolescents, study how state and local governments have enacted legislation to prevent Ku Klux Klan and white supremacist violence, and focus on how those in the Klan and the white supremacist movement have used the techniques of confrontation, consensus building, and media manipulation to achieve their goals. Violence by white supremacists against gays is identified as a new variety of hate crime.

"Final Report." Sacramento, Calif.: California Governor's Advisory Panel on Hate Groups, 2000. A report on the activities of California hate groups during the 1990s, giving findings and recommendations in the areas of existing legislation, law enforcement, education, Internet activity, and the actions of public interest and community groups.

"Hate Groups in America: A Record of Bigotry and Violence." Anti-Defamation League of B'nai B'rith, 1988. A report detailing the history, activities, ideology, and strategies used by the Ku Klux Klan, neo-Nazi groups, the Identity Church movement, and other hate groups in the United States. The report also examines the training methods of these groups, extremist activity in prisons, and methods by which law enforcement, government, the courts, the media, the schools, the armed forces, churches, business, organized labor, and human rights organizations can counter extremism.

"Hate Violence and White Supremacy: A Decade Review, 1980–1990." Montgomery, Ala.: Southern Poverty Law Center, 1999. A nationwide overview of racial violence committed during the 1980s by white supremacist groups.

"Intelligence Report." Montgomery, Ala.: Southern Poverty Law Center, annual. This report covers the subject of hate crimes, hate groups, and the activities of racist and white power groups such as the Ku Klux Klan, as monitored by the organization known as Klanwatch.

Annotated Bibliography

Pantell, L. "Pathfinder on Bias Crimes and the Fight Against Hate Groups." *Legal Reference Services Quarterly*, vol. 11, no. 1, 1991, pp. 39–75. This annotated bibliography presents the user with the burgeoning literature about hate groups and their activities and lists the tools that are available to combat bias crimes. The literature is presented under the following topic areas: hate groups; spreading the message—the voice of hate groups; understanding the motivation for hate crimes; fighting bias crimes; censoring hateful speech—the First Amendment barrier; and research strategy. Each of these broad topic areas is further divided into subtopics. The sources within each subtopic are arranged by type, for example, reports or law review articles. Where appropriate, the sources are listed in order of recommendation within each type of source. There are approximately 200 entries, and most of the publications were published from 1980 through 1990. The bibliography includes an appended map of the location of various hate groups in the United States and a list of the names, leaders, and their addresses for the branches or chapters of various hate groups.

"Poisoning the Web: Hatred Online." New York: Anti-Defamation League of B'nai B'rith, 1999. Available online. URL: http://www.adl.org/poisoning_web/poisoning_toc.asp. A review of right-extremist groups on the Internet, usefully divided into pages on individual organizations, their agendas and philosophies, and their activities; includes the National Alliance, the Ku Klux Klan, neo-Nazi groups, the Christian Identity movement, Holocaust deniers, militias, and patriot groups.

Suall, I. "The Skinhead International: A Worldwide Survey of Neo-Nazi Skinheads." New York: Anti-Defamation League of B'nai B'rith, 1995. Findings of an 18-month survey of the skinhead movement, detailing the structure of an international, 33-country cooperative movement among skinhead groups and drawing conclusions about the ultimate goals of the movement.

"Young and Violent: The Growing Menace of America's Neo-Nazi Skinheads." New York: Anti-Defamation League of B'nai B'rith, 1988. A report that describes the increase in ranks of neo-Nazi skinheads in the United States in 1987 and 1988, which was paralleled by an increase in violent bias-motivated crimes including two homicides; numerous shootings, beatings, and stabbings, mostly directed against minority group members; and vandalism of synagogues and other Jewish institutions. The report finds that neo-Nazi skinheads have close associations with old-line hate groups in the United States and have helped boost the morale and activity level of other white supremacist organizations, including the Ku Klux Klan (KKK) and White Aryan Resistance (WAR).

"Young Nazi Killers: The Rising Skinhead Danger." New York: Anti-Defamation League of B'nai B'rith, 1993. A report on the skinhead movement discussing the organization and operation of neo-Nazi groups and offering recommendations to educators and law enforcement officials for preventing bias-motivated violence.

VIDEOS

Beyond Hate. Washington, D.C.: Public Broadcasting System, 1998. Hosted by Bill Moyers, this video deals with the historical roots of bigotry and extremism and current activities of hate groups. Interviews with neo-Nazis, hate-crime victims and activists, and prominent political leaders such as Jimmy Carter and Vaclav Havel.

Forgotten Fires. Produced by Michael Chandler and Vivian Kleiman. Written and directed by Michael Chandler. University of California Extension Center for Media and Independent Learning, 1998. A documentary about arson committed in 1995 by members of the Ku Klux Klan against two black churches in rural South Carolina.

Hate Crimes. New York: Anti-Defamation League, 1996. A look at hate crimes perpetrated in the name of white supremacy, tracing the activities of the Ku Klux Klan and other groups and presenting interviews with victims as well as perpetrators.

Hate.com: Extremists on the Internet. HBO Films/Southern Poverty Law Center, 2000. A documentary covering extremist groups on the Internet, including the World Church of the Creator, Aryan Nations, Christian Identity, and the National Alliance; as well as profiles of "lone wolves," or individuals who commit violence based on ethnic or religious prejudice. Narrated by Morris Dees.

KKK—Hate Crime in America. American Justice series, A & E Entertainment, 1993. Documentary on the current Ku Klux Klan, its members and activities, and its fragmentation into several rival subgroups that spend as much time infighting as in pursuing the traditional Klan agendas.

Ku Klux Klan: The Invisible Empire. CBS Reports, 1965. A film produced during the turbulent 1960s, when the Civil Rights movement was inspiring a backlash in the form of antiblack violence, much of which was perpetrated by members of the revived Ku Klux Klan. The film includes footage detailing the revival of the Klan early in the 20th century as well as clips from *Birth of a Nation*, the silent film that portrayed the Klan as a protector of traditional white culture and morality.

WEB SITES

Education and Vigilance Network. URL: http://www.evnetwork.net. A site that provides information on racist and neo-Nazi groups, with special emphasis on such groups operating in Pennsylvania and the Northeast.

Hate Crime Network. URL: http://www.hate-crime.website-works.com. Formerly the Hate Crimes Documentation Network, this web site was created by hate-crime victim advocates to allow survivors of bias crimes, who may fear reporting these incidents to the police or the media, an alternative means of reporting their experiences and gaining any assistance they may need. The site offers a discussion forum as well as an archive of current news and events surrounding the issue of hate crimes.

The Hate Directory. URL: www.bcpl.net/~rfrankli/hatedir.htm. Compiled by Raymond Franklin and updated on July 1, 2002, the web site includes a listing of Internet sites of individuals and groups that, in the opinion of the author, advocate violence to others based upon race, religion, ethnicity, gender, or sexual orientation. The organizations are listed with their name, URL, and category devised by the author, including Holocaust Revisionism, Anti-Gay, Anti-Semitic, and so on.

National Coalition of Anti-Violence Programs. URL: http://www.avp.org/ncavp.htm. Formed in 1995, this group represents more than 20 local gay and bisexual agencies, focusing in particular on antiviolence programs throughout the United States and providing contact information for each of the programs. The member agencies focus on domestic violence as well as antigay bias violence.

Stop the Hate. URL: http://www.stop-the-hate.org. Provides resources and links to hate-crime and hate-group-related sites, including neo-Nazi and nationalist hate groups, the Ku Klux Klan, religion-based hate groups, and militia groups. There is also a comprehensive listing of anti-hate resources and support.

HISTORY OF HATE VIOLENCE

BOOKS

Chalmers, David. *Hooded Americanism: The History of the Ku Klux Klan.* Durham, N.C.: Duke University Press, 1987. A comprehensive and detailed history of the Klan from its inception through its expansion in the early decades of the 20th century and its more recent incarnations. Making full use of newspaper and other contemporary accounts, the author details how the Klan moved outside of its regional home in the South to other sections of the country. It also describes the legislative reaction against the Klan in the form of antimask and antilynching laws, precursors to modern hate-crime statutes targeting bias crimes and racial violence.

Ferrell, Claudine L. *Nightmare and Dream: Anti-Lynching in Congress, 1917–1922.* New York: Garland, 1986. A scholarly study of congressional debate and federal measures taken to combat lynching in the turbulent years following World War I.

Kennedy, Stetson. *The Klan Unmasked*. Boca Raton, Fla.: Atlantic University Press, 1990. The author describes his infiltration of the Ku Klux Klan in the 1940s and 1950s and his experiences as an accepted member of the group.

Lutz, Chris. *They Don't All Wear Sheets: A Chronology of Racist and Far Right Violence, 1980–1986*. Atlanta, Ga.: Center for Democratic Renewal, 1987. A short, straightforward, and selective listing of bias incidents through the early 1980s, divided first among states and then chronologically.

MacLean, Nancy. *Behind the Mask of Chivalry: The Making of the Second Ku Klux Klan*. New York: Oxford University Press, 1994. A description of the revived Ku Klux Klan of the 1920s, when the organization expanded out of the South and took advantage of a nationwide animosity toward unassimilated immigrant groups and African Americans, as well as of middle-class fears of the disruptions that came with Prohibition, labor trouble, a call for women's rights, and the loss of prewar comforts and certainties. The author claims that crusades over morals have served the Klan's larger agenda of virulent racial hatred. Comparing the Klan to European fascist movements that grew out of World War I, the book maintains that the Klan's rise was a reaction to African Americans, immigrants, Jews, Catholics, labor, and white women and youth who challenged traditional institutions and did not obey the Klan's rules of conduct.

Madigan, Tim. *The Burning: Massacre, Destruction, and the Tulsa Race Riot of 1921*. New York: St. Martin's Press, 2001. An account of the burning of the Greenwood neighborhood of Tulsa, in which hundreds of African-American residents were murdered by white mobs enraged by a black man's accidental bumping into a white woman. The author conveys a pervasive atmosphere of suspicion and racial hatred and relates many carefully researched stories of individuals involved in the bloody events.

Moore, Jack B. *Skinheads Shaved for Battle: A Cultural History of American Skinheads*. Bowling Green, Ohio: Bowling Green State University Popular Press, 1993. An exploration of the skinhead phenomenon as it arose among the working class in Great Britain and as it was exported to the United States during the 1970s and 1980s, when it was diverted into a neo-Nazi and racist subculture.

Nelson, Jack. *Terror in the Night: The Klan's Campaign Against the Jews*. Jackson: University of Mississippi Press, 1996. An account of a Klan assault against several small Jewish communities in Mississippi during the 1960s, undertaken in reprisal for Jewish support of civil rights workers and overshadowed by the turmoil over desegregation then taking place in the Deep South.

Newton, Michael, and Judy Ann Newton. *Racial and Religious Violence in America: A Chronology*. New York: Garland, 1991. A comprehensive 728-

page timeline of more than 8,000 hate crimes and bias-related incidents in the United States, dating from the European discovery of the New World in the 16th century. The book is particularly useful for scholars of the civil rights era of the 1950s and 1960s, as it covers not only hate crimes but also hundreds of lesser-known incidents of riot and mayhem that manifested the racial malaise of the time.

Newton, Michael, and Judy Newton, eds. *Ku Klux Klan: An Encyclopedia.* New York: Garland, 1991. A reference work of some 8,000 entries on the Ku Klux Klan. The author includes both pro- and anti-Klan organizations, victims and opponents of the Klan, and entries for states and nations that have Klan groups and Klan-related activities. The work spans the Klan's prehistory in the American colonial era and continues up to the current Klan organization and its various subgroups and activities.

Quarles, Chester L. *The Ku Klux Klan and Related American Racialist and Antisemitic Organizations: A History and Analysis.* Jefferson, N.C.: McFarland and Company, 1999. The author traces the complete history of the Ku Klux Klan, including the organization's predecessors in the 18th and early 19th centuries. The book describes how the group is organized, who joins it, what it hopes to achieve, and what its ideology has been over the many years of its existence. Quarles reveals the changeable nature of the organization and its varying modern manifestations, from benign social gathering to violent, revolutionary hate group.

Ruiz, J. *Black Hood of the Ku Klux Klan.* Bethesda, Md.: Austin and Winfield, 1998. This book chronicles the 1922 murder of two white men by the Ku Klux Klan. Klan violence against whites, particularly respected members of their communities, was virtually unknown until 1922. In the summer of that year, two white men in Morehouse Parish, Louisiana, were kidnapped by the Klan, tortured and murdered. Autopsies of the bodies revealed they had been extensively mutilated. The book presents a detailed examination of the investigation that followed the murders and develops a picture of the Klan's grip on the South of the time, a society muted by fear and intimidation. The book includes a historical profile of northeastern Louisiana; an introduction to the Ku Klux Klan; a description of the social setting and other events in the South in the summer and fall of 1922; the search and subsequent discovery of the two bodies; the open hearing and its aftermath; and an account of the present-day Klan in Louisiana.

Stanton, Bill. *Klanwatch: Bringing the Ku Klux Klan to Justice.* New York: Samuel Weidenfeld, 1991. The author, a hate-crimes investigator, describes the efforts of the organization Klanwatch and attorney Morris Dees to prosecute crimes committed by members of the Klan during the organization's resurgence in Alabama during the 1970s and 1980s.

Swinney, Everette. *Suppressing the Ku Klux Klan: The Enforcement of the Reconstruction Amendments, 1870–1877*. New York: Garland, 1987. A book describing the original civil rights laws written to combat Klan violence in the wake of the Civil War, and often cited by scholars of modern hate-crimes lawmaking and litigation.

Tucker, R. K. *Dragon and the Cross: The Rise and Fall of the Ku Klux Klan in Middle America*. Hamden, Conn.: Shoe String Press, 1991. The writer gives an overview of the powerful Klan movement of the 1920s, which is described as a mix of 19th century nativism, provincial Puritanism, and frontier vigilante tradition that was fueled by a nationalist fever left over from World War I. The author details the establishment, operation, and legislative and political influence of the Ku Klux Klan in Indiana, concluding with a 1925 murder case in which a Klan Grand Dragon enticed a young woman to his mansion, where he raped and brutalized her. The perpetrator was convicted of murder and sentenced to life in prison; the case did permanent damage to the Klan among the large percentage of its members who considered themselves members of the respectable middle class.

Wade, Wyn Craig. *The Fiery Cross: The Ku Klux Klan in America*. New York: Simon and Schuster, 1987. A complete history of the Ku Klux Klan from its beginnings in Pulaski, Tennessee, through its 1920s resurgence and its modern incarnations in response to the Civil Rights movement of the 1960s. The author also describes the links between the Klan and white supremacist and neo-Nazi organizations in the West and Northwest.

Walker, Samuel. *Hate Speech: The History of an American Controversy*. Lincoln: University of Nebraska Press, 1994. The author reviews the history of racist and bigoted expression and symbols in the United States and analyzes legal challenges to and limits on the First Amendment protection of free speech.

Whitfield, Stephen. *A Death in the Delta: The Story of Emmett Till*. New York: Free Press, 1988. A detailed book on the murder of Emmett Till, a black teenager lynched in Mississippi in 1955 whose death gave vital impetus to the Civil Rights movement.

LEGAL AND CONSTITUTIONAL ASPECTS OF HATE-CRIME LEGISLATION

BOOKS

Bell, Derrick A. *Race, Racism, and American Law*. 4th ed. New York: Aspen Publishers, 2000. The originator of critical race theory prepared this extensive casebook and study of race and the American legal system for use by law professors and students. The fourth edition includes expanded coverage of Latino and Asian minorities and the law, a discussion of the high percentage of blacks and Hispanics in American prisons, and an examination of the media's role in current race issues.

Cleary, Edward J. *Beyond the Burning Cross: The First Amendment and the Landmark R.A.V. Case.* New York: Random House, 1994. An analysis of the Supreme Court's *R.A.V. v. St. Paul* decision, written by the lawyer who took the case for the original defendant, Robert Viktora, and who argued, successfully, that the St. Paul city ordinance under which Viktora was prosecuted was unconstitutional.

Hentoff, Nat. *Free Speech for Me—But Not for Thee: How the American Left and Right Relentlessly Censor Each Other.* New York: HarperCollins, 1992. A description of efforts to intimidate, censor, ban, and criminalize thought and opinion on both sides of the political spectrum, and a critique of laws targeting hate speech and hate crimes.

Jacobs, James, and Kimberly Potter. *Hate Crimes: Criminal Law & Identity Politics.* New York: Oxford University Press, 1998. A New York law professor argues against hate-crime legislation, suggesting that as written, hate-crimes laws violate the First Amendment protection of free speech.

Jenness, Valerie. *Making Hate a Crime: From Social Movement to Law Enforcement.* New York: Russell Sage Foundation, 2001. The author focuses on the concept of hate crime and how this relatively new legal category, a redefining of violence motivated by innate human prejudices, has emerged in the United States over the past two decades. The author speculates on the origins of this category in social movements, in modern political debate, and in the American system of lawmaking and the criminal justice system.

Jenness, Valerie, and Kendal Broad. *Hate Crimes: New Social Movements and the Politics of Violence.* New York: Aldine de Gruyter, 1997. Discusses the rise of hate-crimes laws and the more general issue of identity politics in the 1990s, and how social movements give rise to new categories and new definitions of age-old human actions. The author explores the question of why bias-motivated crimes against certain groups have been classified as hate crimes, while similarly motivated crimes against other groups have not.

Lawrence, Frederick M. *Punishing Hate: Bias Crimes Under American Law.* Cambridge, Mass.: Harvard University Press, 1999. The author argues strongly for hate-crimes laws and provides his own model of such a law that he believes would pass constitutional muster. The author also opines that hate crimes are in fact a growing problem in the United States that should be dealt with by law enforcement at the federal level.

Matsuda, Mari J., Charles R. Lawrence, and Richard Delgado. *Words that Wound: Critical Race Theory, Assaultive Speech, and the First Amendment.*

Denver, Colo.: Westview Press, 1993. The authors create a theory of assaultive hate speech and argue that such speech should not enjoy First Amendment protections.

Perry, Barbara. *In the Name of Hate: Understanding Hate Crimes*. New York: Routledge, 2001. The author creates a comprehensive theory of hate crimes, supports an expansion of the definition of hate crimes in the law, and argues that the hate-crime phenomenon is the result of a long history of racism within the United States.

Rauch, Jonathan. *Kindly Inquisitors: The New Attacks on Free Thought*. Chicago: University of Chicago Press, 1993. An argument for increased tolerance for diverse opinion, in which the author maintains that an increasing number of groups are calling for censorship and punishment of hurtful speech.

Waldrep, Christopher. *Racial Violence on Trial: A Handbook with Cases, Laws, and Documents*. On Trial series. Santa Barbara, Calif.: ABC-CLIO, 2001. A useful reference book detailing prominent bias-motivated crimes and the trials associated with them, offering transcripts and other primary-source documents associated with the cases, alphabetical listings of important laws, concepts, and individuals, a chronology, and an annotated bibliography.

Wang, Lu-In. *Hate Crimes Law*. Deerfield, Ill.: Clark Boardman Callaghan (annual). A reference book and legal treatise detailing federal and state hate-crimes laws, updated annually by a nationally recognized expert on the subject.

Winters, Paul A. ed. *Hate Crimes*. San Diego, Calif.: Greenhaven Press, 1996. Written for the school/library market, this book offers a useful anthology of articles from different perspectives on hate crimes and affiliated topics such as hate speech, anti-Semitism, and censorship.

PERIODICALS

Alexander, Larry. "ADL Hate Crime Statute and the First Amendment." *Criminal Justice Ethics*, vol. 11, no. 2, Summer/Fall 1992, pp. 49–51. This article reviews the theories of one scholar on the ADL model hate-crime statute and the First Amendment. The article cites a scholar who questions why an assault or other similar crime is more serious when it is committed with a bigoted motive. The article concludes that the greater power to punish conduct does not include the lesser power to punish it more when it expresses an unwelcome message.

Anonymous. "Hate Is Not Speech: A Constitutional Defense of Penalty Enhancement for Hate Crimes." *Harvard Law Review*, vol. 106, no. 6, April 1993. A long and comprehensive editorial responding to the First

Amendment critique of hate-crimes laws, making the point that denying the constitutionality of such laws in effect will make certain criminal acts a form of protected speech.

Brown, Ralph S. "Susan Gellman Has It Right." *Criminal Justice Ethics*, vol. 11, Summer/Fall 1992, p. 46. A discussion of author Gellman's attack on hate-crimes legislation, which was then receiving wide notice among scholars, lawyers, and politicians debating the constitutionality of new laws that set enhanced penalties for bias-motivated violence.

Byers, Bryan, and Benjamin Crider. "Hate Crimes Against the Amish: A Qualitative Analysis of Bias Motivation Using Routine Activities Theory." *Deviant Behavior*, vol. 23, no. 2, March/April 2002, pp. 115–48. The article uses the narratives of eight hate-crime perpetrators to examine hate crimes committed against Amish citizens and the particular bias motivations involved in such incidents.

Byers, Bryan D., and Richard A. Zeller. "Official Hate Crime Statistics: An Examination of the 'Epidemic Hypothesis.'" *Journal of Crime & Justice*, vol. 24, no. 2, 2001, pp. 73–85. A study that examines the "epidemic hypothesis" with regard to hate crime. The author draws on data from the Uniform Crime Reports, which show a relatively steady frequency of hate crimes reported by police departments to the FBI. The author suggests that any changes from year to year may result from variations in reporting and/or measurement practices, and that the rhetoric over the hate-crime problem was not supported by statistical evidence.

Cacas, Samuel R. "Hate Crime Sentences Can Now Be Enhanced Under a New Federal Law." *Human Rights*, vol. 22, Winter, 1995, pp. 32–33. The author reviews the 1994 federal anticrime legislation that included a provision for sentence enhancement in cases of bias-motivated crimes.

Chilton, Bradley S., Gail Caputo, James Woods, and Holly Walpole. "Hate Beyond a Reasonable Doubt: Hate Crime Sentencing After *Apprendi v. N.J.*" *Corrections Compendium*, vol. 26, no. 8, August 2001, pp. 1–3, 20–21. This article presents an analysis of the Supreme Court decision in *Apprendi v. N. J.*, focusing on the implications of this decision for hate-crime legislation and for law enforcement, courts, sentencing, and corrections. The author finds that the decision will reduce the processing of hate crimes and the number of sentencing enhancements, and decrease the number of inmates and state and federal funding that flows from inmate counts. The article also predicts that thousands of appeals will be filed under the *Apprendi* doctrine in areas of hate crime.

Chorba, Christopher. "The Danger of Federalizing Hate Crimes: Congressional Misconceptions and the Unintended Consequences of the Hate Crimes Prevention Act." *Virginia Law Review*, vol. 87, no. 2, 2001, pp. 319–79. The author believes that the incidence of hate crimes is being distorted by faulty statistics, that hate-crimes laws may do more harm than good (citing the higher incidence of interracial violence committed by minority groups), and that hate crimes should not involve the federal government and federal laws.

Cockburn, Alexander. "Hate Crimes Follies." *The Nation*, May 21, 2001, p. 10. The writer discusses why he believes that hate-crimes laws are both pointless and dangerous and contends that the promotion of hate-crimes legislation wastes time that should be spent on urgent issues, including the cases of innocent people on death row.

Decter, Midge. "Crimes du Jour." *National Review*, September 13, 1999, p. 22. Article describing hate crimes as simply a new and redundant category of crime and as a notion that criminalizes thoughts and emotions. The writer also maintains that crimes considered worthy of this designation will come to be defined simply and solely as crimes committed against members of minorities.

Dority, Barbara. "The Criminalization of Hatred." *The Humanist*, May/June 1994, pp. 38–39. The writer contends that state and federal measures against hate crimes are incompatible with a free society, and reviews the fact that state hate-crimes laws are being challenged in courts on the grounds that they are vague, overbroad, discriminatory, or in conflict with the First Amendment right of free expression.

Dunbar, Edward. "Defending the Indefensible: A Critique and Analysis of Psycholegal Defense Arguments of Hate Crime Perpetrators." *Journal of Contemporary Criminal Justice*, vol. 15, no. 1, February 1999, pp. 64–77. An article concerning the strategies used by defense attorneys when handling hate-crimes cases. The author considers the validity of these strategies according to current research in psychology and behavioral science, and in more general terms how such research is used in the courtroom.

Feingold, Stanley. "Hate Crime Legislation Muzzles Free Speech." *National Law Journal*, vol. 15, no. 45, July 12, 1993, p. 15. Analyzing the case of *Wisconsin v. Mitchell*, the author argues against hate-crimes laws as a violation of the First Amendment protection of free speech.

Freeman, Steven M. "Hate Crime Laws: Punishment Which Fits the Crime." *Annual Survey of American Law*, 1992–93, pp. 581–85. A review of the ADL's efforts to create a model hate-crimes law, the Supreme Court decisions on such laws, and the author's case for hate-crimes laws to combat particularly heinous crimes.

Gellman, Susan. "Brother, You Can't Go to Jail for What You're Thinking: Motives, Effects, and Hate Crime Laws." *Criminal Justice Ethics*, vol. 11, no. 2, Summer/Fall 1992, pp. 24–29. The article considers First Amendment challenges to the ADL model hate-crimes statute and laws written according to the model. The author claims that the model statute addresses a serious problem in a way that infringes not only upon speech, but upon freedom of thought, and concludes that an "effects-based statute" serves the state's interest in punishing the special harms of bias crimes and ensures maximum protection of speech, thought, and belief.

———. "Sticks and Stones Can Put You in Jail, But Can Words Increase Your Sentence? Constitutional and Policy Dilemmas of Ethnic Intimidation Laws." *UCLA Law Review*, December 1991, pp. 333–96. A seminal and widely influential article on hate-crimes law, written after the passage of the Hate Crimes Statistics Act but before the major Supreme Court decisions regarding the constitutionality of the new laws. The author argues vigorously on constitutional grounds against creating a new class of criminal act.

Gerstenfeld, Phyllis B. "Smile When You Call Me That: The Problems with Punishing Hate-Motivated Behavior." *Behavioral Sciences and the Law*, vol. 10, no. 2, Spring 1992, pp. 259–85. The author believes that hate-crimes laws are ineffective and largely symbolic, that they muzzle free speech, that they punish motive rather than conduct, and that they actually may encourage bias-motivated violence and intensify prejudicial attitudes toward minorities.

Gondles, James A., Jr. "Hate Crime: Not New, But Still Alarming." *Corrections Today*, August 1999, p. 6. The writer discusses the hate-crime problem, arguing that although it is not new nor unique to the United States, this does not make it less of a concern to those in the corrections profession. He considers some of the findings of the FBI's most recent study on hate crimes, some federal laws that address this issue, and some of the recommendations on the topic of hate crime that have been made by the Leadership Conference on Civil Rights.

Grattet, Ryken, and Valerie Jenness. "The Criminalization of Hate: A Comparison of Structural and Political Influence on the Passage of 'Bias-Crime' Legislation in the United States." *Sociological Perspectives*, vol. 39, no. 1, pp. 129–54. Using a complete statistical analysis of hate-crimes statutes as they stood at the time of writing, this article analyzes the political and social motivation of such legislation and analyzes the reasons for the criminalization of hate as it progressed in the mid-1990s.

Grattet, Ryken, Valerie Jenness, and Theodore Curry. "The Homogenization and Differentiation of Hate Crime Law in the United States, 1978–1995: Innovation and Diffusion in the Criminalization of Bigotry." *American Sociological Review*, vol. 63, April 1998, pp. 286–307. The authors examine the process of "diffusion" of the laws and legal procedures. Hate crimes laws in the individual states, as they analyze them, have been affected by the state's particular political culture as well as by its location. At the same time, the variety of hate crime laws has lessened: The laws become more homogenized as they spread and are generally accepted as the norm.

Grigera, Elena. "Hate Crimes: State and Federal Responses to Bias-Motivated Violence." *Corrections Today*, August 1999, pp. 68–69. The writer analyzes hate-crimes legislation at both state and federal levels and discusses the need for hate-crimes legislation, looking at the diversity of approaches as each state struggles to respond effectively to hate-motivated violence.

Grigg, William Norman. "Hate Crimes." *The New American*, November 16, 1992, pp. 23–28. The author opines that the phrase "hate crimes" is used not to deter crime but to label and suppress politically unacceptable speech, and that the political establishment has an interest in hate crimes as a convenient forum to gain votes and sympathy.

Haider-Markel, Donald P. "The Politics of Social Regulatory Policy: State and Federal Hate Crime Policy and Implementation Effort." *Political Research Quarterly*, March 1998, pp. 69–88. An effort to determine the factors influencing hate crime policy and implementation efforts. The characteristics and extent of hate crime are discussed, and the author also describes hate crime policy as social regulatory policy.

"Hate Crimes: Should They Carry Enhanced Penalties?" *ABA Journal*, May 1993, pp. 44–45. A point-counterpoint piece by two noted commentators. In "Yes: Discriminatory Crimes," Nadine Strossen, an attorney and the president of the American Civil Liberties Union, argues that expression can be used as circumstantial evidence, as the Constitution does not bar the use of words to prove criminal intent; also that lawmakers have every justification to treat discriminatory criminal acts more severely than other criminal acts. In "No: Equality Among Victims," political commentator Nat Hentoff argues against hate-crimes law as an abridgement of First Amendment rights and as a precursor to the policing of thought and opinion by the state.

Hentoff, Nat. "Letting Loose the Hate-Crimes Police." *Village Voice*, July 13, 1993. The author protests that hate crimes unfairly create a special category of crime victim and will ultimately do the most damage to the civil rights of minorities.

———. "Hate Crimes: Should They Carry Enhanced Penalties?" *ABA Journal*, vol. 79, no. 45, 1993, pp. 116–21. A consideration of the penalty-enhancement provisions of new hate-crime laws.

Hernandez, T. K. "Bias Crimes: Unconscious Racism in the Prosecution of 'Racially Motivated Violence.'" In *Criminal Justice and Latino Communities*. Antoinette S. Lopez, ed. New York: Garland, 1995. This chapter analyzes hate crimes and focuses on the need for carefully drafted laws against bias-related violence at the state level. The author points out the limitations of current federal criminal and civil rights laws and believes that state criminal codes leave too much discretion to the prosecutor. As a result, the author states, bias crimes are unlikely to be prosecuted. The author proposes a model state law is one that defines a bias crime as any act or threat made due to some immutable characteristic that the victim possesses or is perceived to possess as a member of a disfavored group.

Jacobs, James B. "Should Hate Be a Crime?" *The Public Interest,* vol. 113, Fall 1993, pp. 3–14. The author argues that the notion of hate crimes is an artificial, politically motivated, and unnecessary legal construct that suffers from vagueness, from illogical and inconsistent application by prosecutors and the courts, and unconstitutionality. He also contends that writing new criminal law is not the proper means to combat social problems such as prejudice against ethnic and religious minorities.

Jacobs, James B. and Barry Eisler. "Hate Crime Statistics Act of 1990." *Criminal Law Bulletin,* March/April 1993, pp. 99–123. Detailed discussion and legal analysis of the federal act passed in 1990 mandating the collection of hate crime statistics by the Department of Justice.

Jacobs, James B., and Jessica S. Henry. "The Social Construction of a Hate Crime Epidemic." *Journal of Criminal Law and Criminology,* vol. 86, no. 2, Winter 1996, pp. 366–91. The authors investigate hate-crimes statistics as they are offered by advocacy groups such as the Southern Poverty Law Center and the Anti-Defamation League, then take issue with the notion that the United States has been going through an epidemic of hate crimes, refuting statistics and claiming that the nation is enjoying a period of heightened racial tolerance and sensitivity on race issues.

Jasket, Kristen. "Racists, Skinheads and Gay-Bashers Beware: Congress Joins the Battle Against Hate Crimes by Proposing the Hate Crimes Prevention Act of 1999." *Seton Hall Legislative Journal,* vol. 24, no. 2 (2000), pp. 509–40. The author believes that the rising rate of hate crimes warrants the inclusion of bias against sexual orientation in hate-crimes statutes, and that a more comprehensive federal law is needed to close loopholes in the existing law and supplement inadequate or nonexistent state hate-crimes laws.

Jenness, Valerie. "Managing Differences and Making Legislation: Social Movements and the Racialization, Sexualization, and Gendering of Federal Hate Crime Law in the U.S." *Social Problems,* vol. 46, no. 4, pp. 548–71. A study of the various federal hate-crimes laws passed in the 1990s and the origins of such legislation in the activities of nongovernmental organizations and interest groups.

———. "Social Movement Growth, Domain Expansion, and Framing Processes: The Gay/Lesbian Movement and Violence Against Gays and Lesbians as a Social Problem." *Social Problems,* vol. 42, 1995, p. 145. The author reiterates an important thesis of her books on the subject of hate crimes: that hate-crimes law originates with new social movements imitative of the Civil Rights movement of the 1950s and 1960s, and that the phenomenon of "domain expansion" tends to bring about new statutes that extend protection to newly defined minority groups.

Jenness, Valerie, and Ryken Grattet. "The Criminalization of Hate: A Comparison of Structural and Polity Influences on the Passage of 'Bias-Crime' Legislation in the United States." *Sociological Perspectives*, Spring 1996, pp. 129–54. The writers describe the content and distribution of hate-crimes law, and using a complete inventory of U.S. hate-crimes statutes and social indicator data, they investigate the social forces shaping the adoption of one particular form of hate-crime legislation—"bias-motivated violence and intimidation" statutes.

———. "Examining the Boundaries of Hate Crime Law: Disabilities and the 'Dilemma of Difference.'" *Journal of Criminal Law and Criminology*, vol. 91, no. 3, Spring 2001, pp. 653–97. The authors argue against new hate-crimes law to protect those with disabilities, on the grounds that creating such a protected group tends to reinforce society's negative stereotypes about such a group, making the disabled more vulnerable to discrimination.

Jones, Joyce. "The Debate over Hate." *Black Enterprise*, December 1998, p. 26. An account of the House and Senate Judiciary Committees debate over the Hate Crimes Prevention Act of 1998. According to the author, the legislation has faced resistance on both sides of the aisles for a variety of reasons: Democrats such as Representative Maxine Waters are concerned about the violation of the First Amendment, and some Republicans question the legislation's protection of sexual orientation.

Jost, Kenneth. "Hate Crimes: Are Longer Sentences for Hate Crimes Constitutional?" *CQ Researcher*, January 8, 1993, pp. 1–24. The writer offers an overview and analysis of the *R.A.V. v. St. Paul* decision reached by the Supreme Court in 1992, and a useful general discussion of the history of hate-crimes legislation.

Kleinig, John. "Penalty Enhancement for Hate Crimes—Editor's Introduction." *Criminal Justice Ethics*, vol. 11, no. 2, Summer/Fall 1992, pp. 3–6. This article examines the concept of penalty enhancement for hate crimes by reviewing a 1991 article by Susan Gellman in which she argued that penalty enhancement statutes have a chilling effect on speech, thought, and expression, and deny equal protection. She also claimed that such statutes would exact significant costs from both society as a whole and the disempowered groups they were intended to protect, and would do so without commensurate benefits.

Knoll, Erwin. "A Matter of Intent." *The Progressive*, August 1993, p. 4. The author warns against the backlash that he feels will be caused by the passage of penalty-enhancement provisions, and believes that such new laws will effectively curtail speech and harm most those groups they were intended to protect.

Lawrence, Charles R. "Crossburning and the Sound of Silence: Antisubordination Theory and the First Amendment." *Villanova Law Review*, vol. 37, no. 4 (1992), pp. 787–804. A consideration of the effect of hate-crimes laws on the free speech rights of crime victims, in which the author considers a Supreme Court opinion written by Justice Antonin Scalia and avers that hate-crimes laws undermine core values of the U.S. Constitution.

Lawrence, Frederick M. "The Punishment of Hate: Toward a Normative Theory of Bias-Motivated Crimes." *Michigan Law Review*, November 1994, pp. 320–81. The author gives the legal reasoning behind hate-crimes laws, offering his support to such measures and describing a method by which they can be made consistent and constitutional.

———. "Resolving the Hate Crimes/Hate Speech Paradox: Punishing Bias Crimes and Protecting Racist Speech." *Notre Dame Law Review*, vol. 68, no. 4, 1993, pp. 673–721. The author supports hate-crimes law, seeing in it society's greater commitment to racial harmony, and analyzes the legal distinction between hate crimes and hate speech.

Leo, John. "A Sensible Judgment on Hate." *U.S. News and World Report*, July 6, 1992, p. 25. The author editorializes in support of the Supreme Court's decision in the case of *R.A.V. v. St. Paul*, and argues that hate-crimes laws such as the St. Paul ordinance in question are an unconstitutional restriction on speech and opinion.

———. "Punishing Hate Crimes." *U.S. News & World Report*, October 26, 1998. p. 20. The writer stands against penalty-enhancement laws, arguing that such laws violate the principle of equality under the law, have no deterrent effect, and are unnecessary and arbitrary.

Levin, Brian. "A Dream Deferred: The Social and Legal Implications of Hate Crimes in the 1990s." *Journal of Intergroup Relations*, Fall 1993, pp. 3–27. The author discusses the Supreme Court's *Wisconsin v. Mitchell* decision and offers a general analysis on the phenomenon of hate crime in the contemporary United States.

———. "Bias Crimes: A Theoretical and Practical Overview." *Stanford Law and Policy Review*, vol. 4, 1992–93, pp. 165–81. The author gives a general overview of the nature of bias crimes, stating that bias crimes are more likely than other crimes to involve physical assault and they tend to be more severe than other assaults. In addition, gay men seem to be the group most often targeted for violent assault, while Jews tend to report bias crimes more often than other victimized groups. The author believes that the unprovoked nature of these attacks and the likelihood of further victimization intensifies the psychological damage inflicted by hate crimes. The article recommends improved data collection; coordination between police, prosecutors, private agencies, and other government officials; and bias crime training.

———. "From Slavery to Hate Crime Laws: The Emergence of Race and Status-Based Protection in American Criminal Law." *Journal of Social Issues*, vol. 58, no. 2, Summer 2002, pp. 227–245. The author takes a historical perspective on modern hate-crime law, tracing the new statutes back to the remedies for slavery that underlay the post–Civil War civil rights amendments and federal laws. Historic cases, laws, and constitutional changes describe the gradual evolution of modern hate-crime law.

———. "Hate Crimes: Worse by Definition." *Journal of Contemporary Criminal Justice*, vol. 15, no. 1, February 1999, pp. 6–21. An article supportive of hate-crimes law as a necessary approach to criminal actions that cause a greater danger to the society at large than ordinary crimes.

Lieberman, Michael. "Beating Back the Power of Hate: The Federal Government's Critical Role in Confronting Bias Crime." *Legal Times*, November 24, 1997, p. 19. An attorney working on behalf of the Anti-Defamation League, the author comes out in strong support of hate-crimes legislation and advocates the role of the federal government in support of the new laws.

———. "Enforcing Hate Crime Laws: Defusing Intergroup Tensions." *The Police Chief*, October 1994, pp. 18–23. The author gives his opinion of the proper role of the police in recording and deterring hate crimes, and in improving community relations, and advocates tougher enforcement of such acts by police departments and prosecutors.

Liebmann, George. "Clinton's Police State." *American Enterprise*, vol. 11, number 4, June 2000, p. 12. The Clinton administration, according to the author, promoted a sort of liberal police state through the creeping federalization of criminal law. The author believes that new hate-crimes laws would mean more of the same. "The result of all this would mean that the degree of punishment for a crime would rest not on how evil the crime is, but on the religion, race, or sexual practices of the victim or the politics of the perpetrator."

McKenna, Ian B. "Canada's Hate Propaganda Laws: A Critique." *Ottawa Law Review*, vol. 26, no. 1., pp. 159–85. The author describes and compares hate-crimes statutes north of the border, where such laws have found wider public acceptance and have brought about tougher enforcement measures than in the United States.

McPhail, Beverly. "Gender-Bias Hate Crimes: A Review." *Trauma, Violence & Abuse: A Review Journal*, vol. 3, no. 2, April 2002, pp. 125–43. The article reviews the debate over including gender as a status category in hate-crimes law, giving arguments both for and against. The author cautions against the inclusion of an entire gender as a protected status, as it may simply overgeneralize the hate-crime category as it applies to true minority groups, making it nothing more than a symbolic gesture.

———. "Hating Hate: Policy Implications of Hate Crime Legislation." *Social Service Review*, vol. 74, no. 4, 2000, pp. 635–53. The author describes the current state of hate-crimes law and policy from a social worker's perspective, controversies surrounding and unintended consequences of the new laws, and the debate between those who see in hate-crimes law the further balkanization of America and those who see the laws as necessary to promote social harmony.

Mjoseth, Jeannine. "Psychologists Call for Assault on Hate Crimes: Hate Crimes Demand Unique Legal, Psychological and Policy Responses." *APA Monitor*, vol. 29, no. 1, January 1998. The author gives conclusions reached at a briefing on hate crimes cosponsored by the American Psychological Association and the Society for the Psychological Study of Social Issues. The article describes the distinct motives behind hate crimes against ethnicity and gender, the effects of hate crimes on the victims, the reasons for the underreporting of hate crimes, and hate-crimes legislation and resolutions. Available online at http://www.apa.org/monitor/jan98/hate.html.

Murphy, Jeffrie G. "Bias Crimes: What Do Haters Deserve?" *Criminal Justice Ethics*, vol. 11, no. 2, Summer/Fall 1992, pp. 20–23. The author objects to several points in Susan Gellman's paper on hate crimes. This author finds that (1) it is false that criminal law never takes account of motives as elements; (2) even if this is a true description of criminal law to date, it simply shows that criminal law should be improved by allowing motives sometimes to count; and (3) at least in some instances, the very concept of harm or injury cannot be understood independent of motives and other mental states.

Niederpruem, Kyle E. "British Columbia's Hate Literature Laws Targeting Journalists." *The Quill*, July/August 1998, p. 44. The author contends that British Columbia's law intended to halt the spread of hate crimes is effectively gagging the press, and that those who publish hate literature, loosely defined as anything anyone finds objectionable in a printed medium, are subject to injunctions and unlimited fines.

Nier, Charles Lewis. "Racial Hatred: A Comparative Analysis of Hate Crime Laws of the United States and Germany." *Dickinson Journal of International Law*, Winter 1995, pp. 241–79. The author gives an absorbing description of the hate-crimes problem in modern Germany and compares and contrasts hate-crimes laws in Germany and the United States.

Palmer, Carolyn J., Sophie W. Penney, and Donald D. Gehring. "Hate Speech and Hate Crimes: Campus Conduct Codes and Supreme Court

Rulings." *NASPA Journal*, Winter 1997, pp. 112–22. Description of a study that examined the use of language prohibiting hate crimes in campus codes of conduct and the familiarity of senior student affairs officers with the Supreme Court's decisions in *R.A.V. v. St. Paul* and *Wisconsin v. Mitchell*.

Pendo, Elizabeth A. "Recognizing Violence Against Women: Gender and the Hate Crime Statistics Act." *Harvard Women's Law Journal*, vol. 17, Spring 1994, pp. 157–83. The author discusses recent hate-crimes legislation passed at the federal and state levels and advocates including gender bias as an element of hate-crimes laws.

Phillips, Scott, and Ryken Grattet. "Judicial Rhetoric, Meaning-Making, and the Institutionalization of Hate Crime Law." *Law & Society Review*, vol. 34, 2000, pp. 567–606. This article examines the transformation of the concept of hate crime into a concrete legal construct that has, over time, been accepted as legitimate. The authors track changes in judicial rhetoric in 38 appeals court opinions that examined the constitutionality of hate crimes from 1984 through 1999. They conclude that the meaning of hate crime had become richer in expression than the words found in the statutes themselves, while the domain of hate crime gradually came to include broader ranges of behavior. The authors demonstrate how lawmakers and the court system tend to fix a legal definition of a term by developing a standard interpretation of that term.

Pollitt, Katha. "Hate Crimes Legislation." *The Nation*, November 29, 1999, p. 10. The author describes the debate over whether hate-crimes laws favor some victims over others, and contends that hate-crimes legislation deals with a class of motives rather than people on the grounds that bias crime perpetrators try to intimidate an entire community.

Potok, Mark. "Ten Years After Federal Officials Began Compiling National Hate Crime Statistics, the Numbers Don't Add Up." *Southern Poverty Law Center's Intelligence Report*, no. 104, Winter 2001, pp. 6–15. An article focusing on the problems of compiling hate crime statistics. The author believes that the national effort to document hate-motivated crime is inadequate, pointing out how the reporting system is riddled with errors and outright falsification of data. The author believes that while the published hate crime totals have been running at some 8,000 cases a year, the real figure is probably closer to 50,000. In some jurisdictions, the article claims, opposition or indifference towards data-collection has compromised the effort and has discouraged already reluctant victims from coming forward.

Ray, Larry, and David Smith. "Racist Offenders and the Politics of 'Hate Crime.'" *Law and College*, vol. 12, no. 3, December 2001, pp. 203–21. The authors examine the political trends and climate that has given rise to the emergence of hate crime as a new category of public controversy and of criminal conduct in the United States and the United Kingdom. The author uses data from the English city of Manchester to examine trends in hate crimes, describing hate-crime laws as a result of the increasingly legalized self-management of a complex modern society. "Hate crimes have thus acquired powerful rhetorical focus for mobilization of victim and identity politics," he states.

Redish, Martin H. "Freedom of Thought as Freedom of Expression: Hate Crime Sentencing Enhancement and First Amendment Theory." *Criminal Justice Ethics*, vol. 11, no. 2, Winter/Spring 2002, pp. 29–42. This article examines "free speech theory," claiming that, whether viewed as a catalyst or as a fundamental element, protection of freedom of thought is essential to the free speech right. In addition, penalty-enhancement laws punish the holding of political or social attitudes that the government deems offensive or unacceptable. The author believes that these laws are a serious threat to the values of free expression.

Rosen, Jeffrey. "Bad Thoughts." *The New Republic*, July 5, 1993, pp. 15–18. The author argues that the penalty-enhancement law enacted in Wisconsin and put to the test in the Supreme Court case of *Wisconsin v. Mitchell* was a carefully drafted statute that does not unconstitutionally suppress speech or thought. He also takes issue with Justice Rehnquist's opinion in this case.

Rushdy, Ashraf H. A. "Reflections on Jasper: Resisting History." *The Humanist*, March/April 2000, pp. 24–28. The author contends that politicians have not taken the opportunity to improve hate-crimes legislation following the conviction of the killers of James Byrd, Jr., of Jasper, Texas. The need to strengthen federal hate-crimes legislation is discussed, and the historical precedent of responding to violent crime with calls for laws with harsher penalties is examined.

Schauer, Frederick. "Messages, Motives, and Hate Crimes." *Criminal Justice Ethics*, vol. 11, no. 2, Summer/Fall 1992, pp. 52–54. This article discusses the claim that penalty enhancement is problematic under the First Amendment. One scholar claims that the First Amendment does not allow a government entity to ban conduct because of a concern with the message sent out by the conduct. The article asserts that there are many reasons to proscribe race-based motives that are not message dependent, and that chief among these is retribution.

Seligman, Dan. "The Perfect Crime." *Forbes*, December 15, 1997, pp. 138–39. A discussion of the possibly unintended consequences of the Violent Crime Control and Law Enforcement Act of 1994, which the author believes may lead to a disproportionate number of African Americans being prosecuted.

Shaughnessy, Edward J. "Hate Speech, Bias Crime and the Law." *New York State Bar Journal*, November 1994, pp. 14–17. A legal analysis of Supreme Court decisions on hate-crimes statutes and a review of the controversy and the viewpoints of those either opposed to and supportive of such laws.

Shaw, Millicent. "Hate Crime Legislation and the Inclusion of Gender: A Possible Option for Battered Women." *Domestic Violence Report*, vol. 6, no. 5, June–July 2001, pp. 65–78. The author presents an analysis of hate crime legislation that focuses on the inclusion of gender as an option for battered women. The article finds that including gender has not resulted in an overwhelming number of gender-based crimes reported as an extension of domestic violence and rape cases. The analysis concludes that the majority of rape, domestic violence, and stalking cases will not become hate-crime cases, but that having the statute available for certain gender-bias cases will aid prosecutors in their decisions.

Shuman-Moore, Elizabeth, and Darren B. Watts. "Bias Violence: Advocating for Victims." *Clearinghouse Review*, vol. 14, no. 5, 1994, pp. 4–18. A two-part article detailing a victim-assistance program for those experiencing bias-motivated violence, and the civil remedies available under federal and state law for such victims.

Simons, Kenneth W. "Equality, Bias Crimes, and Just Deserts." *Journal of Criminal Law and Criminology*, vol. 91, no. 1, Fall 2000, pp. 237–67. An article on victims' rights and criminal justice theory in which the author analyzes legislation regarding hate crimes and discusses "retributivist focus," which measures the culpability of the offender and the wrongdoing the offender commits. The analysis concludes that retributivist theory can justify higher sanctions for bias crimes and can do so more easily than can the principle of fair protection.

Spillane, Lori A. "Hate Crimes: Violent Intolerance." *Prosecutor*, July/August 1995, p. 20. An editorial supporting hate-crime laws and arguing for more vigorous prosecution of the same by district attorneys.

Spong, John. "The Hate Debate." *Texas Monthly*, April 2001, pp. 64–67. The author discusses the prospects for passage of the James Byrd Hate Crimes Act, named for the Jasper, Texas, man who was dragged to death in 1998 by three white supremacists. The act increased the punishment for crimes whose victims were targeted due to their race, religion, or sexual preference.

Stinski, Brent F. "Can Hate Be Controlled? A Clouded Issue." *Human Rights*, Spring 1993. An analytical overview of the penalty-enhancement statutes and the arguments of supporters and opponents of such laws.

Sullivan, Andrew. "What's So Bad About Hate?" *New York Times Magazine*, September 26, 1999, pp. 50–57. The author argues that laws prescribing special punishments in hate-crimes cases make little sense. Hatred, he argues, is a very vague concept—"far less nuanced an idea than prejudice, or bigotry, or bias, or anger, or even mere aversion to others." And if hate instead is restricted to "a very specific idea or belief, or set of beliefs, with a very specific object or group of objects," then the antihate war will "almost certainly" be unconstitutional.

Weinstein, James. "First Amendment Challenges to Hate Crime Legislation: Where's the Speech?" *Criminal Justice Ethics*, vol. 11, no. 2, Summer/Fall 1992, pp. 6–20. The author reviews Susan Gellman's 1991 article in which she claimed that hate crime legislation violated the First Amendment. This paper challenges the claim that such laws are invalid on their face—that is, regardless of the circumstances in which they are applied, a statute that enhances the punishment for racially motivated crimes violates the First Amendment. The author believes that an attack on the constitutionality of hate-crime legislation undermines the validity of all antidiscrimination laws.

Weisburd, Steven B., and Brian Levin. "On the Basis of Sex: Recognizing Gender-Based Crimes." *Stanford Law and Policy Review*, vol. 7, no. 2, Spring 1994, pp. 21–47. An essay on the question of including gender bias, rape, and spousal abuse in the category of hate crimes, in which the author also details the community-wide effect of hate crimes.

Wilson, James Q. "Hate and Punishment." *National Review*, September 13, 1999, p. 18. Prompted by neo-Nazi Buford O. Furrow's murder of a letter carrier and shooting of several children in Los Angeles, the author states that hate-crime laws are an attempt to make the subjective motive matter but that it is not clear why it should, as "making the probability of punishment greater is more vital than stigmatizing the motive of the criminal." The writer discusses the drawbacks of the proposed Hate Crimes Prevention Act of 1999.

Young, Cathy. "Gender War Crimes." *Reason*, January 1999, pp. 55–57. Discussion of the radical feminist theory of gender violence, a theory incorporated within the Violence Against Women Act (VAWA), which allows federal civil rights suits for violent crimes "motivated by gender." The writer reveals that the application of the VAWA is, however, limited by the fact that it provides only for monetary damages. By contrast, the passage of the federal Hate Crimes Prevention Act would allow federal criminal prosecutions for sexual assault or domestic violence.

WEB DOCUMENTS

Gardner, Dan. "Hate Crime Panic Is the Real Threat." *Ottawa Citizen*. Available online. URL: http://www.media-awareness.ca/eng/issues/internet/

resource/gardner.htm. Posted on April 29, 1998. Downloaded on February 7, 2003. The editorialist describes the hate-crime phenomenon as a creation of ethnic identity politics, used by activists, the media, and politicians to advance their own interests. Ultimately, the author believes, the greatest threat posed by the false epidemic of hate crimes will be civil liberties, eroded by new statutes that corrode basic legal principles and diminish individual freedom.

REPORTS

American Prosecutors Research Institute (APRI). "A Local Prosecutor's Guide for Responding to Hate Crimes." The APRI is the research arm of the National District Attorneys Association (NDAA). This resource guide was originally created for use by local district attorneys and lists agencies and organizations specializing in hate crimes, case management methods for prosecutors, and prevention measures. Model procedures used by district attorneys in the prosecution of hate crimes are given, as well as a list of individuals who are currently prosecuting hate crimes.

Center for Democratic Renewal. *When Hate Groups Come to Town: A Handbook of Model Community Responses.* 1992. A handbook for local law enforcement and citizens in dealing with outside hate groups, such as the Ku Klux Klan, that gather for meetings or parades and tend to incite violence and division in the community.

Copeland, Lois. *Violence Against Women as Bias-Motivated Hate Crime: Defining the Issues.* Violence Against Women Policy Studies. Center for Women Policy Studies, 1991. A 26-page report on the issue of gender-based crimes and their proper legal definition.

U.S. Department of Justice. *Stopping Hate Crime: A Case History from the Sacramento Police Department.* Washington, D.C.: Department of Justice, 1997. A six-page brochure detailing the efforts of the Sacramento police to deal with a wave of bias-motivated arsons in 1993. The successful effort to identify the individual responsible inspired the department to issue a set of detailed recommendations, published in this pamphlet, for other local law enforcement groups facing hate crimes.

U.S. Department of State, International Information Programs. "The Need for Hate Crime Legislation: White House Fact Sheet." Available online. URL: http://usinfo.state.gov/usa/race/hate/hate6190.htm. Posted on June 19, 2000. A memorandum from the Clinton White House detailing hate crime statistics and highlighting the provisions of the Local Law Enforcement Act of 2000, which the administration was supporting in Congress. The memo maintains that the legislation is constitutional, that it will keep the primary role of state and local law enforcement, and does not threaten free speech.

U.S. Department of State, International Information Programs. "Remarks by the President at White House Conference on Hate Crimes." Available online. URL: http://usinfo.state.gov/usa/race/hate/cl1197.htm. Posted on November 10, 1997. In this brief speech, President Bill Clinton summarizes the testimony given at the 1997 White House Conference on Hate Crimes, informs listeners of new steps taken by the Department of Justice and the FBI to combat hate crimes, and describes new initiatives undertaken by the Justice Department and the Department of Housing and Urban Development.

MAJOR CONGRESSIONAL HEARINGS

U.S. House of Representatives Judiciary Committee. 1985. *Crimes Against Religious Practices and Property: Hearings on H.R. 665 Before the Subcommittee on Criminal Justice.* Superintendent of Documents #Y4.J89/1:99/134.

————. 1993. *Crimes of Violence Motivated by Gender.* Superintendent of Documents #Y4.J89/1:103/51.

————. *Hate Crimes Prevention Act of 1997: Hearing Before the Committee on the Judiciary, House of Representatives, One Hundred Fifth Congress.* Washington, D.C.: Government Printing Office, 2000. From hearings held July 22, 1998. Available online. URL: http://www.access.gpo.gov/su_docs/.

————. *Implementation of the Church Arson Prevention Act of 1996: Hearings, March 19, 1997.* Superintendent of Documents #Y4.J89/1:105/4. Hearings convened during a period of concern on arson and bombings of African-American churches. The testimony includes the implementation of Church Arson Prevention Act, covering the role of federal and local law enforcement agencies in preventing church arson.

U.S. House of Representatives Judiciary Committee, Subcommittee on Civil and Constitutional Rights. *Anti-Asian Violence: Hearings, November 10, 1987.* Superintendent of Documents #Y4.J89/1:100/116. Hearings on the problem of anti-Asian hate crimes and violence, covering the mid-1980s and including witnesses from the Asian American Legal Defense and Education Fund and other nongovernmental organizations dedicated to the rights and defense of Asian Americans.

U.S. House of Representatives Judiciary Committee, Subcommittee on Crime and Criminal Justice. *Bias Crimes: Hearings, May 11, 1992.* Superintendent of Documents #Y4.J89/1:102/80. Hearings on hate crimes in general, including witnesses from gay rights, Asian-American, Jewish, women's rights, and African-American organizations, as well as the FBI. The agenda also included witnesses and testimony on the Hate Crimes Sentencing Act of 1992.

————. U.S. House of Representatives Judiciary Committee, Subcommittee on Crime and Criminal Justice. *Hate Crimes Sentencing Enhancement Act of 1992: Hearing, July 29, 1992.* Superintendent of Documents #Y4.J89/1:102/64. Hearings on proposed legislation that would provide for enhanced penalties when defendants were found to have committed a bias-motivated crime.

U.S. House of Representatives Judiciary Committee, Subcommittee on Criminal Justice. *Anti-Gay Violence: Hearings, October 9, 1986.* Superintendent of Documents #Y4.J89/1:99/132. Hearings on antigay violence, with testimony from scholars, public officials, and ordinary citizens who had been victimized by antigay hate crime.

————. *Hate Crime Statistics Act: Hearing, March 21, 1985.* Superintendent of Documents #Y4.J89/1:99/137. Hearings convened on the Hate Crimes Statistics Act, which upon passage would mandate reporting of hate crimes data by local law enforcement agencies to the federal Department of Justice.

U.S. Senate Judiciary Committee. *Combating Hate Crimes: Promoting a Responsive and Responsible Role for the Federal Government. United States Senate, One Hundred Sixth Congress.* Washington, D.C.: Government Printing Office, 2000. From hearings held May 11, 1999. Available online. URL: http://www.access.gpo.gov/su_docs/.

————. *Combating Violence Against Women: Hearing, May 15, 1996.* Superintendent of Documents #Y4.J89/2:S.Hrg 104-842. Hearing on the incidence of gender-based violence against women and implementation of the Violence Against Women Act of 1994.

————. *Hate Crime on the Internet: Hearing Before the Committee on the Judiciary, United States Senate, One Hundred Sixth Congress.* Washington, D.C.: Government Printing Office, 2001. From hearings held September 14, 1999. Available online. URL: http://www.access.gpo.gov/su_docs/. The hearing report is further subtitled Ramifications of Internet Technology on Today's Children, Focusing on the Prevalence of Internet Hate, and Recommendations of How to Shield Children From the Negative Impact of Violent Media.

————. *Violence Against Women: Victims of the System; Hearing, April 9, 1991.* Superintendent of Documents #Y4.J89/2:S.hrg.102-369. Testimony concerning the proposed Violence Against Women Act of 1991.

U.S. Senate Judiciary Committee, Subcommittee on the Constitution. *Hate Crimes Statistics Act: Hearing, August 5, 1992.* Superintendent of Documents #Y4.J89/2:S.hrg.103-1078. Hearings on the implementation of this 1990 law by local law enforcement agencies, including testimony from officials of the FBI, local police departments, authors, and representatives of nongovernmental organizations involved in the anti–hate crime effort. Superintendent of Documents #Y4.J89/2:S.hrg. 102-1131. A similar agenda was followed at Senate Judiciary Committee hearings on the Hate Crimes Statistics Act, conducted June 28, 1994.

CRIMINOLOGY, LAW ENFORCEMENT, AND RESEARCH

BOOKS

Bell, Jeannine. *Policing Hatred: Law Enforcement, Civil Rights, and Hate Crime.* New York: New York University Press, 2002. The author takes the perspective of law enforcement in the investigation and prosecution of hate crimes. The handling of hate crimes by the police is analyzed, as well as the practice of reporting and classifying—or not classifying—certain incidents and criminal acts as hate crimes. The author also describes the experiences of police and detectives belonging to minority groups in their handling of hate crimes and considers the impact of race—of victim, perpetrator, and investigator—in the handling of a hate-crimes prosecution.

Best, Joel. *Random Violence: How We Talk About New Crimes and New Victims.* Berkeley: University of California Press, 1999. The creation and treatment of what the author terms "new crimes" such as wilding, freeway violence, and hate crimes, in American society; the development of a "victim industry"; and how institutions such as government and the media manufacture new social problems to further their own interests.

Ferber, Abby L., Ryken Grattet, and Valerie Jenness. *Hate Crime in America: What Do We Know?* Washington, D.C.: American Sociological Association, 2000. A brief volume providing expert testimony on several areas of research and data on hate crimes, including summaries of recent legislation, and a useful list of experts working in the field.

Hamm, Mark S. *American Skinheads: The Criminology and Control of Hate Crime.* Westport, Conn.: Praeger, 1993. The author, a professor of criminology at Indiana State University, explores the origins of skinheads as a social subgroup; a description of the neo-Nazi skinhead movement in the United States and its leaders, Tom Metzger and Clark Martell; and a consideration of the definition of hate crime.

———. *Hate Crime: International Perspectives on Causes and Control.* Cincinnati, Ohio: Anderson Publishing Company, 1994. A study of hate-crimes legislation and law enforcement methods in the United States and abroad, providing useful comparisons and parallels for researchers.

Kelly, Robert J., ed. *Bias Crime: American Law Enforcement and Legal Responses.* Chicago: University of Illinois Press, 1993 (revised second printing). An anthology of 22 essays describing methods of hate-crimes law enforcement and prosecution in the 1980s and early 1990s. This new edition outlines the historic contexts of bias crime against gays and Jews in the Stonewall Riot—which took place in New York City on June 27, 1969—and the Holocaust, respectively. The legal resolutions are discussed for both of these cases. Updated materials have also been added on David Duke's career, the Rodney King case, bias confrontations, and hate crimes on college campuses. The first section of the book, which deals with law enforcement responses, describes police efforts to form bias crime units and legislative efforts to address these crimes specifically in statutes. In a second, completely new section on legal responses, a representative of the Anti-Defamation League discusses the legislation enacted to address bias crime, sentencing measures by the states, and the 1992 Supreme Court decision on hate crime.

Quarles, Chester L. and Paula L. Ratliff. *Crime Prevention for Houses of Worship.* Alexandria, Va.: American Society for Industrial Security, 2001. A handbook for houses of worship of all faiths, aiming to prevent vandalism, arson, and other bias-motivated crimes against property and against congregation members.

Turnbull, Linda S., and Elaine Hallisey Hendrix, eds. *Atlas of Crime: Mapping the Criminal Landscape.* Phoenix, Ariz.: Oryx Press, 2000. In the chapter entitled Hate Crime, author Damon Camp charts the occurrence of hate crimes and hate groups across the country, concluding that hate groups are more prevalent east of and along the Mississippi and on the Pacific Coast. In addition, the majority of hate-crime activity is associated with right-wing extremists and white supremacist groups, which are tied to survivalism, paramilitarism, neo-Nazism, and Holocaust revisionism. The chapter also reviews hate crime legislation in the states, dividing criminal laws into institutionalized violence and intimidation/harassment.

PERIODICALS

Balboni, Jennifer, and Jack McDevitt. "Hate Crime Reporting: Understanding Police Officer Perceptions, Departmental Protocol, and the Role of the Victim: Is There Such a Thing as a 'Love' Crime?" *Justice Research and Policy*, vol. 3, no. 1, Spring 2001, pp. 1–27. The authors discuss the impact on hate-crime reporting of various factors: lack of infrastructure to support accurate reporting, lack of training, disincentives to police officers to accurately report, and hesitation on the part of victims to involve the police. The authors draw on a sample of data taken from police departments across the nation as well as interviews with law enforcement officials and government and private-sector professionals involved with the issue.

Barnes, Arnold, and Paul H. Ephros. "The Impact of Hate Violence on Victims: Emotional and Behavioral Responses to Attacks." *Social Work*, vol. 39, no. 3, May 1994, pp. 247–52. A description of the experiences of hate-crime victims, taken from interviews and focus groups, in which the author advocates greater awareness of the effect of dealing with hate crimes on social workers.

Blanchard, Robert O. "The 'Hate State' Myth." *Reason*, May 1999, pp. 34–40. The writer describes what he calls the hate-crime lobby and how it feeds a perception of ordinary crimes as symptomatic of larger national issues such as sexism, racism, and homophobia. He defends his home state of Wyoming from the charge that it is a breeding ground for prejudice, pointing out the state's record as the first to grant women the right to vote, own property, and hold office. The author also points out the media's selective coverage of the Matthew Shepard murder and its self-interested sensationalism, which turns ordinary crimes into forums for the advancement of a liberal political agenda.

Boyd, Elizabeth A., Richard A Berk, and Karl M. Hamner. "Motivated by Hatred or Prejudice: Categorization of Hate Motivated Crimes in Two Police Divisions." *Law & Society Review*, vol. 30, no. 4, November 1996, pp. 819–50. The writers explore the decision-making practices of police detectives responsible for gathering official hate crime data in two divisions of a large urban police department. They describe the routines followed and how the procedures and hierarchy in the police administration affect the statistical outcomes and conclusions.

Byers, B., and R. A. Zeller. "Examination of Official Hate Crime Offense and Bias Motivation Statistics for 1991–1994." *Journal of Crime and Justice*, vol. 20, no. 1, 1997, pp. 91–106. This study analyzes secondary data from the Uniform Crime Reporting Division of the FBI. The analysis reveals that data covering 1991 to 1994 show remarkable stability when examining both bias motivation and type of offense. Additionally, the official data show that harassment and intimidation are the most frequently reported hate-crimes and that racial bias is one of the most commonly occurring reasons.

Cathcart, Brian. "Cock-up, Corruption or Racism?" *New Statesman*, June 5, 1998, p. 20. The writer raises the question of whether sabotage was involved in the investigation into the murder of Stephen Lawrence, which has become Great Britain's most notorious race killing.

Cooke, Leonard. "Fighting Hate Crimes: The Eugene Model." *The Police Chief*, October 1994, pp. 44–47. The article describes the effective methods of the Eugene, Oregon, Police Services Department in deterring hate crimes.

Craig, Kellina. "Examining Hate-Motivated Aggression: A Review of the Social Psychological Literature on Hate Crimes as a Distinct Form of Aggression." *Aggression and Violent Behavior*, vol. 7, no. 1, January-February 2002, pp. 85–101. This article reviews the literature on hate crimes in social psychology and other related fields. The author attempts to identify factors common to the various types of hate crimes to clarify the nature of hate-motivated crimes, their prevalence, and causes. The paper also discusses membership in organized hate groups, religious values, psychopathology and deviancy, the authoritarian personality and right-wing authoritarianism, and the decision to join a hate group.

Deirmenjian, John M. "Hate Crimes on the Internet." *Journal of Forensic Sciences*, vol. 45, no. 5, 2000, pp. 1020–22. Offering six case studies in electronic hate crime, the author describes the effort to investigate and prosecute such acts, the difficulties of combatting hate crime in the anonymous and borderless world of the Internet, and the intervention efforts against hate groups and hate sites on both local and national levels.

Edwards, Jim. "Statistics Don't Bear Out Feared Wave of Bias Cases Against Muslims, Arabs." *New Jersey Law Journal*, vol. 168, no. 11, June 10, 2002, p. 1. The author investigates complaints of bias incidents and racial profiling against Arab Americans after the September 11, 2001, terrorist attacks, claiming that although there was a rise in such incidents, the increase was not serious or "statistically significant."

Godwin, Cory A. "Applying Correctional Intelligence to Law Enforcement Investigations." *Corrections Today*, August 1999, p. 94. A special section on hate crimes in the United States, discussing the need to gather gang intelligence and to establish formal intelligence units within sheriffs' offices and police departments.

Haider-Markel, Donald P. "Implementing Controversial Policy: Results from a National Survey of Law Enforcement Department Activity on Hate Crime." *Justice Research and Policy*, vol. 3, no. 1, Spring 2001, pp 29–61. This research report explores the implementation of hate crime policy by police departments, emphasizing policies and procedures related to anti-homosexual bias crimes. The author sampled 250 of the nation's largest cities and concludes the support of police leaders and officers, the presence of state hate crime policies, police resources, and public opinion all shaped the effectiveness of local efforts to deal with hate crimes.

Hamm, Mark S. "Terrorism, Hate Crime, and Antigovernment Violence: A Review of the Research." Thousand Oaks, Calif.: Sage Publications,

1998. A report presented at a March 1996, meeting on terrorism and hate crime research to the Committee on Law and Justice of the National Research Council's Commission of Behavioral and Social Science Education. The author reviews the definition of domestic terrorism as used by the federal government and the FBI, contrasting this term with the term *hate crime* as used in data collection by the FBI. The article claims that timely and comprehensive statistics on domestic terrorism, modeled on those associated with hate crimes, could help law enforcement.

Isaacs, Tracy. "Domestic Violence and Hate Crimes: Acknowledging Two Levels of Responsibility." *Criminal Justice Ethics*, vol. 20, no. 2, Summer/Fall 2001, pp. 31–43. The author believes that counseling should be mandatory in cases of hate-crime conviction, with the goal of erasing negative stereotypes and misconceptions about minorities among hate-crime perpetrators.

Jacobs, James. "Rethinking the War Against Hate Crimes: A New York City Perspective." *Criminal Justice Ethics*, vol. 11, no. 2, Summer/Fall 1992, pp. 55–61. The author questions the effectiveness of motivation-specific criminal laws, arguing they will do little to remedy longstanding social problems such as racism and homophobia. The article reviews New York City's Bias Crime Unit, which the author believes has become politically oversensitive, and argues that the criminal justice system should strive for an evenhanded treatment of all crimes without subjective consideration of motive.

Kelly, Michael. "Playing with Fire." *The New Yorker*, July 15, 1996, pp. 28–36. In the midst of what many reporters described as an epidemic of church burning, the author analyzes the news and police reports and contends that rather than instances of hate crime and racism, many were the acts of vandals and common criminals.

Levine, Art. "The Strange Case of Faked Hate Crimes: An Ugly Form of Fraud Seems to Be on the Rise." *U.S. News & World Report*, November 3, 1997, p. 30. Article describing the incidence of faked hate crimes which may have been carried out as a form of insurance fraud. According to Arthur Teitelbaum of the Anti-Defamation League, these incidents injure the real victims of hate crimes, as it can make them less credible.

Lieberman, Joel D., Jamie Arndt, Jennifer Personius, and Alison Cook. "Vicarious Annihilation: The Effects of Mortality Salience on Perceptions of Hate Crimes." *Law and Human Behavior*, vol. 25, no. 6, December 2001, pp. 547–66. The article describes terror management theory, which maintains that intolerance toward those who are different stems from personal vulnerability and fear of mortality. The paper reports on research that explored this theory by examining perceptions of hate crimes among 140 undergraduate students at the University of Nevada.

The author suggests that the solution to intolerance lies in education to supplant deeply rooted prejudices.

Lynch, Michael F. "Responding to Hate Crime and Bias-Motivated Incidents on Campuses." *Campus Law Enforcement Journal*, vol. 31, no. 3, May/June 2001, pp. 23–25. The author reviews the diverse cultural landscape of college campuses, which often brings about bias-motivated incidents as well as exacerbated racial and ethnic tensions. The article reviews the proactive role of campus law enforcement in dealing with hate crimes emphasizing standard operating procedure, training and education, and the use of conciliation on the part of law enforcement. The author also discusses the role of college administrations in formulating hate-crime policies, in agreements with victim-support agencies, and in cooperation with local police departments.

Marcus-Newhall, Amy, and Laura Palucki Blake, with Julia Baumann. "Perceptions of Hate Crime Perpetrators and Victims as Influenced by Race, Political Orientation, and Peer Group." *American Behavioral Scientist*, vol. 46, no. 1, January 2002, pp. 108–35. The authors present three studies of the influence of bias factors—race of victim, race of perpetrator, and political orientation—on the decisions made by mock jurors in hate-crimes cases. The results generally revealed that guilty verdicts and higher sentences were reached when the victim was African American and the perpetrator white.

Martin, Susan E. "Police and the Production of Hate Crimes: Continuity and Change in One Jurisdiction." *Police Quarterly*, vol. 2, no. 4, 1999, pp. 417–37. A study of hate crimes from 1987 through 1996 in Baltimore County, Maryland, and the actions of the Baltimore police in reporting, community outreach, training, and investigation of hate crimes. The author describes the ambiguities in the system of reporting hate crimes, showing that it may lead to distortion and uncertainty in statistics reported by local police departments.

Medoff, Marshall H. "Allocation of Time and Hateful Behavior: A Theoretic and Positive Analysis of Time and Hate Crime." *Journal of Economics and Sociology*, vol. 58, no. 4, October 1999, pp. 959–73. A statistical analysis of hate-crime data for 1995, this article concludes that hate crimes were positively related to the unemployment rate, the percentage of population between 15 and 19 years old, the extent of a state's liberal ideology, and educational levels. Hate crimes were negatively related to wage rates, while law enforcement efforts, religious belief, urbanization, low occupational status, and downward social mobility did not have a statistically significant impact.

Miller, Alexandra J. "Student Perceptions of Hate Crimes." *American Journal of Criminal Justice*, vol. 25, no. 2, Spring 2001, pp. 293–305. The author studies criminal justice majors and non–criminal justice majors, using the hypothesis that criminal justice majors would have a better understanding of hate crimes and be more likely to identify incidents as such. This hypothesis was proven wrong. While criminal justice majors tended to be older and more likely male, both groups had similar portions of whites and blacks. It was also found that females and non–criminal justice majors are more likely to disagree over all types of hate crimes, while criminal justice majors were less likely to identify sexual minorities, females, or Jews as victims. According to the author, the findings demonstrate the need for separate courses within the criminal justice curriculum to address the issues of gender and multiculturalism.

Murphy, Clyde E. "Civil Rights Lawyers Organize a National Response to Hate Crime." *Corrections Today*, August 1999, p. 88. Part of a special section on hate crimes in the United States. The writer shows that reports of bias violence are underreported by victims and underrecorded by law enforcement agencies. He argues that to tackle bias violence, attorneys and other advocates must work with law enforcement officials to guarantee input from survivors and to see that perpetrators are brought to justice. He discusses several of the elements of the national response that must be developed to combat hate crimes and outlines the features of the Lawyers Committees' 1999 initiative.

Nolan, James J., Yoshio Akiyama, and Samuel Bernahu. "The Hate Crimes Statistics Act of 1990: Developing a Method for Measuring the Occurrence of Hate Violence." *American Behavioral Scientist*, vol. 46, no. 1, January 2002, pp. 136–53. The authors describe the FBI's hate-crime data-collection program, which was developed as an adjunct to its annual Uniform Crime Reports. The article examines trends in local law enforcement participation in the program, as well as trends in hate crimes revealed by the more comprehensive collection of data on the local level.

Parks, Carlton, and Kamilah M. Woodson. "Anxiety Symptoms Among Sexually Abused Ethnic Minority Male Survivors of Racially Motivated Hate Crimes: An Exploratory Study." *Family Violence & Sexual Assault Bulletin*, vol. 18, no. 2, Summer 2002, pp. 13–19. A study documenting the psychological impact of forced sexual activity within the context of racially motivated hate crimes. The study sample was composed of 187 men of color (47 percent African American, 21 percent Latino, 18 percent Asian American/Pacific Islander, 8 percent American Indian, and 6 percent biracial/multiracial). Eighteen of the men reported having a history of male sexual assault during racially motivated hate crimes. Compared with men who did not report having a sexual assault history, these men were more likely to have involvement with both male and female survivors of child sexual abuse and sexual assault. The authors discuss the implications of these findings for future research.

Smith, Kyle. "The Day the Children Died." *People*, August 11, 1997, pp. 87–90. A review of the Birmingham church bombing that took place on September 15, 1963, in which four African-American girls were killed, and the current legal maneuverings to apprehend accomplices in that crime.

Soule, Sarah A., and Nella Van Dyke. "Black Church Arson in the United States, 1989–1996." *Ethnic and Racial Studies*, vol. 22, no. 4, 1999, pp. 724–42. A study based on competition theory as applied to church arson, finding that, in addition to straightforward bigotry, more subtle ethnic, political, and economic competition between whites and African Americans can contribute to the incidence of such crimes.

Strandberg, K.W. "Hate Crime: Strategies Used by Bias Crime Units." *Law Enforcement Technology*, vol. 19, no. 9, September 1992, pp. 40–46. The author reviews the nature and functions of law enforcement bias-crime units. These special units are different from other police details because, although they concentrate on the crimes themselves, they are also aware of their responsibility to the victims and to the community as a whole. The unit should receive specialized training, and its racial makeup should match that of the community. The special unit should aim to communicate to the community, offenders, and potential offenders that hate crimes will be promptly and expertly investigated so that offenders may be identified and prosecuted.

Umemoto, Karen, and C. Kimi Mikami. "Profile of Race-Bias Hate Crime in Los Angeles County." *Western Criminology Review*, vol. 2, no. 2, 2000, pp. 1–34. The authors study hate crimes based on racial bias in Los Angeles County, based on law enforcement statistics collected 1994–97. The article maps 1,837 reported bias incidents and locates areas where hate crimes occur in relatively high density; in addition, the authors conducted interviews and undertook archival research. Their results suggest that hate crimes committed in cluster locations more often involve perpetrators who are members of gangs. A related finding was the strong indication of race-bias hate crime among minority-based gangs in which the motive was hatred toward the victim's ethnicity and not the defense of territorial boundaries against other gangs.

Vogel, Brenda L. "Perceptions of Hate: The Extent to Which a Motive of 'Hate' Influences Attitudes of Violent Crimes." *Journal of Crime and Justice*, vol. 23, no. 2, 2000, pp. 1–25. The author described a survey of 450 undergraduates to determine the varying perception of the hate-crimes issue among different ethnic groups. The survey questions involved the relative seriousness of various motives in the commission of a crime; the answers were then correlated to the ethnic group to which respondents belonged.

Walker, S., and C. M. Katz. "Less Than Meets the Eye: Police Department Bias-Crime Units." *American Journal of Police*, vol. 14, no. 1, 1995, pp. 29–48. This article studies bias-crimes units in 16 municipal police agencies. Data were collected through telephone interviews with the police officer directly responsible for the bias crime unit. Results revealed that only four of the agencies had a special bias crime unit, while another six departments did not have a special unit but designated officers in other units to handle the crimes. Six agencies had neither a special unit nor special procedures for handling hate crimes. The 10 agencies with a special unit or procedure varied greatly in their procedures. The 16 agencies also varied greatly in their awareness and commitment to bias crimes units.

Waxman, Barbara. "Hatred: The Unacknowledged Dimension in Violence Against Disabled People." *Sexuality and Disability*, vol. 9, no. 3, Fall 1991, pp. 185–99. The author describes bias incidents directed against the disabled and argues that such acts should be included in those punished by hate-crimes laws.

White, Rob, and Santina Perrone. "Racism, Ethnicity and Hate Crime." *Communal/Plural: Journal of Transnational & Cross-Cultural Studies*, vol. 9, no. 2, 2001, pp. 161–81. The authors explore street fights involving ethnic-minority youth in Melbourne, Australia, attempting to show how marginalization could serve to fuel racist political attacks on such groups. Two main types of group conflict are addressed: street fights and school fights. The author finds that while racism was implicated in street violence, the main variable was that of power, and that fights among groups of relatively powerless sections of the community were less a matter of hate crime than of social dislocation. In addition, street violence tended to reinforce the stereotypes and social divisions which racial and hate crime feeds.

REPORTS

"Audit of Violence Against Asian Pacific Americans: Continuing the Campaign Against Hate Crimes, Fifth Annual Report 1997." National Asian Pacific American Legal Consortium, 1998. Based on 1997 FBI hate-crime statistics, which revealed 481 incidents against Asian Pacific Americans, this study notes a significant increase in reports of anti-Asian violence in California and New Jersey. The report notes that xenophobia and hate groups are primary motives for such acts, as are rapid changes in the ethnic makeup of neighborhoods and cities. The report advocates more comprehensive data collection by law enforcement, further hate-crimes statutes in each state, and more effective federal legislation.

"Bias Crimes Annual Report: Race, Religion, Ethnicity, Sexual Orientation." Connecticut State Police, 1993. This report breaks down Connecticut's hate-crime data from 1993, when 137 crimes motivated by bias against another's race, religion, ethnicity, or sexual orientation were reported in Connecticut, a 52.2-percent increase over 1992. Crime motivated by racial bigotry accounted for 56.2 percent of bias crimes, while 2.9 percent appeared to target both racial and religious groups. Crimes motivated by religious bigotry accounted for 25.5 percent of bias crimes, with anti-Semitism motivating 29 of 35 religious bias crimes. Physical force or a dangerous weapon was used in 24.1 percent of bias crimes. The report also reveals that two training sessions were held in 1993 to help police officers determine whether a crime was motivated by bias may have affected the increased number of police departments submitting bias crime reports in 1993. Connecticut legislation relevant to bias crime is noted, and the Bias Crime Report used by Connecticut's Department of Public Safety is included.

Garafolo, J., and S. E. Martin. "Bias-Motivated Crimes: Their Characteristics and the Law Enforcement Response." Southern Illinois University Center for the Study of Crime, Delinquency, and Corrections, 1993. This report presents the results of a study of the characteristics of bias-motivated crime and the law enforcement response to it in New York City and Baltimore County, Maryland. The research focused on the nature of bias-motivated crimes (event characteristics, victims, offenders) in comparison with samples of similar nonbias crimes, as well as the law enforcement response to bias-motivated crimes. The study found clear differences between bias crimes, which were more likely to occur in public places; be less serious in terms of weapon use and injury; involve younger, multiple victims; involve offenders who were strangers to the victims; and elicit stronger, more emotional, longer-lasting reactions from victims.

"Hate Crimes: An Overview of Numbers and Statutes." *Alaska Justice Forum*, vol. 18, no. 1, Spring 2001, pp. 1–8. Prepared by the University of Alaska School of Justice, this report reviews hate crime legislation and statistics for Alaska for 1999. At that time, only the Anchorage Police Department participated in the FBI crime reporting program. For 1999, racial bias was by far the most common bias involved in hate crimes reported. Of the 4,295 incidents for which racial bias was noted, 2,958 (68.9 percent) were designated as anti-black. There were 1,411 incidents in which a religious bias was determined, and 1,317 showed a sexual-orientation bias. Among the incidents of religious bias, 78.6 percent were anti-Jewish, and antimale homosexual incidents involved 69.4 percent of the incidents with sexual-orientation bias. Over two-thirds of the hate crimes were against persons, with 50 percent categorized as intimidation. A little less than one-third of the total number of hate crimes consisted of property crimes, with the majority listed as destruction/damage/vandalism.

Holmes, W. M. "Responding to Hate Crime and Bias Incidents: An Institutional Checklist." Massachusetts Committee on Criminal Justice, Statistical Analysis Center, 1992. This document contains information to be used by academic institutions to assess their readiness and ability to respond to hate crime reports and bias incidents. It presents a checklist of issues that should be examined when considering an institution's response to hate crimes and bias incidents. Assessment questions on training consider knowledge objectives, attitude objectives, and behavioral objectives. Assessment of institutional policies considers criteria for identifying a hate or bias incident, the handling of ambiguous cases, charges of police bias, and group and individual hate crime.

Levin, B. "Practical Approach to Bias Crimes: How Police and Government Can Coordinate to Fight Violent Bigotry." National Institute of Justice, 1992. This article identifies the unique characteristics of bias crimes and presents a model for police policy, organization, and activities to respond to such crimes in cooperation with appropriate agencies. Particular attention is paid to the role law enforcement can play as part of an organized and cooperative system that addresses these crimes and its victims. The author analyzed data collection, statutes, sentencing, outreach, policy, training, coordination, and the implementation of antibias efforts by police.

Tomsen, Stephen. "Hate Crimes and Masculinity: New Crimes, New Responses and Some Familiar Patterns." Griffith, Australia: Australian Institute of Criminology, 2000. Available online. URL: http://www.aic.gov.au/conferences/outlook4/Tomsen.pdf. A paper presented at a crime symposium held in Canberra, Australia, this document examines current research in antihomosexual and race-related crime committed by working-class and socially disadvantaged males. Using his own study of antihomosexual murders in New South Wales, the author argues that prejudice toward racial and sexual minorities is linked to the attainment of masculine identity. The author believes that *hate crime* has become an overly simplistic term that misses the true motivation of offenders, and advocates antipoverty and family support measures, schooling for the disadvantaged, or employment/diversion programs for young men.

Wessler, Stephen, and Margaret Moss. *Hate Crimes on Campus: The Problem and Efforts to Confront It.* Washington, D.C.: U.S. Department of Justice, Office of Justice Programs, Bureau of Justice Assistance, 2001. The director and associate director of the Center for the Prevention of Hate

Hate Crimes

Violence in Portland, Maine, describe prejudice, hate crimes, and bias incidents in campus settings. The authors note that even statistics based on a small number of reporting schools indicate that hate crimes on campus were a significant problem. Hate crimes occurred relatively infrequently on most campuses, but bias incidents (acts of prejudice not accompanied by crimes) were far more common. Students consistently reported the widespread use of degrading language and slurs by other students directed toward people of color, women, homosexuals, Jews, and others who belong to groups that have traditionally been the target of bias, prejudice, and violence. The book offers strategies to counter hate crimes and implement prevention programs.

WEB DOCUMENTS

California Attorney General's Civil Rights Commission on Hate Crimes. "Reporting Hate Crimes: Final Report." Available online. URL: http://caag.state.ca.us/publications/civilrights/reportingHC.pdf. Posted in 2001. The commission's report on hate crimes in nearly two dozen communities throughout the state, finding that hate crimes often go unreported, for a variety of reasons, and that many law enforcement agencies have a credibility problem over the issue of hate-crimes reporting, investigation, and prosecution. The commission found, in addition, that hate crimes based on gender and/or disability are not generally reported. The report carries several recommendations: establishing a hot line, setting standards for local hate violence prevention and response networks, setting statewide campus hate-crime policies, and improved hate-crime reporting by law enforcement.

Center for Criminal Justice Policy Research (Boston, Mass.) and Justice Research and Statistics Association (Washington, D.C.). "Improving the Quality and Accuracy of Bias Crime Statistics Nationally: An Assessment of the First Ten Years of Bias Crime Data Collection." Available online. URL: http://www.ojp.usdoj.gov/bjs/abstract/iqabcsn.htm. Posted on September 20, 2000. This report describes a project funded by the Bureau of Justice Statistics and includes a review of national hate crime trends, a summary of results from a national law enforcement survey of police officers' attitudes about hate crime, and other information. The report summarizes the first decade of data collection under the Hate Crimes Statistics Act and offers suggestions on how to improve the work.

U.S. Department of Justice, Community Relations Service. "Hate Crimes: The Violence of Intolerance." (Revised December 2001.) This paper describes the local projects of the Community Relations Service in defusing racial tensions and dealing with racial incidents and details its various

practices in preventing such occurrences from escalating into civil disturbances. These practices include model ordinances for local government,
the building of coalitions among community groups, dealing with local
media, investigating and reporting hate crimes, establishing task forces
and training programs, and offering appropriate assistance to victims,
witnesses, and offenders.

Federal Bureau of Investigation. "Hate Crime Data Collection Guidelines:
Uniform Crime Reporting." Available online. URL: http://www.fbi.gov/
ucr/hatecrime.pdf. Updated on October 1999. The FBI published this set
of guidelines for the use of local law enforcement agencies attempting to
comply with the Hate Crimes Statistics Act of 1990 and provide hate-
crimes data to the bureau for its annual Uniform Crime Reports. The
guidelines include the criteria to be applied to hate crimes (such as how
to determine bias motivation), example forms for submitting hate crime
data to the UCR program as well as the National Incident-Based Reporting System (NIBRS), the text of the Hate Crimes Statistics Act, and
"offense definitions."

Grattet, Ryken. "Hate Crimes: Better Data or Increasing Frequency?" Population Reference Bureau, July 2000. Available online. URL: http:/www.prb.
org/Content/NavigationMenu/PT_articles/July-September_2000/
Hate_Crimes_Better_Data_or_Increasing_Frequency_1.htm. Downloaded
October 2002. The author gives a summary of hate-crime data collection efforts, analyzing the numbers through 1998 and revealing that "some of the
best information comes from local rather than national sources." From this
information, several researchers have pointed out the importance of "territorial defense as a key underlying factor in the commission of hate crime."
The author includes a short bibliography of academic articles on hate crime.

Justice Research and Statistics Association. "Hate Crime Reporting: Understanding Police Officer Perceptions, Departmental Protocol, and the
Role of the Victim." Available online. URL: http://www.jrsainfo.org/pubs/
journal/past_issues/Spring2001/balboni_etal.html. Posted Spring 2001.
A paper exploring the problems in reporting hate crime—including the
"disincentives to accurately report" among the police and hesitation of
victims—and how these problems affect published statistics. The report
uses a survey of police officers and interviews with advocacy and human
rights professionals, and makes suggestions for improvements in po-
lice/community relations and in "appropriate department infrastructure."

Justice Research and Statistics Association. "Implementing Controversial Policy: Results from a National Survey of Law Enforcement Department
Activity on Hate Crime." Available online. URL: http://www.jrsainfo.
org/pubs/journal/past_issues/Spring2001/haider-markel.html. Posted
Spring 2001. A survey and research paper on the implementation of

federal, state, and local policies by the police in dealing with hate crimes, with particular focus on hate crimes against homosexuals. The report finds that the tractability of the problem, the support of police leaders, the presence of state hate-crime policies, police resources, and public opinion all affect this implementation.

Sincere, Richard E. "Hate Crimes and Individual Rights." Available online. URL: http://www.indegayforum.org/authors/sincere19.html. Downloaded October 2002. The author believes the passage of hate-crimes law is the wrong response to the murder of Matthew Shepard, describing such laws as feel-good measures that violate constitutional guarantees of free speech and freedom of conscience. Hate-crimes laws, in the author's opinion, set up privileged categories of people defined by their membership in a group, thus bringing about unequal protection under the law.

Miami University, Oxford, Ohio. "No Hate." Available online. URL: http://www.ucm.muohio.edu/documents_and_policies/NoHate/index.cfm. Downloaded October 2002. This page provides the researcher with a useful example of one university's approach to the hate-crime issue. The page offers a basic explanation of the university's procedures and policies on hate crimes and hate incidents, answers to frequently asked questions, resources for those who have been the victim of hate crimes, and Action Steps suggested to students to combat what the page defines as hate crimes and bias-motivated incidents on campus.

U.S. Department of Justice, Civil Rights Division. "Civil Rights Division National Origin Working Group Initiative to Combat the Post-9/11 Discriminatory Backlash." Available online. URL: http://www.usdoj.gov/crt/nordwg.html. Posted on July 30, 2002. In the wake of the September 11, 2001, terrorist bombing, the United States experienced a rise in bias incidents directed against Muslims and Arabs. This document describes the federal initiative undertaken against this backlash, updates current activities by the Civil Rights Division, describes the procedure for filing a complaint of discrimination, and provides links to statements from government offices, and to information from federal agencies on civil rights and the available responses to discrimination.

CURRICULUM AND TRAINING MATERIALS

Malloy, Stephanie. *Reviving Hope in the Face of Hate: A Guide for Countering Juvenile Hate Crime.* Newton, Mass.: National Center for Hate Crime Prevention, Education Development Center, Inc. A guide written for educators and juvenile justice professionals, offering a range of strategies for dealing with juvenile hate-crime offenders. Included are general background and current trends on the hate-crime issue, offender motivations, hate-crime diversion programs, and a description of nine innovative model programs.

McLaughlin, Karen A., Kelly J. Brilliant, and Cynthia Lang. *National Bias Crimes Training Manual for Law Enforcement and Victim Assistance Professionals.* National Center for Hate Crime Prevention, Education Development Center, Inc. 1995. A two-day course for law enforcement professionals on responding to hate crimes, including background notes for trainers, a list of recommended videos, and suggested activities. Available free of charge from the Office for Victims of Crime Resource Center, U.S. Department of Justice, P.O. Box 6000, Rockville, MD 20849-6000; phone (800) 627-6872.

McLaughlin, Karen A., Stephanie M. Malloy, Kelly J. Brilliant, and Cynthia Lang. *Responding to Hate Crime: A Multidisciplinary Curriculum for Law Enforcement and Victim Assistance Professionals.* Newton, Mass.: National Center for Hate Crime Prevention, Education Development Center, Inc. 2000. An updated and condensed version of the *National Bias Crimes Training Manual,* this is a course on responding to hate crime. Included are suggested actions to investigate and respond to hate crimes, victim assistance, reproducible materials such as handouts and transparencies, and background notes for training law enforcement professionals in this field. Also available as a Portable Document Format (.pdf) or ASCII file (without tables) at http://www.edc.org/HHD/hatecrime/id3_m.htm.

Southern Poverty Law Center. "Online Hate-Crime Training Course." This page provides a link to an Introduction to Hate and Bias Crimes course offered by the SPLC in conjunction with Auburn University, Montgomery, and the Federal Law Enforcement Training Center. The tuition course encompasses 12–15 hours of online work, including participation in live chat sessions. URL: http://www.splcenter.org/cgi-bin/goframe.pl?refname=/intelligenceproject/ip-hatetraining.html. Posted on October 2002.

U.S. Department of Justice. "Hate Crime Training: Core Curriculum for Patrol Officers, Detectives and Command Officers." A model curriculum, 280 pages in length, with instruction on law enforcement procedures and practices, victim assistance programs, and community relations for the use of patrol officers, detectives, and policy-level officers. Available online. URL: http://www.usdoj.gov/crs/pubs/hct.pdf. (1999).

Wiley-Cordone, Jennifer. *Preventing Hate Crime Through Community Action.* National Center for Hate Crime Prevention, Education Development Center, Inc. The author presents strategies for communities dealing with the occurrence or threat of hate crimes. Written for juvenile justice, education, law enforcement, and social service professionals, the guide offers examples of successful hate-crime prevention strategies, and gives tips on victim assistance, coalition building, and media relations.

Wiley-Cordone, Jennifer. *Preventing Youth Hate Crime*. Newton, Mass.: National Center for Hate Crime Prevention, Education Development Center, Inc. 1998. A training manual on hate-crime response and prevention, offering a variety of successful practices in juvenile and criminal justice, education, law enforcement, victim assistance, and community organizing.

ANTIHOMOSEXUAL BIAS CRIME

BOOKS

Comstock, Gary David. *Violence Against Lesbians and Gay Men*. Between Men/Between Women: Lesbian and Gay Studies series. New York: Columbia University Press, 1991. An analysis of data collected on antihomosexual violence, a general profile of the perpetrators, and a consideration of the source of this violence in public attitudes toward gays and lesbians.

Herek, Gregory, and Kevin T. Berrill, eds. *Hate Crimes: Confronting Violence Against Lesbians and Gay Men*. Newbury Park, Calif.: Sage Publications, 1992. An anthology of articles on antigay hate crimes, in which the contributors consider psychology, social context, and mental health. The book includes research findings and professional practice, as well as first-person accounts by survivors of hate crimes.

Israel, Constance Denney. *Hate Crimes Against Gays/Lesbians in the Mainstream Press: An Examination of Six Texas Dailies*. Las Colinas, Tex.: Monument Press, 1992. An exposé of press treatment of hate crimes committed against homosexuals, with the author asserting that editors and journalists in Texas are conspiring to whitewash, belittle, or ignore such incidents.

Loffreda, Beth. *Losing Matt Shepard: Life and Politics in the Aftermath of Anti-Gay Murder*. New York: Columbia University Press, 2000. A University of Wyoming professor describes the society of Laramie, Wyoming, the experience of homosexuals in the state, the impact of the Matthew Shepard murder on the community, the trial of those charged with the crime, the consequences for proposed hate-crime legislation, and the role of religious organizations in supporting and opposing homosexuals.

Sloan, Lacey M., and Nora S. Gustavsson, eds. *Violence and Social Injustice Against Lesbian, Gay, and Bisexual People*. New York: Haworth Press, 1998. Not a book on hate crimes per se, this volume explores pervasive, everyday discriminatory acts and attitudes against homosexuals. The author suggests that complacency and apathy contribute to a general social milieu in which truly violent acts, including the most famous incidents covered and analyzed in the national media, can take place.

Swigonski, Mary E., Robin S. Mama, and Kelly Ward, eds. *From Hate Crimes to Human Rights: A Tribute to Matthew Shepard.* New York: Harrington Park Press, 2001. Twelve essays on antihomosexual prejudice and violence. Published simultaneously as *Journal of Gay & Lesbian Social Services,* vol. 3, nos. 1/2, 2001.

PERIODICALS

Anderson, George M. "People Are Getting Hurt." *Commonweal,* February 23, 1993, p. 16. A description of an increase in gay-bashing and intimidation, caused, the author maintains, by increased visibility of gays in public and the debate over ballot initiatives and legislation concerning civil rights for homosexuals.

Anonymous. "The Hate Debate." *The New Republic,* vol. 219, no. 18, November 2, 1998, pp. 7–8. Editorial prompted by the debate over the proposed Hate Crimes Prevention Act stating that hate-crimes laws are the wrong solution to crimes against gays and lesbians. The writer stands against making a distinction among criminals according to their motives and beliefs.

Anonymous. "Laying Down the Law." *National Review,* November 23, 1998, pp. 17–18. Discusses the reaction to the murders of Dr. Barnett Slepian and gay student Matthew Shepard among liberals and their association of such murders to the pro-life and pro-family beliefs of conservatives.

Anonymous. "Murder of Gay Student Sparks Outrage, Debate." *Christian Century,* October 28, 1998, pp. 991–92. The murder of Matthew Shepard and the debate over new hate-crimes legislation urged on the U.S. Congress by President Clinton.

Anonymous. "Preachers of Hate: Violence Against Homosexuals and Abortion Providers." *The Progressive,* December 1998, pp. 8–9. The murders of Matthew Shepard and Dr. Barnett Slepian, the ongoing violence against homosexuals and abortion providers, and whether the United States is heading toward a theocracy, laying the blame on conservative evangelicals and politicians for inspiring the violence.

Anonymous. "Spurred to Action: Laramie Wyo. Police Officer D. O'Malley Becomes Advocate for Hate Crimes Legislation After Murder of M. Shepard." *People Weekly,* vol. 54, no. 25, December 11, 2000, pp. 99–102. An account of a police officer involved in the investigation of the Matthew Shepard case. After the case closed, Officer O'Malley lobbied vigorously for the addition of sexual orientation and gender as categories of protected status within federal hate-crimes law.

Bohn, T. "Homophobic Violence: Implications for Social Work Practice." *Journal of Social Work and Human Sexuality*, vol. 2, no. 3, 1984, pp. 91–110. The author describes research on violence against homosexuals, which indicates that 38 percent of a sample of white gay men and 21 percent of a sample of black gay men reported that they had been robbed or assaulted at least once in connection with their homosexuality. The article states that social workers can help to prevent violence against homosexuals by community organizing and education, emphasizing such victims' assistance as information gathering, hot lines, self-defense classes, and advocacy before law enforcement organizations and courts. In addition, legislation can be supported to establish strong criminal penalties for homophobic assault.

Colgan, J. "Hate Crime Victimization Among Lesbian, Gay, and Bisexual Adults." *Journal of Interpersonal Violence*, vol. 12, no. 2, 1997, pp. 195–215. The authors collect data from surveys of lesbians, gay men, and bisexuals on their experience of bias-motivated violence and offer statistics drawn from the surveys that relate to the lasting effects of such violence.

Herek, G. M. "Hate Crimes Against Lesbians and Gay Men: Issues for Research and Policy." *American Psychologist*, vol. 44, 1989, pp. 948–55. In an analysis of trends in antigay hate crimes, the author maintains that most antigay hate crimes are not reported, that there have been no comprehensive surveys of the problem, and that antigay hate crimes have become a serious national problem.

Jordan, Patrick. "Call Haters to Account." *Commonweal*, November 20, 1998, pp. 6–7. The author describes the murder of Matthew Shepard, which touched off a renewed debate over hate-crimes legislation, and opines that the proposed Hate Crimes Prevention Act of 1998 and other such legislation may have the beneficial effect of deterring the prejudiced against committing violence.

Kibelstis, Teresa Eileen. "Preventing Violence Against Gay Men and Lesbians: Should Enhanced Penalties at Sentencing Extend to Bias Crime Based on Victims' Sexual Orientation?" *Notre Dame Journal of Law, Ethics, and Public Policy*, vol. 9, no. 1, 1995, pp. 309–43. The author provides statistics and background data on crimes against homosexuals and analyzes the legal problems and debate over including homosexual bias within hate-crimes legislation.

Kim, Richard. "The Truth About Hate Crimes Laws." *The Nation*, July 12, 1999, p. 20. Although national lesbian and gay groups are pursuing hate-crimes laws with single-minded zeal, the author believes there is nothing to suggest that such laws actually put a stop to hate crimes. The author also points out that antiviolence programs that are focused on community organizing, outreach, and education are struggling with few resources.

Annotated Bibliography

Kirp, David L. "Martyrs and Movies: *Boys Don't Cry.*" *American Prospect*, December 20, 1999, pp. 52–53. The writer reviews the movie *Boys Don't Cry*, based on the life of Teena Brandon (Brandon Teena), a woman living as a man who was shot and stabbed to death at the age of 21. Outlining the plot of the movie and the facts of the case, he considers newly proposed laws that would make violence on the basis of sexual orientation a hate crime.

Locke, Michelle. "Slaying of Teen May Be Hate Crime." Associated Press, October 19, 2002. Available online at http://www.sltrib.com/10192002/nation_w/8670.htm. Account of a murder in the San Francisco suburb of Newark, California, in which a 17-year-old boy dressed as a girl was beaten to death and buried in a shallow grave. Police were investigating the murder as a hate crime. The crime took place during a controversy over the performance of "The Laramie Project," a play based on the killing of Matthew Shepard, at Newark Memorial High School.

McCarthy, Thomas J. "From This Clay." *America*, November 14, 1998, p. 8. Prompted by the murder of the gay University of Wyoming student Matthew Shepard, the writer reflects on his own attitudes to homosexuality. He recalls how he responded with revulsion and fear to a gay man whom he encountered while a graduate student, which led him to reappraise what he had thought of as his enlightened view of homosexuality.

Peters, Jeff. "When Fear Turns to Hate and Hate to Violence: The Persecution of Gays Is Increasing." *Human Rights*, vol. 18, no. 1, February 1996, pp. 22–30. Using statistics and victim accounts, the author contends that antigay violence is on the rise and offers a survey of federal and state legislature designed to stem the tide.

Rauch, Jonathan. "Beyond Oppression." *The New Republic*, May 10, 1993, pp. 18–23. The author objects to the notion that homosexuals form an oppressed minority and to the phrase hate crime as it is applied to antigay violence. He maintains that crime should be treated as a problem shared by society as a whole and that hate-crimes laws are unconstitutional.

Ricks, Ingrid. "Crying Wolf." *Advocate*, November 29, 1994, pp. 32–36. The author reports a case of insurance fraud perpetrated by several women claiming antigay violence and vandalism.

Winer, Anthony S. "Hate Crimes, Homosexuals, and the Constitution." *Harvard Civil Rights/Civil Liberties Law Review*, Summer 1994, pp. 387–438. An essay on the incidence of bias crimes against homosexuals and a legal brief in support of including homosexual bias under hate-crimes statutes.

Zwerling, Martin S. "Legislating Against Hate in New York: Bias Crimes and the Lesbian and Gay Community." *Touro Law Review*, vol. 11, 1995, p. 529. The author describes trends in antihomosexual violence and advocates for the inclusion of sexual orientation as a protected status within new hate-crime legislation.

REPORTS

Amnesty International. *Breaking the Silence: Human Rights Violations Based on Sexual Orientation*. New York: Amnesty International Publications, 1994. A report on discrimination and persecution of homosexuals around the world.

———. *Crimes of Hate, Conspiracy of Silence: Torture and Ill-Treatment Based on Sexual Identity*. New York: Amnesty International USA, 2001. Available online. URL: http://www.amnesty-usa.org/stoptorture/lgbt/. A report on the torture and abuse of gay, lesbian, bisexual, and transgender individuals, on legal and economic discrimination directed at homosexuals, and the efforts of Amnesty International to address and solve these issues around the world.

Moore, Ken. *Anti-Lesbian, Gay, Bisexual and Transgender Violence in 1998: A Report of the National Coalition of Anti-Violence Programs*. New York: New York City Gay and Lesbian Anti-Violence Project, 1999. Analysis of statistics concerning antigay hate crimes in 1998.

National Asian Pacific American Legal Consortium. *Anti-Asian Violence*. A 45-page report of testimony of Karen Narasaki, the consortium's executive director, before the U.S. Senate concerning reauthorization of the Hate Crimes Statistics Act.

National Coalition of Anti-Violence Programs. *Anti-Lesbian, Gay, Transgender and Bisexual Violence in 2000*. Available online. URL: http://www.avp.org/publications/reports/2000ncavpbiasrpt.pdf. A report based on data collected during 1999 and 2000 from 11 organizations affiliated with the National Coalition of Anti-Violence Programs, and finding that violence against gay, lesbian, bisexual, and transgender individuals increased significantly during that reporting period.

VIDEOS

The Brandon Teena Story. New Video, 1999. Produced and directed by Susan Muska and Greta Olafsdottir. A documentary on the case of Teena Brandon (Brandon Teena), a woman living as a man who was raped and murdered in rural Falls City, Nebraska, in 1993.

Investigative Reports: Anti-Gay Hate Crime. A & E Home Video, 1999. Originally broadcast on July 6, 1999, this documentary hosted by Bill Kurtis details antigay hate crimes, including the beating death of Matthew Shepard and the lesser-known murder of Alan Walker of Arkansas. The film also investigates right-wing and fundamentalist religious groups that encourage or support antigay discrimination.

Licensed to Kill. DeepFocus Productions, 1997. An in-depth look at antigay murders directed by Arthur Dong, whose own encounter with antigay violence in San Francisco inspired the film. *Licensed to Kill,* which includes interviews with criminals convicted of antigay crimes, won the Director's Award and Filmmaker's Trophy at the Sundance Film Festival.

Pink Triangles: A Study of Prejudice Against Lesbians and Gay Men. Cambridge Documentary Films, 1982. A study of antihomosexual prejudice and more generally the origins of bigotry and discrimination as suffered by other minority groups throughout history and at the present time.

CURRENT HATE CRIME JOURNALISM

Borisova, Yevgenia. "Report: Racist Attacks on Rise." Moscow Times.com. Available online. URL: http://www.themoscowtimes.com/stories/2002/10/16/001.html. Downloaded on October 16, 2002. Coverage of bias-motivated incidents in Moscow and the rise of ethnic and religious intolerance throughout Russia, according to a 400-page report by the Moscow Helsinki Group. Despite the signing into law of an anti-extremism bill, the number of racist and anti-Semitic attacks has not declined. The most vulnerable groups, according to the report, are Chechens, Gypsies, Turks, and Jews, with Chechens being the most targeted group after the 1994–96 military campaign by Russia against Chechen rebels in the Caucasus region.

Chibbaro, Lou, Jr. "Democrats Petition for House Vote on Hate Crimes: Measure Would Bypass Opposition by House GOP Leadership." *Southern Voice.* Available online. URL: http://www.southernvoice.com/national/021004hatecrimes.php3?pub=atl. Posted on October 21, 2002. News article describing the efforts by Democratic leaders to get a floor vote on what the author calls the "Local Law Enforcement Hate Crimes Prevention Act." Democrat John Conyers and six of his House colleagues were the first to sign a discharge petition, which must be signed by a simple majority of House members in order to force the Speaker of the House, Republican Dennis Hastert, to bring the bill to a vote. House Republicans have blocked a final vote on the bill since it was introduced in the mid-1990s.

Cope, Ryan. "Definition of Hate Crime Ambiguous." *The Penn.* Available online. URL: http://www.thepenn.org/vnews/display.v/ART/2002/10/18/3db06827a9523. Posted on October 18, 2002. The writer reviews campus statistics showing no hate crimes occurring at the Indiana University of Pennsylvania and the fine distinctions between hate crime and hate acts or incidents.

Crary, David. "'Closet' Survives in Politics: In Many Contests, Gay Rights Is No Issue Among Candidates." *Boston Globe.* Available online. URL: http://www.boston.com/dailyglobe2/294/nation/_Closet_survives_in_politics+.shtml. Posted on October 21, 2002. Openly gay politicians debate the issues during the 2002 campaign season, and the hate-crimes issue proves a hot debating point between Tammy Baldwin, a white Democrat, and Ron Greer, an African-American Republican, who claims that homosexuals have "hijacked" the civil rights movement and strongly opposes the writing of any legislation or the formulation of new public policy dealing with sexual orientation.

DeLeon, Virginia. "Profanity Keeps Play Off LC Stage." *Spokesman-Review.* Available online. URL: http://www.spokesmanreview.com/news-story.asp?date=101602&ID=s1235579&cat=section.spokane. Posted on October 16, 2002. At the Lewis and Clark High School in Spokane, Washington, controversy swirls around the performance of "The Laramie Project," which is canceled by school administrators objecting to the play's use of profanity. The teacher in charge of the production believes that the importance of the message delivered by the play, based on the murder of Matthew Shepard, outweighs any objection to strong or offensive language, which students have heard before.

Edwards, Andrew. "Zero-Tolerance of Anti-Semitic Acts Declared." *Daily Bruin.* Available online at http://www.dailybruin.ucla.edu/news/articles.asp?id=21034. Posted on October 10, 2002. The UCLA campus newspaper covers the signing of a statement by the chancellor of UC Berkeley and more than 300 other heads of American colleges condemning anti-Semitic acts. Taking exception to the statement, UCLA chancellor Albert Carnesale comments that the statement should not have focused on anti-Semitism but instead should have condemned hate crimes against any and all students. The chancellor's action came amidst controversy on the campus over the escalating Palestinian/Israeli conflict and what many university leaders see as a growing trend of anti-Semitism, expressed in speech and in hate incidents.

Fienberg, Howard. "America the Tolerant." *Tech Central Station.* Available online. URL: http://www.techcentralstation.com/1051/techwrapper.jsp?PID=1051-250&CID=1051-102102A. Posted on October 21, 2002. The author believes that despite the occurrence of anti-Arab and anti-Muslim bias crimes in the wake of the September 11, 2001, terrorist attacks, America remains by and large a country tolerant of differences. The author describes a report of the Council on American Islamic Relations, a nonprofit organization, which accounted for 1,516 incidents of anti-Arab bias and violence after September 11, 2001, including denial of religious accommodation, harassment, discrimination, bias, threat, assault, and several murders. Many of these incidents, according to the author, can be discounted as either not bias-related, as ambiguous, or as concerning a lack of religious accommodation rather than outright discrimination or bias.

Greenhouse, Linda. "Justices Seek Federal Guidance on Sentencing." *New York Times*. Available online. URL: http://www.nytimes.com/2002/10/22/national/22SCOT.html?ex=1035950400&en=35345c2de7b625e3&ei=5062 (by subscription). Posted on October 21, 2002. Article detailing the fallout of the Supreme Court's *Apprendi v. New Jersey* decision, which held that evidence used to increase a sentence beyond the statutory maximum must be subject to a jury verdict. The finding of biased motivation that brings a hate-crimes penalty enhancement, for example, must be proven to a jury and cannot be left up to a judge during the sentencing phase. The Supreme Court asks for guidance from the federal government on the question of whether penalty enhancement based on prior offenses, which had been the single exception to this rule, are out of place in the jury-based sentencing procedure established by *Apprendi v. New Jersey*.

Hufstader, Louisa. "Hate Becomes Transparent at NVC." Napanews.com. Available online. URL: http://napanews.com/templates/index.cfm?template=story_full&id=5AD0A6578ACA-4641-A7B9-7787D32119C9. Posted on October 16, 2002. Description of an exhibition, "Hate Is Transparent," mounted by Constance Shipman on the campus of the Napa Valley College. The exhibition consisted of more than 100 hate crimes documented on transparent plastic, hung by a fishing line at eye level. Although the exhibition received favorable comments, others criticized the work as unduly negative. The exhibition was part of the college's Tolerance Week, which offered films, a performance of "The Laramie Project," and a panel discussion.

Hutchinson, Earl Ofari. "Sniper Killings Toss Ugly Glare on Home Grown Terrorism." *The Black World Today*. Available online. URL: http://athena.tbwt.com/content/article.asp?articleid=1780. Posted on October 17, 2002. The author uses the Washington, D.C., area sniper killings of Fall 2002 to describe the daily terror felt by members of ethnic and religious minorities when faced with bias-motivated violence at the hands of racists and skinheads. Police and local officials are reluctant to profile or monitor those who are prone to hate violence, and the federal laxity on gun laws allows "home-grown" killers to terrorize entire metropolitan areas.

Johnson, Julie. "Increase in Hate Crimes Spur Legislation." *New California Media*. Available online. URL: http://news.ncmonline.com/news/view_article.html?article_id=5234e4bb865edfdad9afb6565780a703. Posted on October 8, 2002. The author covers an increase in reported hate crimes in California for 2001, a trend attributed to backlash in the wake of the

September 11, 2001, terrorist attacks. Outside of bias-motivated crimes against Muslims and Arab Americans, the overall rate of hate crimes decreased in the state by 5 percent. Governor Gray Davis signed the Hate Crimes Prosecution Bill on September 23, 2002, placing hate crimes in the same category as other highly sensitive crimes such as stalking, child abuse, and domestic violence, and putting in place a system of "vertical prosecution," in which a single prosecutor is kept on the case through the preliminary hearing, plea bargaining, and trial. Two additional bills pending at press time were the Youth Anti-Bias Pilot Project and Repeat Hate Crime Offender Felony Enhancement.

Kinder, Elizabeth. "Interfaith Group Allied in Eradicating Hate: Muslim Is Honored for Promoting Peace in Peoria Community." PJStar.com. Available online. URL: http://www.pjstar.com/news/topnews/g130895a.html. Posted on October 18, 2002. The author covers the fourth annual Stop the Hate vigil in Peoria, Illinois, attended by members of the city's Muslim, American Indian, Jewish, African, Buddhist, Christian, and pagan communities. The vigil and the Interfaith Alliance, a nonpartisan religious organization, are credited with helping to eradicate prejudice and hate crimes in central Illinois.

Knight, Robert H. "Hate Crimes." *Washington Times*. Available online. URL: http://www.washtimes.com/op-ed/20020621-61753105.htm. Posted on June 21, 2002. The author believes that the Local Law Enforcement Act is a federal power grab that would create a new federal civil right based on sexual behavior, recasting traditional morality as a form of bigotry. The article warns against the route followed by Canada, where free speech, the author contends, has been drastically curtailed by the passage of hate-crime legislation.

Matier, Phillip, and Andrew Ross. "Long, Strange Journey of Hate-Crime Case." *San Francisco Chronicle*. Available online. URL: http://www. sfgate.com/cgi-bin/article.cgi?file=/chronicle/archive/2002/10/07/ BA223469.DTL. Posted on October 7, 2002. The curious case of John Henning III, a respected San Francisco lawyer who was accused of bias-motivated assault after a fistfight with two Hasidic Jews outside the city's Schneerson Synagogue. The Anti-Defamation League labeled the incident an "act of terror," but Henning benefited from a plea bargain in which the hate-crime charge was dropped and the charges reduced to misdemeanors. The deal was labeled a political payoff by critics of the San Francisco district attorney's office, which is considered one of the most zealous in the country in prosecuting hate crimes.

McCurtis, James. "Activists Target Hate Crimes." Available online. URL: http://www.lsj.com/news/local/021008vigillb-2b.html. Posted on October 21, 2002. *Lansing State Journal*. News coverage of an anti-hate crimes rally at the Michigan state capitol in Lansing, part of an 18-hour vigil commemorating the fourth anniversary of the death of Matthew Shepard. Protesters focused on the ongoing efforts of state Republican lawmakers to block hate-crimes legislation in the Michigan House of Representatives. The representatives reply that the bills lack support.

O'Neill, Tom. "Neighborhood Clash in Court: Civil Rights Violations Claimed." *Cincinnati Enquirer.* Available online. URL: http://enquirer.com/ editions/2002/10/18/loc_kyhate18.html. Posted on October 18, 2002. A case of federal civil-rights violations is brought after a clash between white and African-American neighbors in Covington, Kentucky. A mother and two sons were accused of hurling racial epithets, breaking windows and lights, loudly playing neo-Nazi music, and giving the Nazi salute outside the house of the neighboring black family. The bringing of federal civil rights charges in a dispute between neighbors represents a departure from the norm, in which such charges usually involve the police, the prison system, or public schools.

Ortiz, John. "Details about Clery Disclosure." *The State Hornet.* Available online. URL: http://www.statehornet.com/vnews/display.v/ART/2002/ 10/16/3dac9da5467f1. Posted on October 22, 2002. The author gives details on the Clery Act, which requires colleges to report crime statistics including incidents of hate crimes, which are defined as crimes motivated by a victim's race, gender, religion, sexual orientation, ethnicity, or disability.

Ramroop, Tara. "City Staff Refers Hate Crimes Issue to Police Department." *The California Aggie Online.* Available online. URL: http://www. californiaaggie.com/_articles/3926.taf. Posted on October 21, 2002. Coverage of the hate-crimes issue at the University of California, Davis, and the surrounding community, a locus of controversy over the treatment of hate crimes by local police and university officials. Bullying and bias-related incidents at elementary and junior high schools add to the controversy, and many parents feel the city is purposely avoiding the issue.

Richardson, Valerie. "Wichita to Revisit Brutal Slayings as Testimony Begins." *Washington Times.* Available online. URL: http://www.washtimes. com/national/20021007-5521566.htm. Posted on October 7, 2002. A story covering the multiple-murder charges against Reginald and Jonathan Carr, who were accused of kidnapping, rape, robbery, and five murders in connection with a rampage that took place in Wichita, Kansas, in December 2000. The crime brought controversy over hate-crime legislation, as the perpetrators were black and the victims white; opponents of hate-crimes law pointed out that media coverage of the killings was almost nonexistent and that the Carrs were not charged under any civil rights or bias-crime statutes.

Shaffer, Stefanie. "Hate Crimes Cause for Concern in LaPlata." *The Diamondback*. Available online. URL: http://www.inform.umd.edu/News/Diamondback/archives/2002/10/18/news3.html. Posted on October 18, 2002. The author describes the most recent hate incidents in LaPlata Hall on the campus of the University of Maryland. The incidents consist of messages scrawled on doors, walls, and dry-erase boards and are treated by the university police as bias-motivated acts; while in past years the motivation of similar incidents was based on ethnicity or religion, the most recent incidents were targeted at sexual orientation.

Szaniszlo, Marie. "Sept. 11 Backlash Unleashes Hate Crimes in Bay State." Boston Herald.com. Available online. URL: http://www2.bostonherald.com/news/local_regional/hate09252002.htm. Posted on September 25, 2002. The author reports a dramatic increase in hate crimes in Massachusetts in 2001, largely as the result of a backlash against Muslims and Arabs in the wake of the September 11, 2001, terrorist attacks. In all, 576 incidents were reported in 2001, up 24 percent from the 463 reported in 2000. Many occurred as perpetrators targeted the readily accessible owners and employees of Arab- or Muslim-owned gas stations or convenience stores.

Wallace, Amy. "AG Tags Boys with 'Hate' Label. *Portsmouth Herald*. Available online. URL: http://www.seacoastonline.com/news/10192002/news/30168.htm. Posted on October 19, 2002. The author covers New Hampshire attorney general Ann Larney's filing of a civil rights case against four boys aged 12 to 14 for assaulting and taunting a 13-year-old for his suspected homosexuality. In New Hampshire, according to the hate-crime statute which went into effect in 2000, police are not permitted to prosecute civil rights violations; instead an assault charge was filed and the attorney general's office then followed up with the civil charge, which allows the office to issue a protective order and levy a $5,000 fine.

Westhoff, Julia. "University Officials Deny Ignoring Hate Crime." *The Badger Herald*. Available online. URL: http://www.badgerherald.com/vnews/display.v/ART/2002/10/17/3dae2537f37e5. Posted on October 17, 2002. Covers a hate-crime incident at the University of Wisconsin, in which a student was the victim of written and verbal racial slurs, and controversy surrounding the university's handling of the incident. Although the university runs a program known as Speak Up, in which students can report bias-motivated harassment, many do not take advantage of the system, as they do not expect the university administration to take any action on their behalf.

Wynn, Kelly, and Mark Fisher. "Forum Targets Hate Crimes, Racism." *Dayton Daily News*. Available online. URL: http://www.activedayton.com/ddn/local/daily/1011forum.html. Posted on October 11, 2002. Coverage of a two-hour public hate-crimes forum, Call For a Healthy Community, held at the Dayton Convention Center. Panelists addressed hate crimes in the wake of the September 11, 2001, terrorist attacks as well as the issues of racial profiling and language barriers.

Zibrowski, Jamie. "Indiana, Nation Need to Pass, Enforce Hate Crimes Legislation." *Indiana Statesman Online Edition.* Available online. URL: http://www.indianastatesman.com/vnews/display.v/ART/2002/10/02/ 3d9af3c396dd1. Posted on October 2, 2002. In this opinion piece, the author strongly supports hate-crime legislation on the state and federal levels and criticizes Indiana's failure to pass any laws on hate crimes except a data-collection statute. The author also takes to task those who oppose hate-crimes laws dealing with bias against sexual orientation.

CHAPTER 8

ORGANIZATIONS AND AGENCIES

This chapter presents a list of organizations directly or indirectly concerned with hate-crimes-related law, monitoring, data collection, lobbying, education, and prevention. The list is broken down into federal government organizations, academic organizations, national advocacy organizations, and state and local advocacy organizations. The URL address, which allows a researcher to locate the organization's World Wide Web site, is provided where available. As web addresses frequently change, and as these organizations may change their names and their missions, the researcher should consult a good search engine for up-to-date information.

FEDERAL GOVERNMENT ORGANIZATIONS

Bureau of Justice Assistance
URL: http://www.ojp.usdoj.gov/
  BJA
Phone: (202) 616-6500
Fax: (202) 305-1367
810 Seventh Street, NW
Fourth Floor
Washington, DC 20531
The Bureau of Justice Assistance (BJA) is a component of the Office of Justice Programs, U.S. Department of Justice, which also includes the Bureau of Justice Statistics, the National Institute of Justice, the Office of Juvenile Justice and Delinquency Prevention, and the Office for Victims of Crime. According to its public mission statement, BJA's mandate is "to provide leadership and assistance in support of local criminal justice strategies to achieve safe communities. . . . To achieve these goals, BJA programs emphasize enhanced coordination and cooperation of federal, state, and local efforts." Under a grant provided by the BJA, the National Criminal Justice Association prepared *A Policymaker's Guide to Hate Crimes*, a report on federal, state, and local response to hate-crime incidents, on hate-crime cases, and on the

methods used by local law enforcement in investigating and prosecuting hate crimes. The BJA has also funded training curricula for local law enforcement and hosts conferences such as the Hate Crime Summit, organized by the International Association of Chiefs of Police, which took place in June 1998.

Bureau of Justice Statistics
URL: http://www.ojp.usdocj. gov/bjs
E-mail: ASKBJS@ojp.usdoj.gov
Phone: (800) 732-3277
633 Indiana Avenue, NW
  #1142
Washington, DC 20531
This site offers a comprehensive collection of crime statistics reported to the Justice Department, including hate crimes reported to the FBI's National Incident-Based Reporting System (NIBRS), at http://www.ojp.usdoj.gov/bjs/abstract/hcrn99.htm. The report analyzes NIBRS hate-crime incidents from jurisdictions in 17 states reporting such data to the FBI over the three-year period, including information on the type of bias motivation, the offenses committed during these incidents, the presence and use of weapons, and the location and the time of day of these crimes. Information is also provided on the characteristics of hate-crime victims, suspected hate-crime offenders, and the reported relationship between victims and suspected offenders. The Bureau of Justice Statistics has also made an important grant to researchers at the Center for Criminal Justice Policy Research at Northeastern University in Boston, who carried out a survey of hate-crime collection methods nationwide and made recommendations for sustaining participation by local reporting agencies.

Community Relations Service
URL: http://www.usdoj.gov/crs/ crs.htm
Phone: (215) 597-2344
Second and Chestnut Street
  #208
Philadelphia, PA 19106
The Community Relations Service is a federal agency charged with mediating intergroup disputes. The CRS employs a staff of trainers and mediators whose job it is to resolve conflicts and prevent violence when racial tensions begin to occur. When a community is asked to host a Klan rally, or a march by another group likely to cause some kind of public disorder or racial tension, CRS personnel are often called in to provide assistance. The CRS was established by Title X of the Civil Rights Act of 1964. In 2000, the CRS staff of 37 mediators received more than 5,000 requests for their services, and responded to more than 1,200 such requests. The CRS has developed a national hate-crimes response training curriculum that trains police and community leaders in the prevention of and response to hate-crimes incidents.

Federal Bureau of Investigation (FBI)
URL: http://www.fbi.gov
Phone: (202) 324-3691
935 Pennsylvania Avenue, NW
Washington, DC 20535-0001

Uniform Crime Reporting Section
Phone: (202) 324-5015
409 Seventh Street, NW
Suite 4
Washington, DC 20004

The FBI and its 11,400 special agents are charged with investigation of violations of federal law, including federal hate-crimes statutes. FBI headquarters in Washington, D.C., provides program direction and support services to 56 field offices, approximately 400 satellite offices known as resident agencies, four specialized field installations, and more than 40 foreign liaison posts. Under the Hate Crimes Statistics Act, the FBI is charged with training local law enforcement in the investigation of hate crimes and the collection of hate-crime statistics. The agency publishes *Training Guide for Hate Crime Data Collection* as well as *Hate Crime Data Collection Guidelines*, which are regularly updated. The annual Uniform Crime Report (UCR), a national snapshot of crime broken down by category and location, is a useful reference tool for researchers, scholars, and the public. The UCR currently includes comprehensive statistics on the occurrence of hate crimes, state by state, county by county.

Office for Victims of Crime
URL: http://www.ojp.usdoj.gov/ovc
Phone: (202) 307-5983
633 Indiana Avenue
Washington, DC 20531

The Office for Victims of Crime (OVC) was established by the 1984 Victims of Crime Act (VOCA) to oversee diverse programs that benefit victims of crime. OVC provides substantial funding to state victim assistance and compensation programs. In 1994, the agency created a training program, *Bias Crimes: National Bias Crime Training for Law Enforcement and Victim Assistance Professionals*, designed to educate criminal justice and allied professionals regarding the rights and needs of crime victims.

Office of Community Oriented Policing Services (COPS)
URL: http://www.usdoj.gov/cops
E-mail: egov.issues@usdoj.gov
Phone: (202) 514-2058
Fax: (202) 616-8594
1100 Vermont Avenue, NW
Washington, DC 20530

This office is dedicated to community policing practices, in which law enforcement personnel take a more active and public role in the communities they serve. The COPS office provided funding for the Hate Crime Summit held in June 1998 by the International Association of Chiefs of Police as well as funding for bias-crime prevention initiatives under a grant program known as the Problem-Solving Partnership.

Office of Juvenile Justice and Delinquency Prevention
URL: http://ojjdp.ncjrs.org/about/about.html
E-mail: Askjj@ncjrs.org
Phone: (202) 307-5911
Fax: (202) 307-2093
810 Seventh Street, NW
Washington, DC 20531

The Office of Juvenile Justice and Delinquency Prevention is a bureau of the federal Department of Justice. In 1992, the OJJDP was charged with conducting a national assessment of the motives and characteristics of youths who commit hate crimes. Begun in 1993, the survey was finally completed in July 1996 as the *Report to Congress on Juvenile Hate Crime*. The OJJDP also has developed a curriculum called Healing the Hate for the purpose of the prevention of hate crimes by juveniles.

U.S. Commission on Civil Rights
URL: http://www.usccr.gov
Phone: (202) 376-8317
624 Ninth Street, NW
Washington, DC 20425

The U.S. Commission on Civil Rights is an "independent, bipartisan, fact-finding agency" of the executive branch established under the Civil Rights Act of 1957. The commission investigates complaints of discrimination against eligible voters, collects information relating to discrimination or a denial of equal protection of the laws, and issues public service announcements to discourage discrimination or denial of equal protection of the laws. In the wake of the September 11, 2001, terrorist attacks against the United States, the UCCR set up a hot line (800-552-6843) for reporting hate crimes against Muslims and Arab Americans.

U.S. Department of Education
URL: http://www.ed.gov/index.jsp
E-mail: customerservice@inet.ed.gov
Phone: (800) 872-5327
400 Maryland Avenue, SW
Washington, DC 20202

Through the 1990s, this federal cabinet-level department has played an increasingly active role in hate-crimes prevention and hate-crimes initiatives. In 1992, Congress incorporated antiprejudice initiatives into the Elementary and Secondary Education Act (ESEA), legislation that provides federal funding for public schools. By its Title IV, the ESEA created a hate-crimes prevention initiative that promoted teacher training and the development of curricula specifically designed to combat hate crimes. The DOE provided $2 million in grants in 1996 to fund initiatives for hate-crimes prevention, and continues to organize conferences on hate-crime and bias-related school violence, such as the 1998 White House Conference on School Violence.

U.S. Department Of Justice
URL: http://www.usdoj.gov
E-mail: ASKDOJ@doj.gov
950 Pennsylvania Avenue
Washington, DC 20530-0001
Office of the Attorney General:
(202) 353-1555
The stated mission of the U.S. Department of Justice, the federal agency charged with enforcing federal laws, is "to enforce the law and defend the interest of the United States according to the law, to provide Federal leadership in preventing and controlling crime, to seek just punishment for those guilty of unlawful behavior, to administer and enforce the Nation's immigration laws fairly and effectively, and to ensure fair and impartial administration of justice for all Americans." The Department of Justice includes the Civil Rights Division, the Community Relations Service, the Office of Juvenile Justice and Delinquency Prevention, and the Office for Victims of Crime.

U.S. House of Representatives Judiciary Committee
URL: http://www.house.gov/
judiciary
E-mail: judiciary@mail.
house.gov
Phone: (202) 225-3951
2138 Rayburn Office Building
Washington, DC 20515
The committee debates and considers new federal legislation. Hearings held before the committee bring important hate-crimes issues to the media forefront, allowing the public a glimpse of academic, legal, and law enforcement experts and a consideration of the issues and opinion on proposals for new hate-crimes law.

U.S. Senate Judiciary Committee
URL: http://www.senate.gov/
~judiciary
E-mail: webmaster@judiciary.
senate.gov
Phone: (202) 224-5225
Dirksen Office Building
Room SD-224
Washington, DC 20510-6275
The committee debates proposed new federal laws. This website and the parallel site belonging to the House Judiciary Committee allow users to track the status of pending legislation.

ACADEMIC ORGANIZATIONS

Northeastern University Brudnick Center on Violence and Conflict
URL: http://www.violence.neu.
edu
E-mail: jlevin1049@aol.com
Phone: (617) 373-4983
Fax: (617) 373-8646
569 Holmes Hall
Boston, MA 02115
The Brudnick Center seeks solutions to problems of hostility and hatred based on group differences. The center involves faculty from a range of disciplines and initiates research

projects and educational endeavors in the area of intergroup tensions and violence in the schools, state-sponsored terrorism, hate crimes, international conflict and warfare, hate speech on campus, skinhead activity, religious persecution, organized hate groups, and so on.

Gonzaga University Institute for Action Against Hate
URL: http://guweb2.gonzaga.edu/againsthate
Seattle, WA 99258
Phone: (509) 323-3484
This organization was founded in 1997 at this Jesuit university to combat hate crimes on campuses and in communities, with a special focus on the Northwest region. The stated goal of the institute is to "focus multi-disciplinary academic resources on the causes and effects of hate as well as potential strategies for combating hate." The institute develops courses and course materials, publishes the *Journal of Hate Studies* and a newsletter, and provides advocacy to victims of hate crimes.

NATIONAL ADVOCACY ORGANIZATIONS

American-Arab Anti-Discrimination Committee (ADC)
URL: http://www.adc.org
Phone: (202) 244-2990
Fax: (202) 244-3196
4201 Connecticut Avenue, NW
Suite 500
Washington, DC 20008
Founded by Senator James Abourezk in 1980, the ADC, according to its Mission Statement, "is a civil rights organization committed to defending the rights of people of Arab descent and promoting their rich cultural heritage." The ADC claims to be nonsectarian and nonpartisan and offers advocacy in cases of defamation, legal action in cases of discrimination, and counseling in matters of immigration. The ADC has published a series of reports on anti-Arab hate crimes and has organized departments of legal services, media and publications, educational programs, and a research institute.

American Citizens for Justice, Inc.
Phone: (313) 557-2772
15777 West Ten Mile Road
Suite 108
Southfield, MI 48075
This organization seeks to combat harassment and discrimination against Asian Pacific Americans and other ethnic groups through advocacy and legal consulting. The group monitors anti-Asian violence, carries out community education programs, and offers the Vincent Chin Justice scholarship in memory of a prominent victim of anti-Asian bias crime.

American Civil Liberties Union (ACLU)
URL: http://www.aclu.org

E-mail: aclu@aclu.org
Phone: (212) 549-2500
Fax: (212) 549-2646
Washington, DC 20002
This organization was founded in 1920 to advocate constitutional freedoms and civil liberties under attack in the wake of World War I. ACLU attorneys appear in court and in state and federal legislatures to, as the organization states, "defend and preserve the individual rights and liberties guaranteed . . . by the Constitution and laws of the United States." The ACLU has filed briefs and appeared as counsel in several important hate-crimes cases on behalf of defendants whose First Amendment free-speech rights it sees threatened by hate-crimes laws and prosecutions. It also involves itself in cases concerning the death penalty, police procedures, religious liberty, prisons, national security, and gay rights.

American Jewish Committee
URL: http://www.ajc.org
Phone: (212) 751-4000
Fax: (212) 838-2120
165 East 56th Street
New York, NY 10022
An organization seeking to safeguard the welfare and security of Jews around the world, with chapters in several dozen U.S. cities. Although principally concerned with Middle East problems and policy and ties between American Jews and Israel, the AJC also tracks anti-Semitic hate crimes and offers several publications and reports on the

subject, including "Skinheads: Who They Are and What to Do When They Come to Town" and "Bigotry on Campus: A Planned Response."

American Psychological Association (APA)
URL: http://www.apa.org
Phone: (202) 336-6062
Fax: (202) 336-6063
750 First Street, NE
Washington, DC 20002-4242
An organization of academic and clinical psychologists, actively involved in the matter of hate crimes through research and publications and by providing assistance to individuals suffering prejudice and hate-motivated violence. The APA also organizes law enforcement training focusing on understanding the causes and effects of hate-related criminal behavior.

Anti-Defamation League (ADL)
URL: http://www.adl.org
Phone: (212) 490-2525
Fax: (212) 867-0779
823 United Nations Plaza
New York, NY 10017

ADL Government Affairs
Phone: (202) 986-0375
Fax: (202) 775-7465
1629 K Street, NW
Suite 802
Washington, DC 20006
Founded in 1913 to fight discrimination in schools and workplaces against Jews, the Anti-Defamation League now advocates more generally against hate crimes, having writ-

ten a model hate-crimes statute in 1981 that has been adopted by many state legislatures and local governments. The ADL has also produced an anti-hate-crime training video, a handbook of existing hate-crime policies and procedures at various police departments, and a training program in discrimination and bias-motivated behavior for law enforcement. The organization operates 31 regional offices; its web site offers hate-crimes data, press releases and reports, a hate symbols database, and a HateFilter to be used on Internet-connected computers.

Arab American Institute (AAI)
Phone: (202) 429-9210
Fax: (202) 429-9214
918 16th Street, NW
Suite 601
Washington, DC 20006
The Arab American Institute was cofounded in 1985 to serve as a national organization for Americans of Arab descent. The AAI lobbies Congress on behalf of Arab Americans and has been most recently concerned with an anti-Arab backlash inspired by the September 11, 2001, terrorist attacks on the United States.

Asian Law Caucus (ALC)
URL: http://www.asianlawcaucus.
org
Phone: (415) 391-1655
Fax: (415) 391-0366
720 Market Street, Suite 5000
San Francisco, CA 94102
This organization describes its mission as follows: "To promote, ad-

vance and represent the legal and civil rights of the Asian and Pacific Islander communities." To this end, the organization integrates legal services, education programs, community organizing, and advocacy. The specific program areas include anti-Asian violence.

Asian American Legal Defense
and Education Fund
(AALDEF)
99 Hudson Street
12th floor
New York, NY 10013
Phone: (212) 966-5932
Fax: (212) 966-4303
The AALDEF was founded in 1974 to protect and promote the civil rights of Asian Americans through litigation, legal advocacy, and community education. In the wake of the September, 11, 2001, attacks, the AALDEF is, according to its website, "providing legal representation to victims of racial/religious violence, police violence, racial profiling, immigration detainment and other forms of discrimination."

Asian Pacific American Legal
Center of Southern California
(APALC)
Phone: (213) 748-2022
Fax: (213) 748-0679
1010 South Flower Street
Suite 302
Los Angeles, CA 90015-1428
This organization works with the city of Los Angeles and the Los Angeles Police Department to improve responses to and prevention

of hate crimes against Asian Americans. APALC also participates in the Hate Violence Monitoring program of the LAPD, which streamlines the tracking of hate violence and trains officers in the investigation of hate violence cases.

**Association of State Uniform
  Crime Reporting Programs
Utah Bureau of Criminal
  Identification
URL: http://www.asucrp.org./
  mission/index.html
E-mail: statistics@asucrp.org
Fax: (801) 965-4749
3888 West 5400 South
P.O. Box 148280
Salt Lake City, UT 84118**
This organization includes participants of the National Uniform Crime Reporting Program (UCR) and the National Incident Based Reporting System (NIBRS) on the state, regional, and national levels. The introduction of NIBRS in member states provides additional data to define levels and types of violent and property crime and address current criminal justice issues, including hate crimes.

**Center for Democratic Renewal
  (CDR)
URL: http://www.publiceye.org/
  pra/cdr/cdr.html
Phone: (404) 221-0025
Fax: (404) 221-0045
P.O. Box 50469
Atlanta, GA 30302-0469**

An information-gathering organization, the CDR bills itself as a "community-based coalition fighting hate-group activity." The organization serves as a clearinghouse for information on the white supremacist movement. It conducts research and provides training for law enforcement, schools, churches, and community organizations. The CDR has produced more than 40 publications, including the resource manual *When Hate Groups Come to Town*, to assist communities experiencing hate-motivated violence or intimidation.

**Center for Women Policy
  Studies
URL: http://www.
  centerwomenpolicy.org
Phone: (202) 872-1770
Fax: (202) 296-8962
1211 Connecticut Avenue, NW
Suite 312
Washington, DC 20036**
Founded in 1972 as the nation's first feminist policy research organization, the Center for Women Policy Studies provides reports and information resources for academics, community leaders, advocates, and policy makers. The group supports the inclusion of gender bias as a criterion for hate-crimes law and has made violence against women a key area of interest; in 2001, the center published an updated report, "Violence Against Women as Bias-Motivated Hate Crime: Defining the Issues."

Coalition for Human Dignity Information Center
URL: http://www.halcyon.com/chd
Phone: (360) 756-0914
Fax: (360) 738-3034
P.O. Box 36
Bellingham, WA 98227
An organization that tracks the activities of far right and hate groups in the Pacific Northwest and disseminates news reports and research through a quarterly report.

Educators for Social Responsibility
URL: http://www.esrnational.org
E-mail: educators@esrnational.org
Phone: (800) 370-2515
Fax: (617) 864-5164
23 Garden Street
Cambridge, MA 02138
Educators for Social Responsibility states its mission as "to make teaching social responsibility a core practice in education so that young people develop the convictions and skills needed to shape a safe, sustainable, democratic, and just world." To that end, the group offers a variety of curriculum materials, including lesson plans focused on the issue of race discrimination and bias crimes, as well as training materials for educators dealing with the issue of racism, intergroup conflict, and hate violence.

Gay Lesbian Straight Education Network (GLSEN)
URL: http://www.glsen.org
Phone: (212) 727-0135, ext. 110
Fax: (212) 727-0254
121 West 27th Street
Suite 804
New York, NY 10001
This organization was formed to combat discrimination and antigay violence against students and school personnel. Its mission statement includes the following: "GLSEN believes that the key to ending antigay prejudice and hate-motivated violence is education. And it's for this reason that GLSEN brings together students, educators, families and other community members—of any sexual orientation or gender identity/expression—to reform America's educational system." Volunteers from the organization participate in a national network of chapters and work with local schools, teachers, administrators, and librarians; a public policy department works with public officials at local, state, and federal levels.

Ministries in the Midst of Hate and Violence
Hate Crime Data Collection Project
URL: http://gbgm-umc.org/programs/antihate/trackingproject.stm
United Methodist Church
475 Riverside Drive
Room 1502
New York, NY 10115-0050
Believing that hate crimes are underreported to the authorities and the media, this organization collects clippings and information on hate

crimes from volunteers through its web site. The site states that "this project will help us understand the current situation, accumulate data nationwide, do trend analysis, report on the findings and initiate a dialogue based upon empirical data to address underlying causes." As of May 2003, the project was still in the planning stages, with a database and chronology to be published as the work proceeds.

Human Rights Campaign (HRC)
URL: http://www.hrc.org
Phone: (202) 628-4160
Fax: (202) 347-5323
919 18th Street, NW
Suite 800
Washington, DC 20006

The HRC is an advocacy organization for gay and transgender issues. Its HRC Action Center works to pass the Hate Crimes Prevention Act, the pending federal hate-crimes legislation that would bring up to date the 34-year-old hate-crimes law by adding real or perceived gender, sexual orientation and disability to categories currently covered.

International Association of Chiefs of Police
URL: http://www.theiacp.org
Phone: (703) 836-6767
Fax: (703) 836-4543
515 North Washington Street
Alexandria, VA 22314

The International Association of Chiefs of Police is the world's oldest and largest nonprofit membership organization of police executives. The organization's web site includes links, resources, and publications dedicated to the subject of hate-crimes investigation and reporting.

Japanese American Citizens League
URL: http://www.jacl.org
E-mail: jacl@jacl.org
Phone: (415) 921-5225
P.O. Box 7144
San Francisco, CA 94120-7144

The Japanese American Citizens League was founded in 1929 to address issues of discrimination against persons of Japanese ancestry residing in the United States. The current organization, which includes 113 chapters and five regional offices, states that its mission is "protecting the rights of all segments of the Asian Pacific American community." The organization provides scholarships and grants and advocates for legislation concerning Asian Americans. It has created an active hate-crimes program that includes the production of anti-hate-crime brochures, community outreach programs, and digital hate conferences focusing on hate groups on the Internet.

Justice Research and Statistics Association (JRSA)
Phone: (202) 624-8560
Fax: (202) 624-5269
444 North Capitol Street, NW
Suite 445
Washington, DC 20001

A national nonprofit organization that provides statistics and analysis on criminal justice issues for use by state and federal agencies. The organization also provides training in records management, data analysis, and forecasting, as well as reports on the latest research on criminal justice issues being conducted by local, state, and federal agencies. JRSA has published several papers on the hate-crime data collection efforts mandated by the Hate Crimes Statistics Act of 1990.

Lawyers' Committee for Civil Rights Under Law
URL: http://www.lawyerscomm. org
Phone: (202) 662-8600
1401 New York Avenue, NW
Suite 400
Washington, DC 20005
The nonprofit Lawyers' Committee for Civil Rights Under Law was formed in 1963 at the request of President John F. Kennedy to involve the private bar in providing legal services to address racial discrimination. The organization's mission statement reads in part, "Given our nation's history of racial discrimination, de jure segregation, and the de facto inequities that persist, the Lawyers' Committee's primary focus is to represent the interest of African Americans in particular, other racial and ethnic minorities, and other victims of discrimination, where doing so can help to secure justice for all racial and ethnic minorities." The organization provides a hate crimes page linked to a number of useful press and informational releases, speeches, and a hate crimes resource list at http://www. lawyerscomm.org/publicpolicy/ hatecrimeresourcelist.html.

Leadership Conference on Civil Rights (LCCR)
URL: http://www.civilrights.org/ lccr
Phone: (202) 466-3311
Fax: (202) 466-3435
1629 K Street, NW
Suite 1010
Washington, DC 20006
The Leadership Conference on Civil Rights was founded during the era of new civil rights legislation of the 1960s and today describes itself as "the nerve-center for the struggle against discrimination in all its forms." Beginning with 30 civil rights and labor groups, the LCCR has grown to more than 185 national organizations, representing ethnic minorities, women, children, labor unions, individuals with disabilities, older Americans, major religious groups, gays and lesbians, and civil liberties and human rights groups. The LCCR states as one of its primary goals "a strong and effective federal policy against hate crimes."

The Matthew Shepard Foundation
URL: http://www.matthewsplace. com/foundtext.html
Beech Street Law Office

123 South Durbin
Casper, WY 82601
The Matthew Shepard Foundation was founded to memorialize its namesake, the victim of a widely reported antigay murder in Wyoming. On its web site, the foundation states, "The Shepard family has created this Foundation to help people abandon ignorance, prejudice and hate. . . . The energy and resources of the Matthew Shepard Foundation, in conjunction with the Matthew Shepard Memorial Fund, will be devoted to public awareness and education programs to ensure that what Matt lived for and believed in will help others believe as well."

National Asian Pacific American Legal Consortium (NAPALC)
URL: http://www.napalc.org
Phone: (202) 296-2300
Fax: (202) 296-2318
1140 Connecticut Avenue, NW
Suite 1200
Washington, DC 20006
The NAPALC is dedicated to preserving the civil rights of citizens of Asian-Pacific descent. In cooperation with similar organizations across the country, it conducts regular surveys of anti-Asian violence in the United States.

National Association for the Advancement of Colored People (NAACP)
URL: http://www.naacp.org
Phone: (410) 358-8900
Fax: (410) 486-9255

4805 Mount Hope Drive
Baltimore, MD 21215
Since its founding in 1909, the National Association for the Advancement of Colored People has grown to 2,200 chapters and claims more than 500,000 members. The NAACP represents the country's original civil rights organization, founded to protect and preserve legal rights of African-American citizens. The NAACP actively lobbies on behalf of new hate-crimes bills.

National Center for Victims of Crime
URL: http://www.ncvc.org
Phone: (202) 467-8700
Fax: (202) 467-8701
2000 M Street, NW
Suite 480
Washington, DC 20036
A nonprofit organization founded in 1985 and dedicated to services and programs for crime victims, including training and technical assistance to victim service organizations, attorneys, and other individuals and groups associated with the criminal justice system. The organization offers hate crimes information and links at http://www.ncvc.org/9-11/hate_crimes.htm.

National Conference for Community and Justice (NCCJ)
URL: http://www.nccj.org
E-mail: nationaloffice@nccj.org
Phone: (212) 545-1300
Fax: (212) 545-8053
475 Park Avenue South

19th Floor
New York, NY 10016
Founded in 1927 as the National Conference of Christians and Jews, this group combats racial and religious bigotry through educational programs, campaigns and special events, policy research, and legal advocacy. The group also offers a range of publications and annual reports on the topics of intergroup relations and bias.

National District Attorneys Association
American Prosecutors Research Institute (APRI)
URL: http://www.ndaa.org
Phone: (703) 549-9222
Fax: (703) 836-3195
99 Canal Center Plaza
Suite 510
Alexandria, VA 22314
Information and resources for local prosecutors, including the report "A Local Prosecutor's Guide for Responding to Hate Crimes." The organization also holds conferences such as a national training for hate-crimes prosecutors, investigators, and victim/witness advocates, which took place in June 2000 at the National Advocacy Center in Columbia, South Carolina.

National Gay and Lesbian Task Force (NGLTF)
URL: http://www.ngltf.org
Phone: (202) 332-6483
Fax (202) 332-0207
1700 Kalorama Road, NW
Washington, DC 20009-2624

Founded in 1973, the NGLTF is a national advocacy organization dedicated to promoting civil rights for homosexuals. The NGLTF is active in promoting new hate-crimes legislation at the state and federal level that targets antihomosexual prejudice and recognizes homosexuals as a protected group. The Anti-Violence Project of the NGLTF promotes an appropriate official response to antigay violence, strives to improve the treatment of lesbians and gay men by the criminal justice system, and assists communities combatting prejudice and bias-motivated violence. The organization also publishes annual reports on antigay violence and harassment.

National Hate Crime Prevention Center
Phone: (617) 969-7100
55 Chapel Street
Newton, MA 02458-1060
An organization that trains law enforcement personnel and public-sector workers in recognizing, preventing, and investigating cases of bias-motivated violence.

National Organization for Women (NOW)
URL: http://www.now.org
NOW Legal Defense and Education Fund
URL: http://nowldef.org
Phone: (212) 925-6635
Fax: (212) 226-1066
395 Hudson Street
New York, NY 10014

NOW was founded in 1966 to combat discrimination against and promote full equal rights for women. The organization supports the effort to make antigender prejudice a component of hate-crimes laws. The NOW web site features several articles and news on the current hate crimes debate. The NOW Legal Defense Fund works within the justice system and among the members of Congress to further the parent organization's mission.

National Organization of Black Law Enforcement Executives
Phone: (202) 546-8811
Fax: (202) 544-8351
908 Pennsylvania Avenue, SE
Washington, DC 20003
This organization provides training for law enforcement executives in the matter of bias violence, conducts research on law enforcement practices and policies, and works with victim assistance organizations.

National Rainbow Coalition
URL: http://www.rainbowpush. org
Phone: (202) 728-1180
Fax: (202) 728-1180
1700 K Street, NW
Suite 800
Washington, DC 20006
The National Rainbow/PUSH Coalition (RPC) is a multi-issue organization founded by Rev. Jesse L. Jackson, Sr., with headquarters in Chicago. The organization was cre-

ated through the merger of Jackson's Operation PUSH, founded in 1971, and the National Rainbow Coalition. The RPC advertises its mission as "uniting people of diverse ethnic, religious, economic and political backgrounds to make America's promise of 'liberty and justice for all' a reality." The RPC has lobbying bodies at the state and federal levels and has long been a strong advocate of tougher hate-crimes laws.

Not in Our Town
URL: http://www.pbs.org/niot
E-mail: hometeam@kvcr.pbs.org
Phone: (909) 888-6511
Fax: (909) 885-2116
701 South Mount Vernon Avenue
San Bernardino, CA 92410
According to its web site, this organization "promotes public dialogue and provides a model for community response to hate crimes and other associated problems." The web site offers educational resources such as classroom discussion guides that cover hate crimes and community response handbooks, which allow local civic leaders to formulate a response to hate groups.

Partners Against Hate
URL: http://www. partnersagainsthate.org
E-mail: webmaster@ partnersagainsthate.org
Phone: (202) 452-8310
Fax: (202) 296-2371

**1100 Connecticut Avenue, NW
Suite 1020
Washington, DC 20036**
Partners Against Hate is a joint effort of the Anti-Defamation League, the Leadership Conference Education Fund, and the Center for the Prevention of Hate Violence. This collaboration implements programs of outreach, public education, and training to prevent and reduce juvenile hate crimes. The organization's web site offers a useful and very thorough hate crimes database with updated statistics and related information on bias crimes, including a state-by-state breakdown of hate crimes laws and hate-crime incidents.

**People for the American Way
URL: http://www.pfaw.org
Phone: (202) 476-4999
Fax: (202) 293-2672
2000 M Street, NW
Suite 400
Washington, DC 20036**
An organization that takes part in current debates over constitutional issues, religious freedom, judicial appointments, civil liberties and civil rights and is generally supportive of new hate-crimes laws.

**PFLAG (Parents and Friends of
   Lesbians and Gays)
URL: http://www.pflag.org
Phone: (202) 467-8180
Fax: (202) 467-8194
1726 M Street, NW
Suite 400
Washington, DC 20036**
PFLAG is a national nonprofit organization of parents, families, and friends of lesbian, gay, bisexual, and transgendered persons. The organization states part of its mission as "to cope with an adverse society; education, to enlighten an ill-informed public; and advocacy, to end discrimination and to secure equal civil rights." The web site's hate crimes information page, with links, press releases, events, and legislative information and updates, is located at http://www.pflag.org/education/hatecrimes.html.

**Police Executive Research
   Forum
URL: http://www.policeforum.
   org
Phone: (202) 466-7820
Fax: (202) 466-7826
2300 M Street, NW
Suite 910
Washington, DC 20037**
An organization of police executives dedicated to improving police services, PERF supports and promotes hate-crime law and assists local law enforcement in the reporting of hate crime. The organization has been advocating hate-crime data collection since 1987, when it became one of the first national police associations to endorse the Hate Crimes Statistics Act. PERF offers a "cultural differences" training curriculum for law enforcement officials.

**Political Research Associates
URL: www.publiceye.org/pra**

120 Beacon Street
Suite 202
Somerville, MA 02143-4304
"An independent, nonprofit research center, based on progressive values, that serves as a national resource for information on antidemocratic, authoritarian and other oppressive movements and trends." The organization's web site, The Public Eye, carries articles, links, and resources on the consequences of the September 11, 2001, terrorist attacks on the United States, including in particular bias crimes against Arab Americans. The site also offers printed resources, activist resource kits, online resources, including *Public Eye Magazine*, and links to books, articles, reports and research studies.

Prejudice Institute
URL: http://www.
   prejudiceinstitute.org
E-mail: prejinst@aol.com
Phone: (410) 243-6987
2743 Maryland Avenue
Baltimore, MD 21218
The Prejudice Institute is a nonprofit, nonpartisan research organization, the successor to the National Institute Against Prejudice and Violence. The work of the institute is organized around several projects, including studies of the social and psychological effects of victimization; the nature of violent attitudes and behavior; the nature of prejudice, conflict, and ethnoviolence as they are played out in college campus and workplace settings; and the role of the news media in communicating prejudice.

Public Good Project
URL: http://www.nwcitizen.
   com/publicgood
Phone: (360) 734-6642
P.O. Box 28547
Bellingham, WA 98228
Public Good advertises itself as "a research and education network illuminating conflicts where democratic values are being challenged." The organization began as a 1993 investigation into political extremism in Whatcom County, Washington. It has since become a network of contributors who find and upload primary source documents on political extremism, the militia movement, white supremacists, and hate groups. The indices to the available documents are located at http://nwcitizen.us/publicgood/reports.

Recovering Racists Network (RRN)
URL: http://www.rrnet.org/rrn
E-mail: info@rrnet.org
Phone: (925) 682-4959
Fax: (925) 687-4437
670 West Washington Avenue
Kirkwood, MO 63122
The Recovering Racists Network is a project founded by John McKenzie. The organization holds workshops on overcoming racism, publishes books and pamphlets on intolerance and prejudice, and works actively on conflict resolution and

hate-crimes related issues on a local level.

Simon Wiesenthal Center
URL: http://www.wiesenthal.
  com
E-mail: information@wiesenthal.
  net
Phone: (800) 900-9036
Fax: (310) 553-4521
1399 South Roxbury Drive
Los Angeles, CA 90035
Established in 1977, the Simon Wiesenthal Center is an international Jewish human rights organization. The center concerns itself with the issues of racism, anti-Semitism, and terrorism. The center closely interacts with a variety of public and private agencies, meeting with elected officials, U.S. and foreign governments, diplomats, and heads of state. Other issues that the center deals with include the prosecution of Nazi war criminals; Holocaust and tolerance education; Middle East affairs; and extremist groups, neo-Nazism, and hate on the Internet.

Security on Campus, Inc.
URL: http://www.campussafety.
  org ·
Phone: (888) 251-7959
Fax: (610) 768-0646
601 South Henderson Road
Suite 205
King of Prussia, PA 19406
This nonprofit organization is dedicated to reporting and fighting crime on university campuses. The web site provides links to statistics collected by the FBI (Uniform Crime Reports) and the Department of Education. By the Crime Awareness and Campus Security Act of 1990, colleges and universities must disclose annual information about campus crime and security policies; the act was championed by the originators of this web site, Howard and Connie Clery, after their daughter Jeanne was murdered at Lehigh University in 1986 (the act was renamed in memory of Jeanne Clery in 1998 and is now known as the Clery Act). Campus Crime Statistics, which include the subcategory of hate crimes, are reported to the Department of Education and published on the World Wide Web at http://www.campussafety.org/crimestats/doe2001.pdf. The hate-crimes statistics are also summarized at the Security on Campus site.

Southern Christian Leadership
  Conference (SCLC)
Phone: (404) 522-1420
Fax: (404) 659-7390
334 Auburn Ave, NE
Atlanta, GA 30312
The SCLC was founded by Dr. Martin Luther King, Jr., and others, and became the leading organization in the Civil Rights movement of the 1950s and 1960s. King and the SCLC adopted nonviolent tactics and spearheaded a mass political movement against prejudice, lynchings, Jim Crow policies, and institutionalized racism, particularly in the South. The SCLC survived King's assassination in 1968, and currently

takes part in legislative and judicial actions concerning prejudice, hate crimes, and racism; publishes a magazine; and offers informational resources at http://www.sclcmagazine.com/index.htm.

Southern Poverty Law Center (SPLC)
URL: http://www.splcenter.org
Tolerance.org, A Project of the Southern Poverty Law Center
URL: http://www.tolerance.org
Phone: (334) 264-0286
Fax: (334) 264-0629
400 Washington Avenue
Box 548
Montgomery, AL 36104

The Southern Poverty Law Center began as a small civil rights law firm in 1971 and has remained a nonprofit organization that combats racism through litigation and educational projects. Founders Morris Dees and Joe Levin have successfully prosecuted several hate groups through civil lawsuits, and they track hate groups and their activities throughout the country. Most recently, the center has become internationally known for its success in developing novel legal strategies to shut down extremist activity and to help victims of hate crimes win monetary damages against groups such as the Ku Klux Klan. The SPLC project known as Klanwatch monitors hate crimes and hate groups throughout the nation, publishing *The Intelligence Report*, a bimonthly review of hate crimes and activities of white su-

premacist groups. Klanwatch also provides training for law enforcement and seminars on white supremacist groups for community organizations.

STATE AND LOCAL ADVOCACY ORGANIZATIONS

CALIFORNIA

Asian Pacific American Legal Center of Southern California
Phone: (213) 748-2022
Fax: (213) 748-0679
1010 South Flower Street
Suite 302
Los Angeles, CA 90015

Established in 1983, this group provides legal services and education programs geared to Southern California's Asian-American community. Attorneys working on behalf of this program are involved in immigration, education, and interethnic relations and take part in prominent race-violence and hate-crimes cases such as the murder of Joseph Ileto in 1999.

ILLINOIS

Chicago Lawyers' Committee for Civil Rights Under Law, Inc.
Project to Combat Bias Violence
URL: http://www.clccrul.org/
E-Mail: info@clccrul.org
Phone: (312) 630-9744

Fax: (312) 630-9749
100 North LaSalle Street
Suite 600
Chicago, IL 60602-2403
A public interest legal consortium of Chicago's leading law firms, the Chicago Lawyers Committee for Civil Rights Under Law, Inc., claims 48 member firms, whose attorneys logged 15,000 hours of pro bono legal services on civil rights cases and issues in 2001. The Project to Combat Bias Violence provides representation for people targeted for crime because of race, religion, ethnic origin, sexual orientation, disability, and gender. The project promotes improvements in hate-crimes legislation and law enforcement and also provides hate-crimes educational programs.

MASSACHUSETTS

Massachusetts Governor's Task Force on Hate Crimes
URL: http://www.magnet.state.ma.us/StopHate
E-mail: cbouras@stopthehate.org
P.O. Box 4547
Salem, MA 01970
Commissioned in 1991 and reconstituted in the fall of 2001, the Governor's Task Force on Hate Crimes coordinates law enforcement agencies with local organizations and community advocates. The task force includes police representatives, members of the state attorney general's office, local district attorneys' offices, educators, and civic leaders. The task force also works for full voluntary reporting of hate crime information by cities and towns.

NEW YORK

New York City Gay and Lesbian Anti-Violence Project
URL: http://www.avp.org
E-mail: webmaster@avp.org
Phone: (212) 714-1184
240 West 35th Street
Suite 200
New York, NY 10001
The project provides free and confidential services, including counseling, legal advocacy, referrals, and information to victims of bias-motivated violence. The group's web site mission statement also states that "by documenting violence motivated by hate against the lesbian, gay, transgender, bisexual and HIV-positive communities . . . the Project works to change public attitudes that tolerate, insulate or instigate hate-motivated violence, and to promote public policies designed to deter such violence."

INTERNATIONAL ADVOCACY ORGANIZATION

civilrights.org
URL: http://www.civilrights.org
Phone: (202) 466-3311
Leadership Conference on Civil Rights
1629 K Street, NW
Washington, DC 20006
This organization is an Internet-based civil rights network, linking

users to a wide variety of groups and publications working in the area of civil rights, immigration, labor, voting rights, criminal justice, education, and poverty/welfare issues. A section on hate crimes offers reports, resources, and news updates on hate crimes and hate crimes law.

***Searchlight* magazine**
URL: http://www.
searchlightmagazine.com
Phone: 020 7681 8660
Fax: 020 7681 8650
P.O. Box 1576
Ilford IG5 0NG
United Kingdom

Founded in London in 1962 in a response to a resurgence of neo-Nazi activities, *Searchlight* bills itself as an "international anti-fascist magazine." The monthly magazine documents hate crimes around the world, while the organization also serves as an information clearinghouse for academics, schools, journalists, and investigators. According to the organization's home page, "Any organisation with a genuine interest in fighting racism or fascism cam come to Searchlight for information about racist organisations and individuals and for advice on how to deal with the problem."

PART III

APPENDICES

APPENDIX A

HATE CRIMES PREVENTION ACT (2003)

The following is the full text of the Hate Crimes Prevention Act of 2003 (H.R. 80) as reintroduced on January 7, 2003, in the House of Representatives.

A BILL

To enhance Federal enforcement of hate crimes, and for other purposes. Be it enacted by the Senate and House of Representatives of the United States of America in Congress assembled.

SECTION 1. SHORT TITLE.

This Act may be cited as the 'Hate Crimes Prevention Act of 2003'.

SECTION 2. FINDINGS.

Congress finds that —

(1) the incidence of violence motivated by the actual or perceived race, color, national origin, religion, sexual orientation, gender, or disability of the victim poses a serious national problem;

(2) such violence disrupts the tranquility and safety of communities and is deeply divisive;

(3) existing Federal law is inadequate to address this problem;

(4) such violence affects interstate commerce in many ways, including —

    (A) by impeding the movement of members of targeted groups and forcing such members to move across State lines to escape the incidence or risk of such violence; and

    (B) by preventing members of targeted groups from purchasing goods and services, obtaining or sustaining employment or participating in other commercial activity;

(5) perpetrators cross State lines to commit such violence;

(6) instrumentalities of interstate commerce are used to facilitate the commission of such violence;

(7) such violence is committed using articles that have traveled in interstate commerce;

(8) violence motivated by bias that is a relic of slavery can constitute badges and incidents of slavery;

(9) although many local jurisdictions have attempted to respond to the challenges posed by such violence, the problem is sufficiently serious, widespread, and interstate in scope to warrant Federal intervention to assist such jurisdictions; and

(10) many States have no laws addressing violence based on the actual or perceived race, color, national origin, religion, sexual orientation, gender, or disability, of the victim, while other States have laws that provide only limited protection.

SECTION 3. DEFINITION OF HATE CRIME.

In this Act, the term 'hate crime' has the same meaning as in section 280003(a) of the Violent Crime Control and Law Enforcement Act of 1994 (28 U.S.C. 994 note).

SECTION 4. PROHIBITION OF CERTAIN ACTS OF VIOLENCE.

Section 245 of Title 18, United States Code, is amended —

(1) by redesignating subsections (c) and (d) as subsections (d) and (e), respectively; and

(2) by inserting after subsection (b) the following:

    '(c)(1) Whoever, whether or not acting under color of law, willfully causes bodily injury to any person or, through the use of fire, a firearm, or an explosive device, attempts to cause bodily injury to any person, because of the actual or perceived race, color, religion, or national origin of any person —

    '(A) shall be imprisoned not more than 10 years, or fined in accordance with this title, or both; and

    '(B) shall be imprisoned for any term of years or for life, or fined in accordance with this title, or both if —

'(i) death results from the acts committed in violation of this paragraph; or

'(ii) the acts committed in violation of this paragraph include kidnapping or an attempt to kidnap, aggravated sexual abuse or an attempt to commit aggravated sexual abuse, or an attempt to kill.

'(2)(A) Whoever, whether or not acting under color of law, in any circumstance described in subparagraph (B), willfully causes bodily injury to any person or, through the use of fire, a firearm, or an explosive device, attempts to cause bodily injury to any person, because of the actual or perceived religion, gender, sexual orientation, or disability of any person —

'(i) shall be imprisoned not more than 10 years, or fined in accordance with this title, or both; and

'(ii) shall be imprisoned for any term of years or for life, or fined in accordance with this title, or both, if —

'(I) death results from the acts committed in violation of this paragraph; or

'(II) the acts committed in violation of this paragraph include kidnapping or an attempt to kidnap, aggravated sexual abuse or an attempt to commit aggravated sexual abuse, or an attempt to kill.

'(B) For purposes of subparagraph (A), the circumstances described in this subparagraph are that —

'(i) in connection with the offense, the defendant or the victim travels in interstate or foreign commerce, uses a facility or instrumentality of interstate or foreign commerce, or engages in any activity affecting interstate or foreign commerce; or

'(ii) the offense is in or affects interstate or foreign commerce.'

SECTION 5. DUTIES OF FEDERAL SENTENCING COMMISSION.

(a) AMENDMENT OF FEDERAL SENTENCING GUIDELINES—Pursuant to its authority under section 994 of title 28, United States Code, the United States Sentencing Commission shall study the issue of adult recruitment of juveniles to commit hate crimes and shall, if appropriate, amend the Federal sentencing guidelines to provide sentencing enhancements (in addition to the sentencing enhancement provided for the use of a minor during the commission of an offense) for adult defendants who recruit juveniles to assist in the commission of hate crimes.

(b) CONSISTENCY WITH OTHER GUIDELINES—In carrying out this section, the United States Sentencing Commission shall —
  (1) ensure that there is reasonable consistency with other Federal sentencing guidelines; and
  (2) avoid duplicative punishments for substantially the same offense.

SECTION 6. GRANT PROGRAM.

(a) AUTHORITY TO MAKE GRANTS—The Administrator of the Office of Juvenile Justice and Delinquency Prevention of the Department of Justice shall make grants, in accordance with such regulations as the Attorney General may prescribe, to State and local programs designed to combat hate crimes committed by juveniles.
(b) AUTHORIZATION OF APPROPRIATIONS—There are authorized to be appropriated such sums as may be necessary to carry out this section.

SECTION 7. AUTHORIZATION FOR ADDITIONAL PERSONNEL TO ASSIST STATE AND LOCAL LAW ENFORCEMENT.

There are authorized to be appropriated to the Department of the Treasury and the Department of Justice, including the Community Relations Service, for fiscal years 1998, 1999, and 2000 such sums as are necessary to increase the number of personnel to prevent and respond to alleged violations of Section 245 of Title 18, United States Code (as amended by this Act).

APPENDIX B

ADVOCACY AND DEBATE OVER PENDING LEGISLATION: THE LOCAL LAW ENFORCEMENT ENHANCEMENT ACT

Following are samples of the wide range of opinion over the proposed federal legislation currently known as the Hate Crimes Prevention Act (formerly the Local Law Enforcement Enhancement Act).

POLICE EXECUTIVE RESEARCH FORUM LETTER OF SUPPORT FOR THE LOCAL LAW ENFORCEMENT ENHANCEMENT ACT

July 24, 2001
U.S. Senate Judiciary Committee
Washington, DC 20510

Dear Senator:

On behalf of the members of the Police Executive Research Forum (PERF), a national organization of police professionals who represent more than 50 percent of the nation's population, we urge you to support the Local Law Enforcement Enhancement Act of 2001. As police professionals, we see the devastating effects hate crimes can have on victims and the public. This measure will assist local law enforcement in its response to hate crimes.

In the past, PERF has opposed efforts to expand the federal government's authority over traditional local crimes. However, given the unusual nature of hate crimes and the substantial gaps in state laws, PERF believes that there should be a significant federal role in combating hate crimes. In addition, PERF acknowledges that while local police should have primary responsibility in these cases, sometimes local authorities lack the resources or expertise in investigating hate crimes. The Local Law Enforcement Enhancement Act would provide needed technical support to state and local police, as well as U.S. Justice Department grants to cover costs associated with investigating and prosecuting these crimes. This Act would provide necessary assistance when local authorities are unwilling or unable to act, or when they require additional resources.

We are asking that this session, Congress pass the Local Law Enforcement Enhancement Act and that you support this piece of critical legislation.

Sincerely,
Chuck Wexler
Executive Director

"SPECIAL REPORT: HATE CRIMES." UPDATED MAY 21, 2002 RELIGIOUS ACTION CENTER OF REFORM JUDAISM

BACKGROUND

Jews around the world have watched in horror as anti-Semitism has terrorized Europe over the last few months. Gunmen in Toulouse opened fire on a kosher butcher shop. Synagogues in Antwerp, Brussels, and Marseilles were fire-bombed. A cemetery in Strasbourg was vandalized. Attacks against Jewish institutions and individuals send us reeling, disgusted by these blatant and brutal displays of ignorance and hatred. In this troubled time for Jews throughout the world, we must voice loudly our desire for our government to take the moral lead in the crusade to quell the violence stemming from hatred.

The United States is no stranger to anti-Semitism. It has been almost three years since the arson attacks at three Sacramento synagogues and the shooting spree at the Los Angeles JCC, but these and other similar events are still fresh in our minds. In 2001 alone, 1,432 anti-Semitic hate crimes were reported in the FBI's hate crimes statistics survey. Although anti-Semitism is included under federal hate crimes law, a number of groups remain unprotected.

The Local Law Enforcement Enhancement Act (S. 625), introduced by Senators Edward Kennedy (D-MA), Arlen Spector (R-PA), and Gordon Smith (R-OR), would expand federal hate crimes law to add sexual orientation, gender, and disability to race, color, religion and national origin as protected classes. Moreover, it would remove the current requirement that the victim must be involved in a federally protected activity. Ultimately, the

LLEEA would increase the number of hate crimes indictments and prosecutions to more accurately reflect the number of hate crimes committed in the United States.

A vote on the LLEEA is imminent; the Senate leadership has indicated that the LLEEA will be brought to the floor before Memorial Day. There are currently 51 cosponsors in the Senate and the target of 60 cosponsors, the necessary number of votes to avoid a filibuster, is within reach . . .

SERMON TALKING POINTS ON THE LLEEA

The Jewish people have been victims of persecution, discrimination, and hate crimes throughout history. Whether it be the destruction of the First and Second Temples, the Inquisition, or the Shoah, we understand the terrible effects of hatred.

Hate crimes are not a thing of the past for Jews. Abroad, a wave of anti-Semitism has terrorized the European Jewish community. Torched synagogues, vandalized cemeteries, and destroyed stores remind us of the horrendous events we were forced to endure during the Shoah. In the United States, anti-Semitic hate crimes occur at a rate of over four per day. This does not include the significantly larger number of hate-motivated incidents, acts or comments derived from hate that do not qualify as crimes.

Terrorism and hate crimes are effective in the same way: they both target an entire community. Any given hate crime may only have one direct victim, but anyone that shares the targeted characteristic is affected by the crime. For instance, if a Jew is attacked on the street for being Jewish, other Jews in that particular community will fear victimization as well. The fear generated by hate crimes is devastating.

Currently, federal hate crimes law is incomplete. As it stands now, race, color, religion, and national origin are the only protected classes under the law. If a hate crime is committed based on a bias against gender, sexual orientation, or disability, the crime cannot be prosecuted as a hate crime.

Federal hate crimes law is ineffective. Currently, the law contains a provision requiring that the victim be participating in a federally protected activity (asserting the right to speak, assemble, pray, etc.) for the crime to be prosecuted as a hate crime. This is an extremely difficult standard to meet, resulting in an extremely low number of hate crimes actually being prosecuted as hate crimes.

The Local Law Enforcement Enhancement Act (S. 625), introduced by Senators Edward Kennedy (D-MA), Arlen Spector (R-PA), and Gordon Smith (R-OR), would expand federal hate crimes law to include sexual orientation, gender, and disability as protected classes. Moreover, it would remove the current requirement that the victim must be involved in a federally protected activity.

Senate Majority Leader, Tom Daschle (D-SD) has promised that the LLEEA will come to the Senate floor for a vote before Memorial Day. It is critical that Senators hear from their constituents.

Opponents of hate crimes legislation argue that it limits speech. They suggest that a murder regardless of motive is murder and should be punished equally. We disagree. Murdering someone because of an inherent characteristic of theirs that serves to designate them within a community is significantly worse than a standard murder motive. The crime affects everyone with the same characteristic, instilling fear into an entire community . . .

ORGANIZATION OF CHINESE AMERICANS PRESS RELEASE: JUNE 12, 2002

Washington, DC – The Organization of Chinese Americans (OCA), a national Asian Pacific American (APA) civil rights and education group with over 85 chapters and affiliates nationwide, is outraged by the recent events in the Senate surrounding the Local Law Enforcement Enhancement Act (S. 625). A vote was taken on Tuesday over "cloture," a process that would have closed debate on the bill and brought it to a vote on the Senate floor. The vote was 54 to 43 in favor of ending debate, but a vote of 60 or more is required to actually close debate through cloture; thus the Local Law Enforcement Enhancement Act (LLEEA) is not on the Senate floor and cannot be considered for a vote at present.

Current federal law states that a crime cannot be investigated as a hate crime unless the victim is targeted because of his or her race, ethnicity, religion or national origin AND because he or she is engaged in a federally protected activity (i.e. voting, public education). The Local Law Enforcement Enhancement Act (LLEEA) would broaden the current law to cover all crimes motivated by a person's real or perceived race, ethnicity, religion, national origin, sexual orientation, gender or disability when the defendant causes bodily injury or, through the use of fire, a firearm, or an explosive device, attempts to cause injury.

Hate-motivated violence is nothing new to the APA community. Next week will mark the 20th anniversary of the death of Vincent Chin, a Chinese American who was killed in a hate crime during a time of severe anti-Japanese sentiment. The legislation is especially relevant since September 11, because countless APAs, especially South Asian Americans, Muslims and Sikhs, as well as Arab Americans and others have been brutally attacked and murdered for no other reason but their race or religion, sometimes the race or religion they are perceived to be.

The LLEEA has widespread bipartisan support; the vote for cloture, however, was decided quite rigidly along party lines; only four members of the minority party voted in favor of ending discussion: Senators Lincoln

Chafee (R-RI), Susan Collins (R-ME), Gordon Smith (R-OR), and Olympia Snowe (R-ME). OCA finds it morally reprehensible that certain opponents of the bill – most notably Senators Trent Lott (R-MS) and Orrin Hatch (R-UT) – have used their influence to negatively affect a bill that is tremendously important to the APA community and all Americans.

"It is disheartening to see a bill as widely supported and urgent as the LLEEA get bogged down by petty partisan bickering," stated George M. Ong, OCA National President. "Our nation needs comprehensive hate crimes legislation immediately. A hate crime is even more heinous than a crime not motivated by bias; a hate crime is meant to send a message to an entire community. Passing the Local Law Enforcement Enhancement Act would help our government investigate and prosecute perpetrators of these atrocious acts."

OCA encourages all Americans to contact their Senators and urge them to support any action in favor of the LLEEA.

POSITION STATEMENT
NEW YORK CHRISTIAN COALITION
THE PROBLEM WITH HATE CRIME LAW

In recent weeks there has been a lot of talk, and a lot of confusion about proposed "Hate Crimes" legislation. On its surface it would seem only appropriate to support such legislation. After all, who would oppose the idea of preventing "hate?" The problem is that this legislation is not what it purports to be. It's a trojan horse intended to invade our culture with the legitimization of homosexuality.

Here are specific reasons why we oppose "Hate Crime" legislation, and we hope that after reading this you will agree with us and call your representatives in Washington D.C. to encourage them to oppose such legislation.

1. With the exception of discerning the difference between an intentional crime or an accident, American jurisprudence was always intended to regulate behavior, not one's perceived bias. By regulating perceived bias we accept the idea of commissioning "thought police." Not only are actions judged, but so are one's very thoughts.

2. The bill legitimizes homosexuality by creating special victim categories, not only for those of minority races, but also for those who are homosexuals, transsexuals, and other "sexual orientations." This bill equates sexual preference with race and religion. This is precisely why the radical homosexual lobby is pushing so hard for this bill. It will forever entrench homosexuality as a "civil right" instead of the self-destructive, immoral, sinful behavior which it is. It is a stealth attempt to legislate a new morality.

3. This bill legitimizes what the Bible clearly teaches to be wrong, and puts the civil government in direct opposition to traditional religious institutions. Furthermore, it brings the full power of federal law to bear against those in society who advocate a Judeo-Christian belief against homosexual behavior.

4. It represents a further step toward totalitarianism by centralizing more power in Washington D.C., taking authority away from local authorities. Kennedy's hate crimes measure, for example, would add "actual or perceived" gender, sexual orientation or disability to federal hate crimes law, which currently covers race, color, religion and national origin. It would also allow federal investigators and prosecutors to intervene in local communities when suspected hate crimes take place, including those against homosexuals.

5. It makes one life worth more than another. If a young 12-year-old girl is raped and murdered, and a homosexual is murdered in a city park by the same man who happens to call him a fag before he murders him, the murder of the homosexual is a federal offense with a stiffer punishment than the murder of the 12-year-old girl which remains "just" a rape and murder. Why should her life be worth any less than his? We contend that all murder is a hate crime against society. There must be no special classes which serve to devalue the others. All men, women and children are created equal in the eyes of the law. An offense against one is as serious as an offense against any other. Justice must be blind and non-discriminatory.

6. Hate crimes laws are unneeded. Every crime they cover is already illegal under existing state and local laws; indeed, Matthew Shepard's alleged killers were prosecuted under those laws.

MEMORANDUM
THE IMPACT OF HATE CRIMES LAWS UPON RELIGIOUS ORGANIZATIONS AND CLERGY
BY: ERIK W. STANLEY, ESQ. AND MATHEW D. STAVER, ESQ.

This memorandum addresses the impact of the enactment of the "Local Law Enforcement Enhancement Act of 2000" which is currently pending as Senate Amendment No. 3473 to S.2549, the National Defense Authorization Act for Fiscal Year 2001. The Local Law Enforcement Enhancement Act of 2000 (hereafter "Hate Crimes Bill") contains a number of troubling provisions for religious organizations and clergy. The stated goals of the Hate Crimes Bill is addressed in Section I. The immediate impact of the Bill on religious organizations and clergy is addressed below in Section II. The Bill elevates sexual orientation to a protected status—a step never before taken in federal law. The implication of elevating sexual orientation to a protected status is discussed in greater detail below. The immediate impact also contains possibilities for conspiracy prosecutions and increased federal involvement in hate crimes prosecutions against religious organizations and clergy. The long term impact of the Bill is addressed below in Section III.

The religious organizations and clergy that would be impacted by this Bill are those who have a sincere belief that homosexuality, lesbianism, transgenderism and bisexuality violate their religious tenets. This encompasses a wide group of religions and religious beliefs.

Those religions that believe these alternative lifestyles are wrong are compelled by their religious beliefs to speak out and to actively oppose the promotion of such lifestyles. Therefore, the Hate Crimes Bill must be viewed from the perspective of those who believe they must actively oppose the gay lifestyle. Care should be taken to distinguish those who advocate bodily harm and even death for those who participate in the gay lifestyle from those who hold a sincere religious belief that they can do nothing to promote or accept the gay lifestyle, and indeed, must actively, though legally, oppose such lifestyles. The latter and not the former are the subject of this memorandum as it is never justifiable to inflict bodily harm on another if the only justification for the harm is simply because an individual does not agree with another's lifestyle. The Hate Crimes Bill must be assessed in its legal impact on this latter group who attempt to peacefully and lawfully live out their religious beliefs and advocate against what their religious beliefs prohibit.

APPENDIX C

IDENTIFYING A HATE CRIME
IN NEW YORK

Since the 1980s, New York City has played a prominent role in the issue of hate crime. Bias-motivated violence in the 1980s gave strong impetus to the first state and federal hate-crime laws, and New York was the first city to establish a separate police unit dealing specifically with bias crimes. The city's various interest groups and communities remain closely attuned to the presence and prosecution of such crimes, and the issue of whether or not a crime should be identified as a hate crime often sparks heated debate.

Following are the official guidelines used by the New York City Police Department Bias Unit for identifying a hate crime.

CRITERIA

1. The motivation of the perpetrator.
2. The absence of any motive.
3. The perception of the victim.
4. The display of offensive symbols, words, or acts.
5. The date and time of occurrence (corresponding to a holiday of significance, i.e, Hanukkah, Martin Luther King Day, Chinese New Year, etc.).
6. A common-sense review of the circumstances surrounding the incident (considering the totality of the circumstances).
   A. The group involved in the attack.
   B. The manner and means of the attack.
   C. Any similar incidents in the same area or against the same victim.
7. What statements, if any, were made by the perpetrator.

Appendix C

QUESTIONS TO BE ASKED

1. Is the victim the only member or one of a few members of the targeted group in the neighborhood?
2. Are the victim and perpetrator from different racial, religious, ethnic, or sexual orientation groups?
3. Has the victim recently moved to the area?
4. If multiple incidents have occurred in a short time period, are all the victims of the same group?
5. Has the victim been involved in a recent public activity that would make him/her a target?
6. What was the modus operandi? Is it similar to other documented incidents?
7. Has the victim been the subject of past incidents of a similar nature?
8. Has there been recent news coverage of events of a similar nature?
9. Is there an ongoing neighborhood problem that may have spurred the event?
10. Could the act be related to some neighborhood conflict involving area juveniles?
11. Was any hate literature distributed by or found in the possession of the perpetrator?
12. Did the incident occur, in whole or in part, because of a racial, religious, ethnic, or sexual orientation difference between the victim and the perpetrator, or did it occur for other reasons?
13. Are the perpetrators juveniles or adults, and if juveniles, do they understand the meaning (to the community at large and to the victim) of the symbols used?
14. Were the real intentions of the responsible person motivated in whole or in part by bias against the victim's race, religion, ethnicity, or sexual orientation, or was the motivation based on [something] other than bias, for example: a childish prank, unrelated vandalism, etc.?

Note: If after applying the criteria listed and asking the appropriate questions, substantial doubt exists as to whether or not the incident is bias motivated or not, the incident should be classified as bias motivated for investigative and statistical purposes.

Source: Jacobs & Potter: *Hate Crime: Criminal Law and Identity Politics*, pp. 97–98.

APPENDIX D

POLICE RESPONSE TO HATE CRIME INCIDENTS (1999)

The following document was published in 1999 by the International Association of Chiefs of Police (IACP), providing guidelines for the prevention, investigation, and handling of hate crimes by law enforcement.

RESPONDING TO HATE CRIMES: A POLICE OFFICER'S GUIDE TO INVESTIGATION AND PREVENTION BY NANCY TURNER

WHAT IS A HATE CRIME?

Hate crimes and hate incidents are major issues for all police because of their unique impact on victims as well as the community. This guidebook will explain the differences between hate crimes and hate incidents and how to respond to both.

A hate crime is a criminal offense committed against persons, property or society that is motivated, in whole or in part, by an offender's bias against an individual's or a group's race, religion, ethnic/national origin, gender, age, disability or sexual orientation. (Definition developed at the 1998 IACP Summit on Hate Crime in America.)

Legal definitions of hate crimes vary. The federal definition of hate crimes addresses civil rights violations under 18 U.S.C. Section 245.

As of 1999, 41 states and the District of Columbia have hate crime statutes that provide enhanced penalties for crimes in which victims are selected because of a perpetrator's bias against a victim's perceived race, religion or ethnicity. Many states also classify as hate crimes those in which a victim is selected based on a perception of his/her sexual orientation.

Appendix D

Hate crime definitions often encompass not only violence against individuals or groups but also crimes against property, such as arson or vandalism, particularly those directed against community centers or houses of worship. Check your state statutes for the definition of hate crime in your jurisdiction.

Accurate and comprehensive police reporting is essential to understanding the prevalence and patterns of hate crimes both locally and nationally.

The federal Hate Crimes Statistics Act of 1990 (Public Law 102-275 April 23, 1990) encourages states to report hate crime data to the Federal Bureau of Investigation (FBI). Twenty-three states and the District of Columbia require the collection of hate crime data. In 1997, 11,211 state and local law enforcement agencies voluntarily reported 9,861 hate crime offenses to the FBI.

WHY IS IT IMPORTANT TO RESPOND TO HATE CRIMES QUICKLY AND EFFECTIVELY?

Hate crimes differ from other crimes in their effect on victims and on community stability:

- Hate crimes are often especially brutal or injurious.
- Victim(s) usually feel traumatized and terrified.
- Families of victims often feel frustrated and powerless.
- Others in the community who share the victim's characteristics may feel victimized and vulnerable.
- Hate incidents can escalate and prompt retaliatory action.
- Hate crimes and hate incidents create communitywide unrest.

A swift and strong response by law enforcement can help stabilize and calm the community as well as aid in a victim's recovery. Failure to respond to hate crimes within departmental guidelines may jeopardize public safety and leave officers and departments open to increased scrutiny and possible liability.

WHAT IS THE DIFFERENCE BETWEEN A HATE INCIDENT AND A HATE CRIME?

Hate incidents involve behaviors that, though motivated by bias against a victim's race, religion, ethnic/national origin, gender, age, disability or sexual orientation, are not criminal acts. Hostile or hateful speech, or

261

other disrespectful/discriminatory behavior may be motivated by bias but is not illegal. They become crimes only when they directly incite perpetrators to commit violence against persons or property, or if they place a potential victim in reasonable fear of physical injury. Officers should thoroughly document evidence in all bias-motivated incidents. Law enforcement can help to defuse potentially dangerous situations and prevent bias-motivated criminal behavior by responding to and documenting bias-motivated speech or behavior even if it does not rise to the level of a criminal offense.

WHAT IS AN EFFECTIVE POLICE RESPONSE TO HATE CRIMES?

Police officers and investigators have important roles to play in responding to hate incidents and crimes. By doing the job efficiently and carefully, police can reinforce the message that hate crimes will be investigated aggressively, thus enhancing the likelihood of a successful prosecution.

POLICE OFFICERS ARRIVING ON THE SCENE SHOULD ACT IMMEDIATELY TO

- secure the scene
- stabilize the victim(s) and request medical attention when necessary
- ensure the safety of victims, witnesses and perpetrators
- preserve the crime scene; collect and photograph physical evidence such as
  — hate literature
  — spray paint cans
  — threatening letters
- symbolic objects used by hate groups (e.g., swastikas, crosses)
- identify criminal evidence on the victim
- request the assistance of translators when needed
- conduct a preliminary investigation; record information on
  — identity of suspected perpetrators(s)
  — identity of witnesses, including those no longer on the scene
  — prior occurrences, in this area or with this victim
  — statements made by suspects—exact wording is critical
- arrest the perpetrator(s) if probable cause exists

Appendix D

Note: In the presence of the victim, the officer should neither confirm nor deny that the incident is a hate crime—that determination will be made later in the investigative process. After taking immediate action, police officers should

- assign only one officer to interview the victim(s) whenever practical in order to minimize trauma
- protect the anonymity of victim whenever possible
- explain to victim and witnesses the likely sequence of events, including contact with investigators and the possibility of media coverage
- refer victim to support services in the community; provide written resource lists when possible
- tell victim how to contact the police department to obtain further information on the case
- report the suspected hate crime to the supervisor on duty
- refer media representatives to the supervisor on duty or public information officer
- document the incident thoroughly on department report forms, noting any particular hate crime indicators and quoting exact wording of statements made by perpetrators
- assist investigators in making any other reports that may be required under federal or state guidelines and laws

When conducting a thorough follow-up investigation, officers should

- interview victims(s) and witnesses thoroughly and respectfully
- secure evidence by taking photos of offensive graffiti or other symbols of bias
- document the circumstances and apparent motives surrounding the event
- locate and arrest any suspected perpetrators not apprehended at the scene
- provide their supervisor or public information officer with information that can be responsibly reported to the media
- inform victim of what is likely to happen during the continuing investigation
- appeal to witnesses to come forward by canvassing the community
- offer rewards for information about the incident when possible
- coordinate with other law enforcement agencies in the area to assess patterns of hate crimes and determine if organized hate groups are involved

- collaborate with the responding officers to complete any written reports required by their department, state and federal agencies
- notify the FBI if further assistance with investigations is needed

WHAT ARE THE KEY INDICATORS THAT A HATE CRIME MAY HAVE BEEN COMMITTED?

The main difference between a hate crime and other crimes is that a perpetrator of a hate crime is motivated by bias. To evaluate a perpetrator's motives, you should consider several bias indicators:

- perceptions of the victim(s) and witnesses about the crime
- the perpetrator's comments, gestures or written statements that reflect bias, including graffiti or other symbols
- any differences between perpetrator and victim, whether actual or perceived by the perpetrator
- similar incidents in the same location or neighborhood to determine whether a pattern exists
- whether the victim was engaged in activities promoting his/her group or community—for example, by clothing or conduct
- whether the incident coincided with a holiday or date of particular significance
- involvement of organized hate groups or their members
- absence of any other motive such as economic gain

The presence of any of these factors does not confirm that the incident was a hate offense but may indicate the need for further investigation into motive.

A victim's perception is an important factor to consider, but be aware that victims may not recognize the crime as motivated by bias. Victims should not be asked directly whether they believe they were the victim of a hate crime, but it is appropriate to ask if they have any idea why they might have been victimized.

Victims and perpetrators may appear to be from the same race, ethnicity/nationality, or religion, but it is the perpetrator's perception of difference (whether accurate or not) motivating his or her criminal behavior that would constitute a hate crime.

WHAT ARE THE BEST APPROACHES FOR WORKING WITH VICTIMS OF HATE CRIME?

Hate crimes are unique. Victims of hate crimes are targeted because of a core characteristic of their identity. These attributes cannot be changed.

Appendix D

Victims often feel degraded, frightened, vulnerable and suspicious. This may be one of the most traumatic experiences of their lives. Community members who share with victims the characteristics that made them targets of hate (race, religion, ethnic/national origin, gender, age, disability or sexual orientation) may also feel vulnerable, fearful and powerless. In this emotional atmosphere, law enforcement officers and investigators must attend carefully to the ways they interact and communicate with victims, their families and members of the community.

EFFECTIVE WAYS FOR POLICE TO SUPPORT VICTIMS WHILE INVESTIGATING THE CRIME

- remain calm, objective and professional
- ask victim(s) how they want you to help them
- request the assistance of translators when needed
- let victim(s) defer answering questions if they are too distraught
- ask them if they have any idea why this happened to them
- reassure victim(s) that they are not to blame for what happened
- voice your support of the actions the victim(s) took to protect themselves and defuse the situation
- allow them to vent feelings about the incident or crime
- encourage victim(s) to tell the story in their own words
- ask them to recall, to the best of their ability, the exact words of the perpetrator(s)
- ask victim(s) if they have family members or friends who can support them
- inform them of what efforts can be made to enhance their safety
- reassure them that every effort will be made to protect their anonymity during the investigation
- tell victim(s) about the probable sequence of events in the investigation
- provide information about community and department resources available to protect and support victim(s), their families and members of the community

AVOID:

- being abrupt or rushed
- telling victim(s) that you know how they feel
- asking them whether they think this was a bias or hate crime

- criticizing the victim's behavior
- making assumptions about the victim's culture, religion, sexual orientation or lifestyle choices
- allowing personal value judgements about the victim's behavior, lifestyle or culture to affect your objectivity
- using stereotyped or biased terms
- belittling the seriousness of the incident, especially if the perpetrator was a juvenile

REASONS WHY VICTIMS MAY BE RELUCTANT TO REPORT OR PARTICIPATE IN THE INVESTIGATION OF A HATE CRIME:

- fear of re-victimization or retaliation
- fear of having privacy compromised
- for gays and lesbians, fear of repercussions from being "outted" to family and employers
- fear of law enforcement and uncertainty about justice agency responses
- for aliens, fear of jeopardizing immigration status, being reported to INS or deportation
- humiliation or shame about being victimized
- lack of a support system
- cultural and language barriers

WHAT IS THE ONGOING ROLE THE POLICE PLAY WITH HATE CRIME VICTIMS AND THE COMMUNITY?

By providing a continuing point of contact throughout the investigation and prosecution phase, police can facilitate a victim's cooperation with the justice system, assist with the healing process and promote law enforcement's credibility. In the following ways, officers and their departments can support hate crime victims and members of the community:

- Provide victim(s) a point of contact in the department to whom they can direct questions or concerns.
- Inform them on case progress including the end result of the investigation and/or prosecution
- Help to connect them with appropriate support services, victim advocates and community-based organizations when needed
- Protect the privacy of victim(s) and their families as possible

- Engage the media as partners in restoring victimized communities through sensitive and accurate reporting
- Support or coordinate community clean-up efforts
- Participate in meetings or other forums designed to address the communitywide impact of hate incidents or crimes
- Share information, as appropriate, with schools about cases where students or staff were victims or perpetrators of hate crimes
- Collaborate with community leaders to mobilize resources that can be used to assist victims and prevent future hate incidents and crimes

POLICE OFFICERS AND THEIR AGENCIES CAN ASSUME A LEADERSHIP ROLE IN THEIR COMMUNITY TO PREVENT HATE INCIDENTS AND CRIMES

Police officers can . . .

- Help to ensure that victims of hate crimes will report their victimization by demonstrating that law enforcement will respond swiftly and compassionately to all reports
- Participate in hate crime training
- Serve as positive role models, exemplifying tolerance of and respect for others
- Maximize cultural awareness to better communicate and work with citizens from diverse ethnic, racial and religious backgrounds
- Collaborate with community leaders to increase tolerance and promote peaceful conflict resolution among community members
- Support and participate in school programs and curricula intended to reduce prejudice and prevent bias-motivated crimes
- Work with citizens and community organizations to identify and address bias incidents and make referrals to state and local agencies (housing, employment and civil rights) to resolve problems
- Encourage the media to highlight community successes in preventing and responding to hate crimes and incidents
- Contribute to tracking and monitoring organized hate groups by gathering, documenting and reporting information about their criminal activities in affected communities

Police agencies can . . .

- Establish a policy of "zero tolerance" for prejudice throughout the department

- Ensure police are trained to recognize and respond appropriately to hate crimes
- Provide officers with user-friendly hate crime incident report forms that comply with state and national reporting standards
- Sponsor and participate in community events and activities that promote diversity, tolerance, bias reduction and conflict resolution
- Track the criminal activities of organized hate groups
- Collaborate with community organizations, schools, and other public agencies to develop coordinated approaches to hate crime prevention and response
- Engage the media as partners in restoring victimized communities and preventing bias-motivated incidents and crimes
- Document the positive outcomes of hate crime prevention and response strategies

Police officers and their agencies can accomplish much by working in partnership with citizens to implement the American vision of diverse and tolerant communities that offer freedom, safety and dignity for all.

APPENDIX E

MEMO FROM
PRESIDENT CLINTON (2000)

SEPTEMBER 13, 2000
MEMORANDUM FOR THE ATTORNEY
GENERAL SUBJECT: IMPROVING HATE
CRIMES REPORTING

Unfortunately, each year our country experiences a number of hate crimes. We have all heard about the heinous incidents such as the dragging death of James Byrd, Jr., in Jasper, Texas, in June 1998. In October of that same year, Matthew Shepard, a gay college student, died after being beaten and tied to a fence. In July 1999, Benjamin Smith went on a racially motivated shooting spree in Illinois and Indiana. At the end of this rampage fueled by hate, Ricky Byrdsong, an African American who was a former basketball coach at Northwestern University, and Won-Joon Yoon, a Korean graduate student at Indiana University, were killed, and eight others were wounded. In August 1999, Joseph Ileto, an Asian American and U.S. postal worker, died at the hands of a gunman in Los Angeles. This same gunman also injured five persons, including three children, at a Jewish community center. Finally, this year there were two rampages in Pennsylvania in which several people of various ethnic, racial, and religious backgrounds were killed or injured. These crimes affect the entire Nation, the communities in which they occur, and the victims and their families in ways fundamentally different from other crimes. People are targeted simply because of who they are—whether it is because of their race, religion, color, sexual orientation, gender, or disability.

During my Administration, we have worked hard to fight hate crimes. I established the National Church Arson Task Force in June 1996 to oversee the investigation and prosecution of arson at houses of worship around the country. I held the first-ever White House Conference on Hate Crimes in November 1997. At the conference, I announced that the Department of Justice would establish Hate Crimes Working Groups in the U.S. Attorneys' districts across the country. These working groups, essentially federal-state-local partnerships, typically include representation from the U.S. Attorney's Office, the Federal Bureau of Investigation (FBI), state and local law enforcement and prosecutors' offices, educators, and community groups. The groups work to ensure close coordination on hate crimes investigations and prosecutions among responsible law enforcement agencies; promote training of police, investigators, and prosecutors in identifying and dealing with hate crimes; encourage victims to report hate crimes; and educate the public about the harm they cause. In April of this year, I held a strategy session with some representatives of these Hate Crimes Working Groups at which law enforcement officials—at the federal, state, and local levels—reported that they coordinate closely on hate crimes investigations and prosecutions.

In 1998, the last year for which FBI figures are available, 7,755 hate crimes were reported—nearly one hate crime every hour of every day. Of these hate crimes reported, 56 percent were motivated by race, 18 percent by religion, and 16 percent by sexual orientation. However, there was certainly an underreporting of hate crimes.

Today, I announced a new report, "Improving the Quality and Accuracy of Bias Crime Statistics Nationally: An Assessment of the First Ten Years of Bias Crime Data Collection," which was funded by the Department of Justice. This report noted that over 10,000 city, county, and State law enforcement agencies now participate in the FBI's Uniform Crime Reporting (UCR) Hate Crime Data Collection Program. Although 83 percent of participating agencies reported that no hate crimes had occurred in their jurisdiction during the previous year, follow-up surveys with line officers showed that 31 percent of those agencies had investigated one or more incidents of hate crimes. These data indicate a disconnect between what line officers believe are hate crimes and what is reported to the FBI. Extrapolating from this data, the report estimates that between 5,000 and 6,000 additional agencies may have encountered hate crimes that were not reported to the national program. In addition, the report noted that 85 percent of law enforcement officers responding to a survey believed that hate-motivated crimes are more serious than similar crimes that are not motivated by bias.

Based on the results of this report, I hereby direct the Department of Justice to work with state and local law enforcement agencies, as well as relevant law enforcement organizations, to come up with a plan to improve hate crimes reporting, within 120 days. I understand that the department already plans to meet with representatives of state and local law enforcement organizations later this month.

In addition to this meeting, the department should consider in its plan whether various actions, such as the following, would improve hate crimes reporting:

- Pilot programs in jurisdictions where law enforcement agencies reported zero incidents of hate crimes;
- A study to analyze the role that juvenile offenders play in the number of hate crimes committed each year;
- Training sessions by federal law enforcement on identifying and reporting hate crimes; and
- Activities by the U.S. Attorney Hate Crimes Working Groups to work with community groups and local law enforcement to improve hate crimes reporting in their areas, including helping to bring more victims forward to the police.

In carrying out these activities, I know that you will continue your leadership on fighting and preventing hate crimes in order to make this country a safer place for all Americans.

WILLIAM J. CLINTON

APPENDIX F

HATE CRIME: THE CANDIDATES DEBATE (2000)

The following is the transcript of a short debate on hate-crimes law between Democratic Party presidential candidate Vice President Al Gore and Republican Party candidate George W. Bush, then-governor of Texas. At the time, the issue of hate crimes and race relations in general had become a prominent topic and article of difference between the two candidates, with Gore being generally in favor of new hate-crime legislation and Bush standing generally against, positions that reflected the planks of their respective parties. The debate, the second to take place during the campaign, was held on October 11, 2000, at Wake Forest University, in Winston-Salem, North Carolina, and moderated by journalist Jim Lehrer.

Gore: . . . as for singling people out because of race, you know James Byrd was singled out because of his race, in Texas. And other Americans have been singled out because of their race or—or ethnicity. And that's why I think that we can embody our values by passing a hate crimes law. I think these crimes are different.
Gore: I think they're different because they're based on prejudice and hatred, which is—which gives rise to crimes that have not just a single victim, but they're intended to stigmatize and dehumanize a whole group of people.
Lehrer: Do you have a different view of that?
Bush: No, I don't really.
Lehrer: On hate crimes violence?
Bush: No, I—we got one in Texas, and guess what? The three men who murdered James Byrd, guess what's going to happen to them? They're going to be put to death. A jury found them guilty and I—it's going to be hard to punish them any worse after they get put to death. And it's the right cost; it's the right decision . . .

Lehrer: Vice President Gore, what would be on your racial discrimination elimination list as president?

Gore: Well, I think we need tough enforcement of the civil rights laws. I think we still need affirmative action. I would pass a hate crimes law, as I said . . . And I guess I had misunderstood the governor's previous position. The Byrd family may have a misunderstanding of it in Texas also. But I'd like to shift, if I could, to the big issue of education.

Lehrer: Well, no, hold on one second. What is the misunderstanding? Let's clear this up.

Gore: Well, I had thought that there was a controversy at the end of the legislative session where the hate crimes law in Texas was—failed and that the Byrd family, among others, asked you to support it, Governor, and it died in committee for lack of support. Am I wrong about that?

Bush: Well, you don't realize we have a hate crime statute. . . .

Gore: I'm talking about the one that was proposed to deal . . .

Bush: Well, what the vice president must not understand is we got a hate crimes bill in Texas. And secondly, the people that murdered Mr. Byrd got the ultimate punishment. . . .

Lehrer: But they were . . .

Bush: . . . the death penalty.

Lehrer: They were prosecuted under the murder laws, were they not . . .

Bush: Well . . .

Lehrer: . . . in Texas?

Bush: In this case, when you murder somebody, it's hate, Jim.

Lehrer: No, but . . .

Bush: Crime is hate. And they got—and they got the ultimate punishment. I'm not exactly sure how you enhance the penalty any more than the death penalty. Well, we happen to have a statute on the books that's hate crimes statute in Texas.

Gore: May I respond?

Lehrer: Sure.

Gore: I don't want to jump in. [LAUGHTER] I may have been misled by all the news reports about this matter, because the law that was proposed in Texas, that had the support of the Byrd family and a whole lot of people in Texas, did in fact die in committee. There may be some other statute that was already on the books, but certainly the advocates of the hate crimes law felt that a tough new law was needed.

Gore: And it's important, Jim, not only—not just because of Texas, but because this mirrors the national controversy. There is pending now in the Congress a national hate crimes law because of James Byrd, because of Matthew Shepard, who was crucified on a split-rail fence by bigots, because of others. And that law has died in committee also because of the same kind of opposition.

Lehrer: And you would support that bill?

Gore: Absolutely.

Lehrer: Would you support a national hate crimes law?

Bush: I would support the Orrin Hatch version of it, not the Senator Kennedy version. But let me say to you, Mr. Vice President, we're happy with our laws on our books. That bill—there was another bill that did die in committee. But I want to repeat, if you have a state that fully supports the law like we do in Texas, we're going to go after all crime, and we're going to make sure people get punished for the crime. And in this case, we can't enhance the penalty anymore than putting those three thugs to death. And that's what's going to happen in the state of Texas.

APPENDIX G

U.S. DEPARTMENT OF JUSTICE, OFFICE OF JUSTICE PROGRAMS/ BUREAU OF JUSTICE STATISTICS SPECIAL REPORT: HATE CRIMES REPORTED IN NIBRS, 1997–99 (SEPTEMBER 2001)

HIGHLIGHTS

NIBRS hate crime data from 1997–99 showed that

- In 60% of hate crime incidents, the most serious offense was a violent crime, most commonly intimidation or simple assault.
- Intimidation, defined as verbal or related threats of bodily harm, is one of the additional offenses collected in NIBRS.
- In nearly 4 out of 10 incidents the most serious crime was a property offense, 73% of which were damage, destruction, or vandalism of property.
- Sixty-one percent of hate crime incidents were motivated by race, 14% by religion, 13% by sexual orientation, 11% by ethnicity, and 1% by victim disability.
- The majority of incidents motivated by race, ethnicity, sexual orientation, or disability involved a violent offense, while two-thirds of incidents motivated by religion involved a property offense, most commonly vandalism.

Hate Crimes

- Of incidents motivated by hatred of a religion, 41% targeted Jewish victims and 31%, unspecified religious groups.

- Racially motivated hate crimes most frequently targeted blacks. Six in ten racially biased incidents targeted blacks, and 3 in 10 targeted whites.

- Younger offenders were responsible for most hate crimes. Thirty-one percent of violent offenders and 46% of property offenders were under age 18.

- Thirty-two percent of hate crimes occurred in a residence, 28% in an open space, 19% in a retail/commercial establishment or public building, 12% at a school or college, and 3% at a church, synagogue, or temple.

Over the past decade, federal and state legislation has mandated the identification and reporting of offenses known as hate crimes. Today nearly every state and the federal government have laws which require sentencing enhancements for offenders who commit hate crimes. These incidents, also referred to as bias crimes, are criminal offenses motivated by an offender's bias against a race, religion, disability, sexual orientation, or ethnicity (FBI, 1999). Bias crimes are not separate types of offenses but are crimes against persons, property, or society identified by a specific motivation of the offender.

The Hate Crime Statistics Act of 1990 (P.L. 101-275) required the establishment of a system to provide information on the nature and prevalence of hate crimes. This responsibility was given to the Federal Bureau of Investigation's (FBI) Uniform Crime Reporting (UCR) program, which began compiling hate crime statistics reported to law enforcement departments in 1990. The UCR data reflected aggregate counts of incidents, victims, suspected offenders, and categories of bias motivation.

In recent years a growing number of law enforcement agencies have reported incident-level crime data to the FBI's National Incident-Based Reporting System (NIBRS).

NIBRS represents a more comprehensive and detailed crime reporting system, with the ability to capture a wide range of information on specific incidents. In 1997, 1,878 agencies from 10 States submitted NIBRS data to the FBI, representing 6% of the U.S. population. In 1999, 3,396 agencies submitted NIBRS data, from 17 states (Colorado, Connecticut, Idaho, Iowa, Kentucky, Massachusetts, Michigan, Nebraska, North Dakota, Ohio, South Carolina, Tennessee, Texas, Utah, Vermont, Virginia, and West Virginia) representing 13% of the total population.

This report analyzes those NIBRS cases identified by law enforcement agencies as hate crimes from 1997 to 1999. Overall, bias crimes accounted for a relatively small percentage of all criminal incidents reported in NIBRS during this period. Of the nearly 5.4 million NIBRS incidents reported by law enforcement agencies between 1997 and 1999, about 3,000 were identified as hate crimes.

BIAS MOTIVATION

NIBRS reporting requirements dictate that hate crimes be categorized according to the perceived bias motivation of the offender. Due to the difficulty in determining an offender's motivations, law enforcement agencies record hate crimes only when investigation reveals facts sufficient to conclude that the offender's actions were bias motivated. Evidence used to support the existence of bias could include oral comments, written statements, or gestures made by the offender at the time of the incident or drawings or graffiti left at the crime scene. Other factors, including victim reporting and law enforcement procedure, can also impact the quality and accuracy of hate crime reporting. (See Methodology.)

Among those bias incidents reported by NIBRS-participating states from 1997 to 1999, 61% were motivated by racial bias, 14% by religious bias, 13% by sexual orientation bias, 11% by ethnicity or national origin bias, and 1% by disability bias.

- Among racially motivated hate crimes, 6 in 10 targeted blacks and 3 in 10 targeted whites.
- Among crimes motivated by bias against a religion, the majority were anti-Jewish crimes or crimes against unnamed religious groups.
- Almost all incidents resulting from bias against a sexual orientation were committed against male or female homosexuals.
- Crimes motivated by hatred of an ethnicity or national origin most frequently targeted Hispanics.

OFFENSE COMMITTED DURING HATE CRIME INCIDENTS

The majority of offenses committed during NIBRS hate crimes were violent. This compared to all NIBRS offenses reported between 1997–99, of which about 1 in 5 involved a violent offense. In 60% of hate crime incidents, the most serious offense was a violent crime while property crimes were the most serious offenses reported in 38% of incidents. In about 2% of hate crime incidents the most serious crime reported was a drug, weapon, or other type of offense.

Intimidation, simple assault, and aggravated assault were the most commonly reported violent hate crime offenses, representing the most serious offense in nearly 6 in 10 of all bias incidents combined. Intimidation, which refers to verbal or related threats of bodily harm, was the most serious offense reported in 23% of incidents. Simple assault, which defines physical attacks without a weapon or serious victim injury, was the most serious offense recorded in 22% of incidents.

Aggravated assault, which refers to attacks in which the offender uses or displays a weapon and/or the victim suffers serious injury, was the most serious offense reported in 13% of incidents. In an additional 1% of hate crime incidents, the most serious offense was robbery, and in less than 1%, murder and nonnegligent or negligent manslaughter.

Property crimes were the most serious offense recorded in nearly 4 in 10 hate crime incidents, most commonly involving the damage, destruction, or vandalism of personal or public property. Overall, damage, destruction, or vandalism of property was the most serious offense recorded in 28% of all bias incidents. Arson was the most serious crime reported in nearly 1% of bias incidents.

OFFENSE TYPE BY BIAS MOTIVATION

While hate crimes predominantly involved assault-related or vandalism offenses, the type of offense differed by bias motivation. Racially and ethnically motivated incidents were the most likely to be violent. Overall, 66% of race-related incidents and 69% of ethnic-related incidents involved a violent crime. In a quarter of racial or ethnically motivated incidents, intimidation was the most serious offense.

Among crimes motivated by sexual orientation bias, 56% were violent and 42% were property offenses. Simple or aggravated assault was the most serious offense recorded in 37% of these incidents, intimidation in 16%, and rape or sexual assault in 2%. Violent crimes were reported in 12 of the 17 incidents motivated by disability bias recorded in NIBRS between 1997 and 1999.

In contrast to other bias crimes, the majority of crimes motivated by religious bias involved property offenses. In 53% of these incidents the most serious offense reported was damage, destruction, or vandalism of property.

MEASURING HATE CRIME VICTIMIZATIONS NOT REPORTED TO THE POLICE

In general, the majority of crimes experienced by the public are not reported to the police. To examine both reported and unreported crime, BJS has collected data through its National Crime Victimization Survey

(NCVS) since 1972. In the NCVS, representative national samples of the population are interviewed, with each victim of a crime queried about whether the victimization they experienced was reported to a law enforcement agency. In 2000 just under half of violent crimes and just over a third of property crimes were brought to the attention of the police.

NIBRS hate crime data reflect only those incidents in which a law enforcement agency was notified and properly recorded the event (see Methodology for further discussion). On July 1, 2000, BJS initiated the addition of new items to the NCVS designed to uncover hate crime victimizations which go unreported to law enforcement agencies. The NCVS hate crime questions ask victims about the basis for their belief that the crime they experienced was motivated by prejudice or bigotry, as well as the specific behavior of the offender or evidence which may have led to the victim's perception of bias.

Preliminary data from the first 6 months of fielding these questions indicate that the majority of hate crime victims, like victims of many other crimes, do not report the incident to law enforcement . . .

VICTIM CHARACTERISTICS

TYPE OF VICTIM

The targets of hate crimes were most commonly individuals (84%) as opposed to targets such as businesses or religious organizations. Businesses or financial institutions represented 6% of bias victims, governments 4%, religious organizations 2%, and society or the general public represented 2%.

VICTIM DEMOGRAPHICS

Overall, victims of bias crimes were relatively evenly distributed by age, with slightly smaller percentages reported among victims age 45 or older. The age of hate crime victims varied according to the nature of the offense, as a larger percentage of victims of violent hate crime were young. More than half of victims of violence were age 24 or under, and nearly a third were under 18. In comparison, of all violent crime victims reported in NIBRS between 1997–99, about 2 in 10 were under age 18 and more than 4 in 10 were under age 25.

Among hate crime victims of aggravated assault, 30% were under 18, as were 34% of victims of simple assault (not shown in table). Victims of intimidation tended to be older, as nearly 40% were age 35 or over. About 3 out of 4 property crime victims were 25 or older, and nearly a third were 45 or older.

Forty percent of all hate crime victims were white males, 25% white females, 20% black males, and 12% black females. An additional 2% of victims were Asian, and nearly 1% were American Indian. Overall, blacks represented 36% of violent hate crime victims and 22% of property crime victims. Whites represented 62% and 74%, respectively.

VICTIM-OFFENDER RELATIONSHIPS

NIBRS allows specification of the relationship between the victim and offender for violent offenses and nonviolent sex offenses. Among victims of violent hate crimes, 38% listed their attackers as acquaintances, 26% as strangers, and 7% as intimates, relatives, or friends. The victim-offender relationship remained unknown or unreported for 30% of bias victims. Among cases in which the victim and offender were acquaintances, 82% provided no additional information other than the offender was known to the victim, 16% reported that the offender was a neighbor, and 2% that the offender was an employer or employee (not shown in table).

Younger victims were more likely to be victimized by persons known to them (not shown in table). Of violent victims age 12 or younger, 61% were victimized by an acquaintance, 20% by a stranger, and 2% by a relative or friend. For the remainder, the victim-offender relationship was unknown. Among victims age 13 to 17, 51% were victimized by an acquaintance, 21% by a stranger, and 4% by a relative or friend. In comparison, 31% of victims age 21 or older were victimized by an acquaintance, 29% by a stranger, and 7% by an intimate, relative, or friend.

GROUP VICTIMIZATION PATTERNS

More than 4 out of 5 violent hate crime incidents reported in NIBRS involved the victimization of a single individual within a single incident. Two or more victims were involved in nearly a quarter of incidents in which the most serious offense was aggravated assault (23%). Violent incidents in which the most serious offense was rape (0 cases out of 6), robbery (13%), or intimidation (14%) were the least likely to involve multiple victims.

OFFENDER CHARACTERISTICS

OFFENDER DEMOGRAPHICS

Similar to characteristics of the victims, the characteristics of hate crime offenders varied according to offense. Among all NIBRS hate crime incidents, 33% of known offenders, which implies only that some characteristic of the suspect was identified, were age 17 or younger; 29%, age 18 to 24; 17%, age 25 to 34; and 21%, age 35 or older. Violent offenders were generally older than property offenders. Of violent offenders, 31% were age 17 or younger and 60% were age 24 or younger. Of property offenders, 46% were age 17 or younger and 71% were age 24 or younger.

The majority of persons suspected of committing hate crimes were white males. Among those suspected of violent hate crimes, 60% were white males, 21% black males, 10% white females, and 6% black females. Whites also represented a larger share of persons suspected of committing property-related hate crimes, as 69% of property offenders were white males and 15% were white females.

By bias motivation, whites represented the majority of offenders suspected of committing hate crimes: religious, (88%), disability (85%), sexual orientation (84%), ethnic (82%), and racial (66%) (not shown in table). Among racially motivated incidents, 55% of suspected offenders were white males, 25% black males, 11% white females, and 6% black females.

GROUP OFFENDING PATTERNS

About 3 in 4 violent hate crimes involved a single offender in a single incident. Two or more offenders were involved in 66% of robbery incidents, in 33% of aggravated assaults, in 30% of simple assaults, and 15% of intimidation incidents.

INCIDENT CHARACTERISTICS

LOCATION OF HATE CRIME INCIDENTS

Of all bias incidents reported in NIBRS, 32% were committed in a residence, 28% in an open space, 19% in a commercial/retail business or public building, 12% in a school or college, 7% in another or unknown location, and 3% in a church, synagogue or temple. (See Methodology for definitions.) Open spaces primarily refer to roadways and parking garages or parking lots. Thirty percent or more of racial, ethnic, and disability-biased incidents were committed in an open space. Among incidents motivated by sexual orientation bias, 41% occurred at a residence, 23% in an open space, 16% at a school or college, and 15% at a commercial/retail business or public building. A third of religious-biased crimes occurred at an educational or religious institution.

WEAPONS IN HATE CRIMES

Weapons were used in about 18% of all violent hate crimes. Firearms were used or brandished in 4% of violent incidents, knives or sharp objects in

4%, and a blunt object in 4%. By specific offense, homicides (3 out of 3 incidents) and aggravated assaults were the most likely to involve the use or presence of a weapon. Firearms were used or brandished in 17% of aggravated assault incidents, knives in 17%, and blunt objects in 19%.

The differences in weapon use and offense type correspond to victim injury, with aggravated assault victims the most likely to sustain a serious injury (not shown in table). Among all hate-related violent cases that provided information on injury outcome, 47% reported no injury to the victim, 45% a minor injury, 3% a severe laceration, 2% broken bones, and 3% some other type of major injury. In comparison, more than half of aggravated assault victims sustained some type of injury and 1 in 5 reported a more serious injury such as broken bones, an internal injury, or a severe laceration.

TIME OF DAY OF HATE CRIME INCIDENTS

The time of day at which violent hate crimes were reported to have occurred was related to the age of the victim. Victims age 17 or younger were most likely to be victimized during the day, as nearly two-thirds of these incidents occurred between 7 A.M. and 6 P.M., with a peak between 2 P.M. and 4 P.M.

Other research has also reported this afternoon period as a peak time for juvenile victimization . . . In comparison, violent hate crimes involving victims age 18 to 24 were more likely to occur in the late evening, with a peak around midnight. More than a quarter of violent incidents involving victims age 18 to 24 occurred between 10 P.M. and 1 A.M.

LAW ENFORCEMENT RESPONSE

CLEARANCE RATES

NIBRS data indicate that 1 in 4 hate crime incidents were cleared either by arrest or exceptional means. Overall, an arrest was made in about 20% of hate crime incidents. An additional 5% of cases were cleared by exceptional means, which most commonly refers to cases in which either the victim refused to cooperate or prosecution was declined because of a lack of evidence.

Crimes in which the most serious offense was homicide (67% of cases cleared), forcible rape (67% cleared), kidnapping (50% cleared), aggravated assault (40% cleared), simple assault (39% cleared), or forgery/fraud (39% cleared) were the most likely to be cleared through arrest or exceptional means. In comparison, cases in which the most serious offense was intimidation (21%), vandalism (10%), arson (10%), or burglary (15%) were the least likely to be cleared.

Appendix G

ARRESTEE CHARACTERISTICS

In NIBRS, more than a third of persons arrested for hate crimes were under 18, and over a half were under 25 at the time of arrest. Younger persons were more likely to be arrested for property-related offenses. Fifty-six percent of persons arrested for property offenses were age 17 or younger compared to 28% of persons arrested for violent hate crimes.

Offenders under age 18 comprised sizable proportions of persons arrested for simple assault (29%), intimidation (33%), and damage, destruction, or vandalism of property (66%) offenses. Three-fourths of hate crime arrestees were white. Eighty-five percent were male, including 66% white males and 18% black males.

The vast majority (93%) of persons arrested for hate crimes were not armed at the time of arrest. About 2% of arrestees were armed with a firearm, 2% with a knife, and 3% with another type of weapon such as a blunt object (not shown in table).

About 38% of hate crime arrests reported in NIBRS were listed as on-view arrests, suggesting that the officer caught the offender during or shortly following the incident (not shown in table). An additional 25% of arrests involved the issuance of a citation or summons in which the offender was not taken into custody, and 37% involved apprehensions in which suspects were taken into custody in connection with warrants or earlier crime incidents.

Of cases providing data, two-thirds indicated that arrestees were residents of the locality in which the crime occurred. Among persons under 18 at the time of arrest, nearly 3 out of 4 were residents of the locality where the incident took place.

APPENDIX H

FBI UNIFORM CRIME REPORT SECTION ON HATE CRIME (2000)

The FBI's annual Uniform Crime Report includes a section on hate crimes. Following is a summary of the most recent such report, for the year 2000, available at http://www.fbi.gov/ucr/cius_00/00crime212.pdf. Further interpretation and discussion of the agency's hate crime statistics, including a breakdown by each reporting agency (county, police agency, and city) can be found within the 130-page document "2000 Hate Crime Statistics" at http://www.fbi.gov/ucr/cius_00/hate00.pdf.

BACKGROUND

In response to mounting national concern over crimes motivated by bias, Congress signed into law on April 23, 1990, the Hate Crime Statistics Act of 1990 (the Act). This law required the Attorney General to collect data "about crimes that manifest evidence of prejudice based on race, religion, sexual orientation, or ethnicity." The Attorney General delegated the responsibilities of developing the procedures for and managing the implementation of the collection of hate crime data to the Director of the FBI, who in turn assigned the tasks to the Uniform Crime Reporting (UCR) Program. In September 1994, the Violent Crime Control and Law Enforcement Act amended the Act to include both physical and mental disabilities as potential bias factors, and the actual collection of disability-bias data began in January 1997. Additionally, the Church Arson Prevention Act of 1996 mandated that hate crime data collection become a permanent part of the UCR Program. . . .

NATURE

In 2000, there were 8,152 hate crime incidents reported to the FBI. The incidents involved 9,524 separate offenses, 10,021 victims, and 7,642 known offenders. Of the single-bias incidents reported, 4,368 were motivated by racial bias; 1,483 by religious bias; 1,330 by sexual-orientation bias; 927 by ethnicity/national origin bias; 36 by disability bias. Additionally, 8 incidents involved multiple biases. (See Table 2.33.)

TABLE 2.33
NUMBER OF INCIDENTS, OFFENSES, VICTIMS, AND
KNOWN OFFENDERS
by Bias Motivation, 2000

Bias Motivation	Incidents	Offenses	Victims[1]	Known Offenders[2]
Total	8,152	9,524	10,021	7,642
Single-Bias Incidents	8,144	9,507	10,003	7,632
Race:	4,368	5,206	5,435	4,498
Anti-White	886	1,061	1,091	1,182
Anti-Black	2,904	3,433	3,562	2,832
Anti-American Indian/Alaskan Native	57	62	64	58
Anti-Asian/Pacific Islander	281	317	339	273
Anti-Multi-Racial Group	240	333	379	153
Religion:	1,483	1,568	1,711	590
Anti-Jewish	1,119	1,172	1,280	417
Anti-Catholic	56	61	63	33
Anti-Protestant	59	62	62	23
Anti-Islamic	28	33	36	20
Anti-Other Religious Group	173	188	211	78
Anti-Multi-Religious Group	44	46	52	18
Anti-Atheism/Agnosticism/etc.	4	6	7	1
Sexual Orientation:	1,330	1,517	1,589	1,471
Anti-Male Homosexual	925	1,052	1,089	1,112
Anti-Female Homosexual	181	213	230	173
Anti-Homosexual	182	210	226	153
Anti-Heterosexual	22	22	24	18
Anti-Bisexual	20	20	20	15
Ethnicity/National Origin:	927	1,180	1,232	1,037
Anti-Hispanic	567	745	773	711
Anti-Other Ethnicity/National Origin	360	435	459	326
Disability:	36	36	36	36
Anti-Physical	20	20	20	22
Anti-Mental	16	16	16	14
Multiple-Bias Incidents[3]	8	17	18	10

[1] The term *victim* may refer to a person, business, institution, or society as a whole.

[2] The term *known offender* does not imply that the identity of the suspect is known, but only that an attribute of the suspect is identified which distinguishes him/her from an unknown offender.

[3] A *multiple-bias incident* is any hate crime in which two or more offense types were committed as a result of two or more bias motivations.

Racial bias represented the largest percentage of single bias-motivated offenses in 2000. Of the reported offenses, 54.8 percent were motivated by racial bias, 16.5 percent by religious bias, 16.0 percent by sexual-orientation bias, 12.4 percent by ethnic/national origin bias, and 0.4 percent by disability bias. Seventeen offenses were associated with multiple-bias incidents. (See Table 2.33 and Chart 2.19.)

Considering victims of single-bias motivated hate crimes, a total of 54.3 percent of victims were attacked because of their race, with bias against blacks accounting for 35.6 percent of all hate crime victims. (See Table 2.33.)

Overall, intimidation was the most frequently reported offense. Intimidation accounted for 34.6 percent of the total, followed by damage, destruction, or vandalism of property, 29.0 percent; simple assault, 17.0 percent; and aggravated assault, 13.4 percent. (See Table 2.34.)

TABLE 2.34
NUMBER OF OFFENSES, VICTIMS, AND KNOWN OFFENDERS
BY OFFENSE, 2000

Offense	Offenses	Victims[1]	Known Offenders[2]
Total	**9,524**	**10,021**	**7,642**
Crimes against persons:	**6,223**	**6,223**	**6,266[3]**
Murder and nonnegligent manslaughter	19	19	26
Forcible rape	4	4	5
Aggravated assault	1,274	1,274	1,734
Simple assault	1,616	1,616	2,062
Intimidation	3,294	3,294	2,421
Other[4]	16	16	18
Crimes against property:	**3,242**	**3,739**	**1,653[3]**
Robbery	139	160	327
Burglary	138	158	76
Larceny-theft	114	121	81
Motor vehicle theft	11	12	10
Arson	52	70	48
Destruction/damage/vandalism	2,766	3,193	1,092
Other[4]	22	25	19
Crimes against society[4]	**59**	**59**	**78[3]**

[1] The term *victim* may refer to a person, business, institution, or society as a whole.

[2] The term *known offender* does not imply that the identity of the suspect is known, but only that an attribute of the suspect is identified which distinguishes him/her from an unknown offender.

[3] The actual number of known offenders is 7,642. (See Table 2.33.) Some offenders, however, may be responsible for more than one offense and are, therefore, counted more than once in this table.

[4] Includes additional offenses collected in NIBRS.

Appendix H

Law enforcement agencies reported 7,642 known offenders in conjunction with the 8,152 incidents recorded in 2000. (See Table 2.33.) Of the known offenders, 6,266 were associated with crimes against persons, 1,653 were linked to crimes against property, and 78 were connected with crimes against society. The single most reported offense, intimidation, was committed by 38.6 percent of known offenders involved in crimes against persons. (See Table 2.34.) By race, 64.2 percent of the known offenders were white, 18.9 percent were black, 9.7 percent were of unknown races, and 7.2 percent were of other race categories. (See Table 2.35.)

TABLE 2.35
NUMBER OF KNOWN OFFENDERS
by Race, 2000

Known Offender's Race[1]

Total	**7,642**
White	4,905
Black	1,441
American Indian/Alaskan Native	49
Asian/Pacific Islander	109
Multi-Racial Group	393
Unknown Race	745

[1] The term *known offender* does not imply that the identity of the suspect is known, but only that an attribute of the suspect is identified which distinguishes him/her from an unknown offender.

LAW ENFORCEMENT PARTICIPATION

Hate crime data for 2000 were supplied by 11,690 law enforcement agencies in 48 states and the District of Columbia. These agencies represented approximately 84.2 percent of the nation's population, nearly 237 million people. (See Table 2.40.) Of the participating agencies, 83.8 percent reported that no hate crimes occurred in their jurisdiction, and the remaining 16.2 percent reported that at least one hate crime occurred.

287

APPENDIX I

List of State Hate-Crime Statutes (2000)

The following is a list of state hate-crime statutes, listed by statute number and by type, from the web site of the Center for the Study of Hate and Extremism, located at http://www.hatemonitor.org/other_states/state_statutes_by_type.html#alas.

ALABAMA

Ala. Code § 13A-5-13 (Penalty Enhancement) (1993)
Ala. Code § 13A-11-12 (Institutional Vandalism, Desecration of Religious Institutions) (1977)

ALASKA

Alaska Stat. § 12.55.155 (Penalty Enhancement) (1996)

ARIZONA

Ariz. Rev. Stat. Ann. § 13-1604 (Institutional Vandalism, Desecration of Religious Institutions) (1994)
Ariz. Rev. Stat. Ann. § 13-1702 (Penalty Enhancement) (1997)
Ariz. Rev. Stat. Ann. § 41-1750 (Data Collection) (1991)
Ariz. Rev. Stat. Ann. § 41-1822 (Training Law Personnel) (1991)

ARKANSAS

Ark. Code Ann. § 5-71-207 (Disturbing Religious Worship) (1975)

Ark. Code Ann. § 5-71-215 (Institutional Vandalism and Desecration of Religious Institutions) (1993)

Ark. Code Ann. § 16-123-105 (Civil Action, Private, Damages) (1995)

Ark. Code Ann. § 16-123-106 (Civil Action, Private, Damages and Injunction) (1993)

Ark. Code Ann. § 16-123-107 (Civil Action, Private, Damages and Injunction) (1995)

CALIFORNIA

Cal. Civil Code § 52 (Civil Action, Private and Attorney General, Damages and Injunction) (1994)

Cal. Penal Code § 51.7 (Independent Criminal Civil Rights with Categories) (1994)

Cal. Penal Code § 136.2 (Stay Away Order once criminal charges filed) (1996)

Cal. Penal Code § 302 (Disturbing Religious Worship) (1994)

Cal. Penal Code § 422.6 (Independent Criminal Civil Rights with Categories and Institutional Vandalism) (1994)

Cal. Penal Code § 422.75 (Penalty Enhancement) (1995)

Cal. Penal Code § 422.9 (Violation of Civil Injunction is a Criminal Penalty) (1987)

Cal. Penal Code § 422.95 (Sensitivity Training) (1995)

Cal. Penal Code § 594.3 (Institutional Vandalism and Desecration of Religious Institutions) (1983)

Cal. Penal Code § 11410 (Declaration of Purpose for Criminal Sanctions)

Cal. Penal Code § 11411 (Cross Burning) (1991)

Cal. Penal Code § 11412 (Obstructing Exercise of Religion) (1984)

Cal. Penal Code § 1170.75 (Penalty Enhancement) (1994)

Cal. Penal Code § 13519.6 (Data Collection and Training Law Personnel) (1992)

COLORADO

Colo. Rev. Stat. § 18-9-113 (Institutional Vandalism and Desecration of Religious Institutions) (1991)

Colo. Rev. Stat. § 18-9-121 (Independent Criminal Civil Rights with Categories and Institutional Vandalism) (1988)

CONNECTICUT

Conn. Gen. Stat. § 29-7m (Data Collection) (1987)
Conn. Gen. Stat. § 33-37 (Independent Criminal Civil Rights with Categories) (1949)
Conn. Gen. Stat. § 46a-58 (Independent Criminal Civil Rights with Categories, Cross Burning and Desecration of Religious Institutions) (1984)
Conn. Gen. Stat. § 46a-64 (Independent Criminal Civil Rights with Categories—Public Accommodation Discrimination) (1990)
Conn. Gen. Stat. § 46a-64c (Independent Criminal Civil Rights with Categories—Housing Discrimination) (1992)
Conn. Gen. Stat. § 52-571(a) (Civil Action, Private, Injunction) (1993)
Conn. Gen. Stat. § 52-571(c) (Civil Action, Private, Damages) (1995)
Conn. Gen. Stat. § 53-37(a) (Mask or Hood Wearing) (1982)
Conn. Gen. Stat. § 53-37(b) (Independent Criminal Civil Rights without Categories) (1993)
Conn. Gen. Stat. § 53a-40a (Penalty Enhancement) (1990)
Conn. Gen. Stat. § 53a-181b (Independent Criminal Civil Rights with Categories and Institutional Vandalism) (1990)
Conn. Gen. Stat. § 562-251b (Civil Action, Private, Damages) (1984)

DELAWARE

De. Code Ann. tit. 11, § 304 (Independent Criminal Civil Rights without Categories and Independent Criminal Civil Rights with Categories) (1997)
De. Code Ann. tit. 11, § 805 (Cross Burning) (1993)
De. Code Ann. tit. 11, § 1301(1)(g) (Mask Wearing) (1953)
De. Code Ann. tit. 11, § 4209(e)(1)(v) (Penalty Enhancement—Aggravating Circumstance in Death Penalty Statute) (1995)

DISTRICT OF COLUMBIA

DC Code Ann. § 22-3112.2 (Cross-Burning and Desecration of Religious Institutions) (1983)
DC Code Ann. § 22-3112.3 (Mask Wearing) (1983)
DC Code Ann. § 22-4001 (Defines Bias-Related Crimes)
DC Code Ann. § 22-4002 (Data Collection) (1990)
DC Code Ann. § 22-4003 (Penalty Enhancement) (1990)
DC Code Ann. § 22-4004 (Civil Action, Private, Damages and Injunction) (1990)

FLORIDA

Fla. Stat. Ann. § 760.51 (Civil Action, Attorney General, Damages and Injunction) (1994)

Fla. Stat. Ann. § 775.085 (Penalty Enhancement and Civil Action, Private, Damages and Injunction) (1992)

Fla. Stat. Ann. § 775.0845 (Penalty Enhancement for Mask Wearing) (1995)

Fla. Stat. Ann. § 806.13 (Institutional Vandalism and Desecration of Religious Institutions) (1995)

Fla. Stat. Ann. § 876.17 (Cross Burning, Public Place) (1993)

Fla. Stat. Ann. § 876.18 (Cross Burning, Another's Property) (1993)

Fla. Stat. Ann. § 877.19 (Data Collection) (1996)

GEORGIA

Ga. Code Ann. § 16-7-26 (Desecration of Religious Institutions) (1968)

Ga. Code Ann. § 16-11-37(b)(1) (Cross Burning) (1974)

Ga. Code Ann. § 16-11-38 (Mask Wearing) (1968)

HAWAII

Haw. Rev. Stat. § 711-1107 (Institutional Vandalism and Desecration of Religious Institutions) (1993)

IDAHO

Idaho Code § 18-2915 (Data Collection) (1995)

Idaho Code § 18-7301 (Independent Criminal Civil Rights with Categories) (1972)

Idaho Code § 18-7901 (Declaration of Purpose for Criminal Sanctions) (1983)

Idaho Code § 18-7902 (Independent Criminal Civil Rights with Categories, Desecration of Religious Institutions, Institutional Vandalism, Cross Burning) (1983)

Idaho Code § 18-7903 (Civil Action, Private, Damages and Injunction) (1983)

ILLINOIS

20 Ill. Comp. Stat. 2605/55a(A)31 (Data Collection and Training Law Personnel) (1995)

720 Ill. Comp. Stat. 5/12-7.1 (Independent Criminal Civil Rights with Categories and Civil Action, Private, Damages and Injunction) (1996)
720 Ill. Comp. Stat. 5/21-1.2 (Institutional Vandalism and Desecration of Religious Institutions) (1994)
730 Ill. Comp. Stat. 5/5-5-3.2(a)(10) (Penalty Enhancement) (1996)

INDIANA

Ind. Code Ann. § 22-9.5-10-1 (Independent Criminal Civil Rights with Categories—Fair Housing) (1993)
Ind. Code Ann. § 35-43-1-2 (Institutional Vandalism and Desecration of Religious Institutions) (1996)

IOWA

Iowa Code § 692.15 (Data Collection) (1996)
Iowa Code § 708.2C and 229A.2 (Independent Criminal Civil Rights with Categories) (1995)
Iowa Code § 712.9 and 729A.2 (Penalty Enhancement) (1992)
Iowa Code § 716.6A and 729A.2 (Penalty Enhancement) (1992)
Iowa Code § 729.4 (Independent Criminal Civil Rights with Categories—Fair Employment Practices) (1987)
Iowa Code § 729.5 (Independent Criminal Civil Rights without Categories—Institutional Vandalism) (1992)
Iowa Code § 729A.1 (Independent Criminal Civil Rights with Categories) (1992)
Iowa Code § 729A.4 (Training Law Personnel) (1992)
Iowa Code § 729A.5 (Civil Action, Private, Damages and Injunction) (1992)

KANSAS

Kan. Stat. Ann. § 21-4003 (Independent Criminal Civil Rights with Categories) (1993)
Kan. Stat. Ann. § 21-4111 (Institutional Vandalism and Desecration of Religious Institutions (1994)
Kan. Stat. Ann. § 21-4716 (Penalty Enhancement) (1994)

KENTUCKY

Ky. Rev. Stat. Ann. § 15.331 (Training Law Personnel) (1992)
Ky. Rev. Stat. Ann. § 17.1523 (Data Collection) (1992)
Ky. Rev. Stat. Ann. § 344.450 (Civil Action, Private, Damages and Injunction) (1996)
Ky. Rev. Stat. Ann. § 525.110 (Institutional Vandalism and Desecration of Religious Institutions) (1992)

LOUISIANA

La. Rev. Stat. Ann. § 14:107.2 (Penalty Enhancement) (1997)
La. Rev. Stat. Ann. § 14:225 (Institutional Vandalism and Desecration of Religious Institutions) (1984)
La. Rev. Stat. Ann. § 15:1204.2(B)(4) and 1204.4 (Data Collection) (1997)
La. Rev. Stat. Ann. § 40:2403(H) (Training Law Personnel) (1997)

MAINE

Me. Rev. Stat. Ann. tit. 5, § 4681 (Civil Action, Attorney General, Injunction; Violation of Injunction is a Criminal Penalty) (1995)
Me. Rev. Stat. Ann. tit. 5, § 4682 (Civil Action, Private, Damages and Injunction, and Violation of Injunction is a Criminal Penalty) (1995)
Me. Rev. Stat. Ann. tit. 17, § 2931 and tit. 5, § 4684A (Independent Criminal Civil Rights with Categories) (1987) and (1993)
Me. Rev. Stat. Ann. tit. 17-A, § 507 (Institutional Vandalism and Desecration of Religious Institutions) (1976)
Me. Rev. Stat. Ann. tit. 17-A, § 507A (Desecration of Religious Institutions—Cemetery/Burial Ground) (1987)
Me. Rev. Stat. Ann. tit. 17-A, § 1151(8)(B) (Penalty Enhancement) (1995)
Me. Rev. Stat. Ann. tit. 25, § 1544 (Data Collection) (1991)

MARYLAND

Md. Code Ann. art. 27, § 470A (Independent Criminal Civil Rights with Categories, Institutional Vandalism and Desecration of Religious Institutions) (1994)
Md. Code Ann. art. 88B, § 9 (Data Collection) (1992)

MASSACHUSETTS

Mass. Gen. Laws Ann. ch. 12, § 11H (Civil Action (Attorney General, Injunction) (1982)

Mass. Gen. Laws Ann. ch. 12, § 11I (Civil Action (Private, Damages and Injunction) (1982)

Mass. Gen. Laws Ann. ch. 12, § 11J (Violation of Injunction is a Criminal Penalty) (1985)

Mass. Gen. Laws Ann. ch. 22C, §§ 33 to 35 (Data Collection) (1991)

Mass. Gen. Laws Ann. ch. 265, § 37 (Independent Criminal Civil Rights without Categories)(1979)

Mass. Gen. Laws Ann. ch. 265, § 39 (Independent Criminal Civil Rights with Categories and Diversity Awareness Program) (1997)

Mass. Gen. Laws Ann. ch. 266, § 98 (Institutional Vandalism and Desecration of Religious Institutions) (1960)

Mass. Gen. Laws Ann. ch. 266, § 116B (Training Law Personnel) (1991)

Mass. Gen. Laws Ann. ch. 266, § 127A (Institutional Vandalism and Desecration of Religious Institutions) (1989)

Mass. Gen. Laws Ann. ch. 268, § 34 (Mask Wearing) (1902)

Mass. Gen. Laws Ann. ch. 272, § 38 (Disturbing Religious Worship) (1970)

Mass. Gen. Laws Ann. ch. 272, § 98 (Independent Criminal Civil Rights with Categories—Public Accommodations Discrimination) (1970)

MICHIGAN

Mich. Comp. Laws. Ann. § 14.101 (Civil Action, Attorney General, Damages and Injunction) (1970)

Mich. Comp. Laws Ann. § 750.147b (Institutional Vandalism, Desecration of Religious Institutions, Cross Burning, Independent Criminal Civil Rights with Categories and Civil Action, Private, Damages and Injunction) (1989)

Mich. Comp. Laws Ann. § 752.525 (Disturbing Religious Worship) (1994)

Mich. Executive Order (Data Collection) (1996 and 1997)

MINNESOTA

Minn. Stat. Ann. § 363.12 (Declaration of Policy for Criminal Sanctions) (1993)

Minn. Stat. Ann. § 609.2231 (Independent Criminal Civil Rights with Categories) (1989)

Minn. Stat. Ann. § 609.28 (Disturbing Religious Worship) (1994)
Minn. Stat. Ann. § 609.595 (Institutional Vandalism) (1989)
Minn. Stat. Ann. § 609.749(3)(1) (Penalty Enhancement) (1995)
Minn. Stat. Ann. § 611A.79 (Civil Action, Private, Injunction and Damages) (1996)
Minn. Stat. Ann. § 626.5531 (Data Collection) (1997)
Minn. Stat. Ann. § 626.8451 (Training Law Enforcement) (1993)

MISSISSIPPI

Miss. Code Ann. § 97-17-39 (Institutional Vandalism and Desecration of Religious Institutions) (1993)
Miss. Code Ann. § 97-35-17 (Disturbing Religious Worship) (1993)
Miss. Code Ann. § 99-19-301 and § 99-19-307 (Penalty Enhancement) (1994)

MISSOURI

Mo. Ann. Stat. § 537.523 (Civil Action, Private, Damages and Injunction) (1988)
Mo. Ann. Stat. § 574.085 (Institutional Vandalism and Desecration of Religious Institutions) (1997)
Mo. Ann. Stat. § 574.090 (Penalty Enhancement) (1988)
Mo. Ann. Stat. § 574.093 (Penalty Enhancement) (1988)

MONTANA

Mont. Code Ann. § 45-5-221 (Independent Criminal Civil Rights with Categories, Institutional Vandalism, Cross Burning) (1989)
Mont. Code Ann. § 45-5-222 (Penalty Enhancement) (1989)
Mont. Code Ann. § 49-2-601 and § 49-2-602 (Independent Criminal Civil Rights with Categories—Housing Discrimination) (1993)

NEBRASKA

Neb. Stat. Ann. § 28-101 (Penalty Enhancement and Civil Action, Private, Damages) (1997)
Neb. L.B. 90, 1997 Legislative Session (Data Collection) (1997)

NEVADA

Nev. Rev. Stat. Ann. § 41.690 (Civil Action, Private, Damages) (1995)
Nev. Rev. Stat. Ann. § 193.1675 (Penalty Enhancement) (1997)
Nev. Rev. Stat. Ann. § 201.270 (Disturbing Religious Worship) (1995)
Nev. Rev. Stat. Ann. § 206.125 (Institutional Vandalism and Desecration of Religious Institutions) (1995)
Nev. Rev. Stat. Ann. § 207.185 (Independent Criminal Civil Rights with Categories) (1995)

NEW HAMPSHIRE

N.H. Rev. Stat. Ann. § 651.6 (Penalty Enhancement) (1995)

NEW JERSEY

N.J. Stat. Ann. § 2A:53A-21 (Civil Action, Private and Attorney General, Damages and Injunction) (1995)
N.J. Stat. Ann. § 2C:12-1(b)(6)(e) (Penalty Enhancement) (1995)
N.J. Stat. Ann. § 2C:33-4 (Penalty Enhancement) (1995)
N.J. Stat. Ann. § 2C:33-9 (Desecration of Religious Institutions) (1979)
N.J. Stat. Ann. § 2C:33-10 (Independent Criminal Civil Rights without Categories) (1995)
N.J. Stat. Ann. § 2C:33-11 (Institutional Vandalism and Desecration of Religious Institutions) (1995)
N.J. Stat. Ann. § 2C:44-3 (Penalty Enhancement) (1995)
Attorney General Directive No. 1987-3 (Data Collection) (1987)
N.J. Bias Incident Investigation Standards (Training Law Personnel) (Sept. 1991)

NEW MEXICO

N.M. Stat. Ann. § 30-13-1 (Disturbing Religious Worship) (1963)
N.M. Stat. Ann. § 30-15-4 (Desecration of Religious Institutions) (1965)

NEW YORK

N.Y. Civ. Rights Law § 40-c to -d (Independent Criminal Civil Rights without Categories and with Categories) (1981)
N.Y. Exec. Law 63 (Civil Action, Attorney General, Damages) (1993)

N.Y. Penal Law 240.21 (Disturbing Religious Worship) (1967)
N.Y. Penal Law 240.30 (Independent Criminal Civil Rights with Categories) (1992)

NORTH CAROLINA

N.C. Gen. Stat. § 14-3 (Penalty Enhancement) (1993)
N.C. Gen. Stat. § 14-12.12 (Cross Burning) (1967)
N.C. Gen. Stat. §§ 14-12.13 and 14-12.14 (Mask Wearing) (1993)
N.C. Gen. Stat. § 14-49 (Institutional Vandalism, Desecration of Religious Institutions) (1993)
N.C. Gen. Stat. § 14-62.2 (Church Burning) (1997)
N.C. Gen. Stat. § 14-144 (Institutional Vandalism and Desecration of Religious Institutions) (1995)
N.C. Gen. Stat. § 14-199 (Obstructing Religious Worship) (1993)
N.C. Gen. Stat. § 14-401.14 (Independent Criminal Civil Rights with Categories) (1993)
N.C. Gen. Stat. § 15A-1340.16 (Penalty Enhancement) (1995)
N.C. Gen. Stat. § 15A-1340.16(d) (Penalty Enhancement) (1994)

NORTH DAKOTA

N.D. Cent. Code § 12.1-14-04 (Independent Criminal Civil Rights with Categories) (1973)
N.D. Cent. Code. § 12.1-14-05 (Independent Criminal Civil Rights without Categories) (1973)

OHIO

Ohio Rev. Code Ann. § 2307.70 (Civil Action, Private, Damages) (1990)
Ohio Rev. Code Ann. § 2909.05 (Institutional Vandalism and Desecration of Religious Institutions – burial) (1993)
Ohio Rev. Code Ann. § 2927.11 (Desecration of Religious Institutions) (1986)
Ohio Rev. Code Ann. § 2927.12 (Independent Criminal Civil Rights with Categories) (1987)

OKLAHOMA

Okla. Stat. Ann. tit. 21, § 850 (Independent Criminal Civil Rights with Categories, Institutional Vandalism and Data Collection) (1992)
Okla. Stat. Ann. tit. 21, § 915 (Disturbing Religious Worship) (1921)
Okla. Stat. Ann. tit. 21, § 1765 (Desecration of Religious Institutions) (1921)

OREGON

Or. Rev. Stat. § 30.190 (Civil Action, Private, Damages and Injunction) (1983)
Or. Rev. Stat. § 166.155 (Independent Criminal Civil Rights with Categories) (1989)
Or. Rev. Stat. § 166.165 (Independent Criminal Civil Rights with Categories) (1989)
Or. Rev. Stat. § 166.075 (Institutional Vandalism and Desecration of Religious Institutions) (1971)
Or. Rev. Stat. § 181.550 (Data Collection) (1989)

PENNSYLVANIA

Pa. Cons. Stat., tit. 18, § 2710 (Penalty Enhancement) (1982)
Pa. Cons. Stat., tit. 18, § 3307 (Institutional Vandalism and Desecration of Religious Institutions) (1994)
Pa. Cons. Stat., tit. 18, § 5509 (Desecration of Religious Institutions) (1973)
Pa. Cons. Stat., tit. 42, § 8309 (Civil Action, Private, Damages and Injunction; Attorney General, Injunction; Violation of an Injunction is a Criminal Penalty) (1997)
Pa. Cons. Stat., tit. 71, § 250 (Data Collection) (1987)

RHODE ISLAND

R.I. Gen. Laws § 9-1-35 (Civil Action, Private, Damages and Injunction) (1985)
R.I. Gen. Laws § 11-5-13 (Penalty Enhancement) (1994)
R.I. Gen. Laws § 11-11-1 (Disturbing Religious Worship) (1994)
R.I. Gen. Laws § 11-42-3 (Independent Criminal Civil Rights with Categories) (1994)
R.I. Gen. Laws § 11-44-31 (Institutional Vandalism and Desecration of Religious Institutions) (1986)
R.I. Gen. Laws § 11-53-1 (Declaration of Purpose for Criminal Sanctions) (1994)
R.I. Gen. Laws § 11-53-2 (Cross Burning) (1994)
R.I. Gen. Laws § 11-53-3 (Independent Criminal Civil Rights with Categories) (1983)
R.I. Gen. Laws § 42-28-46 (Data Collection) (1994)
R.I. Gen. Laws § 42-28.2-8.1 (Training Law Personnel) (1993)

SOUTH CAROLINA

S.C. Code Ann. § 16-5-10 (Independent Criminal Civil Rights without Categories) (1994)
S.C. Code Ann. § 16-17-520 (Disturbing Religious Worship) (1962)
S.C. Code Ann. § 16-17-560 (Independent Criminal Civil Rights with Categories—Political Rights/Opinions) (1994)
S.C. Code Ann. § 16-17-600 (Desecration of Religious Institutions) (1994)

SOUTH DAKOTA

S.D. Codified Laws Ann. § 22-19B-1 (Independent Criminal Civil Rights with Categories and Institutional Vandalism) (1993)
S.D. Codified Laws Ann. § 22-19B-2 (Cross Burning) (1993)
S.D. Codified Laws Ann. § 22-19B-3 (Civil Action, Private, Damages) (1993)
S.D. Codified Laws Ann. § 22-27-1 (Disturbing Religious Worship) (1976)

TENNESSEE

Tenn. Code Ann. § 4-21-701 (Civil Action, Private, Damages) (1990)
Tenn. Code Ann. § 39-17-309 (Independent Criminal Civil Rights without Categories, Institutional Vandalism, Mask Wearing) (1990)
Tenn. Code Ann. § 39-17-311 (Desecration of Religious Institutions) (1989)

TEXAS

Tex. Gov. Code Ann. § 411.046 (Data Collection) (1991)
Tex. Penal Code Ann. § 12.47 and Tex. Code Crim. Proc. art. 42.014 (Penalty Enhancement) (1993)
Tex. Penal Code Ann. § 28.03 (Institutional Vandalism and Desecration of Religious Institutions) (1994)

UTAH

Utah Stat. Ann. § 76-3-203.3 (Penalty Enhancement) (1992)
Utah Stat. Ann. § 76-6-106 (Institutional Vandalism) (1996)
Utah Stat. Ann. § 76-6-107 (Institutional Vandalism) (1996)

VERMONT

Vt. Stat. Ann. tit. 13, § 1455 (Penalty Enhancement) (1990)
Vt. Stat. Ann. tit. 13, § 1456 (Cross Burning) (1990)
Vt. Stat. Ann. tit. 13, § 1457 (Civil Action, Private, Damages and Injunction) (1990)

VIRGINIA

Va. Code Ann. § 8.01-42-1 (Civil Action, Private, Damages and Injunction) (1988)
Va. Code Ann. § 18.2-57 (Penalty Enhancement) (1997)
Va. Code Ann. § 18.2-127 (Desecration of Religious Institutions) (1990)
Va. Code Ann. § 18.2-138 (Institutional Vandalism) (1990)
Va. Code Ann. § 18.2-422 (Mask Wearing) (1986)
Va. Code Ann. § 18.2-423 (Cross Burning) (1983)
Va. Code Ann. § 52-8.5 (Data Collection) (1988)

WASHINGTON

Wash. Rev. Code Ann. § 9.61.160 (Threats to Bomb or Injure Religious Institutions and Public Property) (1977)
Wash. Rev. Code Ann. § 9A.36.078 (Declaration of Findings/Policy for Criminal Sanctions) (1993)
Wash. Rev. Code Ann. § 9A.36.080 (Independent Criminal Civil Rights with Categories, Institutional Vandalism and Cross Burning) (1993)
Wash. Rev. Code Ann. § 9A.36.083 (Civil Action, Private, Damages) (1993)
Wash. Rev. Code Ann. § 36.28A.030 (Data Collection) (1993)
Wash. Rev. Code Ann. § 43.101.290 (Training Law Personnel) (1993)

WEST VIRGINIA

W. Va. Code § 5-11-20 (Civil Action, Attorney General, Injunction and Civil Penalties) (1998)
W. Va. Code § 15-2-24(i) (Data Collection) (1977)
W. Va. Code § 61-6-13 (Disturbing Religious Worship) (1993)
W. Va. Code § 61-6-21 (Independent Criminal Civil Rights with Categories and Penalty Enhancement) (1993)
W. Va. Code § 61-6-22 (Mask Wearing) (1993)

WISCONSIN

Wis. Stat. Ann. § 895.75 (Civil Action, Private, Damages) (1996)
Wis. Stat. Ann. § 939.641 (Penalty Enhancement for Mask Wearing) (1996)
Wis. Stat. Ann. § 939.645 (Penalty Enhancement) (1996)
Wis. Stat. Ann. § 943.012 (Institutional Vandalism and Desecration of Religious Institutions) (1996)

WYOMING

Wy. Stat. Ann. § 6-9-102 (Independent Criminal Civil Rights with Categories) (1982)

INDEX

Page numbers in **boldface** indicate biographical entries. Page numbers followed by *g* indicate glossary entries.

Index

Index

Index

Index

Index